1,001

The "Hire Me"
Words That Set Your
Cover Letter, **Resume**,
and **Job Interview**
Apart

PHRASES
YOU NEED TO
GET A JOB

NANCY SCHUMAN, CSP, Vice President of Lloyd Staffing, and BURTON JAY NADLER

Aadamsmedia
Avon, Massachusetts

Published by
Adams Media, a division of F+W Media, Inc.
57 Littlefield Street, Avon, MA 02322. U.S.A.
www.adamsmedia.com

Contains material adapted and abridged from *The Resume and Cover Letter Phrase Book* by Nancy Schuman, CSP, Vice President of Lloyd Staffing, and Burton Jay Nadler, copyright © 2010 by F+W Media, Inc., ISBN 10: 1-4405-0981-6, ISBN 13: 978-1-4405-0981-0; *The Everything® Cover Letter Book, 2nd Edition* by Burton Jay Nadler, copyright © 2005 by F+W Media, Inc., ISBN 10: 1-59337-335-X, ISBN 13: 978-1-59337-335-1; *The Everything® Resume Book, 3rd Edition,* by Nancy Schuman, copyright © 2008 by F+W Media, Inc., ISBN 10: 1-59869-637-8, ISBN 13: 978-1-59869-637-0; *Resume Buzzwords* by Erik Herman and Sarah Rocha, copyright © 2004 by F+W Media, Inc., ISBN 10: 1-59337-114-4, ISBN 13: 978-1-59337-114-2; and *The Job Interview Phrase Book* by Nancy Schuman, CSP, Vice President, Lloyd Staffing, copyright © 2009 by F+W Media, Inc., ISBN 10: 1-4405-0184-X, ISBN 13: 978-1-4405-0184-5.

ISBN 10: 1-4405-3887-5
ISBN 13: 978-1-4405-3887-2
eISBN 10: 1-4405-3950-2
eISBN 13: 978-1-4405-3950-3

Printed in the United States of America.

10   9   8   7   6   5   4   3   2   1

Library of Congress Cataloging-in-Publication Data
is available from the publisher.

This book is available at quantity discounts for bulk purchases. For information, please call 1-800-289-0963.

CONTENTS

THE WINNING WORDS

Excess e-mail, endless online searches and media subscriptions, 24-7 smartphone access, and the list goes on . . . The information age has created a massive influx of material to wade through on a daily basis to get to the heart of any matter. By necessity, time-strapped employers have become scanners, desperately searching for the juicy nugget that stops them in their tracks because it delivers what they need. This book is packed full of winning phrases that make you stand out in a sea of noise. The right wording can set you apart from hundreds of applicants, all vying for the same position. If you want to ride the fast lane to the job of your choosing, you've got to wow them with words from your cover letter to your resume to the final interview.

What you say and *how you say it* can work for you in powerful ways that you can literally take to the bank. But these words can just as easily work against you if you're unable to cut to the chase and promote your genius in a persuasive manner. That's where this book becomes invaluable. It will teach you how to sell yourself, and inside you'll find the most magnetic keywords and phrases to help you do just that. From the cover letter and resume on to the job interview and the follow-up, you'll discover tested advice that will put you out front in *all* stages of your job search. With 1,001 phrases, keywords, and action verbs that compel employers to give you their undivided attention, you'll never find yourself struggling with writer's block or grasping for the right thing to say. What's more, you'll find the industry-specific terminology that's like music to your employer's ears.

You see, it doesn't matter if sales is the furthest from your chosen career path; for now, you need to acquire the skills of a master salesperson and use them to broadcast your passion, strengths, and unique talents to your prospective employer. By learning how to string together powerful phrases and honing in on the words that employers most want to hear, you will not only get noticed, but you'll bolster your confidence and find a direct path to "You're hired!"

PART I

Cover Letters That Get Noticed

Chapter 1

CRAFTING YOUR COVER LETTER

Dos and Don'ts

The cover letter is the most critical step in the pursuit of a job. It is the first impression you make, and you only get one chance to make a stellar one. Introducing yourself to a stranger whose job it is to critique you can, for some, be paralyzing. Most of us spend way too much time staring at a blank page trying to conjure up the perfect words for the situation. However, writing a cover letter that lands you an interview can be achieved more easily than you think. Following the RIGHT formula, discussed in the next paragraph, can get you started. This formula will guide you through the process of finding those perfect words. Sometimes they are provided in the job posting itself, and other times you can pluck them from the industry samples you owe it to yourself to review. In this chapter, you will also learn about various kinds of cover letters as well as the basic components of a cover letter—each paragraph in the document seeks to communicate specific strategically targeted and job-function-focused information that you don't want to accidentally leave out.

Write Your Cover Letter the RIGHT Way

Writing your cover letter is as simple as following a five-step process. Just think of the acronym R-I-G-H-T. It stands for Review, Identify, Generate, Hone, Transmit. When following this process, you will:

1. Review Samples, Postings, or Descriptions
To inspire initial efforts and motivate actions, review sample cover letters and postings as well as job descriptions. Think about the phrases or special language used in these items. Key phrases in job postings must be transformed into the best paragraphs in your cover letters. If imitation is the most sincere form of flattery, it can be the best cover letter–writing strategy.

 RED FLAG!
DON'T DISPLAY A LACK OF KNOWLEDGE about your industry. Know the buzzwords that get your cover letter noticed.

2. Identify Resume Key Points
Look at your resume and think about how it relates to the job for which you're applying. Identify key points that you wish to highlight in your cover letter. These should be field-focused qualities as well as directly related academic, employment, or co-curricular achievements. What is it about your resume that you think is most strategically linked to targeted career fields and the specific job or particular functional areas of an employer? What two resume entries do you want the cover letter reader to examine in detail?

3. Generate a Draft
Keep your first draft to one page if possible, but don't worry too much about length. Later, you'll edit to the desired word count. Use the examples in the sample cover letters for inspiration, but don't copy word for word any of the samples that inspire you. Just get some ideas down on paper or on screen. Don't feel pressured to generate your final draft first.

4. Hone a Finished Version
This is when you'll edit the content to achieve maximum effectiveness and impact. The finished version should not contain typos or any major grammatical or style errors. Remember, this is your first writing assignment for your prospective employer.

5. Transmit via E-mail or Fax, Then Mail
Once done, don't delay communication. There truly is no reason to wait. Never procrastinate. Proceed to the next section to learn details regarding cover letter format, content, and specifics to completing the five steps to cover letter success.

Which Letter to Send

The lists within this section define different types of cover letters, the circumstances for which they are appropriate, and to whom they are sent. Later, you will review samples phrases to include in each type of letter.

Letters of Application Used When Responding to Postings

These letters target:

- Confidential Postings (when employers are not identified). These letters must focus on the job descriptions and the skills you possess to succeed in the position.

- Employer Identified Postings (with the employer clearly noted, yet a contact name may not be given). These letters should reveal research on the company. If you don't have someone to address letters to, use memo format.

- Employment Agencies (when employers are not identified). When your letter is sent to a search professional, use the phrase "**judge my candidacy worthy of an interview for this position with your client's firm**."

- Executive Search Firms (when employers are not identified). As with positions posted by employment agencies, focus your letter on motivating the reader to support your candidacy and forward documentation to the client who is the hiring organization, with a recommendation to interview. These firms deal with more senior positions.

RED FLAG!

DON'T GET AHEAD OF YOURSELF. Be realistic when you detail your existing career goals to your network contact. Don't say that you want to be CEO someday when your current goal is to snag an entry-level position.

Letters of Introduction Addressed to People and Places

These letters are transmitted:

- As Broadcast Letters. These letters are very popular yet least effective if done as opened and unfocussed letters sent to hundreds of employers. They can be effective if they identify specific career fields, functional areas of interest, and particular firms. Be sure to cite the employer's name in these letters.

- As Cold Communiqués. These letters target individuals or companies with whom the writer has no true connection. These might be addressed to lists of senior executives on websites, names in professional association membership directories, or those in specialized, field-focused directories.

- In Advance of On-Campus Interviews. These letters request an interview or set the scene, impressing employers that you communicated after being selected to meet.

- In Advance of Career Fairs. In these cases, the letters set the scene and increase your chances for being granted an interview for post-baccalaureate jobs or internships.

- To Targeted Employers. These letters are best sent to a particular person, although they can be effective if sent generally to Human Resources when uploaded or e-mailed through a company's website. It's recommended to direct such letters to the attention of a particular person or a connection of some kind.

Networking Notes

These are brief e-mail or faxed messages sent to advocates and network members. In these notes, you ask for consideration, referrals, or support. Resumes are attached, and reference is made to a cover letter that will be sent later. While some people still believe these should be handwritten, e-mail and faxing is faster and, now, most appropriate.

Structure of the Cover Letter

The cover letter should, in most cases, be one page. It should always include the following three elements:

1. Introductory focus paragraph. Remember what you once learned about the five-paragraph essay? Begin with a clear thesis statement supported by two paragraphs and end with a conclusion. Cover letters should include the same. The initial paragraph cites job title or functional area of interest, and requests an interview. This first section can identify the foundations upon which you will rest your candidacy. Is it education? Is it work experience in general, or one or two particular accomplishments? Is it a specific project that matches the position's stated requirements?

2. Qualification and motivation paragraphs. These two paragraphs (sometimes presented in bullet-point lists) detail qualification and motivation connections. They identify examples from your past that project abilities to perform in the future. This is where you apply the first two of the five steps. What key resume points will you present here? How can you connect achievements to job requirements? Be specific! The more you

use the language of the field you wish to enter, special phrases and keywords, the better. Talk the talk to walk the walk. Use appropriate language to ensure that you will soon walk into an interview with confidence. Keep in mind that today many employers read the Twitter streams, blogs, and Facebook pages and other social networking site links posted by candidates. Many times these are used to uncover negative information about a candidate, but you have a real advantage if your blog or Twitter stream is timely to your industry and has relevant information that suggests you're a subject matter expert. Call attention to this in the body of your letter.

💬 Action Speak

Coached	Weighed
Evaluated	Reported
Overcame	Participated
Secured	Honed
Strengthened	Integrated

3. Closing paragraph. Restate your desire for an interview, perhaps suggesting a phone interview as a convenient next communication. State that you will follow up to confirm receipt of the letter and accompanying resume. If you wish, you can close with the most critical point you wish to cover during the interview. Of course, also say thank you.

Special Circumstance Statements

These can be added as postscripts or in the last paragraph. You may share with the reader that you anticipate being in a particular city on a particular date, that you have an offer in hand and limited time to conduct interviews, or that you have also enclosed supporting documents such as writing samples, letters of recommendation, or other materials.

Cover Letter Dos

When writing cover letters, too often candidates second-guess themselves by wondering, "Is this what I want employers to see?" You cannot read the minds of potential employers, but you can conduct field-, function-, and firm-specific research to be very focused. Cover letters are most powerful when they are targeted and clearly present performance potential. Here is a list of Dos to help inspire confidence in your cover letter at the research and rough draft stage:

- Identify samples that you wish to model. Find ones that match your goals or appeal to your sense of style.

- Make sure your samples have objectives, qualification summaries, or achievement summaries.

- Define your objectives clearly and concisely.

- Place your most significant achievements in the document as paragraph text or bullet points. Use your cover letter to connect past achievements to future performance potential.

- Be able to describe the specific job you are seeking. Know the qualification connections that would be associated with this position. Generate a collection of keywords associated with your field- or job-focused goals.

- Keep the final version to one page and meticulously check for spelling and grammar mistakes. Have someone proofread it.

If you abide by the list of Dos from the beginning, you will streamline the writing process for yourself and avoid the most common pitfall of cover letter drafting: insufficient planning and lack of effort. In the following chapters, you will be provided with hundreds of examples of cover letters gone RIGHT. They are industry-specific and they are chock full of winning words and powerful phrases that you can incorporate into your own letter. Before you charge ahead to these glowing examples of cover letter success, there is insight to be gained from reading examples at the opposite end of the spectrum: cover letters gone wrong.

Cover Letter Don'ts

It's important to point out that there are some things *not* to say in your cover letter. It may be true that the line between appropriate and inappropriate is often blurred in both casual and professional settings as people struggle to make themselves stand out from the crowd, but that doesn't mean you should adopt an "anything goes" attitude in an effort to get an interview. The point of this document is to help you secure a job, so be careful not to discuss topics that could potentially detract from that goal. The following phrases detail the major pitfalls to avoid.

1. Don't tell your life story. "I was born in Wisconsin, one of three children. I did well in school. I was on the football team and editor of my school newspaper. I moved to Chicago to go to college and . . ." Keep your answer limited to the parts that will affect your suitability for the job.

2. Don't say "I plan to get my MBA as soon as possible" if that isn't relevant to the job. Avoid describing short-term goals that have nothing to do with the position you're interviewing for.

3. Don't highlight a general trait as your greatest strength. Saying "I'm a hard worker who always get to work on time" leaves the reviewer of your cover letter wondering if you have any specific skills related to the job.

4. Don't overstate your enthusiasm for change. Saying "I love change, and without it I get bored" will make companies wary of your commitment and get you flagged as someone who jumps from job to job every two years.

5. Don't focus on unimportant details. Saying "My ideal work environment is an office with big windows and proximity to the train station" doesn't tell your potential employer what sort of work challenges you and what work pace best suits you.

6. Don't appear uninterested in your chosen field. "I decided to pursue a career in advertising because my dad's friend thought I'd be good at it" shows a lack of concern for your future, and it may cause the interviewer to doubt your decision-making abilities.

7. Don't take the focus off your strengths by emphasizing skills you lack. Telling someone "I haven't worked in this field before, but I'm a fast learner" downplays any strengths you have, such as working well on a team or possessing good communication skills. Accentuate the positive as much as possible.

8. Don't be vague when listing your skills. If you're applying for a teaching position, you'll need to be much more specific than just saying "I love kids, and I'm a good teacher." What's special about the way you interact with children, and what makes you a good teacher?

9. Don't paint a picture of yourself as an iron-fisted ruler. If you're targeting a management position, avoid saying, "I'm strict, and in my office it's my way or the highway." Portray yourself as a hands-on manager who works alongside her employees.

> **Green Light** In all your communications, it helps to show that you are flexible and comfortable with change.

10. Don't leave out the details. Saying "I'm good with patients and insurance" in your cover letter is not going to make you stand out against the candidate who says something like, "I dealt with insurance companies on a daily basis, and I found that if I learned how each one worked, it was a lot easier for the doctors in my practice to get paid and for patients to get reimbursed. I also worked at the reception desk at these jobs and was happy to be able to calm down anxious patients and hopefully offer some reassurance."

11. Don't forget to explain how you progressed in your job. By saying "I started out as an assistant and was promoted to a senior position within one year," you don't give the reviewer much information about what you did in the meantime.

12. Don't confuse personal accomplishments with professional ones. While you may be tempted to boast, "My accomplishments include winning my softball team's biggest game of the season by hitting a grand slam," it's not something to mention in your cover letter.

13. Don't minimize the impact your work has had on your current company. Always highlight and focus on results in your cover letter. For example, "I wrote a manual explaining all bookkeeping department procedures in our company. New employees receive a copy of this manual, which helps them learn their job faster."

14. Don't fail to make the connection between your education and the position you're pursuing. Avoid saying "Even though I have no experience managing media communications, I am eager to learn what the job entails." You must relate your background to the job. If it's a big stretch, reconsider your decision to apply.

15. Don't give the wrong impression of your interest in a particular company. "I'd love to work here because my best friend does" is not a good reason. If it's the only reason, again, rethink your decision to apply.

16. Don't convey a sense of enthusiasm about using skills you don't currently possess. Someone with no prior research experience who says "I am thrilled at the prospect of researching medical issues" will be flagged as a person requiring training or close supervision.

17. Don't display a lack of knowledge about your potential future employer. Instead of saying "I am interested in learning more about your company," say "I am interested in speaking with you further about this position." You won't be expected to know everything about the job from the posting alone.

18. Don't display a lack of knowledge about the industry you seek to join. If you're going to work for a book publisher, don't call the manuscripts *articles*. Know which buzzwords will get your cover letter noticed, and use the language spoken by those already in the industry.

19. Don't say, "This Assistant position is clearly the next step I need to take in order to become a principal." You may think this statement shows ambition, but what it really says is that you don't care how you get the experience you need to advance to a higher position.

Endnote: Now that you can recognize where a cover letter goes right and where it goes wrong, you're better equipped to edit your own cover letter drafts. The more you build confidence in your own ability to produce powerful cover letters, the easier it will be to compose and revise them.

Chapter 2

WRITING TO REACH OUT

Networking

According to the U.S. Department of Labor, 60 to 85 percent of all jobs are secured through networking. This method yields the best results because time-strapped and discerning employers want to hire skilled people who are vetted through friends, colleagues, and professional acquaintances. Many big companies even offer referral bonuses to employees who pass on the names of talented applicants, so it makes sense to focus a good amount of your job search efforts on networking. Think about the contacts you can reach out to in your industry and personal networks; make a list and assign dates to when you will reach out—and how.

    As you will see in this chapter, there are two main ways to connect with people in written form: you can write a networking note (which is a brief and personal note meant to get the job conversation started) or a networking letter (a longer, somewhat more formal letter with a more specific solicitation request). Each has its place, and how you word your correspondence will greatly impact the relationship building process, so it's essential that you phrase your letters meaningfully for the best chance of success. Once you review the phrases in the sample networking notes, it should be easy to transform the following networking dos and don'ts from words into successful actions.

The Dos and Don'ts

When you network, you're engaging in person-to-person communication for a specific purpose. Successful job seekers respond to postings, contact places on their hit lists, and, of course, communicate with people expressing desires to interview and find a great job. Commit these rules to memory for the best possible outcome from your networking effort:

- Don't ever be deceptive and ask for information about a career field when you really want consideration or referrals.

- Do honestly and clearly present goals or desired assistance from all you contact.

- Don't limit networking to existing contacts.

- Do expand your network via personal referrals, membership directories, or other listings.

- Don't be presumptive, thinking all your contacts will respond immediately and positively.

- Do be persistent, patient, and enthusiastic when e-mailing, calling, faxing, or mailing.

- Don't appear impersonal or as if you are conducting a mass-mailing networking campaign.

 RED FLAG!

Don't nag your contacts. While you should be persistent, don't harass people for immediate feedback. Give them plenty of time to respond to your networking communications and you'll get better quality job leads.

Networking Notes: Short & Sweet

These are brief and personal notes that are intended to begin a process that will build momentum with each subsequent communication. Typically, they are brief (one or two paragraphs) and do not contain detailed summaries of qualifications. You may attach or enclose your resume, but this is merely to share biographical information quickly, not to solicit consideration formally. Most notes are e-mailed, but sometimes they are handwritten and mailed when convenient. Either way, you will want to keep yours concise, focused, and enthusiastic.

Here are several examples of networking notes appropriate for different contacts. Pay close attention to the phrasing throughout—you'll want to incorporate this into your own correspondence.

CONTACT: Past Employer

Dear Ms. Green:

I am **very proud** that my accounting career began as an Intern and, after, as an Audit Trainee with Any Corporation. As you know, when I left Any Corporation to earn my MBA at Any University in Boston, MA, **my performance record was strong** and my friends within the organization many. While my postgraduate school achievements with Other Company have been **fulfilling**, and all **documented on the attached resume**, your assistance with my efforts to relocate "home" to the Rochester, NY, area would be most welcomed. Do you know of any companies now seeking someone with my **finance**, **auditing**, **cash flow**, **and strategic planning expertise**? Are there individuals you would encourage me to contact? Are there particular posting sites I should utilize or **professional organization** members I should network with? Last, and most ideal, would Any Corporation consider my candidacy?

Your answers to these queries would be most welcomed and appreciated. A few minutes of your time when I next visit Rochester for a prerelocation trip would be wonderful. Also, please convey my regards to all of my old Any Corporation colleagues. Thank you.

Sincerely,

John Smith

CONTACT: Family Friend

Dear Mr. Jones:

It does seem a bit awkward asking you for assistance with my job search, but mom and dad inspired me to overcome my concerns and do so anyway. As you may know by now, via communications with my family members, I am **actively seeking** new Property Management opportunities that will allow me the chance to relocate to the New York City area. Do you know of any **companies now seeking someone with my real estate background**? Are there individuals you would encourage me to contact and send a copy of the attached resume? Are there particular posting sites I should utilize or **local professional organizations** I should join? Last, and most ideal, would Any Corporation consider my candidacy?

Your answers to these queries would be most welcomed and appreciated. **A few minutes of your time** over the phone would be great. When I am next in New York, for interviews or prerelocation activities, please allow me to purchase you and your family dinner or lunch. Thank you for your assistance now and, sincerely, for being a great family friend for so long.

Sincerely,

John Smith

Green Light DO HONESTLY and clearly present goals or desired assistance to all those you contact.

CONTACT: Professional Group Colleague

Dear Ms. Green:

It was good seeing you at the Association of Computer Professionals conference. As we discussed briefly, I am now actively seeking new software design opportunities. Would you feel comfortable **sharing some contact names** with me? Of course, in addition to the attached resume, I will provide each individual **a detailed cover letter** and cite your referral. You know of my background and abilities, and I am very **appreciative** of our friendship and **respectful** of your professional reputation, so I will handle all communications appropriately. Again, the names of contacts, as well as e-mail or mailing addresses, would be most well-received and appreciated. Thank you in advance for the consideration,

John Smith

CONTACT: Instructor / Professor

Dear Ms. Green,

With commencement near, I wanted to gain your **insights and referrals** regarding potential employers. As you know, my interest in marketing and promotions is quite **strong**, and I am very **proud of my accomplishments** in your Marketing Cases and Strategies course. Our final project is **prominently detailed** on the attached resume, and I hope someday soon I will describe it to prospective employers during interviews. Are there particular companies, contacts, or alumni you would encourage me to communicate with? And can

I **use you as a reference**? I will call to follow up on this e-mail, but because you are so busy, continuing our communications electronically would be fine.

Thank you,
Elizabeth Lee

CONTACT: Professional Group Officer
Dear Alice:

As the Vice President of Membership for Women in Advertising I thought you might be able to assist me with my efforts to begin a post-baccalaureate career in the field of advertising. Does WIA offer any **specialized posting or networking services** to members? Are there particular members in the San Francisco Bay area who you would encourage me to contact? Because I will be graduating in June, I would welcome consideration for **a full-time**, **part-time**, **or internship position**.

The attached resume is intended to quickly inform you of my background, not to solicit consideration. Of course, I will forward an appropriate and detailed cover letter when I send this document to Women in Advertising members you recommend. Your assistance with my efforts would be **most appreciated**. Thank you.

Sincerely,
Elizabeth Lee

CONTACT: Alumni
Ms. Green:

As an alumna of Any College, I thought you might be able to assist me with my efforts to find a Public Relations position in the Chicago, IL, area. Attached is a copy of my resume that clearly **projects my qualifications** for these positions. Any **contacts within your firm**, within other firms in the city, or with search firms specializing in public relations and communications would be appreciated. Of course, I would send a more detailed cover letter with my resume to these individuals. While I do hope your firm might **consider my candidacy**, any referrals to other firms would be welcomed. In advance, thank you for your assistance.

John Smith

RED FLAG!

Don't say, "I'm looking for a nine-to-five job." It shows that you're not willing to put in extra time and effort many employers require.

Networking Letters: Focused and Friendly

Unlike networking notes, networking letters are actual solicitations for particular positions or, in some cases, requests for referrals. Most often, these are proactive documents addressed to people who can grant consideration or offer names of others who might also consider candidates for employment. Occasionally, they are reactive documents, when a particular person's name is cited as supporting your candidacy for a specific job. Regularly the same length as any cover letter, networking letters also include similar format and content. Persuading the recipient to review the attached or enclosed resume is clearly the main purpose of these letters.

Phrases for the Introduction

Networking is all about connections, so be sure to mention who gave you the contact information for the person you're reaching out to. If you established the connection on your own, remind him or her how you met (for example, perhaps you met at a conference or were seated next to each other on a plane) and quote or paraphrase them whenever possible to show that you value their input. Be clear about why you're making contact. These phrases present a variety of ways to initiate a networking letter.

Administrative Assistant

Recently, Francis Williams **suggested I contact you** regarding my job search. I am currently seeking a position that would **use my legal**, **administrative**, **and office management knowledge and experience**.

Auto Salesperson

During a recent visit to Rochester, NY, my long-time friend Francis Williams mentioned your name as a contact in the field of auto sales. I understand that your corporation has contracted Bill's agency several times to promote your regional dealerships. I would like to take this opportunity to **ask for any assistance** or, ideally, consideration you might be able to provide with my job search.

Bank Manager

Francis Williams, **a colleague of mine** at United Bank in St. Louis, MO, mentioned your name as an authority in the Midwest banking industry. Francis met you on a visit to your Omaha, NE, office last month and was **impressed by both the reputation and successful operation of your branches**. I now **respectfully request advice**, **consideration**, **or referrals** as I seek banking opportunities in the Omaha area, where I will be **relocating** next month.

Chief Financial Officer

Ideally upon review of my resume you will feel comfortable identifying a few individuals, perhaps corporate clients of Any Bank, who I can **present my candidacy** to, as well as search professionals who specialize in my field.

Customer Support Representative

I met with Dennis last week while on a business trip to Pittsburgh, PA, and he suggested that **you might have an opening** within the customer support department of your corporation and that as a result of your active involvement in the Pennsylvania Association of Customer Service professionals that **you might have some suggestions** regarding others I can present my candidacy to.

Editor

John Curran, **whom I saw recently** at the ABA convention, spoke highly of your **creative**, **market-sensitive approach to publishing** and the tremendous impact you have had on Any Publishing. He also said you might have plans to expand your editorial team and suggested that I write you.

Finance Manager

Kelly Monroe, of First Avenue Bank, informed me that Any Bank **might be expanding its professional staff**. Kelly once worked for me and can attest to my past performance and potential for future success. Based on my **comprehensive experience in the field of finance**, all detailed in the attached resume, I can offer your bank a **broad range** of management and technical skills.

International Controller

It was a **pleasure meeting you last month** when we were both visiting the Maximillians at their home in Austin. As you may recall, I was then working as international controller of Other Company, a multidivision manufacturer of automatic test equipment. Recent ownership changes prompted me to seek a new position in finance management. When I spoke with Francis Maximillian regarding my search, I was strongly encouraged to request your assistance.

Marketing Assistant

It was a pleasure talking to you during our flight to Chicago last April. I hope you enjoyed your trip! As you may recall, I was then a senior at Harvard University studying marketing and sales. **You were kind enough to give me your business card** with instructions to contact you once I was "liberated from the demands of academia." Finally, that day has arrived.

Marketing Specialist

Thank you for taking the time to speak with me after your sales presentation last Thursday. As you may recall, I am now **actively seeking consideration** for a marketing position within Any Corporation. I have applied for a Marketing Specialist position via the online system, but your advice and support would be much appreciated. **Are there individuals to whom I should send my resume** and cover letter directly?

Mortgage/Loan Officer

Francis Williams, one of your branch office managers and fellow alum of Any University, thought you might be interested in someone with my qualifications. I am **currently seeking a new position** with a bank or specialty lender as a mortgage loan officer. When I **shared my goals** with Francis, I was strongly encouraged to contact you immediately.

Nurse

Kelly Williams, a nurse in your pediatric unit, suggested I contact you regarding the currently posted Nurse position at Any Hospital. Kelly believes that I have the **qualifications**, **motivations**, **and special qualities** needed to join her as a member of your care-focused nursing team or "family" as she called it.

Payroll Supervisor

I received your name from a **mutual friend**, Francis Williams. I was employed at Francis's bank several years ago and we worked closely on several projects. **In a recent conversation**, Francis mentioned that you were actively recruiting candidates for a payroll specialist. I hope upon review of the attached resume that **you will judge my candidacy as worthy of an employment interview**.

Production Manager

As Francis Williams may have informed you, as a result of a dramatic downsizing my production position was eliminated, so **I am immediately available to interview** for the Production Manager position now posted on Any Corporation's website. Francis is familiar with my managerial style and accomplishments, for he started his career in production under my supervision.

> **Green Light** *Remember* to keep your networking communication short and enthusiastic!

Publicist

Francis Williams suggested I write you with regard to **opportunities in advertising**, **public relations**, **and promotions**. I would appreciate any information, advice, or consideration you can provide as I search for Publicist or related positions.

Secretary

Francis Williams suggested I apply for the Secretarial position recently posted on your company's website. **As a current employee of Any Corporation**, she is well aware of the qualifications and motivations you seek in administrative support professionals. As a past coworker, she is **very familiar with my potential** to join her on the Any Corporation team. I hope, after reviewing the attached resume, you will find that my abilities and capabilities suit your needs and that I will be invited to interview for this position.

Staff Accountant

It was a pleasure meeting you at the alumni luncheon last Monday and kind of you to offer your assistance with my job search for a new and challenging accounting position. **As you suggested**, and following the instruction on the handout provided, I did register for and now have access to the online posting system and electronic alumni directory. Any additional assistance, advice, or referrals would be most welcomed.

Telecommunications Specialist

A few years ago, I was your son Dan's classmate at the University of Miami. When I bumped into him last week in Billings, Montana, he informed me that you deal closely with several leading specialists in the telecommunications field and **suggested I contact you immediately**. At present, I am interested in joining a company where **I can contribute strong skills and education** in communications.

💬 Action Speak

Accelerated	Maximized
Catapulted	Oversaw
Earned	Reconciled
Handled	Streamlined
Launched	Vitalized

Phrases for Skills and Passion Paragraphs

In these paragraphs, you can describe your experience and point out key skills or achievements listed on your resume. It's also okay to ask your contact for advice or assistance with your job search. But remember: The main objective is to give your contact a reason to think of you first—above any other candidate—when he or she becomes aware of an open position that matches your experience.

Auto Salesperson

Due to recent downsizing, I am **seeking a new**, **long-term association** with an aggressive, fast-paced dealership.

Bank Manager

As my resume indicates, I am a skilled professional with over **ten years of relevant experience**. In addition to an MBA degree (Executive Program), I have five years' loan officer experience, and **a BA degree in Economics and Finance**.

Marketing Assistant

Enclosed is a copy of my resume for your **reference and referral**. I am wondering if there are any Chicago-based individuals whom you would **encourage me to contact**. In particular, I would like to contact someone at Leo Burnett or Quaker Oats. **Could I use your name** in my correspondence with these persons? In addition, I would like to request consideration for a position with Any Corporation.

Marketing Specialist

Detailed on the attached resume, during the past five years, my experience in my present marketing position **focused on product management**, **strategic planning**, **marketing**, and the sale of equipment, systems, chemicals, and related products and services. I am a **strong contributing member of the team** responsible for the worldwide marketing of bio-instrument chemicals sold to biotech markets, pharmaceutical markets, and research laboratories.

Mortgage/Loan Officer

My current position as a senior collections specialist has provided me with the opportunity to **accomplish and exceed a set objective** of reducing delinquent loans from $24 million to $10 million within six months. At this point, I feel I have successfully **surpassed both company and personal goals** and am **searching for new and greater challenges**, particularly those that would involve marketing and client–relationship building responsibilities.

Payroll Supervisor

My background encompasses **eleven years of progressively responsible and sophisticated hands-on experience**, including serving as a union benefits coordinator and human resources administrator. Most significant, in my present position as payroll administrator, with a special emphasis on the **day-to-day details** of related financial and MIS operations, I have gained particular expertise required of a Payroll Supervisor.

Production Manager

As you can see from my resume, **production-related experience** extends throughout the last two decades. After completing a BS in Management, I entered the Other Company's management development program and found operations and production to be my greatest strengths. **Several titles**, **progressively responsible positions**, **and promotions later** I amassed supervisory and Production Management experience with the same large, Washington, D.C.–based corporation. While the firm is now downsizing, I remain **eager to continue an accomplishment-filled career** with Any Corporation.

Publicist

As you will see after you review this document, I possess **comprehensive experience** supporting a successful direct-mail fundraising effort of a major university. Training and expertise also include publicity and public relations, staff training and supervision, program coordination, budget management, market research, copyediting, and management and administration of related detail.

Secretary

I now offer Any Corporation the **skills I possess**, which include:

- Administrative and customer service achievements spanning over six years.

- Abilities to **use**, **support**, **and teach others** Word, Access, PowerPoint, Excel, and Internet applications.

- Bilingual Spanish–English abilities that have been **used on the job**.

- Awareness of the critical importance of secretarial and administrative staffers.

Telecommunications Specialist

My qualifications, all detailed on the enclosed resume, are as follows:

- A Bachelor of Arts in Communications that included courses, projects, and case studies addressing marketing, public relations, web design, and advertising issues.

- Experience with all **planning and implementation areas** of marketing, public relations, advertising, and sales.

- Experience as an assistant account executive for a major advertising agency, **whose clients include** telecommunication firms, and as promotions intern at a radio station.

- Bilingual German–English skills, and experience living and studying in Europe.

Phrases for the Closer

Don't be shy—ask for a meeting, a referral, or consideration for an existing open position with your contact's company. Here are some tactfully worded examples that show how you can express your interest and enthusiasm.

Administrative Assistant

If you know of any related openings or contacts to whom I should forward a resume, I would appreciate your advice and referrals. Of course, **if your firm needs a person with my background**, your consideration would also be appreciated.

Auto Salesperson

I will be visiting the Rochester, NY, area next week and **I would like to meet with you if your schedule permits**. Your insight into the market, as well as any specific advice or contact names, would be very helpful.

Bank Manager

During a brief telephone or in-person conversation, I could gain contact names within Any Bank, or within other area financial institutions, as well as any search professionals you think might be of assistance. Of course, if Any Bank would **find my candidacy attractive**, I would also welcome your consideration.

Customer Support Representative

Could we meet so that I can further outline my qualifications and how I could **contribute successfully to your firm**? And, if appropriate, could you provide me with a list of additional contacts? I look forward to your advice, referrals, and, ideally, consideration for employment with Any Corporation.

Finance Manager

I am confident I could **contribute my expertise to the continued success of** Any Bank and would welcome the chance to discuss career opportunities. My desire to relocate to the New York City area is strong, as is my **willingness to travel**, solicit new business, and become an **accomplishment-driven professional** on the Any Bank team.

International Controller

Also, I will be visiting Austin, TX, again in two weeks. Should your schedule permit, I would like to meet, perhaps for lunch or dinner. This would allow me to **thank you properly** and personally for your assistance, and provide me the opportunity to **gain additional insights** you might have regarding my search efforts as they focus on Austin.

Green Light *Do use networking websites like LinkedIn to increase your growing pool of network contacts.*

Marketing Specialist

I appreciate your advice, consideration, and support of my candidacy and I look forward to speaking with you regarding appropriate next steps.

Mortgage/Loan Officer

Thank you for your consideration. Of course, **feel free to communicate** with Francis or anyone on my reference list regarding my potential to be a performance-driven and very successful Loan Officer.

Nurse

I trust you will agree with Kelly's views regarding my candidacy, and **grant me the opportunity to interview for this position** and support my credentials in person. Of course, I did complete the online application, but I wanted to personalize my candidacy via this letter, accompanying resume, and letters of recommendation.

Payroll Supervisor

I look forward to speaking with you in detail about **your expectations** for the person who becomes Any Corporation's next Payroll Supervisor and regarding my qualifications for this position.

Secretary

I look forward to interviewing for the Secretarial position now available at Any Corporation. Thank you for your consideration.

Staff Accountant

If you know of Any Corporation in need of an experienced Accountant, in addition to those now posted on Any College's online system, **I would appreciate your letting me know**. Your idea of contacting all past on-campus recruiters was a good one and **I look forward to receiving the listing from you**. And, I will of course begin to network with other alumni in the accounting field to conduct, as you called it, "a proactive networking blitz."

Telecommunications Specialist

I would greatly appreciate any advice or referrals you might be able to provide. A listing of firms and contact names would be wonderful, and I would of course cite your referral in any communications with these individuals.

Endnote: Reaching out and touching as many of your contacts as possible can be a potent way to capture opportunities at companies where you'd like to work. By knowing when to write a note versus when to write a letter, and crafting professional, friendly correspondences to your contacts, you can exponentially increase your odds of landing a job in your given industry.

Chapter 3

WRITING TO RESPOND

Job Postings

It would be great if we had networking contacts at every job we applied to, but realistically this is just not the case. Most of us spend hours online perusing the barrage of open positions, hoping we'll find a suitable match. When you don't know anyone at a prospective company, it's even more important to use wording that captures an employer's attention. This sample collection of cover letter phrases reveals some of the best ways to respond to job postings. Here, the samples are organized by paragraph type (introductory, qualification and motivation, and conclusion).

Phrases for Introductory Paragraphs

These phrases convey a strong sense of enthusiasm and interest.

Administrative Assistant

Upon reading the advertisement in the Jackson Review, I was **inspired to contact you** immediately and offer this cover letter and attached resume **to formalize my interest**.

Assistant Curator

Please **consider me** a strong, enthusiastic, and focused candidate for the Assistant Curator position recently advertised on *www.evansvillecourierjobs.com*.

Assistant Editor

I would like to take all appropriate steps to formalize my candidacy for the position of Assistant Editor. When I reviewed the posting advertised via *www.bostonglobejobs.com*, **I wanted to immediately share** the attached resume and writing samples.

Field Finance Manager

While my current position with Other Company, Inc. is most challenging and rewarding, the **opportunity to serve** within **the capacities described in the posting** is professionally exciting.

Fundraiser

I hope someday my enthusiasm and professionalism **can contribute to the success** of your development campaigns and grant application efforts.

Home Economics Department Coordinator

It would be **with great professional enthusiasm** and the pride of an alumnus that I now formalize my candidacy for the Home Economics Department Coordinator position.

Multimedia Specialist

Please consider me **a strong**, **enthusiastic**, **and qualified candidate** for the Multimedia Specialist position recently posted on Any Corporation's website.

 RED FLAG!

Don't rely on your training or education alone to speak for the skills you possess. Make your talents explicit.

Newspaper Intern

As documented on the enclosed resume, I am currently a junior English major **with a strong interest** in a journalism career.

The following phrases cite specific numbers that communicate a wealth of experience and track record of success.

Administrative Judge

More than ten years of experience as a litigator and **ever-curious** student of the judicial system have, I trust, prepared me to be a competent and appropriately confident candidate for the Administrative Judge position.

Chief Financial Officer

Detailed on the attached resume, I have a ten-year **record of success** managing corporate financial operations for profitable and fast-growing manufacturing companies with multistate and international operations.

Claims Adjuster

During the past fifteen years, I have been with a major insurance company **primarily focusing on** workers' compensation claims. Accomplishments, all cited on the attached resume, required **a sound background** in claims management, cost containment, customer relations, employee training, and administrative support. I am proud that annually, for the past five years, **I have cost-effectively negotiated** well over two hundred claims.

Travel Agent

As the attached resume indicates, I have a decade of **progressive responsible experience** in the travel and tourism field.

These phrases make a connection between the candidates' skills and the skills listed in the job descriptions.

Analyst

Detailed on the attached resume, my current position as an Analyst at Another Company **requires a skill set similar to the one stated** as required for your position.

Campus Police Officer

Your advertisement in *Careers in Law Enforcement* **notes requirements and capabilities that I possess** and would like to discuss during an interview.

Child Care Assistant Director

As a licensed child care provider in the state of Ohio with three years' experience in a private center, the position described in your Child Care Assistant Director posting on *www.toledojobs.com* **is exactly what I seek**.

Hotel Manager

Each step on my current career path has **allowed me to develop qualifications** for the Hotel Manager position announced via the Hospitality Association Newsletter.

International Buyer

As I read the position appearing on Any Corporation's website, I **identified** a number of **specific qualifications** I possess that **match those you seek**.

Park Maintenance Supervisor

As a current town employee, it would be **a wonderful and logical next step** to serve within roles that would ask me to **manage**, **motivate**, **hire**, **and train** others to perform efficiently and professionally.

> **Green Light** Make mention of the particular job or job function you desire in the first paragraph of your cover letter.

This sample calls attention to a portfolio that can be accessed online, which is convenient and easy for the recipient to review.

Associate Desktop Publisher

In support of my candidacy for the Associate Desktop Publisher position on your firm's website, attached is a copy of my resume. Also, please review my portfolio at *www.csmith.com.*

These phrases demonstrate how to call attention to materials you are submitting in addition to your resume.

Cosmetologist

Attached please find my resume, a list of references, and a letter of recommendation. While these documents do inform you of **my professional experiences and capabilities**, through an interview **I can learn more about your vision** for Any Boutique, what you expect of the Cosmetologist, and **the nature of your clientele**.

Director of Public Works

Attached is a resume, a list of references, and performance reviews from the previous two years. All reveal past achievements.

Editor

I am very interested in the Editor position listed on *www.dallasmorningnewsjobs.com*. Attached, please find my resume and a writing sample, both offered to support my candidacy and **request for an interview**.

Meeting Planner

I would like to be Any Corporation's meeting planner. After reading your announcement in the *San Francisco Chronicle*, I was eager to share qualifications via the attached resume and letters of recommendation. After evaluating these documents, I hope you would **allow me the opportunity** to interview for this exciting opportunity.

These phrases show how to word a request to keep your application confidential.

Dental Hygienist

I would like to interview for the Dental Hygienist position you advertised in the *Times-Union*. My concerns for current patients are such that I must ask that my candidacy remain confidential. While I am **eager to interview**, share my motivations and qualifications, and provide you with references, I ask you to please keep our communications private.

Event Planner

Current circumstances require that my interest in this position remain confidential, but **please be assured** I am most definitely **ready to interview** and accept an offer if one were given.

These phrases mention crucial keywords that immediately make the applicants stand out.

Photographer/Writer

Detailed on the enclosed resume and **illustrated via samples of my work**, I am an **accomplished** photographer with over ten years' experience in commercial and industrial photography, portraiture, and wedding photography. Published writings include *A Shutterbug's Notes* and *Picture Your Pet,* and **I have broad experience** creating printed and online newsletters, which involved all copy and graphics.

Production Quality Control Manager

After seven years of **progressively responsible experience** in production, electro-mechanical assembly, soldering, testing, and total quality management with a precision manufacturing operation, I feel **I have all the qualifications you require** for the Production Quality Control Manager position.

Program Coordinator

I am **particularly qualified** for this opportunity as a result of my double language major, my current enrollment in two language-proficiency certificate programs, as well as past experiences within tutorial and teaching roles.

Site Location Supervisor

During the past fifteen years, my experiences as a developer, general contractor, owner, and property manager of residential, commercial, and industrial projects have been extensive. **In conjunction with** these projects, I was **actively involved** in investment analysis, whole loans and structured transactions, and financial control **to assure quality completion within schedules and budgets**.

Technical Writer

As detailed on the attached resume, I am currently a Technical Writer and Senior Project Administrator at Rizzo Associates. **Within these capacities** I complete all research, drafting, editing, and finalizing of documentation for a defense contractor.

This sample mentions a personal connection within the company that may help the applicant get his or her foot in the door.

Senior HVAC Technician

At the suggestion of Donald Lee of your HVAC department, **I am requesting an interview** for the Senior HVAC Technician position recently posted on Any Corporation's website. Donald is **well aware of my background**, so he encouraged me to share my resume and request consideration for this opportunity.

These phrases can help you out if you're responding to a confidential listing. Note that each one mentions where the listing was found, and many focus on education, current employment, and professional achievements.

Applications Programmer

After reviewing your posting in *www.softwarejobs.com*, **I seek to become an active candidate** for this position by submitting the attached resume via this web-based system.

Assistant Personnel Officer

I would like to interview for the Assistant Personnel Officer position recently advertised in the *Washington Post*. As the attached resume indicates, I have extensive experience in personnel, including **my most recent position** as Assistant Staff Manager at Virginia General Hospital. **To succeed in this capacity** I recruited and trained administrative and clerical staffs, ancillary and works department staffs, and professional and technical staffs. I also evaluated personnel, conducted disciplinary and grievance interviews, signed employees to contracts, and advised staff on conditions of employment, entitlements, and maternity leave.

Biomedical Engineer

As I recently **earned** my undergraduate biomedical engineering degree, it is **with great enthusiasm** that I now seek to interview for the Engineering Trainee Position recently posted on *www.biojobs.com*.

Business Consultant

I am responding to your advertisement for a Business Consultant in the *Wall Street Journal.* It is likely that my consulting experience with large and small businesses **matches the requirements for this position**.

Legal Associate

Please consider me a strong candidate for the Legal Associate position advertised in *Lawyers Weekly*. Upon reading this announcement, I wanted to provide you **the enclosed resume**, **recommendations**, **and transcripts**. As you will note from my resume, I hold a Juris Doctor degree and recently received a Master of Tax and Accounting, with a concentration in estates and trust. Described on each of the supporting documents, my career started as a general practitioner, and, with time, became more involved in estate planning activities. Thus, it is with **a comprehensive foundation of knowledge and professional experience** that I now seek to interview for and, I hope, serve within the capacities of the Legal Associate.

Librarian

I would like to apply for the position of Librarian advertised on *www.libraryscience.com*. In addition to an MLS. degree and ALA accreditation, I have **experience in varied settings**. Professionally, experience at the Kathryn Bell Library for the past eight years focused on patron services and education, within circulation and reference desk roles **enhanced the above capabilities**. Prior, working within a private secondary school, **I addressed issues** pertinent to faculty, students, and parents. **In all capacities**, and via academic training, including a graduate degree in library science and undergraduate English major, I **nurtured** research, acquisition, as well as book manuscript, journal, and dissertations archival and retrieval efforts.

Operations Manager

I would like to interview for the Operations Manager position recently posted in the *Arkansas Democrat-Gazette*. While the announcement does reveal some of what you are seeking, **during an interview I can** learn more about what you would expect of the next Operations Manager and **target specific capabilities accordingly**.

Pharmaceutical Sales

After success selling tangible products and software services, it is **with great focus and confidence** that I now seek to interview for the Pharmaceutical Sales position recently posted on *www.pharmjobs.com*.

Phrases for Qualification and Motivation Paragraphs

These phrases communicate current and past job responsibilities by describing key tasks the applicants have performed. Notice how these phrases include strong action verbs and adverbs to grab the recipients' attention. Important job-specific keywords are also used.

Administrative Assistant

By **prioritizing tasks**, **managing time efficiently**, and **communicating effectively** with those to whom I reported, as well as those who reported to me, I **maximized the output** and customer service efforts of a very **demanding** office.

Administrative Judge

In this position, I **utilized** legal knowledge as well as research, analytical, and writing skills in addition to trial and negotiation talents to yield among my office's highest conviction rates.

Analyst

I have **monitored and analyzed** accounts receivable and accounts payable, and I have worked with internal accountants to complete monthly, quarterly, and annual reports.

Assistant Curator

As the Classical Music Listings Coordinator for the Complete Musical Almanac summer and fall supplements, I **updated a comprehensive database** and **oversaw creation of a system** that stores and retrieves past editions, using keywords, dates, composers, and genre.

Associate Desktop Publisher

Ten years of progressively responsible computer experience, all detailed on my resume, include **researching**, **developing**, **and documenting** the operational procedures of a software seller. I was responsible for all aspects of the design, creation, and dissemination of many, many user-friendly, yet state-of-the-art, manuals. I also **coordinated** and published the sales and marketing of a newsletter distributed monthly to **key accounts** and sales representatives.

Campus Police Officer

Described in detail on the attached resume, in my present position I **maintain the highest possible** site and operations security for a defense contractor. Prior, for almost a decade, I served in the United States Army, maintaining **peak** law enforcement/security alertness and the welfare of all personnel. In that capacity, I received numerous letters of commendation for **superior job performance**.

💬 Action Speak

Cemented	Sold
Conceived	Targeted
Enlisted	Transformed
Expedited	Utilized
Presided	Won

Case Manager

Noted on my resume, I have **guided** at-risk youth as well as inmates through individual counseling and structured programs. This involved extensive case documentation, referrals, and **goal identification**, as well as **communication and interaction with** boards of trustees, agency personnel, and others. All cases were **clearly**, **concisely**, **and professionally tracked and documented**, so appropriate groups, including psychologists, teachers, judges, and parole boards, could review them.

Dentistry Department Manager

Through **efficient tracking and control systems**, budget planning, and administration, I have, and can continue to, **generate cost savings and greater profit margins**.

Features Reporter

While earning **dual degrees** in Journalism and Fine Arts at Mount St. Mary's, I worked as editor-in-chief of the yearbook and as layout editor and reporter for the school's weekly newspaper, **where I became proficient in** desktop publishing.

Hospital Administrator

I am a **strong organizer**, **enthusiastic speaker**, **capable leader**, **and team player** who can interface effectively with you, your Any Health Resource colleagues, medical professionals, as well as support staff and vendors.

Legal Assistant

This fall and past summer, I interned for a small general practice firm, where I was **entrusted with a great deal of responsibility**. In paralegal capacities I researched, wrote, and proofed appellate briefs; composed memoranda pertaining to corporate, contract, and criminal law; and drafted complaints and answers. I was an **active participant** in attorney–client conferences, interviewing clients, and addressing how the law affects clients' suits, as well as raising potential consequences of varied legal outcomes.

Occupational Health Manager

I am a certified occupational health nurse with twenty-one years of experience **developing and implementing** occupational health programs. Each related position **required sound knowledge of** OSHA and general occupational health issues in manufacturing, research, and healthcare settings. I have served within diagnostic, patient care, physician support, education, training, and regulatory compliance roles.

Photographer/Writer

Academically, I hold a Bachelor of Arts in English from Reed College, where **relevant coursework** included feature writing, photojournalism, and news reporting. I have **attended seminars and workshops** through the Fred Jones Workshop and the Winona School of Professional Photography. My photos have appeared in the Winona course catalog, BBI Printing Company's catalog, and numerous Smithco publications (including annual reports and newsletters). I wrote all copy for the above-cited books.

Political Staffer

Currently, I am an Administrative Assistant at the State House in Providence, RI. In this role, my **primary**

responsibilities include writing press releases, researching and drafting legislation, and consistent constituent contact. I have also **worked with various committees** and legislators regarding an array of legislative issues. Prior, I worked as an intern at the Lieutenant Governor's office and I actively worked for several political and social causes on campus and in the Boston, MA, area.

Product Developer

I have **more than ten years of experience** in manufacturing R&D, management of new product development, and existing product redevelopment and upgrade. I am especially experienced with complex composite materials, precision metal castings, and PC board industries. In addition, I have **extensive experience** both as a teacher and a lecturer at several well-known universities; and have earned a PhD in Materials Science Engineering and completed undergraduate studies in Mechanical Engineering.

Publisher's Assistant

As a current temporary assignment worker with All-temps in Topeka, KS, I have become **highly computer literate** in both Macintosh and Windows operating systems and software programs. To accomplish all that is cited on my resume, I was organized and accurate, **mastered new information rapidly**, **communicated effectively** with supervisors, peers, and subordinates, and I **work well with diverse individuals**.

Restaurant Manager Trainee

I have held **positions of responsibility** in banquet and special event catering, function management, and restaurant food service operations. I have additional experience in front-desk operation of a conference facility. Within each position, I nurtured **ever-improving organizational**, **leadership**, **training**, **and supervisory skills** in settings dedicated to providing quality service and performance in **high-volume operations**.

Television Camera Operator

At L.A. Productions, I was **involved in all aspects** of video production, **supporting** writing, direction, production, and editing efforts associated with three short 8-mm films and several music videos that were shot and edited using digital equipment.

The following phrases direct attention to specific sections of the applicants' resumes. Taking this approach is helpful when certain aspects (and not necessarily all aspects) of your professional or educational experience directly correlate to the job for which you're applying.

Assistant Hospital Supervisor

Recently, I took a sabbatical and finished my Masters of Public Health at Emerson College, so I am now actively seeking opportunities **to build upon academic and employment skill sets**. Please focus particular attention on the summary of qualification section of my resume, for all **competencies and potential to succeed** as your Assistant Hospital Supervisor are **clearly noted**.

Conference Coordinator

When making determinations regarding interviews, please focus attention on accomplishments associated with my roles as Director of Volunteer Services, specifically those related to **planning and implementing** annual educational, fundraising, and community-awareness events.

Gemologist

The summary of qualification section of my resume **highlights** retail and manufacturing gemology experiences as well as previous public relations, sales, promotions, and retail **achievements**.

These phrases state how the job in question can help the applicants grow professionally.

Athletic Director

Recently, I became responsible for running Yale University's boathouse and two national secondary rowing competitions. Over the past two seasons, I **addressed all** ordering, budgeting, donation solicitation, parts inventory, and travel arrangements for crew teams. I now **wish to continue my relationships with** secondary coaches and educators within administrative roles.

Child Care Assistant Director

As AnyCenter's Assistant Director I will continue **my passionate commitment** to children, yet **expand my efforts** to support the professional growth of my colleagues as well as effective marketing, parent relations, and management undertakings.

These phrases cite continued education and training these applicants have pursued. Including this information in your cover letter lets the recipient know how you've stayed current in your field.

Chief Financial Officer

I have been a Certified Public Accountant for over two decades, completing continued professional studies required of updated certification. I have earned an MBA in Finance and a Bachelor of Arts in Accounting. Most important, I have always supported the educational and professional development of my staff and hired those **committed** to continued learning and professional excellence.

Home Economics Department Coordinator

Academically, in addition to earning a BS in Home Economics and Nutrition Education, I **completed supplemental professional development** with each employer since graduation. Additional training now includes **specialized seminars** in preventative nutrition, community outreach, and budget management, all taught by faculty of a **well-respected** teaching hospital.

Senior HVAC Technician

I possess nine years of experience in after-warranty maintenance, preventive maintenance programs, and complete overhaul of major heating, air conditioning, and ventilation systems. I have **successfully installed and repaired** systems within varied buildings and work settings, often in facilities that are **challenging and requiring creativity** as well as technical know-how. I have also completed extensive and continuous education and training on the latest and most cost-efficient energy and control systems.

These phrases point to figures that support the candidates' successes in their current jobs.

Customer Service Manager

During my tenure, 55 percent of the entry-level staff I trained advanced to managerial positions within Fortmiller. **I instilled within these men and women** that customer service excellence does sustain loyalty, enhance sales, and, ultimately, yield profitability.

Director of Public Works

As featured on my resume, I am an **effective** manager and budget administrator; and I have the ability to work with individuals and groups in construction/public works environments where concentration is on community services, safety, the environment, and constituency concerns.

These phrases provide some insight into the applicants' interests and clarify why the applicants are seeking out these positions considering their work experiences to date.

Park Maintenance Supervisor

For the past twelve years, I have held positions within the Youngstown Fire Department. Although my current position is **secure and rewarding**, it is strictly administrative and does not allow me to physically participate, as I have in the past, in actual firefighting or other hands-on activities that provide the outdoor work environment I most enjoy. The Park Maintenance Supervisor position described in your advertisement **matches motivations and qualifications presented on my resume and in this letter**.

 RED FLAG!
DON'T LEAVE OUT the details. Saying, "I'm good with people" is not ample proof of your interpersonal skills.

Pharmacist

Since graduating from the University of the Pacific School of Pharmacy I have successfully completed all professional roles and responsibilities while working within a hospital setting. While my experiences at the David Grant Medical Center were challenging and rewarding, I now seek a position that will **allow me to continue my career development** within a retail pharmacy setting.

State Administrator

While my previous positions have been challenging, rewarding, and broad in scope, I now wish **my expertise to be utilized** by Any Organization. **Your mission** to provide lobbying and financial support for those individuals and groups committed to the education of deserving students **is one I seek to transform** into record-breaking fundraising, dynamic public relations, and effective policy papers.

The following sample shows phrases used to communicate interest in a job posting with a regional focus, as well a willingness to relocate to the specified region.

Travel Agent

Relocation to Connecticut motivates me to respond enthusiastically to your posting.

Recent efforts coordinating all travel and accommodations for those attending a major conference held at the Mohegan Sun have enhanced my relationship with the Greater Connecticut Convention and Visitor's Bureau and the Connecticut Chamber of Commerce and heightened my awareness of this region. I now **strongly believe in my potential** to market services to people traveling to and from Connecticut, for business as well as personal reasons.

The phrases that follow share a common trait: They are organized in bullet points. Using bullet points in your cover letter communicates information quickly and effectively. That's especially important when you're competing against hundreds of other applicants for the same job. The phrases you use in bullet points need to be short and direct. This is another situation where the use of clear action verbs and adverbs is key.

Assistant Editor

Through internships, co-curriculars, and practical experience, I now offer Any Corporation:

- Writing, editing, and layout **skills gained** as features editor, art editor, graphic artist, and reporter for various college publications.

- Knowledge and technical skills gained from courses and projects associated with advertising art and desktop publishing.

- Experience using PageMaker, Word, WordPerfect, Excel, PowerPoint, and varied graphics software to draft, edit, and finalize publications and presentations and to create dynamic graphics.

Associate Desktop Publisher

Successful completion of **the projects detailed on my resume** require skills that match those stated as required of the Associate Desktop Publisher post. These qualifications include:

- Experience transforming research abilities into factual, detailed, and accurate copy and graphics.

- **Record of success planning, overseeing, and delivering projects on time** and error free.

- Comprehensive graphic and text editing talents, and capacities to **maximize the efforts** of writers, graphic artists, designers, and freelancers.

- Proficiency using, supporting, and teaching others Word, PageMaker, PhotoShop, PhotoShow, Visual Studio, Picture It, QuarkXPress, Illustrator, Front Page, Print Shop, and Publisher.

Claims Adjuster

In summary, **my qualifications, motivations, and achievements include**:

- Over fifteen years of progressively responsible claims experience, encompassing life, health, and auto, but specializing in workers' compensation.

- Knowledge of laws and regulations pertaining to claims and potential outcomes of litigation.

- Experience conducting extensive research, working with investigators, and appropriately interacting with policyholders, physicians, healthcare practitioners, and legal professionals.

- Record of success coordinating detailed data and **negotiating effectively** with claimants, professional peers, corporate management, and others to arrive at **mutually favorable solutions**.

- Experience training, establishing goals for, monitoring, and supervising claims professionals.

Clinical Research Nurse

As a result of patient care- and research-related experiences, I have nurtured the skills stated as required in the posting. These include:

- Past experience in clinical research.

- Capacities to develop and follow detailed protocols, procedures, and database-collection efforts.

- **Commitment to flawless** patient record keeping and confidentiality.

- Knowledge of issues pertaining to AIDS and experience working with this patient population.

- Experience working in research contexts, supporting clinical trials and laboratory research efforts.

- Graduate and undergraduate studies in nursing, including anatomy and physiology.

Cosmetologist

Now, at the Other Boutique, I am proud to say that I have:

- **Developed a strong and loyal clientele.**

- Introduced an exciting new and profitable line of cosmetic products.

- **Expanded** bridal- and wedding-party business.

- Accounted for sales in excess of $4,000 for 14 months.

Dental Hygienist

Summarizing all that appears on the attached resume, I offer:

- Current experience as a Hygienist, Surgical Assistant, and Assistant Office Manager.

- **Success in providing** state-of-the-art prophylaxis treatment to adults and adolescents.

- Capacity to perform presurgical, surgical, and post-operative care roles.

- **Progressively responsible experience** as a Hygienist, Assistant, and Office Administrator.

- Sound knowledge of medical terminology and clinical procedures.

- **Certification** in first aid, cardiopulmonary resuscitations, and electrocardiography.

Editor

Detailed on my resume, specific abilities and achievements of mine that match the stated requirements include:

- Over two years of experience within book acquisition, editorial production, and marketing roles

- **Special knowledge of** youth and adult markets, focusing on lifestyle, sports, and leisure.

- **The commitment to blend creativity with profitability**.

Event Planner

I am confident my six years of experience in public relations with a focus on event planning **have prepared me to succeed** in the position described in the posting. I offer you and your Any Corporation colleagues:

- Experience planning annual marketing, promotions, fundraising, and volunteer recognition events.
- **Proven abilities to negotiate and liaise** with catering, hotel, and travel professionals.
- Capacities to generate corporate partners and individuals willing to share event costs.
- Record of success using events **to mobilize and motivate others** and, ultimately, have **bottom line impact** on sales or donations.

Field Finance Manager

It would be **with great focus and confidence** that I would:

- **Develop new and enhance existing relationships** with dealers who use Any Corporation financing.
- Monitor existing accounts and provide detailed weekly, monthly, quarterly, and annual reports to senior managers and field representatives.
- Hire, train, and motivate field representatives.
- Focus on **profitability**, risk management, and underwriting responsibilities.

RED FLAG!
DON'T DRAW ATTENTION to any weaknesses. Writing, "I haven't worked in this field before, but I'm a fast learner" in your cover letter is honest but damages your credibility.

Loan Officer

Qualifications, capabilities, and achievements all detailed on the resume include:

- **Outstanding record** of achieving sales goals as Branch Manager; successfully conducting residential and commercial mortgage acquisitions and personal and commercial loan transactions.
- Extensive experience developing commercial lending packages for private clientele, including financial restructuring, REFI, equipment financing; coordinating activities with COMIDA, GCIDA, IBDC, and ESDC, and attorneys, appraisers, title companies, and governments.
- Capacity to train, supervise, and motivate others to achieve **maximum performance**.
- **Expertise to develop** marketing strategies and collateral, internal management programs, and professional business plans **through utilization of Word, Excel, and PowerPoint**.
- Successfully **developing and implementing** marketing strategies and collateral material.

Office Receptionist

In summary, my receptionist and administrative skills include:

- Experience using multiple phone lines and serving as telephone and in-person receptionist.
- 70 wpm typing speed and proficiency using word processing programs and spreadsheet applications.
- **Strong worth ethic** and record of success within corporate, medical, and retail settings.

Public Relations Associate

I would like to touch on particular aspects of my background that should be of interest to you. These include:

- Over five years' progressively responsible campaign development experience.
- Undergraduate Public Relations degree from **one of the nation's top** communication program.
- Capacities to **successfully address needs and achieve goals** of corporate and not-for-profit clients.

Purchasing Agent

When starting my career, as purchasing clerk and now as a Senior Buyer who wishes to become your next Purchasing Agent, I have learned to:

- Clarify the needs of end users.
- Source and **communicate effectively** with vendors and suppliers via phone and Internet.

- Create detailed spreadsheet cost-benefit analyses of potential purchases.
- Communicate with end users and negotiate with suppliers and vendors with great focus.
- **Track, store, and retrieve** all purchase documentation, delivery dates, warrantees, and installation agreements.
- Use purchasing, budgetary, and related software systems

Social Worker

Previewing and reviewing what appears on the resume, I offer the following:

- Capabilities to serve within comprehensive social work capacities in school or healthcare settings
- **Experience creating and implementing** treatment plans for clients with psychosocial, behavioral, and health-related disorders.
- **Capacity to manage** cases, maintain accurate case records, and create detailed reports.

Technical Writer

Summarizing what appears on the attached resume, the capabilities and abilities I will use to succeed at Any Tech include:

- Proven abilities to structure technical writing projects and motivate others to complete components **accurately and on time**.
- Capacities to transform technical information into detailed illustrations and documentation.

- **Sensitivities related to** creation of classified training and support materials for military hardware.

- Security Clearance Level IA.

- **Project- and team-management skills nurtured via observation and experience**.

- Capacities to **identify specific task components** and **set realistic deadlines**, then monitor and motivate others.

- Expertise associated with the use of Word, WordPerfect, PowerPoint, Lotus 1-2-3, Excel, and CAD.

Telemarketer

My achievements to date include:

- Induction into performance clubs and **earning of multiple recognitions** over the past three years.

- Personal responsibility for over $500,000 FY annual sales.

- **Record of consistently reaching or exceeding established goals** for over four years.

- Qualifications gained with ESP Telecom and the Test Review Education Group include:

- **Outstanding selling and closing capabilities** illustrated by a proven track record of exceeding goals.

- Active listening techniques, nurturing conversations through appropriate questioning.

- **Drive and focus required** to meet contact and sales quotas, meeting self- and other-established deadlines.

- Confidence in cold calling and direct sales roles, marketing services and products to businesses and clients.

- **Pride associated with** using earnings as a telemarketer to pay for college tuition and expenses.

- Knowledge, concepts, specialized techniques, and vocabulary gained from business administration, public speaking, persuasive writing, and marketing courses.

Phrases for Closing Paragraphs

These phrases show how you could handle wording the request for an interview.

Administrative Assistant

I hope you will give me **the opportunity to discuss the available position** with you.

Administrative Judge

I welcome the opportunity to discuss my qualifications with the selection committee.

Assistant Curator

I have often relied on the resources available at Any Music Library, and I would welcome the opportunity to join your curatorial staff. I would be **happy to discuss the position with you further**.

Assistant Editor

I hope you will give me **the opportunity to discuss your expectations** for this position and the above bullets, point by point.

Assistant Hospital Supervisor

I would be **interested in speaking with you further** regarding this position.

Associate Desktop Publisher

I will be visiting Richmond next week, and I would be **happy to meet with you at your convenience**.

Campus Police Officer

I would like to discuss my qualifications and **outline the potential I have** to be a strong member of your security force.

Case Manager

I would welcome a meeting **to discuss my academic as well as professional background** and to learn more about the undertakings of Any Agency.

Child Care Assistant Director

During an interview I can elaborate upon qualifications cited in this letter and the Summary of Qualification on my resume. **Ideally, we might also discuss** the inspiration I gained and sought to give as the author of the children's book *Home We Go!* I would appreciate the opportunity to speak to you further about this position.

Claims Adjuster

I hope I can share my qualifications for the Claims Adjuster position with Any Insurance. My salary requirements are appropriate for the position, so please let's discuss my desire to become a **strong contributor** to your claims' efforts.

Customer Service Manager

It would be **with enthusiasm and confidence** that I would interview for this exciting opportunity. I do hope that after you review my resume, as well as the attached training memos, that you will wish to discuss my customer service experience.

Dental Hygienist

I look forward to meeting with you and further discussing **my desires to join your team**.

Dentistry Department Manager

Through a telephone or in-person interview, I can detail information regarding the above accomplishments and learn more about your visions for the dentistry department.

Director of Public Works

I am confident of my ability to direct an efficient, cost-effective, and productive department. In order to translate this confidence into performance-focused outcomes, **I must convince you** and your selection committee colleagues of my potential to serve as the next Director of Public Works. I will call your office next week to see if it would be appropriate to schedule a meeting.

Editor
I do **hope to have the chance to expand upon** the above bullets and describe how much my efforts at Books R Cool prepared me to succeed at Any Corporation.

Event Planner
I welcome the opportunity to meet with you **to further discuss my qualifications** and your expectations for Any Corporation's next Event Planner.

Film Archivist
I will call soon to confirm receipt of this e-mail and, **I do hope**, **to arrange** a telephone or in-person interview.

Fundraiser
I look forward to speaking with you about my qualifications and your expectations for the Fundraiser who will be joining you and your Any Organization colleagues.

Gemologist
After you have reviewed my qualifications, **I would appreciate interviewing with you** for this position. Perhaps an initial telephone conversation could be followed by a lengthier in-person discussion?

Home Economics Department Coordinator
I will be in Seattle next week. **Would it be possible to meet** to discuss my qualifications for this position?

Hospital Administrator
Through a telephone or in-person interview I can reiterate the qualifications presented in this letter and on the accompanying resume. Most important, **during our meeting** I can learn about your goals for Any Health Resource Corporation and your expectations for the next Hospital Administrator.

Hotel Manager
I would welcome the chance to speak by phone or in person regarding this position. I will be attending the Hospitality Association Conference next week. If you will be there, **perhaps we could meet then?**

International Buyer
I do hope that you will allow me the opportunity to expand upon the attached resume via an interview.

Legal Assistant
During an initial telephone interview and, subsequent to my relocation, via an in-person meeting, I would be **happy to detail my qualifications** and motivations to join Any Law Firm as a Legal Assistant.

Television Camera Operator
I look forward to sharing my tapes with you and interviewing for this position. I hope to hear from you regarding **a mutually convenient time and date**.

These phrases express the candidates' intentions to make future contact.

Meeting Planner
I will call to discuss your thoughts regarding an interview and, ideally, to creatively share ideas about your next events.

Multimedia Specialist

Of course, **I will call to discuss** your thoughts regarding my candidacy.

Newspaper Intern

I will call your office next week **to confirm receipt of my resume** and inquire about the possibility of an interview.

Office Receptionist

I will call to discuss your thoughts regarding **next steps**.

Pharmacist

I will call to confirm receipt of this e-mail and to arrange either an in-person or telephone interview.

Political Staffer

I will call to discuss your thoughts regarding my candidacy and, **if you believe appropriate**, to arrange an interview.

Production Quality Control Manager

I will call to confirm receipt of this fax (originals to follow in the mail) and to discuss **your assessment of my background**.

Public Relations Associate

I will call to confirm receipt of this letter and, if you judge it appropriate, to arrange an interview at a mutually convenient time and date.

Publisher's Assistant

I will call in a week **to schedule a convenient time** to discuss my qualifications and **your expectations**.

Researcher

I will call to confirm receipt of this letter and to discuss your thoughts regarding whether a phone or in-person interview would be appropriate.

Restaurant Manager Trainee

I will call to confirm receipt of this fax (originals will follow in the mail) and to arrange a mutually convenient time and date for an interview.

> **Green Light** Make sure your cover letter identifies your most significant qualifications in the first two paragraphs.

These phrases show how you might indicate that a reference will be in touch or that transcripts and/or a letter of recommendation is forthcoming.

Biomedical Engineer

I will e-mail a copy of my transcript and a letter of recommendation soon **to further support my candidacy**.

Operations Manager

In addition, soon I will be forwarding a reference list and letters of recommendation to support my candidacy. I trust all documentation assists you with your deliberations.

Preschool Director

To assist with your deliberation, I asked the first person listed on the attached reference page to contact you regarding my abilities.

Translator

Also **find enclosed letters of recommendation** written by several clients.

These phrases very simply thank the reader of the cover letter for their consideration. There are many ways to word this, although the message is more or less the same.

Pharmaceutical Sales

I appreciate your reviewing the attached documents, and I look forward to hearing from you soon.

Purchasing Agent

I appreciate your consideration of my candidacy and **look forward to your reply**. Thank you.

State Administrator

I appreciate your time and look forward to speaking with you.

Store Manager

Thank you for reviewing my credentials. I look forward to speaking with you.

Endnote: You don't have to know your reader to know how to impress him or her. Using the bolded phrases in this chapter will help you capture the reader's attention and, hopefully, get your foot in the door for a first interview.

Chapter 4

WRITING TO ENGAGE

Special Situations

If you have a unique situation that sets you apart from other applicants, do not fear. This chapter will help you find the words and phrases you need to highlight your greatest strengths, embrace your special circumstances instead of hiding behind them, and use the situation to your advantage whenever possible. Are you a recent college grad, looking for your first job or internship? Have you decided to change industries completely? Maybe you're a stay-at-home parent diving back into the work force or someone trying to recover from a recent layoff. While you can take comfort in the fact that you are not alone (as you'll see from the samples that follow), you may be concerned that your unique circumstances will put you at the bottom of the pile. The truth is that you are who you say you are: If you communicate your special situation positively, gracefully, and effectively, then you can elevate yourself to the very top of the applicant pile.

Phrases for Introductory Paragraphs

No matter what your situation, you want to begin your cover letter by alluding to your strengths and stating why you are capable of fulfilling the role for which you're applying. The following samples can help everyone from those who have been in the work force for decades to those who are just starting out.

As a candidate with decades of experience or an employment history at only one company, you have the opportunity to highlight a variety of accomplishments while demonstrating a serious interest in your industry. Here are some phrases you might include in your introductory paragraph.

All Employment at One Company (Materials Manager)

Described with great pride on the attached resume, during the past eighteen years I have **progressed rapidly in positions of responsibility** at This Hospital. As the supervisor of patient transportation, manager of warehousing/distribution, and within my current position as senior buyer and manager of inventory control I have **met budgetary goals** and **provided efficient and mission-driven services**.

Fifty-Plus-Years-Old Job Candidate (Product Manager)

Are you and your colleagues in need of a motivated professional with comprehensive product management experience spanning decades? **I would like to continue my achievement-filled career** with Any Corporation as a full-time, part-time, or contract-based employee. Through this letter, the attached resumes, and ideally an interview, I can present my qualifications for your consideration.

This sample shows how you might present your candidacy for a job within the company where you're currently employed. Be sure to outline key achievements to date.

Application for In-House Position (District Supervisor)

In support of my candidacy for the management job posting for District Supervisor, I present my resume and this memo, summarizing my experience with Any Gas Company and other employers in the gas distribution industry.

When your job has consisted of managing the details of life at home for an extended period of time, your cover letter needs to focus on your experience outside the home. It's essential to communicate your enthusiasm and motivation to continue your career and make a positive contribution to the company.

At-Home Parent Re-Entering the Work Force (Graphic Designer)

I would like to meet to discuss freelance assignments or a part-time position in Graphic Design or Production. During this meeting, **I can show you my portfolio** and discuss how excited I am to continue my career within an industry that is for me **a professional passion**.

Displaced Homemaker (Administrator)

I am highly motivated and qualified to serve within an Administrative position at Any Corporation. Detailed on my resume, I offer **extensive and varied experience** in administrative roles in both employment and community service.

How will you take your experience and apply it to a job in a different field? These sample phrases show how candidates have communicated their intent to potential employers.

Career Changer (Advertising Assistant)

I would like to inquire about and ideally interview for a position at Any Advertising Agency. Detailed on the attached resume, I have over eight years' experience in promotion, communications, and administration. Now, it is with great focus and enthusiasm that **I seek to contribute** as an Assistant supporting client services, traffic, or media planning activities.

> **Green Light** Whether you are changing industries or not, it's always wise to show how the job skills you have earned thus far relate to the job at hand.

Career Changer (Marketing Executive)

As Any Corporation's Dealer Representative, **I will utilize my thorough knowledge of** boating as well as sales, marketing, and communication skills to inspire those who sell your products, educate salespersons, and **promote** product lines directly to consumers. As a semiprofessional sailboat racer, I am very familiar with the Any Corporation line.

Career Changer (Product and Services Developer)

Currently, I am **seeking a career change** and opportunity to associate with a progressive bank, where I can effectively **apply my creative and innovative talents** and capability for developing or increasing and successfully marketing new service products. During the past eight years, I have served as vice president and director of operations of an ever-expanding, quality-driven, function and recreation complex. In these capacities **I had total responsibility for creating** effective sales programs and **assuring** the quality of services provided. Last year, **we exceeded our goals** by 150 percent and grossed more than $1.4 million in sales. Our increased business resulted from **an aggressive marketing effort** targeting local businesses.

Former Small Business Owner (Environmental Advocate)

The article in the May edition of *Save Our Earth* was impressive. In fact, the article and the mission and offerings of Any Environmental, as **dynamically presented on your website**, have inspired me to seek employment with your agency. Do you currently have an opening for an Environmental Advocate, Public Relations or Volunteer Coordinator, Researcher, or Lobbyist?

As a freelancer, you must show some knowledge of and proficiency in the position for which you are applying. These two samples clearly inform potential employers why the candidates should be considered for work.

Freelancer (Editor and Writer)

I am a Freelance Editor and Writer of educational and reference materials targeting college students and adults. Books and articles written or edited to date have been in the areas of careers, self-help, and parenting. Recently, I identified titles by Any Publishing Company that reveal your interest in targeting similar topics and readers as those cited above. Therefore, **I would like to learn more about your** Freelance Writing and Editorial needs and acquisition process.

Freelancer (Production Assistant)

I would like to apply for the Production Assistant position advertised on the *www.pa.com* website and in the *Miami Herald*. While **the attached resume reveals an extensive list of experiences** in all aspects of video production, including positions as writer, researcher, director, and editor, **only through an interview can you** determine if I have what it takes to transform **your vision** into day-to-day production realities.

If you're a recent grad, your goal in writing a cover letter is to highlight your course work and internships as they relate to the position. You can begin by mentioning a mutual connection who recommended you apply for the position or by stating what type of job it is that you hope to find. Consider the following wording in these introductory paragraphs.

Recent Graduate (Assistant to Museum Director)

During my undergraduate years, I sought to learn within the classroom and beyond. I did so via specific courses and, most important, through practical internships and training. Now, I seek an opportunity **to put my newly developed skills and knowledge to use** in a position at Any Museum. Perhaps I can do so as an Assistant to the curator or within patron relations, education, or fundraising roles?

Recent Graduate (Legal Assistant)

Justice Ellen Malone of the Allentown Courthouse suggested that I contact you regarding an opening you may soon have for a Legal Assistant. Judge Malone is aware of my desire to find a challenging paralegal-, legal research-, and administrative-focused position, and **she encouraged me to immediately seek consideration** to join you and your associates at Any Firm.

Recent Graduate (Set Designer)

Lynne Winchester recently indicated that you may have an opening for a Set Designer and suggested that I contact you. **I am seeking a position involving** stage design for television, theater, and video productions.

If your educational background isn't your strong point, don't worry. Take this opportunity to showcase what real-life experience you have. If you display familiarity with and success in a certain area, it's difficult for a potential employer to overlook that.

Weak Educational Background (Parking Supervisor)

Described on my resume, I am currently the Parking Supervisor for the Parkinson Hotel and Conference Center. This position was **a rapid promotion to management** after only one year of service as a parking attendant. As supervisor of parking facilities, **I oversee all** financial collections, maintain customer service standards, resolve problems, and manage a large staff of hourly workers. I also **administer** work schedules, evaluate performance, coordinate payroll matters, assign duties, and interface with hotel management. While I am so very **proud of my achievements to date**, within an area that requires practical knowledge and experience, I do wish to find **expanded challenges and rewards**.

Perhaps you've been laid off or fired. Perhaps your employment history has a few holes. The key to writing an effective cover letter in these situations is to convince your potential employer of your trustworthiness, dedication, and focus. Call their attention to your references, and state your desire to follow a particular career path. Consider the following sample phrases.

 RED FLAG!
KEEP EMOTION OUT OF IT. Never speak poorly of a previous employer, even if you left on unfriendly terms.

Fired/Laid Off (Recruiter)

Attached is a copy of my resume, a list of professional achievements, as well as letters of recommendation written by colleagues, clients, and candidates with whom I've worked. I trust that **these documents will convince you that I am worthy of an interview** and, after you have had the opportunity to evaluate my candidacy, that **I could soon become a strong member** of the Any Executive Search Firm team.

Gaps in Employment History (Assistant Curator)

I am seeking a position blending museum and gallery experience as well as **a keen interest and academic background in** fine art. Ideally that will be as your Assistant Curator. Detailed on the attached resume, I have completed two extensive internships for successful galleries in Alabama. In each position, I **contributed to all aspects of** operations, including artist relations, sales, show planning and implementation, and administrative duties. Responsibilities and accomplishments included assisting customers, setting up displays, and completing mailings for exhibitions.

No Clear Career Path (Accounting)

I am now actively seeking a career-focused position in Accounting that will utilize my experience in both financial management and customer service, as well as my strong academic background. **While researching area firms**, I learned of Any Accounting's training and development program. This opportunity seems an ideal way to begin and build **an accomplishment-filled career with your firm**, and a long-term career is exactly what I seek.

Part-Time Employment History (Store Manager)

I would very much like to join the Any Retail Chain's management team. A very strong and clear sense of **career focus**, previous retail experience, knowledge of your stores and target markets, and **a desire for a full-time management position** have prompted me to forward the attached resume.

If you've been working in the military or overseas, you need to show how your experience relates to the position for which you're applying. What about your experience makes you an asset to the team you want to join? By linking your current experience to the duties of the job you want, you'll convince employers that your unique background will serve them well.

Military Background (Transportation Operator)

Seven of the past twelve years were spent with the United States Army in transportation-related roles and assignments. Since completion of military services I have worked within sales positions. Now, I am very interested in resuming a civilian career in Transportation Operations or in the sale of products or equipment allied to the transportation field. All **pertinent experiences are detailed on the attached resume**.

Overseas Employment History (Marketing Assistant)

Anticipating relocation home to the United States, I am now actively seeking a Marketing Assistant position with Any Corporation. As you review the attached vita, I trust you will conclude that **I can effectively contribute to** an international, service-oriented organization dedicated, **as your mission states**, "to expanding international commerce through effective state of the art and traditional marketing strategies." **I understand you currently have** a number of international clients and anticipate landing new accounts with multinational firms.

Phrases for Motivational and Qualification Paragraphs

This is the part of your cover letter where you need to sell yourself. Tell your potential future employer what you bring to the table. Imagine being asked the question, "What do you have to offer?" Answer it in these paragraphs.

All Employment at One Company (Materials Manager)

Most recently, **I have been able to reduce the expenditures** of all in-house medical and nonmedical supplies substantially each year through **cost-effective negotiations**, purchasing, and control. **I also played a key role** in automating inventories and providing a functional layout for warehouse locations that reduced the selection and distribution process for warehoused materials. This also **enabled me to provide** more stringent controls, reducing shrinkage, damage, and obsolescence—common problems in the healthcare field. Estimated costs and savings are cited on the resume.

Application for In-House Position (District Supervisor)

As you know, these positions required the ability to provide technical support, retain personnel, supervise outside contractors, and work with developers and public officials during the joint work programs and projects. **My performance reviews during my tenure at Any Gas have all been above average** and my current supervisor, Kelly Stevens, has offered to support my desire for this promotion.

As reflected in all past reviews and training evaluations, I have the technical capability to work with and direct company and contractor personnel on all phases of gas distribution systems, from new construction to replacement and operation. Previous accomplishments with Any Gas indicate my strong **communication skills** and **my ability to work with people at all levels of responsibility**, including those who would report to and interact with a District Supervisor.

At-Home Parent Re-Entering the Work Force (Graphic Designer)

Professionally, I offer more than seven years' experience in production and traffic areas of Print and Graphic Design and in related fields, including fundraising and direct- and mass-mailings. After a three-year hiatus, with my family well established, I am **highly motivated to return to the work force** and contribute to the growth of Any Advertising Agency. In addition to my resume and portfolio, **excellent references do support my candidacy**.

Career Changer (Advertising Assistant)

As owner of a successful and profitable housecleaning service for four years, I designed and wrote all promotional materials, including direct-mail coupons. Immediately after my first promotional campaign, the volume of business tripled, resulting in my hiring and overseeing six people. In addition to **supervising employees**, I completed all administrative and budgetary tasks, which entailed handling calls, scheduling, billing, record keeping, ordering supplies, and customer relations. Now, having just sold the business, I am seeking a position in advertising.

Career Changer (Marketing Executive)

A career change that will involve a transition from **a successful management career** to a marketing, promotions, and consumer relations career is most desired. I am confident that my business and boating background **will ensure that I have favorable impact on sales, image, and continued growth**.

Career Changer (Product and Services Developer)

As I will share personally, **if you grant me the opportunity to interview** for a client services, loan officer, or marketing position, **I am adept at making business-to-business contacts**, creating and utilizing promotional advertising and marketing programs, and making **effective presentations**.

Displaced Homemaker (Administrator)

I offer Any Corporation:

- Experience with staff supervision and motivation.

- A record of success within meeting planning and direction, and activities scheduling.

- Confidence within public speaking situations.

- Excellent phone and **correspondence skills**.

- Bookkeeping fundraising, and promotions talents.

Fifty-Plus-Years-Old Job Candidate (Product Manager)

Past experience has provided me many opportunities to implement **profitable Product Management strategies** including those associated with pricing, production, distribution, as well as advertising for existing and new products. Specifically, for pharmaceutical and food products, I have been **involved in all aspects of** product/protocol development and management to obtain FDA product approval. As a Product Manager for Estrade, Inc., I coordinate all product development for a medical supply corporation with annual sales in excess of $400 million. Prior, I served in similar capacities for Vita Thirst, the manufacturer of healthful drink products. My product designs, production planning, and marketing techniques have been **recognized as consistently innovative** and, most important, **profitable**. Over the years, every product I have been associated with **met or exceeded annual profit goals**.

Fired/Laid Off (Recruiter)

As detailed on my resume, recruiting skills and accomplishments were nurtured over seven years while recruiting high technology, support staff, and marketing personnel. Much of this experience involved extensive travel, training program development, and **networking** prospective clients. In addition to **a record of success and a well-earned reputation**, I possess **valuable contacts** within the management information systems, software development, and engineering industries that would prove valuable to Any Firm's client base.

Gaps in Employment History (Assistant Curator)

Academically and personally, I have a Bachelor of Arts degree in Art History, have participated in several related seminars, and I have had occasion to visit many of the world's great museums. I am a frequent visitor to the Any Museum and a member of Friends of Any Museum, so **I am familiar with your mission**, target patronage, and educational and outreach efforts.

Former Small Business Owner (Environmental Advocate)

As described on my resume, and revealed through the annual report also attached, I have **a passion for** environmental concerns and practical experiences in all of the above areas. For the past four years, I have been operating an entrepreneurial venture, Recycling Renegades. I **successfully acquired** the first recycling permit in Cambridge, MA, for ferrous and nonferrous metal, aluminum, high-grade paper, and plastic. As owner and manager, I conducted research, developed pilot programs, formulated networks for voluntary recycling, picked up and processed materials, and distributed proceeds to community associations. While my motives were altruistic, **my accomplishments proved profitable** as well.

Freelancer (Editor and Writer)

The attached resume details my projects to date, **as well as my academic background**, early experiences as an editorial assistant, and current status as a part-time English instructor. Whether editing or writing textbook materials, teacher workbooks, or ancillary activities and worksheets, I can tailor the content, tone, and approach to a variety of purposes and audiences.

Freelancer (Production Assistant)

Summarizing, personal and professional qualities I possess include:

- Three years as a freelance Production Assistant working on several commercial and documentary pieces.

- **Skills and perspectives gained** as chief assistant on Milk Carton Kids: An American Crisis, supporting preliminary research and writing, scheduling location shooting, and screening potential interview candidates.

- **Breadth of administrative and logistical talents** gained completing two public-service announcements for Miami Child Services, which included camera operation and heavy script and video editing.

- **Patience, flexibility, creativity, and active listening skills required to thrive under the pressure of deadlines** and working within the demands of preproduction, shooting, and production stages.

Military Background (Transportation Operator)

Key points on this document and those I would like to discuss during an interview include:

- Experience managing all phases of civilian and tactical Transportation Operations (vehicles from two-and-one-half-ton cargo trucks to ten-ton tractor trailers and petroleum tankers).

- Experience teaching courses and training troops about the total transportation cycle in the United States and abroad.

> **Green Light** Bulleted lists of your qualifications and experience are a succinct and reader-friendly feature for any cover letter.

- **Record of success** contributing toward the efficient military operations and **potential** to do so at an in-house traffic, transportation, and distribution function or a commercial transportation depot.

No Clear Career Path (Accounting)

To this program and your firm, I would bring the following:

- A Bachelor of Science degree, *cum laude*, in Finance.

- Four years of collections experience.

- Successful collecting of 90 percent of overdue accounts.

- Experience in accounts payable and accounts receivable.

- Knowledge of Excel, Lotus 1-2-3, Word, Quick-Books, and varied accounting applications.

- The competencies and commitment required to pass the CPA examination and **adhere to strict professional and ethical standards**.

Overseas Employment History (Marketing Assistant)

Summarizing some of the points I would like to share via phone discussions and in-person interviews, I offer Any Corporation:

- Experience as an interpreter and translator working on international market research with the Marketing Department at the University of Paris, Sorbonne.

- **Knowledge of concepts and terminology** associated with marketing and advertising.

- **Confidence and history of success** as administrative assistant to professors and business executives.

- Trilingual fluency in English, French, and Italian, and strong **proficiency** in Spanish.

- Skills and perspectives gained completing a Bachelor of Arts degree in French, *summa cum laude*, from University of Rochester in Rochester, New York.

- **Communication and presentation skills** gained tutoring individuals in foreign languages and English as a Second Language.

- **Familiarity working and interacting with** multilingual, multicultural individuals and groups.

Recent Graduate (Assistant to Museum Director)

As my resume indicates, I recently participated in a program for art history majors at the Louvre. This involved studying European art and attending seminars on museum operations. Prior, I worked for two summers at the Metropolitan Museum of Art as a Museum Assistant at the information booth.

Recent Graduate (English Teacher)

Supporting special education offerings, I learned of IEPs and district approaches to inclusion. I was **proud to assist** students with learning disabilities, as well as those who needed assistance with physical disabilities. I used lesson planning, instructional as well as tutorial, talents gained in classrooms and other settings. Throughout my undergraduate years I participated in a volunteer literacy program, tutoring both youth and adults struggling with reading difficulties. The **skills and perspectives gained** as a student teacher and tutor will be **foundations upon which I will build a successful teaching career**.

Recent Graduate (Legal Assistant)

Described in great detail on the attached resume, I have worked in a variety of legal settings throughout college. Currently, I am a volunteer for Temple's Student Legal Aid, **supporting the efforts** of law students helping undergraduates and community members with legal problems. I worked part time over the past three years as a peer probation **mentor** for the Allentown, PA, juvenile court. In addition to these experiences, last summer I served as a research assistant for the Chief County Clerk of Allentown, when I met Judge Malone.

Recent Graduate (Set Designer)

As noted on my resume, I graduated recently from Clemson University with a Bachelor of Arts degree in Theater Arts and a concentration in Studio Art. Courses in modern drama, music and sound in theatre, set creation and design, intermediate painting, and woodworking **all contributed to the skills I possess** and **focused my aspirations** toward stage design. As an undergraduate, I designed and helped create props for numerous campus productions, including *The Tempest* and *Marco Polo Sings a Solo*, and I developed many storyboards and set design presentations.

Phrases for Closing Paragraphs

This is your chance to request an interview, reinforce your interest in the job, and quickly summarize why you're a great candidate. Whether you've been working for thirty years, just graduated from college, or never even went to college, your closing statement will generally convey the same thought—you are competent, your interest in the job is serious, you appreciate the company's consideration, and you look forward to future communication.

All Employment at One Company (Materials Manager)

Past achievements within one organization prove my professional competencies and potential to succeed in new roles at Any Hospital. As your healthcare operations grow, since the acquisition of several local HMOs, I know that Materials Management issues will become crucial. Please, **let's discuss how I might help link growth with efficiency**.

Application for in-House Position (District Supervisor)

I feel professionally and personally **ready to handle the challenges** of the District Supervisor position. During an interview I can confidently yet objectively share these qualifications with you and others involved in the selection process. I look forward to meeting with you to discuss my candidacy. Thank you for your consideration.

Career Changer (Advertising Assistant)

I hope we will have the chance to discuss current or future opportunities during an interview. **If no positions are available or anticipated**, **any referrals to other agencies would be welcomed**.

Career Changer (Marketing Executive)

I do hope that I will have the chance to soon present my qualifications and motivations in person. Please, **do not hesitate to e-mail or call to arrange a meeting**. And I have asked some of my boating colleagues to contact you regarding their views of my potential.

Career Changer (Product and Services Developer)

I would welcome your thoughts regarding where I might best contribute to Any Bank. I will call to confirm receipt of this note, to clarify next steps, and, I most sincerely hope, **to arrange a brief meeting**.

Displaced Homemaker (Administrator)

If you are looking for someone with these skills, I hope you will give me the opportunity to speak with you. During a telephone conversation and, ideally, a meeting I can expand upon the above bullets and **personalize my candidacy**. A resume and cover letter can reveal a great deal, but in-person communication is, I believe, best.

Fifty-Plus-Years-Old Job Candidate (Product Manager)

I would appreciate your consideration and look forward to speaking with you, with Sam Smith, or others you deem appropriate **regarding how I might best contribute** to Any Corporation, as you continue to work on the development of your new healthy snack line. I will call to discuss your thoughts regarding my candidacy.

Fired/Laid Off (Recruiter)

Ideally, you and I could meet soon, whenever mutually convenient. I will call to confirm receipt of this fax and to discuss your reactions to my request for an interview. In advance, **thank you for your consideration**.

Former Small Business Owner (Environmental Advocate)

I wish **to utilize skills gained** via this venture, and as an undergraduate environmental engineering major, at Any Environmental Agency. Will you be attending the environmental affairs conference in New York City? If we haven't connected by phone, e-mail, or in person prior, **perhaps we can meet at the conference**.

Freelancer (Editor and Writer)

Could I speak to you about working on some of your projects as either Editor or Author? Attached is a piece written for an online newsletter as well as a brief note written by Kerry Williams, an editor at Textbook Company. **I hope these documents reveal the potential I possess** to contribute to Any Publishing Company's efforts. Of course, I can provide additional writing samples and references, as needed.

Freelancer (Production Assistant)

I've admired Any Production Company's work for some time and attended your screening of Silent Victims at the Miami Crime Awareness Convention last month. **It would be wonderful if I could help on your next project**, and future undertakings.

Gaps in Employment History (Assistant Curator)

In addition to the targeted resume **I have also provided a reference list** of individuals familiar with my past experiences who can **share views regarding my future potential**. I would like to discuss full-time or part-time options. To date, whenever given the opportunity to work in an arts environment, I have succeeded. I hope I have that chance at Any Museum.

Military Background (Transportation Operator)

Also, I am a trained professional, a graduate officer of the U.S. Army Transportation School, and I have completed my bachelor's degree. I would appreciate the opportunity to further describe my qualifications and **the immediate and long-term contributions I could make** to Any Corporation.

💬 Action Speak

Focused	Qualified
Fulfilled	Rendered
Mediated	Shared
Planned	Uncovered
Predicted	Wrote

Overseas Employment History (Marketing Assistant)

I will be in New York from February 14 through February 28 for a prerelocation visit. Would it be possible to schedule an interview for that time? While I hope we will have had telephone and e-mail communications prior, **it would be wonderful if we could meet during my upcoming visit**. Of course, I am eligible to work in the United States and I anticipate paying all relocation expenses.

Part-Time Employment History (Store Manager)

As my resume indicates, and as is the history of many who build successful careers, some of my Retail Management experience has been part time. **I am now seeking a permanent position and the opportunity to build a career** while I contribute to the growth of Any Retail Chain. Please allow me the opportunity to share how past experiences and accomplishments can predict future achievements via an interview.

Recent Graduate (Assistant to Museum Director)

The eyes of a young visitor to your museum have grown into those of a diligent student, recent graduate, and hopeful candidate. While my heart still contains the **enthusiasm** and **excitement** I felt during early visits, my head is now is full of **knowledge and career focus**. Please grant me the opportunity to interview for and, someday, **to become part of your staff**. I will call to see if an in-person interview would be an appropriate next step.

Recent Graduate (English Teacher)

Also attached are letters of recommendation and a favorite lesson plan. As you read these documents I hope you gain a sense of the teacher I wish to be. I know I can instill knowledge, inspire continued learning, and refine writing talents. I will call to confirm that I have completed all required steps and to inquire regarding the interview and selection process.

Recent Graduate (Legal Assistant)

Prior to applying to law school in a few years, I wish to fine-tune my knowledge of law and gain a greater sense of career focus and special interests. Ideally, I can do so at Any Firm. **I will contact you within the week to further discuss the possibility of interviewing** for this position.

Recent Graduate (Set Designer)

Enclosed is a resume as well as some photographs of my work. Of course, **I would like to show you my entire portfolio** and discuss with you **how I might contribute** to Any Production Company's current and future projects. **I have some great ideas for** the sets of *Trivia Tunes* and *Videos after Dark* and hope to have the opportunity to discuss them with you.

Weak Educational Background (Parking Supervisor)

With increased concerns about security has come increased focus on parking operations at facilities like Any Airport. I hope I have contacted you at a time when consideration can be given to **a candidate who has proven by past experience that learning by doing is the best education**. I would like to speak with you about current or future opportunities. Of course, references are available upon request. If you now utilize an outside vendor for parking operations, referrals to the proper person in that organization would be appreciated.

Endnote: Putting a positive spin on a circumstance that could be construed as problematic is an artful dance. The examples you've just read are proof that the right words have the power to transform just about any special situation into an advantage.

Chapter 5

WRITING TO INQUIRE

Targeting Ideal Employers

Do you like things to be on your terms? Job searching does not have to be a passive experience. If you know exactly where you want to be working, don't wait for the right posting to pop up on the job boards. Take the reigns and reach out to the company or companies of your dreams with a targeted cover letter—don't forget to amp it up with an empowering array of "hire-me" phrases from this chapter. Targeted cover letters, when done correctly, are as effective as they are bold. In this section, you'll find sample "hire-me" phrases divided between two types of targeted cover letters.

1. Cold contact letters. When making cold contact in the form of a cover letter, you are not responding to a posting or contacting someone at the advice of others. These cover letters can be effective. The more focused they are, and the more you reveal knowledge of the job and employer, the better. In these cover letters, company-specific information must be changed letter to letter.

2. Broadcast letters. These are distributed to many employers, and they are less focused. Their format may appear similar to other letters, and it is most important to have the company name appear prominently early. While less company-specific information is contained, you must still show readers that you know the organization's name and the nature of the business. Broadcast letters can be good first efforts and momentum builders if you maintain appropriate expectations and follow up effectively.

When broadcasting your availability, share with readers potential titles and functional areas of interest. They must be dynamic *Here I am, here is what I do best, and let's talk about how I can succeed* letters.

Cold Contact Letters—Phrases for Introductory Paragraphs

When you contact a potential employer without responding to a specific job posting, it's important to begin your cover letter by clearly stating your intentions. The phrases that follow contain examples of how individuals have expressed their interest in working for the companies they've contacted. Notice how many examples show that the candidates possess some knowledge of each company's present or future business plans.

Administrative Assistant

Upon review of Any Corporation's website I am motivated to share my availability for an Administrative Assistant position. While no specific opportunities were posted, I want to express my strong desire to meet with you to share motivations and qualifications and to **seek consideration for current or anticipated openings**.

Admissions Counselor

Now, through this letter, I seek consideration for a position within your office.

Advertising Sales Associate

Given past sales achievements and a desire for a future career in advertising, I would like to explore opportunities at Any Station.

Associate Editor

Ideally, **you will find my background strong enough to warrant consideration** for an editorial post at Any Publishing. Specifically, I am seeking a position as an Associate Editor, Project Editor, or equivalent in new book or journal development.

Audiovisual Specialist

To initiate consideration for audiovisual opportunities with your company, attached is a resume for your review.

Chef

As Any Hotel completes its renovations and will soon expand wedding-planning efforts, I seek to join your team and, **as your mission statement cites,** "blend customer service and culinary excellence with profitability."

Computer Software Designer

I do hope Any Corporation is now recruiting or will do so in the near future. **I understand you and your colleagues are now working on** major government contracts for specialized applications, next generations of your popular and profitable Any Software programs, and numerous research and development projects.

Editorial Assistant

I would like to interview for an assistant position or an internship in the editorial department at Any Magazine. It would be wonderful if I could **utilize existing skills and knowledge** within the context of my goal to work for a music- and lifestyle-related publication.

Elementary School Teacher

It is with great enthusiasm for, and commitment to, elementary education that I inquire about teaching positions at Any Private School.

Financial Analyst

Now, **as I seek to relocate** to the St. Louis area, it is with great excitement that I wish to discuss my potential to contribute to the finance area of Any Corporation.

Marketing Director

It would be with continued professional pride, ambition, and goal-direction that I would serve as a Marketing Director, Brand Manager, or related title at Any Corporation. Please grant me the opportunity to discuss my hopes for the future, as well as your goals for your organization during an interview.

Mutual Funds Broker

Described with pride and in detail on the enclosed resume, I have over a decade of experience within the financial services area. Now, as I look ahead to future challenges and, of course, rewards, I seek to focus on a specialized area of expertise—mutual funds. Therefore, **it is with great confidence gained from a history of success** and the enthusiasm of seeking new opportunities that I seek consideration for a brokerage position at Any Brokers.

 RED FLAG!
DON'T FORGET TO CHANGE ALL company-specific information each time you draft a new cold contact letter. Double-check the header before you hit send.

School and Community Counseling

In anticipation of relocation to Dallas, **I have researched a number of facilities and become particularly intrigued by Any Center's offerings**. Therefore, I would welcome consideration for a full-time or part-time counseling position.

Phrases for Motivational and Qualification Paragraphs

In these sample phrases, the candidates describe their interests, experiences, skills, and accomplishments as they relate to the companies' businesses. You might feel a little awkward talking yourself up, but remember —you've reached out cold to a company that doesn't know anything about you. You need to make yourself stand out.

Administrative Assistant

Most recently, I worked as a receptionist with Other Consulting, where I **gained exposure** to all facets of administrative support, specifically for a firm like Any Corporation that markets and provides state-of-the art information technology services. **I am well aware of Any Corporation's commitment to** "excellence in specialized customer service," as stated in your mission statement.

Advertising Sales Associate

I believe the ratings and demographics of the station could be effectively marketed to both large and small local, regional, and national businesses, focusing on youth and male target audiences. The newly acquired WWE programming should be an Advertising Sales Associate's greatest asset.

Computer Software Designer

I am confident I can be a successful Computer Software Designer at Any Corporation. I have **considerable experience** with DBMS packages, like Oracle, Ingres, DB2, FoxPro, and OS/2 Data Manager.

Competencies include Unix, C, SAS, Pascal, and a variety of other programming languages, including (but not limited to) SUNOS, DOS, and VAX operating systems. I have used, taught, and provided user support for graphics, spreadsheet, database, desktop publishing, word processing, and telecommunication applications.

Elementary School Teacher

As you prepare to dedicate the new Blake Entertainment Center I am confident that you and your Any School colleagues, parents, and students anticipate expanded music instruction, choral, and performance offerings. I would like to discuss how my background could address these special goals, as well as those associated with traditional classroom instruction.

Financial Analyst

Any Corporation's growth over the past years, including expansion to Canadian and Mexican markets and the aggressive acquisition of smaller competitors, requires strong financial oversight and flow of information to key decision-makers. I am confident in my ability to set up and manage financial analysis and credit leveraging systems, procedures and controls, and employee-training programs that will address **Any Corporation's expanding needs**.

Fundraiser

Fulfilling Any Organization's mission "to enhance the potential for young men and women to maximize educational and career opportunity" would be **a personal and professional passion**.

Management Consulting Analyst

Ideally, **I will contribute to** the following practice areas: financial analysis, management strategies, and business development. Detailed in the attached resume, I describe my fine-tuned research, analysis, and writing capabilities.

Marketing Director

Qualifications for a related position with Any Corporation, a manufacturer and marketer of optical scanning and mapping devices, are all cited on my resume, along with **details of all achievements**.

> **Green Light** Flattery goes a long way in a targeted cover letter. Include key phrases that reveal your knowledge of the company and convey your excitement.

Public Relations Assistant

Media relationships were developed as I selected and placed models for television commercials. **I have the skills to** coordinate creative programs and innovative functions involving clients and the general public, and, clearly, **I feel confident I could successfully apply my experience to a position in your firm**.

School and Community Counselor

I have counseled clients ranging in ages from four to twenty-four and specifically addressed ADHD, ODD, and learning disabilities within a team context, including teachers, parents, outside professionals, and the student in planning and implementation. So, **it would be an ideal next professional step to work at Any Center** with adolescents dealing with many of the issues cited and using a rational emotive and behavioral approach to treatment.

Television Production Assistant

Last summer, and most relevant to my request to interview for a PA position, I worked as an intern for KBZT-TV's "Island Beat." **In this capacity I had the opportunity to** co-produce a local talk show, which required that I preinterview and schedule guests, handle financial and transportation details, and research show topics. I also networked resource organizations to locate potential guests and panel members. I wish to bring all the talents, ambition, and commitment I nurtured as an intern and a student to Any Station. While most interested in PA opportunities, **I would welcome consideration** for an internship as well.

In some cases, it will be appropriate to describe your accomplishments using a list. The following lists show what the candidates hope to accomplish, what type of work interests them, and what type of work they are qualified to perform. The lists are short in length, and each bullet point is concisely written.

Admissions Counselor

I would like to become associated with Any University and educate potential applicants, parents, and guidance counselors regarding:

- A curriculum that allows students to learn what they love, and love what they learn.

- The challenges and rewards of undergraduate research and Quest courses.

- Specialized offerings like the Early Medical Scholars, Take 5, Study Abroad, Internships, The Senior Scholar Program, 3-2 Programs, and Certificate programs.

Audiovisual Specialist

It would be with great focus and confidence that **I would like to assist Any Corporation** with:

- **Creating and maintaining** multimedia presentations as well as web-based presentations. Purchasing, scheduling, and setting up equipment as needed.

- **Providing** user support for all who develop presentations and use related equipment.

Mutual Funds Broker

Highlighting all **I wish to discuss during an interview**, my qualifications include:

- More than a decade of **progressively significant roles and achievements** within planning portfolio management and client services.

- Personal responsibilities for more than $210 million in **client assets**

- Recognition for **outstanding asset-based performance** and customer services.

- Service as trainer and curriculum developer after completion of the ABC Financial Consultant Sales Training and Advanced Training.

- Licensed Series 6, 7, 63, and health and life insurance.

Phrases for Closing Paragraphs

In this section of your cover letter, your goal is to secure an interview by making yourself appear available and interested. You're reinforcing everything you said in your first and second paragraphs. Naturally, you'll close by thanking your contact for his or her consideration and review.

Admissions Counselor

I will call your office to confirm receipt of this e-mail (originals to follow in the mail) and, I hope, to arrange either a formal employment interview or informal discussion regarding **anticipated opportunities**.

Advertising Sales Associate

I want **to discuss your reactions to this letter and accompanying resume** and assess your thoughts regarding adding a new sales professional to your team.

Associate Editor

I will be relocating to the New York area later this summer, so I will be **available to begin employment** anytime thereafter. I will be in New York next week. Could we meet then?

Audiovisual Specialist

The nature of your manufacturing and marketing of consumer products, specifically all promotions, sales, and marketing efforts, requires a variety of audiovisual needs. **I look forward to speaking with you** about how I can creatively and enthusiastically address those needs.

Chef

Perhaps we could meet at the end of the month when I will be in Kentucky for a conference? Or, **we could begin discussions of potential opportunities by phone**. I will call to confirm receipt of this letter and to discuss next steps.

Computer Software Designer

Please, let's talk soon about **current or future opportunities** at Any Corporation. I look forward to hearing from you and meeting you.

Editorial Assistant

I will call to confirm receipt of my resume and, **at your convenience**, to arrange an initial phone interview and in-person meeting. Chicago is home, so I am **actively exploring opportunities** in the area, and I will be visiting for interviews regularly.

Elementary School Teacher

Please, let's meet to discuss your assessment of **my potential to be a strong member of** Any School's instructional team.

💬 Action Speak

Appointed	Originated
Attained	Persuaded
Convinced	Solved
Formulated	Undertook
Fostered	Used

Financial Analyst

I would appreciate the opportunity to **discuss your visions** for the finance area of Any Corporation and **how I might contribute** as an analyst.

Investment Banking Analyst

I would welcome the chance to discuss my qualifications for an Analyst position when you visit campus. If it would be more convenient for me to visit New York City, I would be happy to do so.

Librarian

Could we arrange an interview **to discuss how I may best contribute** to the staff of Any Library? I will call to confirm receipt of this e-mail and arrange a meeting when we can discuss **any current or anticipated openings** for a librarian.

Mutual Funds Broker

Please, let's talk about **my potential to succeed** at Any Brokers, about my desires to either expand your business on the island, and, if more appropriate, about my willingness to relocate to Southern California.

Public Relations Assistant

Please **allow me the opportunity to directly share** motivations as well as qualifications via an interview. I will be in Los Angeles at the end of the month and wonder if it would be **possible to arrange for an interview?**

School and Community Counseling

I hope we can meet to discuss **anticipated openings** and how my background might match Any Center's needs.

Broadcast Letters

Phrases for Introductory Paragraphs

You're writing a broadcast letter, which means you're probably sending it out to quite a few companies. You'll want to create a descriptive statement about your experience that you can use in most of your letters. For that reason, it should be general enough that it can apply to almost any cover letter you send out, and it should be specific in a way that catches the recipient's eye.

Administrative Assistant

Are you currently in need of an Administrative Assistant with **over a decade of experience** and a commitment to supporting the needs of patients and supervisors, and **working effectively with peers**? If yes, please review the attached resume and consider my candidacy for a position with Any Company.

Admissions and Enrollment Management

I trust the enclosed resume, specifically the Admissions Achievements section, **highlights my capabilities** for an Admissions and Enrollment Management position. Within professional capacities **I have held titles of** Senior Assistant Director and Director of International Recruitment, as well as Assistant Director and Counselor.

Chiropractor

I am a **certified** chiropractor currently exploring affiliations with established practices. Cited on the attached resume, I have worked in the Chicago area for over twenty years and, as a result, **my reputation for** quality care is well known.

Credit Manager

I am seeking a position as Credit Manager, to which I bring many years of successful credit management experience.

Freight Supervisor

During the past thirteen years, I have been **actively involved** in positions as field manager of container operations and night operations supervisor of freight stations and service centers, dealing with domestic and international freight deliveries.

RED FLAG!
DON'T IDENTIFY SALARY as a motivating factor in pursuing a job. Employers want to see that you have a genuine interest in the position.

Senior Vice President (Banking)

As you know, **because of our regular interactions** as members of the Missouri Bankers Association, I am currently a Senior Vice President at Central St. Louis Bank. The recent acquisition of CSB necessitates my communicating with other financial institutions, actively seeking consideration for a SVP position.

Phrases for Motivational and Qualification Paragraphs

This is where you need to expand on your brief descriptive statement that you used in the intro paragraph. You've hooked your reader, now tell them why you're right for the job.

Administrative Assistant

Detailed on the attached resume, I have worked in a hospital setting where I learned all **critical terminology**, how to address specialized billing and support issues, and what is required **to support the needs of** physicians, nurses, and healthcare practitioners. I now am actively seeking the opportunity to return to a challenging and rewarding medical setting.

Admissions and Enrollment Management

With the assistance of colleagues, I doubled the number of international candidates completing applications and interviews and those receiving offers to enroll at Seton Hall University. **In-depth knowledge** of admissions and enrollment strategies and processes and appreciation for how academic, athletic, co-curricular, and residential communities can be marketed make me **an enthusiastic and qualified candidate** for a position at Any School.

Chiropractor

Currently, I work as a chiropractic therapist with the Chicago Chiropractic Center, a position I have held for the past fifteen years. **In this capacity I provide** spinal manipulation and handle necessary musculoskeletal needs of sports injury patients, alleviate pain in elderly and work-related patients, and assist the industrial-accident injured in regaining strength and stamina.

I, like you and your Any Practice colleagues, am **an active member** of the American Chiropractic Association, Illinois Chiropractic Society, Chicago Chiropractic Society, and Sports Injury Council of the American Chiropractic Association.

Credit Manager

During the past ten years, as credit manager with a $20 million manufacturing and distribution firm, **I have successfully set up and enforced** credit controls, resulting in reducing DSO from 60 days to 33. I am continually involved in training personnel in credit and collection policies and procedures, troubleshooting and resolving sales and customer disputes, and making credit and collection decisions to reduce bad debt risk and **increase cash flow**.

Based on **my past contributions** to the credit profession, **I received recognition**, through NACM New England, as Credit Executive of the Year in 2010 and was elected the president of the same professional credit association for the 2009–2010 term.

> **Green Light** Choose two resume entries you are particularly proud of and make them the focus of your cover letter.

Freight Supervisor

In addition to supervising **day-to-day operations**, my experience encompasses hiring, training, and supervising drivers and office and support personnel, and providing **cost-effective**, **quality service** within a multiple-service network. I have sound knowledge of computer systems for freight movement management and I am **skilled** in both troubleshooting and resolving problems relative to the movement of materials and the people to make these activities possible.

Marketing/Sales Executive

During an interview I will share how past successes below required skills that will lead to future achievements with Any Corporation. Sales and marketing accomplishments to date include:

- Developing sales programs and new businesses to increase penetration, market share, and revenue, using **advanced**, **technically sophisticated** systems-management services.

- Participating in development and marketing teams for new service products for a service business generating $3.7 billion worldwide.

- Assuming P&L responsibility for an added-value services business generating $90 million.

- Establishing a record for producing **positive bottom-line results** in a high-tech, service-oriented business with worldwide markets.

Optics Researcher

Noted on the attached resume, I will be graduating in December from the University of Rochester. I have experience working as a researcher and as an optical engineer. Specifically, through experiences at Sine Patterns, I **developed qualifications applicable to Any Corporation**, including:

- Abilities to operate microlithography and photographic equipment.

- **Capacities to transform stated needs of customers into completed products** including optical masks, resolution charts, reticles, and custom film.

- Knowledge of product management and quality control issues.

- Specialized skills associated with **team and independent tasks** and projects.

Phrases for Closing Paragraphs

Keep it simple. The key phrases used in closing paragraphs don't vary much among different types of cover letters. In the case of a broadcast letter, you're requesting to hear from the company based on whether they have a position available that your expertise could serve.

Admissions and Enrollment Management

I will inquire soon to confirm receipt of this letter, to learn if you are currently expanding your operation, and **to identify appropriate next steps**.

Chiropractor

I look forward to hearing from you **if my qualifications are of interest**.

Credit Manager

I look forward to hearing from you **if you have a suitable position** available, or if you have any referrals.

Freight Supervisor

I would welcome the opportunity **to discuss whether Any Corporation has a need for someone with my background** and whether you would be **willing to consider me for immediate or future employment**.

Marketing/Sales Executive

I am well qualified to direct areas that are **key to achieving your sales and profit objectives**. If you have such a position open, I look forward to hearing from you.

Optics Researcher

Because I will be available to start immediately after receipt of my degree, around January 1st, I would certainly **appreciate the opportunity** to speak with you soon regarding your anticipated hiring needs.

Senior Vice President (Banking)

Although my present position is challenging, and I have a record of success within these capacities, **my future is with** another organization, like Any Bank. Ideally, my next position will addresses both national and international banking markets and I will be called upon to **continue an accomplishment-filled career as a leader, motivator, and achiever**. Let's discuss your reactions to my request for consideration.

Endnote: Targeting your ideal employer is a good move. Keep your goals in mind as you are choosing the words and phrases for your cover letter. Aim to impress them with your proactive appeal for employment and use your carefully worded goals to show them how you can contribute to their company.

Chapter 6

WRITING FOR CONSIDERATION

Search Agencies

Building and fostering a network of industry connections can be a part-time job in itself, but what if you could take a shortcut to a vast web of pre-established connections? The right search agency can save you a lot of time and energy by doing just that. These agents are experts in placing quality workers like you with companies who are hungry for them. If your cover letter impresses a headhunter, he or she can match you to a job that those outside the inner circle aren't even aware exists. How do you impress them? Outshine all the other cover letters with your growing arsenal of hire-me phrases.

There are two types of search agencies you may want to impress: employment agencies and search professionals. Employment agencies most often deal with temporary, temp-to-perm, or entry-level opportunities. In truth, they don't find jobs for people, they find candidates for jobs already posted with them. Search professionals, or headhunters as they are called, do regularly source candidates. They also seek retainer or contingency relationships with potential employers. Once employers post, these professionals screen information from candidates to determine those who match. Most often, search professionals deal with management or executive-level candidates and opportunities or with very specialized fields.

Your goal in sending a cover letter to a search professional is to inspire them to interview and, ultimately, select you as worthy of referral to an employer. If you want to motivate them to advocate on your behalf, you need to utilize the kind of wording that gets people job offers. Borrow some power phrases from the samples below and, as they read your cover letter, they will envision their contingency or retainer payment already earned.

Cover Letter Phrases to Use When Contacting Employment Agencies

Phrases for Introductory Paragraphs

What can a staffing/search firm do for you? For the recipient of your cover letter to know the answer to that question, you need to be direct about what type of job you're looking for, and you need to present yourself as a go-getter.

Accounting Manager
The enclosed resume outlines **my diverse and in-depth experience** in accounting and finance management. I am in search of an appropriate opportunity in the greater Missouri area.

Bookkeeper
If one of your clients is in need of a highly motivated bookkeeper with the experience and enthusiasm needed to handle the day-to-day details necessary to insure smooth operation, **I would appreciate your** consideration of my candidacy on behalf of that client.

Claims Processor
As a qualified and motivated candidate, with a record of past achievements, I now seek opportunities to continue **an accomplishment-focused career** in claims with a firm that has now posted an opportunity with Any Staffing Firm. I trust you recall that a number of years ago I communicated with you and your colleague, Francis Williams, regarding my interest in claims, and you placed me at Marifield Rehab. Now, **I seek your professional assistance** again.

Chef
I will be moving to the Dayton area and I would like the assistance of Any Staffing Firm **as I search for exciting new positions**. The advertisement in Today's Cook is most appealing; I would like to be considered for this particular position. Your announcement also inspires confidence that you will have other **client postings that match my qualifications**.

Dental Assistant
I am conducting a search for a full-time or part-time position in the Indianapolis area. **I have heard about your agency's placement record** through several colleagues, so I am very enthusiastic that you may now or soon have client postings that match my professional abilities.

> **Green Light** Include plenty of action words in your cover letter. The more energetic and proactive your writing, the more they'll want to meet you in person.

Executive Assistant

Currently, I am **seeking appropriate career opportunities** in the corporate arena. This particular posting seems ideal, but I would also **welcome your consideration** for any other client postings you believe **match my background**.

Legal Administrator

I have recently relocated to Florida and **I would like the assistance of Any Staffing Firm** to locate a court- or paralegal-related Administrator position with one of your clients.

Research and Development Position

I will be relocating to your area next month and I would be interested in a position in which to apply my chemical, electromechanical, and mechanical research skills. I believe **I would be a good match for** a progressive, technically oriented company seeking support in research, manufacturing, or production. **Your professional views and assistance** with my job search would be most welcomed.

Sales/Customer Service Representative

I enjoyed our brief conversation at the New Jersey Sales and Marketing Expo. As you now know, I am actively seeking new, challenging, and rewarding sales or customer service opportunities. **I am now formally requesting the assistance of your agency** with my search.

Phrases for Motivational and Qualification Paragraphs

In these paragraphs, you'll describe your practical experience. Mentioning your current salary is appropriate here because it will help a recruiter make a better match for you. Be honest about your skills and experience; the more accurately you can communicate your strengths, the better chance you'll have of finding work through a staffing/search firm.

Bookkeeper

Although my preference is to stay in Hawaii, I would consider relocation to California, so referral to one of your California offices would be welcomed. Salary, benefits, and future **opportunity for growth** will influence my enthusiasm for particular **opportunities that may now be available** via Any Staffing Firm. My present salary is $38,000, so I am motivated to maximize my earnings and increase this amount by at least 10 percent.

Chef

Areas of expertise include all aspects of food preparation and presentation, as well as kitchen management including ordering, hiring, and training. I now work at the McGuiness Inn and I will leave this establishment with **positive references** and a history of planning seasonal menus, **overseeing** all preparation of traditional American cuisine. In addition to cooking to order, I

perform in scheduling, controlling inventory, and customer relations roles.

Dental Assistant

Highlighting all that is detailed on the resume and revealed through the attached letter of recommendation, my qualifications are as follows:

- Over six years of experience as a dental assistant, **contributing to** direct patient care and patient relations.

- Recognition from National Education Center as dental assistant honors graduate.

- Sound knowledge of medical terminology and clinical procedures.

- Certification in first aid, cardiopulmonary resuscitation, and electrocardiography.

- **Additional experience** as receptionist/secretary with an executive search/management consulting firm, a financial management company, and realty firms.

Executive Assistant

In addition to five years of staff experience at Bradstreet and Associates, I have worked for three years as Executive Assistant to the president and to the executive vice president of a software development company.

Legal Assistant

As described on the enclosed resume, in Washington, DC, I was a Legal Assistant for **a well-respected** law firm. There my responsibilities included completion of legal research, drafting and proofing documents, interviewing witnesses and clients, and preparing documentation needed to support litigation activities of attorneys.

As a result I have **highly refined technical and organizational skills**, including **comprehensive computer expertise**. I have extensive **experience working on multiple projects and meeting deadlines** in a **team-oriented** legal environment.

RED FLAG!
STEER CLEAR OF putting your desired salary in your cover letter. Reserve salary discussions for a later phase.

Research and Development

Some colleagues identify my greatest strengths as related to building and maintenance of testing equipment, prototypes, and maintenance of manufacturing equipment.

Sales/Customer Service Representative

My current ambition is to gain management and supervisory responsibilities. I am willing to travel and I would be interested in a salary in the $35,000 to $45,000 range. Of course, salary is important, but it is a negotiable issue.

Security Guard

For the past three years as a bank Security Guard, I was **responsible for ensuring the safety** and security of customers, bank employees, and bank assets. My compensation for that position was about $30,000. I am an **experienced, motivated, and well-trained professional**. I do hope that Any Staffing Firm has current clients, and related postings, that match my background.

Phrases to Use for Closing Paragraphs

When writing to a recruitment/talent acquisition firm, a strong closing paragraph requests a meeting (or at least suggests future communication) and communicates confidence in your candidacy for a position that matches your interests. Always be sure to thank the agency for their time and review of the materials you submit.

Accounting Manager

I do hope that you judge me qualified for one or more searches being conducted by Any Employment. After we speak, **I trust you will refer my candidacy** to employers who have posted those opportunities with you.

Claims Processor

I would very much like **to discuss all of my professional and personal goals**, including salary, with you or one of your Any Staffing Firm partners.

Chef

Perhaps we could meet to discuss my ambitions and qualifications? Ideally, you now have employers in search of candidates and **I could also interview with them** during my upcoming visit. Also, please be aware that I would welcome consideration for positions within an hour commute from Dayton.

Dental Assistant

I am available to start as soon as needed, and relocation is easy to arrange. Please, let's talk by phone regarding appropriate next steps and, **should you judge appropriate**, arrange an in-person meeting. I would be happy to travel to Indianapolis **to meet with you or one of your clients** whenever necessary.

Executive Assistant

I hope you identify my candidacy as **worthy of referral** to those who posted the Executive Assistant position, and to other clients. I do believe Any Staffing Firm can help me with my overall job search.

Legal Administrator

I hope you will find me a **qualified candidate** for the position posted and refer me to the client seeking to hire the Legal Administrator. I also hope you have additional clients who have engaged you to find candidates for immediate full-time or part-time opportunities.

Research and Development

Please, let's discuss by phone your thoughts regarding my candidacy and whether Any Staffing Firm might help. Do you know of any openings that match my qualifications? Would you refer me to an employer interview? What are the appropriate next steps?

Sales/Customer Service Representative

I would be interested in further discussing my candidacy and identifying any **employment opportunities you feel would be applicable to my skills**. Please do keep my candidacy confidential, and I respectfully request that you or any prospective employers only contact references cited in the contract.

Cover Letter Phrases to Use When Contacting Executive Search Firms

Phrases for Introductory Paragraphs

These letters begin much like letters to employment agencies. If anything, your introductory paragraph may focus more heavily on your work experience. Check out these samples to see how you might start this cover letter.

Director of Information Services
During our meeting at the Minority Professional Recruiting Expo, we discussed **opportunities with your client firms** that are of great interest to me. As we discussed, I am **currently seeking a challenging environment** where I can apply my combined technical knowledge, experience, and ability to create and implement innovative concepts for greater information systems efficiency.

🗨 Action Speak

Assessed	Pinpointed
Contributed	Reinforced
Enforced	Shaped
Finalized	Trained
Improved	Transmitted

Management Consultant
To date, I have **played a key role** in designing, implementing, reorganizing, and managing a variety of functions—including operations, manufacturing, materials, engineering, and quality assurance—for nationally and internationally recognized corporations. **The attached resume documents past achievements**. My contact with you reveals ambitions for future challenges and rewards.

Operations Manager
Any Search Firm is well known within the industry, so **I am confident that ours will be a positive and mutually beneficial relationship**. I am actively seeking a new and challenging position and I am confident that, ultimately, you will find me a candidate easy to place.

Plant Manager
During the past ten years, I have held positions ranging from production supervisor to plant and operations manager with a $16 million manufacturer and importer of electrical products. I am now seeking a new position where I can **contribute to a company's cost-effective, quality operation and profitability**.

Senior Accountant
The varied accounting, finance, and general management experience **gained over the course of my career** should be of interest to you as you conduct current or future client searches. As you may recall, you once contacted me regarding a Senior Accountant position, but at that time I was not ready to seek new opportunities. Well, now I am ready, willing, and eager to do so.

Phrases for Motivational and Qualification Paragraphs

Why are you qualified for the type of job you seek? What are your areas of expertise? What have you accomplished in past positions? You must highlight this information in your cover letter, specifically in these paragraphs

Director of Information Services

Qualifications, all detailed on the resume attached to this e-mail, include the following:

- Thirteen years of experience with MIS corporate information systems.

- Experience operating and **supervising** administrative functions of several UNIX systems.

- **Skill communicating** with domestic and international networks, mainframes, and network system support.

- Ability to work as a team member, **team leader**, and/or independent contributor, working offsite via modem and data network, to assist users in sales, finance, manufacturing, and production.

- Ability to **generate positive results** in a company's information systems and networks by **streamlining systems** and improving user training and performance.

Management Consultant

Currently, I am seeking a position within management consulting. I strongly believe this firm and their clients **can benefit from** my twenty years of progressively responsible management experience. **Areas of expertise**, and those that can ultimately yield **value-added assets** within consulting roles, are diverse and include the following:

- Five years as director of operations for a $60 million manufacturer.

- Over six years as materials manager with a multi-plant, multiwarehouse, $10 million manufacturer of industrial rubber products.

- Over nine years as manufacturing coordinator with a toy manufacturer, with **responsibilities related to** expansion of existing manufacturing and support facilities, setup of new facilities, manpower planning, union relations, and capital equipment investment and materials purchases.

Operations Manager

Because of diversity of past achievements, I am able to **transfer skills** to marketing, manufacturing, distribution, and service of other products. In addition to a strong marketing and sales background, I have also **established a record** for setting up, staffing, and managing top-producing, profitable district sales and service operations.

Plant Manager

In my current position as plant manager, I **developed a stable work force and environment following a restructuring**. Under my direction, the company has benefited from efficient supervisory staff and support personnel in all phases of plant operations, including production, purchasing, inventory control, warehousing, distribution, and maintenance of a 325,000-square-foot facility.

Senior Accountant

As a manufacturing plant controller, I managed accounting activities of a $35 million manufacturing plant. **Accomplishments include**:

- Preparing, analyzing, and presenting P&L, balance sheet, departmental expense, manufacturing variance, and other operating reports.

- Preparing $2 million annual departmental operating budgets, analyzing results, initiating required **operational improvements**, and preparing forecasts.

- Developing annual strategic and operational improvements, **resulting in a 15 percent increase in efficiency**.

- Overseeing human resources, purchasing, payroll, and other plant administrative functions.

- Maintaining quality accounting operations by implementing internal controls testing programs.

Phrases for Closing Paragraphs

If you're planning a move (or are currently in the process of relocating) or need to keep your search confidential, now's the time to say so. Set the agency's expectations. This includes salary requirements. It should be noted that this is one of the rare times when discussing salary in a cover letter is acceptable. Request a response from the agency, and as usual, be sure to say thank you.

Director of Information Services

Relocation is not a problem; target cities remain Chicago, Boston, and San Francisco, and my compensation requirements are in the low $70,000 range. **Please keep my candidacy confidential** and do let's continue **our conversations regarding opportunities** as they arise.

> **Green Light** There are some things you should reveal in a cover letter. For example, it's okay to disclose that you want to keep your job search confidential or that you are in the process of relocating.

Management Consultant

Please review your current contingency and retainer client relationships to determine those that might match my strengths. I would **greatly appreciate your consideration and**, **ultimately**, **your referrals for interviews with** one, or more of these consulting organizations or with a firm seeking to hire an internal consultant.

Operations Manager

Should you be aware of an advanced marketing and development position in the $100,000–$150,000 range, please consider me **an eager and qualified candidate**. I would welcome your assistance with my search efforts, and I would be **happy to discuss my background** with you or one of your client firms at any time.

Plant Manager

I would welcome the opportunity **to apply my proven track record** to one of your client firms. Relocation is not a problem. While **salary and compensation is negotiable**, my current salary is in the low $70s, so I would anticipate a new position to offer an increase or the potential to earn more. Please, **let's discuss my candidacy** and how Any Search might assist me with my search.

Senior Accountant

While my prime interest is securing a position on the East Coast, I am willing to relocate for the right opportunity and compensation (ideally $85,000–$95,000, annually).

Endnote: Writing to a staffing agency is not unlike writing to a hiring manager. The agent is looking for someone who can advocate well for his or herself, and now you have the sample phrases you need to do so. Because they will be referring you to a client company, you must use your cover letter to prove to a staffing agent that you have the skills that are of greatest value in your industry.

PART II

Resumes That Make a Mark

Chapter 7

CRAFTING YOUR RESUME

Seven Steps to Success

If the cover letter is the appetizer, then the resume is the main course. A well-crafted cover letter warms them up and piques their interest, but a show-stopping resume is the surest way to win an interview. The good news is, by featuring all the right words and phrases and following these seven steps, anyone's resume can be outstanding. Already have a resume? You're ahead of the game. The advice in this chapter will help you revitalize your old resume or build a completely new one using action words, power phrases, and formatting tricks that showcase your professionalism, establish a proactive tone, and play up your greatest strengths.

The Seven Key Steps to Writing a Resume

Gaining focus and creating a strong, content-rich resume is easy when you have a plan to follow. These seven steps can guide you through the process:

Step One: Review Samples

When looking at sample resumes, analyze them like a knowledgeable and focused job seeker, excited about the task at hand. The goal is to identify the qualities you like.

The first thing employers and recruiters do when they want to fill a position is list the qualifications the job requires. They list these traits in order of priority according to which are essential, which are optimal, and which are merely desirable (or optional).

Sometimes job descriptions and postings include detailed qualification criteria, but more often these preferences are expressed vaguely.

It's crucial when you're writing your resume to find the right phrases that convey your goals, objectives, and a clear sense of job purpose. The wording of your resume should echo the qualifications listed in the job posting. You must create a powerful resume that mirrors your qualifications in order to win an interview and impress the employer into giving you the job.

Step Two: Consider Format, Content, and Order of Information

Pick out your two or three favorite sample resumes. Examine them from top to bottom. Once you identify qualities of each you wish to adapt, consider some basic questions:

- What first impression will your resume generate? How is it formatted?

- What will appear first and most prominently on the page?

- How will your resume identify you? Will it include your e-mail address? Will it include your mailing address and all your phone numbers, including cell phone?

- Will you include an objective statement or a qualification summary?

- Will you present educational information before or after a qualification summary? Before or after experience?

- Will you order information about your work history, qualifications, and objectives with the most pertinent appearing earliest and most prominently at the top?

- Will you use as few lines as possible, reserving most of the page for critical content?

- Will you use columns, with dates on the left and descriptions on the right, or a block format?

- Will headlines be centered or left-justified?

Formatting Basics

The font you choose is the key to a well-formatted resume. Fonts should be traditional, easy-to-read, and common. You don't want to create a beautiful resume in some obscure font that will be replaced on your reviewer's computer by an automatic font substitution (probably destroying all your careful line spacing and other formatting work as well). The best fonts and point sizes for resumes are:

- Book Antiqua (9, 10, or 11 point).
- Century Schoolbook (9, 10, or 11 point).
- Garamond (10 or 11 point).
- Palatino (8, 9, or 10 point).
- Times (9 or 10 point).
- Times New Roman (9, 10, or 11 point).

You can highlight important elements with CAPITALIZATION, **bold face**, and *italics,* as well as with indentations, line spacing, and bullet points.

> **Green Light** For headlines, increase the font size two points at a time until the headline is emphasized but not disproportionate.

Identify Yourself

Letterhead is the best and easiest way to do this. You can design your own very simply. Your letterhead should include:

- Your name on the first line.
- Your full mailing address.
- The telephone number(s) where you can be reached during business hours.
- Your e-mail address.

Summarize Yourself

Some resumes use qualification or achievement summaries to present objectives and goals. Summaries follow or even replace objective statements. Sometimes these sections come at the end, providing the resume with a solid bottom line. Note that not all resumes include these elements; it's up to you to decide whether you need them.

Putting Your Experience in Order

The best resumes present the job seeker's most significant experiences first. Entries are grouped under headlines. They include undergraduate and graduate degrees, specialized training, and work history. Education can come at the top, as the first or second category, or you can present it last. Candidates with plenty of valuable on-the-job experience generally list that first, saving the bottom of the page for a summary of their education.

Academic achievements and honors can be presented in a bulleted list. To figure out what belongs on this list, think about courses, papers, and projects with special relevance to this field. You might also have pertinent extracurricular or community experience. In general, these activities should follow your education and employment entries.

💬 Action Speak

Advanced	Pioneered
Boosted	Processed
Consolidated	Simplified
Documented	Spearheaded
Enhanced	Unified
Generated	

Step Three: Identify Your Objectives and Your Audience

What do you aim to achieve with your resume? Answer that question, and you will define your goals. You must also define, as best you can, who will be reading your resume. Your reviewers belong to the field. They use particular words, phrases, and other field-focused terminology when they talk about their work.

Your resume should clearly state your career objectives, but not necessarily with what was once called a *Career Objective*. Instead, your career objective should be conveyed by your content, clearly projecting your firmly focused qualifications as well as achievements.

Step Four: Inventory Your Qualifications and Achievements

The best way to pick out your important achievements is to think in terms of the job or field you're aiming to enter. Free-form lists of random accomplishment are not as effective. You don't want to rely on your reviewer to figure out or analyze the significance of anything in your resume. It's your job to make your value clear.

Achievement summaries are the heart of any good resume. They should be enough to convince the reviewer of your commitment, your qualifications, and your obvious value. It's important not to skimp on the time or energy you put into summarizing your past accomplishments. To a potential employer, your past has everything to do with the future.

Step Five: Analyze Your Competencies and Capabilities

Great resumes reflect past achievements and, via qualification summaries, project ahead to future roles and responsibilities. You are not limited to talking about what has been achieved. Instead, your resume is the perfect platform to express your confidence and competence to tackle the future.

Step Six: Draft and Critique Your Resume

Your first draft should be inspired by the sample resumes you've reviewed and analyzed. They will probably influence your choice of content and the order of your information. Let them. Later on, you can go back and determine the best order of presentation and omit unnecessary entries.

As you put your first draft together, don't worry about keeping it to any particular length. It is better to start long and later edit it down. Write as spontaneously as you can. Don't rewrite as you go; there will be plenty of time for that when your draft is complete. Your finished resume should be concise. If after your best editing efforts it is still longer than one page, so be it! Employers do read two-page resumes, as long as they are well organized, with the most important information on the first page.

Step Seven: Distribute Your Resume

Most of your resumes will probably go out via e-mail or be posted to the Internet, though you will still need a printed version as well. In either case, it's important to keep making a good first impression. Here's how you do it:

- Use a strong format, very simple graphics (as long as they contribute to your statement), and an attractive design.

- Use standard portrait orientation when printing your resume.

- Use bond or linen paper. White, ivory, natural, and off-white are your best color options. Use the same paper for your cover letters and other correspondence.

Your Resume Checklist

Here is an actual step-by-step review of what you must do to create or update your resume today. This list simplifies the actions already outlined and clarified previously. Have your laptop or desktop computer ready. You should soon be writing or typing, not just thinking. Without delay, you should be able to create or update your resume in less than a day.

☐ Identify at least two sample resumes to model. This should take no more than fifteen minutes.

☐ Reflect upon how and when these samples presented their information. Create a draft listing of headlines you might use in the order you want them to appear. This step should take about ten minutes.

☐ Concisely state your job-search goal as it will appear in a statement of objectives or as the headline of a qualification summary. This step should also take ten minutes.

☐ With this goal in mind, make a list of significant, related accomplishments. This should take about thirty minutes.

☐ Review significant, related accomplishments to link past accomplishments with future potential via a qualification summary. It is recommended that you actually draft your entire resume, including the objective, before you take on this task. No matter whether this section is presented first or last, writing this section should be your last, most important, and perhaps lengthiest task. This could take about an hour, but it can be done quicker.

☐ With model resumes in view, type a draft of your version. Don't think, just type. Later, you will complete self-critiquing and copyediting. This should take at most one hour.

☐ Conduct software-linked spell-checking and grammar reviews. Have someone else review for typos and format questions, then make revisions and complete the final version. While you should respect comments of colleagues and friends, remain confident that you are the best and ultimate judge regarding what should appear in your resume and how it should be presented.

☐ Draft and finalize your cover letter. Distribute your resume. The time it takes to complete this step will depend on whether you e-mail your resume or deliver it by hand.

Field Descriptions

Many industry publications compile long lists of criteria to help workers assess their career compatibility and evaluate their potential goals. The following list provides brief descriptions for a variety of fields. With this general idea of what comprises a field, you can more easily determine your particular focus and your qualifications for performing a particular function.

Administration

The administrative field involves general office management as well as oversight of facilities and systems associated with day-to-day organizational activities. No matter their titles, many employees of this field work in administrative, customer service, or general office positions. On the other end of a wide continuum, those serving within these functions are also responsible for large operations and organizations. They generally supervise many individuals, projects, and resources. Job functions include office services, facilities, security, management, and project management roles.

Architecture, Construction, and Engineering

This field is dominated by the principles and theories of science, engineering, mathematics, and design to solve and carry out initiatives within research, development, manufacturing, sales, construction, inspection, and maintenance.

Arts and Media

This field includes the performing and fine arts; broadcast, print, and Internet media; and communication-oriented organizations. Settings include, but are not limited to, galleries, museums, radio and television stations, dot-com organizations, publishers, newspapers and magazines, public relations firms, and advertising agencies.

Business

This sector includes almost any profit-driven activity. Most often, the business world is associated with large publicly or privately held companies that provide services or market products.

Communications

The communications field involves writing, graphics, public relations, publicity, and promotions. It includes all activities associated with creating, distributing, and transmitting text and graphic information via varied print, video, audio, computer, and web-based media.

Education

The education field includes private and public preschools, elementary schools, middle and secondary schools, colleges and universities, as well as tutorial and training operations.

Finance

This field involves accounting, budgeting, treasury, auditing, and information systems activities. It includes collection, documentation, and analysis of financial data and the use of this data to make strategic decisions and share pertinent information with investors, regulators, and government entities. It also includes allocation and growth of capital required for annual operations as well as growth.

RED FLAG!
CUTESY OR GIMMICKY L-MAIL monikers like Partyallnight@ or Muscleman@ do not belong on a resume. It's worth your time to register for a more professional address when you're searching for jobs.

Government

Government includes all local, state, federal, and multinational organizations that pass legislation, offer and regulate services, lobby, and promote specific programs and resources.

Health and Human Services

Usually considered a member of the service sector, this field includes both individuals and facilities that offer medical, psychological, social, and related services. Practitioners can be private, government-affiliated, or have nonprofit status. Hospitals, clinics, residential treatment facilities, agencies, and special programs all fit within this field.

Hospitality

This is a service sector that encompasses a broad variety of industries such as hotels, restaurants, casinos, travel, and tourism.

Human Resources

This field involves recruiting, retention and staffing, compensation and benefits, training and development, as well as employee-relations efforts. It includes all hiring, career development, compensation, and personnel management activities.

Law

The legal field includes services and systems associated with enforcement of laws, such as judicial, regulatory, corrections, investigation, and protection organizations. Employers include government and private agencies, law firms, and nonprofit entities, as well as courts and mediators.

Marketing

Marketing involves new product development, product management, marketing analysis, research, product and sales support, advertising, promotions, and public relations, as well as customer services. These functions can take place in-house, in consumer and industrial product manufacturers, or at specialized consulting firms or agencies.

Sales

The sales field involves direct sales, representative sales, distribution and arbitrage, and retail sales. It includes all activities associated with sales of raw materials used to create products or the sale of products directly to consumers. It can also involve sales of financial or other services.

Science and Technology

The tech sector includes organizations and businesses associated with research, development, manufacturing, and marketing of new technologies. Activities can be purely research-and-development oriented, or they can be product or service oriented. Government, business, and education entities all fit within this specialized category.

Technology and Operations

This field involves production, materials, traffic, and management of information systems. It includes overseeing or participating in the activities associated with producing tangible products and, with purchasing, receiving, storing raw material, components, or finished products. It is also associated with the allocation of human resources to specific assignments and with the operating, programming, or servicing of computers.

Endnote: Stay focused when you craft your resume and choose wisely in terms of what experience and qualifications you feature. Make it easy on yourself and your reviewer by highlighting achievements that clearly connect to the job. Even the small choices you make at this stage of the process can make a big difference in the amount of responses you get later on.

Chapter 8

INFLUENCING WITH PHRASES

Industry-Specific Wordings

Not everyone speaks resume. Even though you know what you did at your last job, you may find it difficult to translate that information into the formal language that a resume requires. To save you a lot of hemming and hawing, this chapter provides a comprehensive collection of phrases organized alphabetically by job industry! The phrases mainly cover common job duties and responsibilities. Use them on your resume when describing your own work experience.

Account Executive

- Marketed loan and financing programs to financial institutions and mortgage brokers.

Accountant

- Assisted with monthly closings and financial reporting.
- **Worked directly with** controller to prepare primary and secondary public stock offerings.
- Implemented Solomon general ledger accounting package.
- Installed and set up modules, **developed procedures** for new system, and trained staff.

Accountant, Senior

- **Oversaw** all accounting and payroll functions **for a $20 million publicly held company** that develops, manufactures, and markets proprietary X-ray systems.
- Assisted controller in preparing financial statements and SEC reports.
- **Prepared budgets** and projections and monthly budget-to-actual reports and **distributed to managers**.
- Reviewed work of staff accountant and approved journal transactions for data entry.
- **Managed** accounting duties of a venture-capital-funded start-up spin-off organization, including financial reporting and coordinating annual audit with external auditors.
- Interacted with systems and payroll services professionals **regarding problems and solutions**.
- Assisted with **analyzing implications**, making final decisions, and completion of consolidation of three European subsidiaries.

Accountant, Staff

- Monitored cash and accounts receivable for venture capital–funded software development firm.
- Assisted in general ledger close, including foreign currency translation of foreign subsidiaries.
- **Trained new employees to** administer the accounts-payable and order-entry functions.
- Completed compilations, reviews, audits, and tax returns for individual and corporate clients.
- **Created** financial schedules and reports using Excel and SuperCalc spreadsheet programs.
- Passed Audit, Law, and Theory portions of CPA exam at first sitting.

Accountant (Supervising), Senior

- **Supervised**, **planned**, **and budgeted** audit engagements.
- Oversaw and completed checks of audit reports, financial statements, and tax filings.

- **Recruited, trained, supervised, and evaluated** staff accountants.

- **Gained experience from** client assignments, including those in oil and gas, manufacturing, real estate, and nonprofit arenas. Proficient training use of spreadsheet packages

- **Served as liaison between** Supervisor, Staff Accountants, and clients.

- Prepared financial statements, tax filings, and audit reports.

Accounting Analyst, Corporate

- Prepared and analyzed income statements, balance sheets, and earnings schedules for $9 billion corporation.

- **Compiled** 10k federal reserve, management, and analyst reports.

- Utilized trend reports to analyze balance sheet and income statement key ratios.

Accounting Assistant

- Compiled daily reports for magazine and advertising revenues.

- Completed Accounts Receivable and Payable efforts.

Accounting Intern

- **Supported efforts of** Relationship Managers, servicing depositors with **accounts in excess of $500,000.**

- Completed compilations, reviews, audits, and tax returns for individual and corporate clients.

- Created financial schedules and reports **using Excel spreadsheet programs.**

- Supported transactions and **addressed inquiries,** developed reports, and assisted colleagues and customers.

Accounting Manager

- Completed SEC Reporting and Disclosure forms.

- Managed general ledger closing and maintenance.

- **Supervised and reviewed all** accounting and finance areas.

- Administrated 401(K) pension plan. Implemented accounting, payroll, and manufacturing software.

- Reported directly to CFO, providing financial data and analytical reports **to maximize profits and support managerial decisions.**

- Hired, trained, evaluated, and supervised accounting, bookkeeping, and analyst professionals.

- Involved with corporate management in areas of acquisition and corporate development.

Accounting Technician

- Maintained and reported on financial records and created financial statements associated with money market mutual fund **for sixty corporate clients.**

- Balanced Trial Balance and generated journal entries.

- **Maintained**, **compared**, **and reconciled** the fund on three computer systems.

- Assisted system analysts in preparation and implementation of new computer system.

Administrative Assistant

- Provided administrative support for new business development group; assisted CFO with **special projects**.

- **Ensured smooth workflow; facilitated effectiveness of** fourteen sales consultants.

- Directed incoming calls; initiated new client application process; maintained applicant record database.

- Aided in **streamlining** application process.

- Assisted in design and implementation of computer automation system.

Administrative Assistant to the President and Chief Executive Officer

- Prioritized daily activities of CEO.

- Set up and maintained tickler system.

- **Composed and edited correspondence for** President.

- Assisted CEO with sensitive customer and employee relationships.

- Recorded and distributed Management Committee minutes.

- **Maintained and distributed monthly department reports**.

Administrative Assistant to the Chief Executive Officer

- Coordinated and prioritized daily activities of Board Chairman.

- Performed administrative functions in support of CEO.

- **Required an in-depth knowledge** of the bank, financial community, investors, and customers.

- Assisted with preparation for Board of Directors and Shareholder meetings.

- Recorded and distributed minutes of Board, Shareholder, and Executive Committee meetings.

- Maintained CEO's travel and appointment schedule, using computerized scheduling system.

Green Light Be sure to list all professional affiliations on your resume. Leave out any that aren't within or directly related to your industry.

Administrator, Central Personnel

- **Coordinated** statewide reclassification study.

- Organized questionnaires and individual interviews.

- **Evaluated**, **analyzed**, and rewrote job descriptions; prepared study package for senior management approval.

- Established related managerial files.

- Dealt with diverse personnel-related projects.

Advertising Account Supervisor and Media Coordinator

- Trained, **guided**, and directed staff of five while monitoring ad placement system.

- **Assisted in creation of** advertising campaigns and acted as liaison between client, agency, and media vendors, including selection, budget, and advertisement placement.

Advertising Media Planner, Senior

- **Directed all phases of** media planning services for **national accounts**, primarily based in eastern region.

- Planned media and placement **for five of the firm's largest clients**, with annual media budgets ranging from $1 million to $7 million, and total media budgets in excess of $15 million.

- Oversaw efforts of two Media Coordinators, a Media Assistant, and two support professionals.

- **Created Excel and Access systems to track** media plans and purchases, client quarterly sales, and profits.

- **Regularly interacted with** account services colleagues and clients to address queries, determine commitment to existing plans, and redirect plans as needed.

Advertising and Public Relations Internship

- Conducted market research, wrote press releases, produced traffic reports, worked media events, and assisted with advertising production.

Architect

- Assisted with development and testing of Computer-Aided Design and Database software.

- Provided demonstration and technical support for **pre- and post-sales activity**.

- Acted as **subject matter expert** for future software enhancements and requirements.

- **Served in leadership roles** for various joint studies teaming with IBM and other major corporations in the evaluation of CDB software for architecture.

- Participated in conceptual design, design development, and construction documentation of architecture and landscape design.

- Created exploration, analytical, and presentation models materially and on computers for residential and commercial projects.

- Fabricated sculptural wood and bronze detail elements installed in varied projects.

Art Assistant, Advertising

- **Produced** paste-ups and mechanicals for full-service advertising agency.

- Operated Photostat camera and coordinated logistics for photo shoots.

- **Brainstormed** with creative team.

Art Instructor, Secondary

- Developed new and **updated existing** curriculum regularly for Studio Art, Art History, and Art Appreciation courses.

- Focused Studio Art projects on composition, color, and **conceptual problem solving**, requiring completion of projects using varied media, including charcoal, pen and ink, acrylics, and airbrush.

- Inventoried, ordered, and controlled budget of approximately $10,000 annually.

- Implemented curriculum with classes for gifted art students, including a district-wide art competition and scholarship in 1993.

Art Instructor, Elementary

- Visited school sites on a regular basis **implementing** a creativity-focused curriculum.

- **Teamed with** teachers to incorporate art projects and related lessons into existing units.

Assistant to the Director of Public Relations

- Assisted in promotion and publicity of special events.

- Developed press kits and releases **to initiate**, **maintain**, **and maximize media relations**.

- Compiled easy-to-access and update computerized publicity files **using FileMaker Pro**.

- Researched prospective consumer markets using Internet and direct-contact techniques.

- Created direct-mail lists, updated media lists, and **maintained task priority lists**.

Audit Trainee

- Conducted audits to complete Federal and State regulatory documentation associated with the FDIC.

- **Assessed efficacy of** policies and procedures related to fiscal, regulatory, and customer service standards.

- **Gained knowledge of operating procedures** associated with departments including Personal Banking, Small Business Banking, and Home Equity Loans.

Auditing Analyst

- **Prepared** contract proposals and illustrative cost calculations.

- Constructed Actuarial Valuation and analyzed actuarial gains and losses.

- **Independently generated regular reports for** forty individual clients and oversaw development of reports for sixty corporate clients.

- Determined the minimum and maximum contribution allowable by law for the IRS.

- Assured accuracy of **comprehensive** financial information database.

Auditor (Internal), Senior

- Conducted operational and financial audits of manufacturing subsidiaries.

- Designed and implemented audit programs **to test the efficiency of** all aspects of accounting controls.

- **Recommended changes and improvements** to corporate and divisional management.

- Trained and supervised staff auditors in all aspects of the audit engagement.

Bank Branch Manager/Commercial Business Development Officer

- Co-managed District Officer Call Program to retain, expand, and track commercial customer base.

- Instituted Branch Neighborhood Equity Call Program, which **enhanced sales of** Home Equity and first and second mortgage products 33 percent over a six-month period.

- **Designed and managed** District Product Development Program, which included development of H.E.L.O.C., Home Equity Loans, residential mortgage products (Two-Year Fixed ARM, Five-Year Fixed ARM), Business Installment Loan (BIL), and marketing collateral.

- Served as one of two Chicago-Area Sales Trainers, **supervising professional sales training program** for twenty-three branch network that included Train-the-Trainer, market identification and definition, needs analysis, program development, implementation, results assessment, and **follow-up** responsibilities.

Bank Branch Manager/IRA Specialist

- Designed brochures for IRA Marketing Program and **instituted** model for customer focus groups.

- Co-designed and managed new IRA Marketing strategies through Customer/Client Focus Groups.

- Managed overall loan **operations** of third-largest branch, **with transactions averaging over $10 million per year**.

Bank Branch Manager/Mortgage Development Specialist

- Developed Branch Neighborhood Equity Call Program to introduce and expand Home Equity Programs **resulting in a 16 percent increase in** Lines and Loans in first month.

- Designed and managed Branch Product Development and Customer Information and Sales incentives.

Bank Teller

- Processed account transactions; **reconciled** and deposited daily funds.

- Informed customers of bank products, referred public to designated personnel, provided account status data, and **handled** busy phone.

- Oriented, trained, supervised, and **delegated tasks** for new hires.

- Assisted with planning and implementing extended-hours customer service strategies.

Barback

- Handled customer service and cash intake.

- Assisted with liquor inventory.

- **Performed** security services.

Bartender and Bar Manager

- Served patrons; purchased wine, alcohol, beer, and mixes.

Bookkeeper

- Supervised general ledger through trial balance, as well as A/P, payroll, and payroll tax returns for construction and home improvement firm with annual revenues in excess of $2 million.

- **Converted** bookkeeping procedures from written documents to in-house computer system.

- **Coordinated department's workflow**, supervising A/R and A/P Clerks.

 RED FLAG!
DON'T INCLUDE YOUR AGE in the contact information section of your resume.

Bookkeeper, Senior

- Oversaw bookkeeping for mortgage and home equity loan firm, **specializing in** addressing first home purchases, debt consolidation, and educational payment needs of clients from diverse financial backgrounds.

- **Generated and presented** general ledger and investors' monthly reports for firm that generated over $10 million in mortgage and loan portfolios annually.

- Oversaw A/R and A/P staff **to ensure accuracy of** accounts.

- Monitored efforts of third-party payroll services checking accuracy of scheduled payments.

- Managed multiple accounts for major investor and real estate developer with commercial and residential properties in several states.

- **Interacted effectively with** all finance-savvy senior managers specifically reporting to CFO.

- Supported annual auditing and tax efforts of CPA firm.

Brand Manager and Director of Marketing Operations for Technical Imaging

- **Spearheaded implementation of** corporate objectives within the Technical Imaging Division.

- Conceived and energized all marketing strategies and **provided feedback on program performance and recommendations to corporate senior managers**.

- Directed and **supervised staff of ten** with responsibilities for generating $250 million in sales with a $150 million margin for core products.

- Prepared and effectively controlled a $7 million marketing expense and a $4 million advertising budget.

- Created first end-user direct-mail strategy **generating a 30 percent response rate** and selling 400,000 units in first year.

- Mounted trade show exhibitions including designing booths, collateral materials, and advertisements. Secured $200,000 in prebooked sales within a month of trade show presentations for four new products.

Budget Analyst

- Balanced $1.3 billion budget using internally developed and regularly revised software.

- Reconciled accounts on ISA/ABC system to other financial systems.

- **Assisted management in** budget preparation.

- **Conducted training classes** on the financial system for upper-level management.

- Prepared comparison of expense to budget reports for executives on demand and on weekly, monthly, and quarterly basis.

- Submitted accounts and IRS filing for the Political Action Committee.

- Generated financial analysis and reporting projects **using Focus Report Writing and Excel, including macro programming, and MS Word**.

- Contributed annually to budget development and **strategic planning processes**.

Busboy

- Set and cleared about twenty tables per evening of large dining room.

- Trained new bus people.

Campaign Assistant

- Supervised chapter campaign duties.

- Assisted the Executive Director with **administrative responsibilities**, such as personnel and budget.

Case Manager

- **Served within** counseling and referral roles for at-risk students and their families.

- Coordinated outreach, intake, and referrals for those with financial, educational, and medical issues.

- **Maintained detailed** case records and statistics for reports distributed to district and state officials.

Case Worker

- Assessed client needs, developed treatment plans, and managed cases.
- **Communicated with** court officials.
- Served as child advocate for court proceedings.

Case Worker, Director (Case Management Services and Legal Advocate)

- Provided counseling and referral services for residents of shelter for abused women and their children.
- Trained and interacted regularly with twenty-four-hour hotline volunteers, supporting telephone crisis counseling and **authorizing** admission of residents on an emergency basis and for long-term transition periods.
- Conducted individual and group orientations, took case histories, and **facilitated** counseling sessions.
- Assisted women completing temporary restraining orders and served as liaison with legal counsel.
- Provided expert testimony during domestic violence legal cases and **reported outcomes** to staff.
- Assisted with public relations and fundraising and **regularly contributed to** grant writing activities.

Chief of Campus Police, Assistant

- Assisted with personnel, budget, and procedural oversights associated with a department of twenty full-time and twenty part-time security professionals.
- **Recruited**, **trained**, **and reviewed** performance of professional and administrative personnel.
- Protected life and property on and about the campus of Johns Hopkins University.
- Patrolled on foot and via automobile, **using strong observational and interaction skills**.
- Upheld laws and codes of the State of Maryland and Johns Hopkins University.
- **Cooperated** with law enforcement agencies, regularly interacting with Deputy Sheriff.
- **Conducted community outreach** and educational efforts, focusing on alcohol use and abuse, safe dating, and property protection.
- Served on Student Life Committees and assisted with judicial investigations.

Civil Litigation Specialist/Office Manager

- Managed office and staff of three secretaries, **ensuring smooth operation of** firm with three attorneys and billings in excess of $1.5 million and awards of over $10 million annually.
- Interviewed clients; **prepared files** and discovery; handled multiple cases.

- Requested and reviewed medical documentation.

- **Negotiated** and settled cases with defense attorney and insurance companies.

- Attend mediations and conciliations.

- **Prepared clients** for depositions and trials.

- Controlled and **maintained** law office accounts utilizing accounting and billing software.

- **Regularly attended** seminars on personal injury law.

Clinic Therapist (Orthopedic In- and Outpatient)

- Developed treatment plans for chronic-pain and cardiac patients.

- Presented regular in-service on hip and knee prostheses.

Computer Systems Analyst

- Completed database management, systems analysis and design, workstation maintenance and repair, and LAN management tasks.

- **Reduced process time and purchasing errors** by developing an online program that allowed the purchasing department to track the status of all purchasing invoices.

- Developed purchase order program that **improved** data entry speed and reduced data entry errors.

Coordinator, Special Events

- Created and coordinated Special Events and Promotions **within $425,000 marketing budget.**

- Selected and wrote event advertising, promotional materials, and publicity copy.

- Handled charity fundraising, corporate image positioning, and community outreach efforts.

> **Green Light** Volunteer experience can really round out a resume. If you regularly volunteer, add the heading "Volunteer Experience" and provide details.

Counseling and Mental Health Services Intern

- Counseled undergraduate and graduate students with personal, academic, and career issues.

- Addressed psychological and developmental needs of multicultural and diverse 3,600 undergraduates and 1,000 graduate students.

- **Assessed** and diagnosed clients on the basis of presenting problem, history, and rating on Personality Assessment Inventory (PAI).

- Participated in two hours of individual supervision and one hour of group supervision per week.

- Served as a liaison between Counseling Center and University Health Services through involvement in the development of Feel Fit in February speakers series and outreach program designed to meet the health needs of student populations.

Counseling Psychologist

- **Facilitated** individual and group counseling for clients diagnosed with varied neurotic, psychotic, developmental, and behavioral disorders.

- **Collaborated with** health-service professionals to development treatment plans for emotionally disturbed adolescents.

- Assisted clients in developing survival skills to aid transition from residential to independent living.

- Coordinated service networks for academic, psychological, and social assistance.

Counselor

- Served as assessment, recruitment, and referral **specialist**.

- Traveled to community sites and **executed presentations** to recruit prospective parents for minority children.

- Conducted testing and home studies of prospective parents to determine eligibility.

- Followed up for evaluation purposes three months, six months, one year, and two years post adoption.

- Served as referral source to private and public mental health services **as needed**.

Counselor, International Primary School

- Administered psychological and educational testing for students ranging from prekindergarten to fifth grades.

- Counseled students, families, and teachers.

- Designed remedial and therapeutic plans.

- **Led group activities for** self-image enhancement and behavior modification.

- Worked with teachers on preventive strategies for social and disciplinary problems.

Counselor, School

- Counseled students individually and in groups; designed specific counseling programs to meet needs.

- **Responded effectively to** various on-campus crises via crisis intervention strategies.

- Coordinated and oversaw IEP meetings and specific meetings designed to help high-risk students become more successful in school.

- Consulted daily with teachers and parents regarding student performance.

- **Teamed with** psychologist presenting information for special education students to parents and teachers.

- Facilitator of workshops, presentations, and programs for students, teachers, and staff.

Counselor (School), Intern

- Counseled students on personal, educational, and career issues.

- **Developed and implemented** guidance services in a multicultural setting; included social skills groups, divorce groups, and disability awareness program.

- Conducted individual and group counseling for students.

- Worked with the "Latinos Unidos" club to improve cultural awareness.

- Developed and implemented preschool curriculum **to enhance** language skills of developmentally delayed students.

- Coordinated with parents on designing an educational plan to facilitate the development of their children.

Dental Assistant

- Assisted dentist in prophylactic procedures: provided necessary tools, sterilized equipment, comforted patients.

- Provided secretarial assistance.

Dental Clinic Director and Clinical Instructor

- Supervised clinic with rotating groups of dental students and support personnel.

- **Evaluated** student performance via videotape voice-overs and written reports.

- Annually **analyzed financial viability of** clinic, instituted regularly revised plans to increase profitability, and managed business related activities.

Dental Hygienist

- Provided prophylaxis treatment, teeth cleaning, oral hygiene education, and periodontal scaling.

- **Administered** Novocain prior to painful procedures.

Dental Hygienist, Surgical Dental Assistant, and Assistant Office Manager

- Provided **state-of-the-art** individualized prophylaxis treatment to adult and adolescent patients.

- Administered teeth cleaning, gum massage, oral hygiene education, and periodontal scaling procedures and **supervised** interns undertaking similar procedures.

- **Scheduled** patients for appointments for surgical procedures and provided presurgical preparation.

- Recorded temperature and blood pressure, inserted intravenous units, and administered sedatives.

- Provided postoperative care in person and via telephone follow-up. **Recorded** vital signs every ten minutes until patients were conscious; established patient comfort; **provided necessary information** to patients regarding new medications and possible side effects.

- Handled accounts payable and receivable and health insurance transactions.

Dental Trainee/Extern

- Served in rudimentary observation and support roles **before advancing to** Dental Assistant.

- Sterilized instruments, processed X-rays, scheduled appointments, maintained patient relations.

💬 Action Speak

Appraised	Explored
Budgeted	Headed
Coordinated	Introduced
Distributed	Proposed
Effected	Sponsored

Dentist

- Provided comprehensive dental care and trained staff members.

- Developed marketing plan, **established and allocated** marketing budget, and **oversaw business operations of** practice composed of one dentist, one hygienist, and one support professional.

Dentist (General Practice), Owner

- Purchased large dental practice through a leveraged buyout.

- Determined and **successfully implemented long-term growth strategies**.

- Supervised a staff consisting of two other dentists and six support personnel.

- Provided comprehensive care for over 2,000 patients.

- Lead the office in **steadily increasing production and revenues**.

- **Updated** practice and computerized equipment.

- Presently facilitating transition of practice to new owner.

Editor, Senior

- Evaluated general trade reference titles and **assess profit potential**, acquire titles, and negotiate contracts.

- **Oversaw** publication, from development and editing to production, publicity, and marketing.

- Served as in-house editor for internal and external newsletters and web documentation.

Editor/Writer

- Edited and wrote large proposals for government contracts.

- **Designed** format and coordinated production.

- **Organized** and maintained up-to-date books through several revision cycles.

- Interpreted client requirements and **determined applicability of** proposal responses.

Engineering Technician

- Prototyped and tested new PC products, drawing schematics and expediting parts for these new PC products. Designed and coded multiuser database management software for engineering use.

- **Expedited** the parts for over twenty-five telecommunications terminal prototypes. Built, **troubleshot**, and transferred those prototypes to various departments for testing.

Finance Assistant, Commercial

- Prepared daily client loan advances and payment activity.

- Maintained client loan/collateral statements.

- Assisted with preparation of departmental reports and loan agreements.

Guidance Counselor and English as a Second Language Instructor

- Counseled students and families **for clientele ranging from** prekindergarten to twelfth grade.

- Administered psychological and educational testing.

- Designed complete record keeping system for all students.

- **Implemented** behavior modification programs

- Administered achievement, vocational, and college prep tests.

- Made policy on admissions and discipline.

- **Worked with** teachers on individual educational and behavioral programs.

- Taught English as a Second Language to students in third–sixth grade.

 RED FLAG!
DON'T CLUTTER YOUR RESUME with redundant phrases, e.g., saying you have a "proven track record of success."

Human Resources, Director of

- Oversaw hiring, training, and all personnel responsibilities **for insurance broker with 400 employees**.

- **Determined technology and procedures related to** maintaining and updating personnel files, ensuring compliance with federal and state regulations pertaining to benefits and wages.

- Supervised grievance adjudication.

- Performed claim payment internal audits.

- **Coordinated activity with** reinsurance carriers.

Human Resources and Staff Development, Director of

- Developed and implemented overall human resource policies.

- **Provided leadership in the areas of** personnel, payroll, labor relations, training, and affirmative action for operations with over 2,000 employees.

- Administer personnel and payroll procedures, policies, and systems to meet management and employee needs.

- **Consulted with Chairman**, **Executive Board**, **managerial staff**, **and supervisors to** ensure policy compliance with applicable statutes, rules, and regulations.

- Advanced agency Affirmative Action Plan.

- Determined appropriate grievance procedures required to resolve labor disputes.

- Acted as liaison for regulatory agencies: EOHS, OER, DPA, State Office of A.A., and PERA.

- Maintained staff training program.

- **Interfaced with** legal staff when addressing discipline and grievances.

Investigator/Case Manager (Human Services)

- **Conducted assessments** and developed treatment plans for family caseload.

- Maintained documentation of contracts and provided crisis intervention and family therapy.

- **Served as advocate for** clients in court and with community agencies.

Laboratory Technician

- Produced and processed blood components.

- Labeled and released for transfusion and manufacture.

- Performed viral immunology testing and irradiation of blood products.

LAN Coordinator

- **Analyzed**, **developed**, **and maintained** application software for multisite engineering LAN.

- Provided training and user support for all applications to LAN users.

- Maintained departmental PC workstations including software installation and upgrades.

- **Reduced data entry errors and process time** by developing an online program allowing program manager to submit model number information.

- Replaced time-consuming daily review board meetings by developing a program that allowed engineers to review and approve model and component changes online.

- Developed an online program that **reduced process time**, standardized part usage, and **allowed** engineers to build part lists for new products and components.

Legal Intern

- **Researched and drafted** motions on criminal law and procedural issues. Interviewed clients at New Mexico correctional institutions.

- Argued bail motions in several state district courts.

- Negotiated plea and bail agreements for defendants accused of misdemeanors. Attended criminal trials and depositions.

Legal Secretary/Legal Assistant

- Greeted clients, maintained files, and **completed administrative tasks**.

- Prepared documents for legal proceedings involving real estate transactions.

- **Entered client information** into Excel- and Access-driven computer system.

Librarian

- Provided excellent patron services when covering circulation and reference desks.

- Gave instructional guidance to patrons, including use of computerized and manual index tools and catalogs.

- Focused interactions on empowering and instructing patrons while **creating positive relationships**.

- Addressed reference questions by demonstrating proper Internet and printed resources.

- Planned and **presented** regular community education programs.

- Recorded incoming periodicals and journals on computerized system and strip resources for security.

- **Compiled** statistics on door count, circulation, photocopies, and reference activities.

- Served on Acquisition Committee and **provide quarterly and annual recommendations to** Budget Committee.

Librarian/Audio Visual Coordinator

- Supervised comprehensive secondary school library, overseeing volunteer, professional, and student staffs.

- Established annual educational plans and **regularly supported** instructional efforts of teachers.

- Completed daily patron services and operations efforts and supervised student study periods.

- Interacted with Budget Committee to establish and monitor annual budgets.

- Ordered publications as well as software, and maintained audio-visual equipment.

Management Consultant

- Provided marketing, behavior, and research counsel for advertising, public relations, and marketing consulting firm.

- **Participated in internal and external strategic planning for** *Fortune* 500 firms, government agencies, nonprofits, and healthcare providers.

> **Green Light** If your GPA was a 3.0 or higher, include that information in the "Education" section of your resume.

Market Research Associate

- Managed behaviorally based research projects including proposal writing; methodology, instrument, and sample development; field coordination; data coding, analysis, and report writing.

- Included customer and employee studies, communication audits, market analysis, name/logo testing, constituency relations, positioning, and consumer studies.

- **Completed projects for** insurance providers, hospitals, and private practices.

Market Research Consultant

- Established firm, conducted client outreach, recruited three associates, and **oversaw all operations activities**.

- **Built** consumer behavior models using multivariate techniques, including regression and discriminate analysis, and cluster analysis.

- **Analyzed data** from national survey to identify purchase intents and patterns for business-to-consumer direct marketers.

- **Presented information to** senior management of client organizations.

- Specialized in entrepreneurial start-up activities, business plan development, and venture capital solicitation.

Market and Strategic Management Research Consultant

- Conducted **large-scale** quantitative research projects based in customer satisfaction measurement and total quality implementation, including design, coordination, statistical analysis, and report generation.

- **Specialized in** business-to-business services, e-commerce, and health care.

Marketing Assistant

- Cold-called high school and college students and parents, marketing college and graduate school entrance exam preparation courses.

- **Yielded 35 percent attendance at seminars and simulations** used to market services.

Marketing Representative, Senior

- Managed assigned territory including **prospecting** new distribution sources, **rehabilitating** nonperforming agencies, and terminating relationships.

- **Served in lead role for** all insured sales presentations by **conducting strategy negotiations**, making presentations, and facilitating actual presentation.

Marketing, Vice President of

- Identified target markets, constructed complex questionnaires, conducted telephone interviews, **compiled and analyzed data for** research activities associated with entrepreneurial start-up.

- Conducted focus groups to identify market segments and penetration.
- **Wrote and presented report to management** including strategic recommendations.
- Addressed all marketing research needs.
- Gathered data to develop comprehensive business plan and marketing reports.

Nanny

- Provided live-in child care for two boys, currently ages two and four.
- Provided environmental enrichment and personal care.
- Supervised play, transported children to preschool and other activities, and assisted with meals.
- **Reinforced** parental rules and values.
- Accompanied family on short and long trips and vacations.

Nurse Practitioner

- Provided gynecologic, obstetric, and primary care **in collaboration with** physicians in private practice
- Evaluated and managed acute and chronic gynecologic and obstetric problems, including: abdominopelvic pain, genitourinary problems, infections, breast concerns, endocrine-related problems, osteoporosis, and postoperative and pregnancy complications.

- **Evaluated and managed** wide array of primary care problems including EENT, allergic conditions, dermatological problems, infectious diseases, chest pain, and respiratory, gastrointestinal, and musculoskeletal problems.
- Performed annual and employment exams and prenatal and postpartum care.
- **Counseled** and prescribed for cholesterol and weight management, contraception, menopause, osteoporosis, and mood disorders.
- Developed health education handouts and presented staff in-service training.
- **Performed** periodic Quality Assurance review for onsite laboratory.
- Acted as preceptor for Nurse Practitioner and Physician Assistant students.

Nurse Practitioner, Senior

- **Evaluated and managed** health problems including: infectious diseases, allergic conditions, dermatological problems, respiratory, gastrointestinal, genitourinary, endocrine, and musculoskeletal problems, traumatic injuries, and occupational health issues.
- Provided routine and preventive care, employment and sports physical exams.
- **Initiated** gynecologic services for Eastman School of Music.
- Made health education presentations, acted as preceptor, and served on Training and HIV Task Force.

- Coordinated University Health Services Library used by nurses, nursing students, and patients.

 RED FLAG!
DON'T WRITE, "I know how to go online, and I can use a PC," when listing technical skills. Mention specific software programs, operating systems, and industry-specific applications.

Pastry Chef, Assistant

- Worked with Executive Pastry Chef, **monitoring** baking, mixing, and finishing of cakes, pastries, and a full range of bakery products on an as-needed basis.

- Completed special orders for banquets, catered functions, and hotel restaurant.

Pastry Chef and Bakery Manager

- **Plan and prepare** desserts on a daily basis for restaurant patrons.

- Oversee all operations of retail bakery and prepare desserts and breads for catered functions.

- Prepared an extensive assortment of desserts, rotating on a weekly basis, including cakes, cookies, cobblers, puddings, tarts, special-order desserts, and wedding cakes.

- Created breakfast pastries and breads for lunch specials.

- **Planned and executed** monthly menu that included six desserts, two sorbets, two ice cream dishes, and two fresh breads daily for lunch and dinner.

- Ordered all bakery and dairy supplies, and prepared desserts for retail store and special orders.

Patrolman

- Performed all standard policing functions, **earning excellent ratings** annually.

- Interacted and communicated with town officials regarding proactive and reactive efforts.

Physical Therapy Aid

- Assisted with ultrasound, muscle stimulation, massage, and interferential treatments.

- Served as translator using Spanish language skills with selected patients.

Production Assistant

- Booked main guests and panelists for weekly topical talk show.

- **Generated** and researched story ideas.

- Conducted video research.

- Edited teasers for show.

- **Organized** production details for studio tapings.

- Coordinated publicity ads in local newspapers.

Production Intern

- Assisted producers of live, daily sports interview and call-in show.

- Researched and generated story ideas.

- Preinterviewed guests.

- Covered shoots and wrote promos.

- Produced five segments.

Professor

- Taught undergraduates Criminal Law, Criminal Procedures, Crime in America, and Business Law.

- **Stimulated** class involvement through use of case studies, mock trials, and law-school simulation.

- Served as Freshman Advisor to diverse students and Faculty Advisor to prelaw majors **on an annual basis**.

Professor, Assistant

- Taught undergraduate courses in Business Administration and Law, including: Criminal Law, Crime in America; Courts and Criminal Law; Criminal Procedures; Crime in America; and the Courts.

- Taught first-year law students Criminal Procedures and Juvenile Procedures.

Programmer Analyst/Senior Programmer

- **Supervised** Junior Programmers on varied System Projects.

- Actively participated in projects involving e-commerce, CRM, BI or ERP functions.

- **Developed**, **maintained**, **and supported** Sales Illustration Systems in "C."

- Wrote "Illustration Software Installation" routine in INSTALIT software.

- **Designed file transfer process** for Mainframe to PC using NDM software. Hands-on experience with PC hardware, Windows, IBM, Novell Software, Emulation Software (Rumba, Extra, etc.), Dial-In Software (SimPC, XTalk, etc.) and have understanding of LAN technologies.

- Developed an Executive Information System on the mainframe using COBOL 2.

- Designed and **implemented system enhancements** and new products.

Promotional Assistant

- Implemented promotional campaigns, wrote copy, and designed advertisements. Enhanced attendance via creative competitions and corporate sponsored give-aways.

Public Relations Manager

- **Served as consultant to** seven state chapters regarding campaign problems and activities.

- Organized regional campaign meetings; **spoke at** several campaign conferences.

- Reviewed legislation and brought specific bills to the attention of the proper committee or individual.

- Staffed the Legislative Advisory Committee and **followed through on** specific bills.

- Developed fundraising programs.

- Conducted the previous two annual campaigns for the newly merged Central Chapter.

Publicist

- **Personally support** media relations, campaign development, and implementation efforts associated with professional athletes, education, and not-for-profit clients.

- Interact with clients regularly to **address needs and fine-tune** annually updated strategic media plans.

- **Draft**, **edit**, **and finalize** news releases, speeches, and press packets.

- Develop and maintain relationships with regional and national print and broadcast media, supporting efforts **to maximize** desired coverage.

- Serve as client spokesperson and as press conference coordinator.

Publicity Assistant

- Publicized new books and authors.

- Assisted with television, radio, and print media tours and individual appearances.

- **Created and implemented** author questionnaire to maximize publicity generated through professional contacts.

- Wrote press releases and designed press packets.

- **Responded to** review copy requests.

Real Estate Loan Officer

- **Originated** real estate loans, developed marketing plan **to expand business in** Santa Clara County.

- Conducted cold calls, created individualized mortgage broker packets.

- Completed individual and group presentations designed to generate loan business.

- **Implemented first-ever** real estate expo promotional event.

Real Estate Sales Associate (Residential and Commercial)

- Served in comprehensive sales as well as mortgage and lease-advisory capacities for residential and commercial clients for one of the Bay Area's largest branch offices.

- **Prospected new buyers and sellers** via monthly seminars, direct-mail, and e-mail campaigns, appearances on radio programs, and print and television ads.

- **Regularly exceeded sales goals**, twice receiving national Gold Jacket recognition for top 10 percent production, three times receiving $100 million

Club recognition for annual sales and leases, and annually receiving Top Producer recognition for regional and state sales figures.

- **Licensed in** residential and commercial sales, property management, and financing and leasing.

Real Estate Territory Manager (Regional)

- Recruited to open and develop Bay Area for multi-line commercial accounts.

- **Generated** territory volume of $4 million from $250,000.

Recruiting Manager (Executive Recruiting)

- Reviewed and revised annual college recruiting strategies and yield targets with VPs of Human Resources, Merchandising, and Operations.

- **Developed**, **proposed**, **and monitored** annual college recruiting budgets of approximately $75,000.

- **Regularly reviewed and established** target school listings, contacts, and recruiting dates.

- Trained college team liaisons and leaders to make effective campus recruitment presentations.

- Organized senior executive involvement in Career Days second interview processes.

- Facilitated College Recruiting Team discussions regarding Management Development Program offers.

- Recruited for, hired, and **oversaw fifteen Summer Interns** and ten Academic-Year Interns annually.

- Assisted training staff with planning educational and social activities associated with initial portions of a ten-week program that blends classroom instruction with career networking and skills training.

Rehabilitation Therapist (Cardiac)

- **Acted as program coordinator for** exercise regimen and provided treatments using ultrasound, electric stimulation, massage therapy, and stretching/strengthening exercises.

- Coordinated aquadynamics program for chronic-pain patients.

Rehabilitation Therapist (Pediatric)

- Coordinated treatment of amputee children and children with congenital birth defects.

- **Created** Alive with Pride program now functional at thirty national hospitals.

- Developed child-oriented play program and trained teachers via elementary school seminars.

Restaurant Manager

- **Oversaw operations of** 250-seat facility averaging over $10,000 daily sales, offering American cuisine luncheon and dinner service to store patrons.

- Scheduled, motivated, and supervised staff of twenty-five full-time and part-time servers per shift.

- **Monitored** daily and monthly receipts and expenditures.

- **Communicated with** store and corporate management regarding sales targets and profit strategies.

> **Green Light** Keep your resume clean and easy-to-read. Remove unnecessary details like street addresses and zip codes when identifying the companies where you've worked.

Restaurant Manager, Assistant

- Oversaw operations of 175-seat facility averaging over $3,000 daily food sales and $3,000 wine and alcohol sales, offering luncheon, dinner, and after-dinner service.

- Supervised staff of thirty employees per shift, controlled inventory, deposited cash, maintained physical plant, and completed daily and weekly reports for after-hours club catering to elite patrons.

- Monitored food costs, effectively communicated with chef and prep staff regarding costs.

- **Prepared and submitted** weekly, monthly, and quarterly reports to owners.

- With chef, planned weekly menus.

- Completed management training program.

Retail Buyer (Apparel Department), Junior

- **Developed sales volume** from $5.5 million to $7.5 million.

- **Consistently achieved** net operating profit of 50 percent, highest in company.

- **Implemented promotional strategies** and developed key classifications directly responsible for volume increase.

- Developed electronic and direct communication networks supplying product knowledge to sales staff and **impacting strategic planning of** vendor programs.

- Instituted e-mail communication strategies and status-tracking efforts.

- Chosen as Merchant of the Year 2008, 2009, and 2010.

Retail Buyer, Assistant

- Acted as liaison with vendors and warehouse to assure timely merchandise delivery of men's coordinates, coats, swimwear, and activewear.

- **Interpreted**, analyzed, and responded to OTB, selling reports, and seasonal plans.

Retail Sales Manager (Divisional)

- Handled furniture, electronics, and basement store with $5.6 million in sales for the year 2008.

- During mall expansion, held store sales volume within plan by achieving **12 percent sales increase**.

- Priorities included constant evaluation of stock levels and content, goal setting, development of key personnel, and **achieving** a high motivational level.

Sales Account Executive (Advertising)

- **Sold** time and production support to potential clients.

- **Assisted with establishment of** all media and production plans, proposals, and budgets submitted to potential and existing clients.

- Implemented existing local, regional, and national strategies and media sales programs.

- **Increased sales and production revenues**.

 RED FLAG!
DON'T INCLUDE PERSONAL achievements like "I bought my first house" in your list of accomplishments. Stick to talking up your strengths as an employee.

Sales Account Executive (Advertising), Senior

- Established and maintained national corporate accounts as well as regional and local accounts.

- Interacted with national sales, regularly identifying and **leveraging** new packages based on demographics and ratings.

- Utilized production experience to establish and grow strategy targeting regional and local revenues, primarily generated from independently owned retailers and service providers.

- **Developed relationships with** regional ad agencies, specifically media planners, to establish client-focused team approach.

- **Accounted for over $2 million in new clients revenues** over four-year period, and average annual revenues of $500,000.

- Initiated and developed marketing strategies and target grid for the second-ranked TV station in fifth-largest market for effective sales programs/promotions.

Sales Account Executive, Dealer

- **Oversaw completion of** relationship building, bidding, delivery, and all sales efforts required to market products and services through dealer locations.

- **Initiated cooperative sales strategy** with reseller business owners.

- Designed marketing promotions and directed reseller's sales efforts into business and education accounts.

- **Grew sales by 400 percent to $20 million**.

- Oversaw training and completed performance reviews of ten–fifteen Sales Representatives.

Sales Account Manager, National

- Developed and implemented national sales strategy for computer and peripheral manufacturer, consultant, and support-service provider.

- Initiated, built, and **nurtured relationships with** several *Fortune* 500 corporations including Ackler Industrial, The Carnulton Group, Hanlon and Associates, and Polamin Company.

- Oversaw resale accounts as well as direct-user accounts. Involved identification and analysis of potential business applications within target accounts and cultivation of key business relationships with senior management **to facilitate sales**.

- **Grew profits** 200 percent over five years to $15 million amidst decreasing unit pricing, increasing sales goals, and enhanced competition.

- Completed all five years in the top 12 percent of the National Account Channel as Golden Star Award winner.

- **Created new revenue streams** resulting in an estimated $30 million in sales and $40 million in new services for the company.

- Regularly reported sales results and status of strategies to senior marketing executives and CEO.

Sales Representative (Corporate Chain)

- Provided administrative and technical sales support to corporate chain account locations, including Power Electronics, Computer Corral, and Circonne Computer.

- Regularly called upon accounts to maximize knowledge of retail personnel, address concerns, and **promote** in-store visibility.

- Developed marketing promotions and trained store personnel.

- Tracked individual store sales and profit data to **determine** efficient coverage schedule and recognize particular achievements.

Secretary (Departmental)

- Answered phones, scheduled appointments, greeted patients and visitors, and prepared and filed charts.

- Typed and printed invoices and requisitions.

- Supervised inventory and general office organization.

- **Served as liaison between** physicians, staff, and patients.

Secretary to Executive Vice President and Senior Loan Officer

- Managed Secretarial Staff supporting commercial loan officers.

- **Coordinated staff meetings** and presentations to Board of Directors.

- Prepared monthly departmental and divisional reports for distribution.

- Updated and maintained Policy and Procedure Manual **on a timely basis**.

Secretary to the Senior Vice President Commercial Division

- Set up Commercial Loans on System.

- Prepared monthly reports for Board of Directors.

- **Updated** financial statements.

- Maintained appraisal files.

- Coordinated loan renewals.

Security, Head of

- **Managed all aspects of** security for hotels and adjoining properties.

- Hired, scheduled, supervised, and **evaluated** personnel.

- Provided all policing functions, with emphasis on defusing potentially violent situations.

- **Cooperated extensively with** Baltimore and Bethesda Police Departments.

Social Worker

- **Provided services for** clients and families with medical, psychological, housing, and financial needs.

- Supervised agency volunteers and graduate student interns.

- **Worked collaboratively with** various community agencies to provide needed serves.

- Conducted in-service training to staff and those from other agencies.

Social Worker, Clinical

- **Diagnosed**, evaluated, and treated children, adolescents, adults, and families living within the guidelines of Care and Protection Petitions.

- Interacted with legal, medical, and psychological professionals.

- Provided individualized social work services for children and adolescents, including pregnant teens, foster-home residents, and those meeting court-mandated criteria.

- **Maintained accurate and thorough documentation** via case records.

Social Worker (District)

- Provide direct social work services to elementary, middle, and high school students and families.

- As member of interdisciplinary team, **establish, implement, and monitor effectiveness of** Independent Educational Programs.

- **Regularly communicate** with parents, teachers, and special-education professionals regarding individual students.

- Conduct group discussions with students and parents pertaining to developmental, behavioral, and medical issues.

Store Manager

- **Manage** Spinner's largest-volume store, with sales of approximately $30,000 per week.

- Handle all merchandising, inventory control, ordering, cash control, and maintenance.

- Oversee store opening and closing procedures.

- Direct sales floor activities, assist customers, and **address customer concerns**.

- **Input data** to prepare daily sales reports and regularly use weekly and monthly data to develop sales and promotional strategies.

- Hire, train, and coordinate a staff of twenty-six.

- Work with Spinner corporate colleagues as well as record company professionals to develop local marketing and advertising strategies, supplementing national campaigns.

- **Inspire** sales staff to develop and implement special promotions and events.

- Won two merchandising display contests.

- Received the Super Spinner Sales Award for exceeding sales goals

Store Manager, Assistant

- **Promoted from trainee to Assistant Manager within twelve months**.

- **Conceptualized** and implemented employee training and effectiveness program.

- Hired, trained, and supervised staff of six serving customers of specialty men's clothing store.

- Provided exceptional customer services to high-end consumers, regularly including direct e-mail and phone contact, and relationship building.

- Tallied daily receipts and made bank deposits.

- Opened and closed store, **handled customer service issues**, and oversaw cash control.

- Maintained inventory levels, monitored merchandise, **provided feedback to** owner/buyer regarding trends and need for reorders.

Student Clinician (Speech Pathology)

- Diagnosed, then planned and administered therapy to children with apraxia, language delay, hearing impairment, and articulation disorders.

- Used Visual Phonics and American Sign Language with hearing-impaired child client.

- Diagnosed, then administered therapy to adult displaying motor speech disorders and aphasia.

- **Established** home programs to effectively train and motivate parents, spouses, and others.

- **Wrote** case summaries documenting clinical goals, approaches, and achievements.

Student Teacher (Third Grade)

- Independently established and presented lesson and unit plans.

- Created specific interdisciplinary Reading and Work unit, focusing on reading skills for varied jobs, and including visiting career field representatives.

Systems Engineer

- **Coauthored** software test plan for computer prototypes.

- Researched, wrote, and edited test procedures.

- Developed computer engineering test tools.

- Wrote database application to track and generate reports on problems found during development.

- **Organized** preproduction testing of prototypes.

- Analyzed requirements for new processes to improve product testing.

- Created software that automated work-related processes, such as generating status- and engineering-change request reports.

Systems Manager

- **Researched, wrote, and edited** proposal used to identify needs and find networks and desktop configurations composed of eight personal computers and two printers

- Supervises three Technology and Systems Consultants for office with thirty full-time employees.

- Planned and **oversaw completion of** special project teams related to existing and **future technology needs** and potential purchases.

- Regularly conducted software- and hardware-related troubleshooting and audit activities.

- **Interacted with** product vendors and customer service and technology support professionals.

- Designed 24/7 backup and retrieval system for accounting databases and word-processing data.

Systems Programmer

- Initiated start-up and **implemented operations**.

- Designed and managed implementation of a network providing the legal community with a direct line to Supreme Court cases.

- Developed a system that catalogued entire library's inventory.

- Used Cs to create a registration system for a university registrar.

Teacher

- Taught infant, preschool, and after-school programs.

- **Planned curriculum**, organized activities, communicated with parents and staff regarding children's growth and development.

- **Enhanced skills development** through interactive play and song.

- Responded to annual increase in students and move to new facility.

- **Worked with owner on** goals and assisted with annual licensing documentation and visitation.

 RED FLAG!
DON'T EXAGGERATE or lie about your past job responsibilities. All it takes is one reference check to get the truth.

Teacher, Substitute

- **Instructed academic lessons** to K–12 population; lesson development and classroom management.

- Worked with developmentally challenged students.

Teacher, Summer School (English)

- Planned and implemented lessons focusing on literature, grammar, writing, and research.
- **Addressed** remedial needs of students.

Teaching Assistant (Biochemistry Laboratory)

- Assisted students in biochemistry laboratory.
- Worked with professors to **prepare materials for** use in the laboratory and graded quizzes and laboratory reports.
- Created web page allowing students access to test results.

Teacher (Voice and Piano)

- Instructed approximately seventy voice, piano, and composition students.
- **Presented** six recitals annually, working with students to select and prepare performance pieces.
- Regularly used video and electronic piano computer system to provide audio and visual feedback.
- **Guided** students through application process for admissions and auditions for music programs and professional performance and composition.

Telemarketing Professional

- Cold-called residential and commercial consumers, assessing domestic and international calling needs, and then recommending and marketing long-distance programs.

- **Consistently achieved at least 125 percent of sales goals**.
- Landed largest commercial accounts during 2008–2009 and 2009–2010 Fiscal Years.

Television and Radio Station Producer (Campus Cable)

- Wrote hard news, feature stories, scheduled/interviewed guests.
- **Responsible for** researching materials for mini-documentary.
- Scheduled and interviewed guests for roundtable discussions.
- Wrote and edited scripts and edited master tape.
- Researched materials and packaged tapes for production.
- Performed as camera technician, stage manager, and teleprompter operator.
- Assembled lighting and audio equipment.

Travel Consultant

- **Arranged** individual and group travel, regularly yielding monthly billings in excess of $10,000.
- **Promoted** agency via weekly visits to senior residences as well as college campuses.
- **Regularly attended training sessions related to** airline offerings and reservation systems updates.

- Coordinated air ticketing requests and tour departures using APOLLO and SABRE systems.

- Served as agency specialized for cruise industry.

- Regularly attended sessions hosted by cruise and air carriers, educating regarding options and plans.

- **Tracked** international and domestic fares, sharing data with colleagues daily.

- Issued tickets and final itineraries for air and cruise customers.

- Maintained and filed pertinent materials and **assisted with updating of** website.

- Assisted with projects associated with marketing of Disney World, Disneyland, and Disney Cruises.

- **Served as group leader for** numerous cruise and resort familiarization trips.

- Prepared detailed financial reports and assisted senior management with development of strategic goals.

Tutor and Advisor (Summer Enrichment Program)

- **Advised**, tutored, and taught specialized courses to selected group of high school students.

- Planned and implemented ten-week Study Skills, SAT Preparation, and Writing Skills seminars, focusing on at-risk students with the potential to succeed in college.

- Created assignments-based "Reality Academy," an ideal high school.

Underwriter (Insurance)

- Analyzed all personal lines of business to determine acceptability and to control, restrict, or decline, **according to company guidelines**.

- Supervised all personal lines of business for Arizona and New Mexico.

- **Kept current with changing policies**, **rates**, **and procedures**, explaining coverage, rules, forms, and decisions to agents, staff, and insured.

Veterinarian's Assistant (Surgical)

- Assisted clinicians and students treating patients, and provided room pre- and postoperative care.

Veterinarian's Assistant (Surgical), Senior

- Perform pre- and postoperative care and emergency care.

- **Monitor** ventilation and vital statistics of premature and critically ill animals.

- Collect and ship blood samples, perform intravenous and arterial catheterization, intubation of endotracheal and nasogastric tubes.

- Organize labs for and oversee veterinary students and clinical instruction sessions.

Veterinary Animal Technician/Research Assistant

- **Directed** hygienic procedures on 300 animals, including surgery and necropsies.

- **Conducted research on** pet food products and analyzed studies on nutrition, zinc, urine, feces, fluid therapy, medication, breeding, and artificial insemination.

- **Collaborated in** testing new vaccine for feline leukemia, submitting reports for FDA approval.

- Supervised and scheduled twenty center and union employees in conducting research.

Veterinary Assistant

- Assisted with daily diagnosis and treatment, and served as ICU specialist, completing oral, IV, IM, SQ, fluid therapy-, radiology-, hematology-, immunology-, chemotherapy-related tasks.

- **Administered**, **assisted**, **and maintained** anesthesia during surgery.

Waiter, Head

- **Managed**, **opened**, **and closed** high-volume four-star restaurant.

- **Hired**, **trained**, **scheduled**, **and supervised** waitstaff.

- **Led** weekly quality assurance and menu discussion sessions.

- Oversaw special catering events held onsite and at residences of patrons.

- **Provided efficient service to** full bar, serving area, and catered affairs.

- **Addressed concerns** and special requests.

- Reconciled gratuity intake in accordance with tax regulations.

Witness Advocate

- Interviewed victims and witnesses, prepared documents, and organized information for court appearances.

- Assisted attorneys during trials, taking notes and **facilitating access to** evidentiary documents.

Writer (Technical) and Senior Project Administrator

- Research data and accurately describe the installation, removal, erection, and maintenance of all military hardware.

- **Outline** wiring diagrams, draw part breakdowns for illustrators, **draft and finalize** all descriptions associated with use of and training to use military hardware.

- **Serve as overall program lead for** specific projects in A-3, EA-3, and EP-3E programs.

- Work on IPB, MIM, and IFMM for all maintenance levels.

- **Transform** various source materials, including engineering drawings and wiring diagrams into user targeted written and disc-driven documentation and illustrations.

- Served as project lead, including editing, layout, and corrections.

Endnote: Terminology varies from industry to industry, but there is one hard and fast rule of resume writing that everyone must follow: active language beats passive language every time. Show them that you make things happen and they will consider you a worthy candidate for employment. Show them that you are fluent in the action phrases of your industry and you are one step closer to the interview.

ADDING SPICE

Chapter 9

The Keywords You Need

One of your goals in writing a resume is to convince your prospective employer that you know your industry well. Buzzwords are a vital tool for anyone hoping to cement their reputation as a connoisseur of their field. Hiring managers and human resource professionals reviewing your resume will expect to see the appropriate terminology in the body of your resume. Not sure if you have enough buzzwords in your resume? Here is a valuable list of them (organized by industry) along with regularly used action verbs.

Accounting and Finance

Accounting and finance buzzwords highlight experience with accounting, budgeting, treasury, auditing, and information systems activities. This includes collection, documentation, and analysis of financial data and the use of this data to make strategic decisions and share pertinent information with investors, regulators, and government entities. It also includes allocation of capital required for annual operations as well as growth.

Resume Buzzwords

1099 Tax Information
A/P
A/R
Absorbing Cost
Abusive Tax Shelter
Accommodative Monetary Policy
Account Aggregation
Accounting
Accounting Software
Accounting Systems
Accounts
Accounts Payable
Accounts Receivable
Accredited Investor
Acid Test
Acquisitions
Actual Reports
Actuarial Department
Actuarial Valuation Report
Adjusted Gross Income
Administrative Leadership
ADP System
Advances
Affiliate
Affinity Investment Scheme
Allotment Needs

Alternative Investment Market
Analysis of Financial Data
Analytical Services
Annual Budget Process
Annual Budgets
Annual Capital Budgets
Annual Operations
Annuity
Appropriation of Money
Asset Management
Asset Reconciliation
Asset Responsibility
Assets
Audit Papers
Audit Requests
Audit Schedules
Auditing
Auditors
Audits
Automated Transmission Process
Balance of Trade
Balance Sheets
Bank Balances
Bank Reconciliations
Bank Training Program
Bar Charts
Bear Market

Bellwether Stock
Benefits Reports
Bids
Big Five
Big Three
Bill Payment
Billing Errors
Billing Systems
Black-Scholes Model
Blue-Chip Stock
Board of Directors
Bond and Corporate Financial
    Services
Bond and Equity Transactions
Bond Market Association
Bonds
Bookkeeping
Boston Stock Exchange
Branch Office
Bridge Financing
Brokerage Firm
Brokerage License
Brokerage Services
Brokers
Budget
Budget Account
Budget and Investigated Variances

Budget Control

Budget Projections

Budgeting

Bull Market

Bureau of Economic Research (BEA)

Bureau of Labor Statistics (BLS)

Burn Basket Execution

Business Administration

Business Cycle

Business Development

Business Experience

Business Model

Business Plan

C.O.B.R.A.

Capital

Capital Budget

Capital Expenditure

Capital Gain

Capital Growth

Capital Surplus Statement

Cash

Cash Account

Cash Availability

Cash Disbursement

Cash Earnings

Cash Flow

Cash Management

CDs

Check Cashing Center

Check Disbursement

Check Verification

Checkbook Maintenance

Check-Cashing Center

Checks

Chicago Stock Exchange

Cincinnati Stock Exchange

Claim Liabilities

Claims Processing

Client Relations

Client's Asset Base

Close the Books

Closet Index

Coding of Receipts

Collections

Commerce Department

Commercial Credit Unions

Commercial Lending

Commercial Loan Operations

Commissions

Commodities

Commodity Futures

Commodity Options

Composite Index

Composite Table

Composite Yield

Compound Interest

Computer Models

Computer Systems

Consulting

Consumer Confidence Index (CCI)

Consumer Credit

Contract Negotiation

Contract Proposals

Contractors

Contracts

Conversion Parity

Convertible Debt

Coordinated Payments

Corporate and Municipal Securities

Corporate Banking Services

Corporate Clients

Corporate Finance

Corporate Financial Data

Corporate Financial Reporting

Corporate Lenders

Corporate Securities

Corporation Account

Cost Estimators

Cost of Living Adjustment (COLA)

Credit Analysis

Credit Balance

Credit Bureau

Credit Reporting

Credit Terms

Currency

Custody Services

Customer Agreement

Customer Inquiries

Customer Relations

Customized Credit Solutions

Customized Investment Portfolios

Data Processing

Database Management

Day Trader

Debt

Debt Consolidation Services

Debt Underwriting

Decimal Pricing

Deferred Compensation Retirement
   Plan

Department of Commerce

Deposit Accounts

Derivatives
Derivatives and Asset Management
Devaluation
Development of a Mission
Direct Deposits
Director Labor and Standard Costs
Disbursement and Tracking of Loans
Disclosure Forms
Discount Brokerage
Discretionary Income
Discretionary Investment
    Management
Disposable Income
Divestiture
Dividend Credit
Dividend Receivables
Dividend Reinvestment Plan
Dividend/Interest Payments
Documentation
Dollar Bond
Donated Stock
Dow Jones Composite Average
Dow Theory
Due Diligence
Dynamic Pricing
Earned Surplus
Earnings Reports
Earnings Schedules
Earnings Season
Economic Indicators
Economics
EDP
Efficient Market Theory (EMT)
Emerging Markets

Employee Benefits Reports
Employer-Employee Relationships
Enforcement Policies
Equity
Equity Funds
Equity Ratio
e-Reporting
Escrow
Escrow Deposit
Estate Planning
Eurobonds
European Union (EU)
Exchange Rate
Excise Tax Laws and Regulations
Expenditures
Expense Recording
Expense Reports
Expenses
Federal/State/Unemployment Taxes
Filing Procedures
Finance
Financial Accounting
Financial Advisory Services
Financial Analysis
Financial Expertise
Financial Modeling
Financial Plan
Financial Reporting
Financial Statements
Financial Strategies
Financial Systems
Financial Trend Analysis
First and Junior Trust Deed Loans
Fixed Assets

Fixed Income Securities
Fixed-Income Sales and Trading
Fleet Financing
Flexible Funding Alternatives
Focus Sessions
Forecasts
Foreign Currency
Foreign Exchange
Foreign Markets
Fraud Account Functions
Fund Coding
Fund Custody Services
Fund Expenses
Fund/Sponsor Investments
Future Sales and Trading
GAAP and SSAP Formats
GCAS Productivity
General Ledger
Global Fund Services
Global Macroeconomics
Global Markets
Global Trade Services
Government Entities
HMO Rates
Home Loans
Homeowners
Illustrative Cost Calculations
Income Statements
Income-Related Statements
Inequities
Information Systems
Institutional Equities
Insurance and Financial Services
Insurance Products

Integrated Financial Solutions

Internal Control Procedures

Internal/External Reporting

International Banking Services

International Bond Funds

International Economics

International Index Assets

Investment Banking

Investor Relations

Investor Services

Investors

Invoices

IRA

IRS Filing

IRS Service Policies

ISA/ABS Systems

Issuance of Policies

Journal Entries

Journal Transactions

Key Ratios

Leasing Companies

Legal and Credit Files

Lending

Liabilities

License Agreements

Lien Mortgage Loans

Line Management

Listed Companies

Loan Documents

Loan Payments

Lotus

Management Information Systems

Management Services

Managerial Accounting

Manual Worksheet System

Manually Issued Policies

Market Averages

Market Awareness

Market Indicators

Market Invoices

Marketing

Markets

Merchant Investment Banking

Mergers and Acquisitions

Middle- and Upper-Income Markets

Money Management

Money Market Account

Money Market Instruments

Month-End Journal

Monthly Closing

Monthly Financial Statements

Monthly Forecasts

Monthly Manufacturing Accounting
   Report

Mortgage Loans

Mortgages

Municipal Securities

Mutual Funds

NASD Regulations

NASDAQ

National/International Markets

New Benefits

New York Stock Exchange

Online Investments

Operating Budget

Operational Support

Options

Originating (Brokering and Funding)

Outstanding Payable Balance

Outstanding Tax Obligations

Overdrafts

Overdue Accounts

Partnerships

Past Due Interest

Payable Vouchers

Payroll

Payroll Coverage

Payroll Functions

Payroll Records

Personnel

Petty Cash

Planning Refinement

Portfolios

Premium-Based Workers'
   Compensation

Pricing Policies

Primary and Secondary Public Stock
   Offerings

Principal Auditor

Private Client Services

Private Companies

Probabilities

Problem Resolutions Skills

Production Costing

Profit Plans

Profit Sharing

Profitability

Pro Forma Statements

Property and Casualty Carrier

Public Companies

Public Finance

Public Relations

Purchase Orders
Purchasing
Quantitative Analysis
Quarterly/Monthly Reports
Real Estate and Mortgage Loans
Real Estate Transactions
Receipts
Record Keeping Services
Record Transactions
Regulators
Regulatory Bodies
Remit Payments
Reports
Repurchase Agreements
Residential Loan Applications
Retail Banking
Retirement Accounts
Retirement Management
Retirement Programs
Retirement Services
Retrospective Refund Liabilities
Revenue Collection
Royalties Computation
Sales
Schedules
SEC Reporting
Secured Business Lending
Secured Loan Programs
Securities
Securities Lending Services
Securities Services
Securities Trading
Security Discrepancies

Self-Insurance Program
Selling
Shareholder Account Activities
Shareholder Inquiries
Shares
Single-Country Funds
Single-Family Residences
Spending Behavior
Spreadsheets
State Insurance Regulations and
   Legislation
Statistics
Stock Brokerage Licensure
Stock Market Investments
Stock Research
Stocks
Strategic Decisions
Strategic Plans
Tax and Insurance Escrow
Tax and Regulatory Requirements
Tax Filings
Tax Forms
Tax Liabilities
Tax Returns
Tax Shelters
Taxable Fixed Income
Tax-Deferred Investments
Tax-Exempt Assets
Telephone Collections
"Tiered" Interview Techniques
Trade Capture Settlement
Trade Management Development
Trade Settlements

Transaction Management
Transfers
Travel and Entertainment
   Reconciliations
Travelers Checks
Treasury
Treasury Bills
Trend Reports
Trial Balance
Trust and Banking Markets
Trust Departments
Unbillable/Uncollectible Business
Underwriting
Underwriting Philosophy
Underwriting Results
Valuation
Variable Annuity Products
Vendor Identification Files
Vendor Payments
Weekly Cash Requirements
Wire Transfers
Workers' Compensation

Administrative

These buzzwords are for applicants looking for general management and office positions. They reflect an involvement and familiarity with general office management as well as oversight of facilities and systems associated with day-to-day organizational activities. Important skills include administrative, project management, customer service, and light labor.

Resume Buzzwords

Account Records Maintenance
Account Transactions
Accounts Payable
Accounts Receivable
Ad Placement
Adding Machines
Administrative Policies and
   Procedures
Administrative Support Services
Advertising
Agendas
Analysis
Appraisal Files
Archives
Articulate/Expressive Speaker
Associates Degree
Association Membership
Bank Services
Banking Processes
Billing
Billing Systems
Bills of Lading
Bookkeeping
Branch Audits
Budget Requirements
Business Administration

Business Forms
Business Letters
Busy Phone Work
Calculators
Certified Mail
Clerical Functions
Clerical Skills
Client Files
Client Relations
Client/Customer Correspondence
Coding
Commercial Loan Files
Company Literature
Computer and Software Applications
Computer Operation
Computer Skills
Conferences
Confidential Records
Contract Bids
Consultant
Correspondence
Courier Services
Credit Checks
Customer Inquiries
Customer Relations
Customer Service
Daily Activities

Daily Deadlines
Daily Deliveries
Daily Fund Deposits
Daily Office Functions
Daily Reporting
Data Entry
Data Gathering
Data Processing
Database Management
Departmental and Divisional Reports
Design Composition
Detail Oriented
Dictaphone
Direct Mail
Dispatch
Documentation
Donor Relations
Editing
e-Mail
Employee Appraisals
Equipment Maintenance
Event Planning
Expense Accounts
Expense Reports
Express Mail
Facilities Management
Fax Messages

Federal Express
File Coding
File Maintenance
Filing Systems
Financial Management
Financial Statements
Forms
General Accounting Procedures
Human Resources
Inbound and Outbound Mail
Incoming Calls
Incoming Mail
Information Trafficking
Inquiry Resolution
Insurance Claims and Payments
Interbuilding Correspondence
Interviews
Inventory
Inventory Analysis
Inventory Control
Inventory Discrepancies
Inventory Systems
Invoicing
Logistics
Mail Processing
Marketing Forecast Reports
Mass Mailings
Material Coordination
Meeting Minutes
Meeting Planning
Meetings
Member Appointments
Membership
Merchandising

Monthly Charges
Monthly Payroll
Monthly Reports
Multiline Phones
Multiple Projects
Newsletter
Office Equipment
Office Management and Operations
Office Procedures
Office Reports
Online Database
Organization Policies and Procedures
Packing Slips
Payable Invoices
Periodical Production
Personnel Functions
Personnel Management
Personnel Records
Petty Cash
Phone Requests
Photo-Typesetting
Physical Inventory
Plan Meetings
Positive Attitude
Presentations
Press Releases
Problem Identification and Resolution
Problem Solving
Procedural Enhancement
Procedure Manual
Procedures
Processing
Product Displays
Production Schedules

Promotions/Contests
Proofreading
Public Inquiries
Public Relations
Purchase Orders
Questions and Complaints
Reconciliation
Record Keeping
Reference Library
Registered Mail
Relocation Policy
Report Generation
Report Writing
Reports
Research
Rules/Regulations
Sales Reports
Sales Support
Schedule Hours
Schedule Management
Secretarial Staff
Seminars
Shipping/Receiving
Shorthand
Site Visits
Special Events
Special Projects
Speed Writing
Spreadsheets
Staff Meetings
Staffing Needs
Statement Transcription
Statistical Typing
Statistics

Stenography
Strict Deadlines
Supervisory Skills
Survey Data
Switchboard
Systems Enhancement
Tax Returns
Telephone Inquiries
Telex

Time Records
Time Sheets
Trade Shows
Training Skills
Transcription
Travel Arrangements
Travel Calendar
Travel Vouchers
Troubleshooting

Typing
UPS
Vendor Relations
Word Processing
Words Per Minute (WPM)
Workers' Compensation
Workflow
Writing Skills

Aerospace

Positions in this field might be in manufacturing, commercial, or military aviation, or research. Aerospace industry buzzwords display experience with manufacturing, engineering, and maintenance of commercial, military, and business aircraft; helicopters; aircraft engines; missiles; spacecrafts; and materials, related components, and equipment. This includes scientific research; hands-on work repairing and constructing aircraft equipment and parts; guaranteeing customer safety through quality assurance testing; and producing reliable, high-quality products.

Resume Buzzwords

ABS Resins
Acquisition Management
Activity Reports
Actuators
Adapter Cards
Advanced Combat Systems
Advanced Fighter Aircraft
Advanced Technology Products
Aerospace Defense Products
Aerospace Ordnance Devices
Aerospace Systems
Aerospace Telemetry
Air Defense Technologies
Air Force Material Command

Air Traffic Control
Air/Coastal Defense Radar Systems
Aircraft
Aircraft Avionics
Aircraft Components
Aircraft Engines
Aircraft Fuel Systems
Aircraft Fuselages
Aircraft Maintenance
Aircraft Modification
Aircraft Refueling
Altitude
Analysis Reports
Appliances
Audio Accessories

Automation
Aviation Communications Products
Avionic Display Systems
Avionic Mechanisms
B-2 Spirit Stealth Bomber
Boeing 747
Braking Control Systems
Broadcasting
Cabin Interior Products
Cabin Video Systems
Capital Services
Casting Foundry
Circuit Breakers
Circuits
Combat Systems

Command/Control Systems
Commercial Aircraft
Commercial Aircraft Parts
Commercial Jet Transports
Commercial Pumping Systems
Computer Bus Structures
Computer Peripheral
Computer Systems Development
Computer-Based Information
Control Equipment
Control Systems
Control Valves
Controls
Corporate Aircraft
Coupling Equipment
Data Communications Hardware
   Products
Data Interchange Services
Database Systems Support
Defense Industry
Defense Systems
Design Activities
Displacement and Pressure
   Transducers
Distribution of Electricity
Ducting Systems
Dynamic Hydraulic and Mechanical
   Testing
Dynamic Testing
Edge-Lighted Plastic Panels
Electric Motors
Electrical Components
Electrical Distribution
Electrical Modules

Electrical Supply Houses
Electromagnetic Parts
Electromechanical Locks
Electronic Components
Electronic Firing Systems
Electronic Industrial Automation
   Products
Electronic Systems
Electronics
Electro-Optics
Emergency Rescue Equipment
Energy Extraction Applications
Engine Components
Engine Instrumentation
Engine Parameters
Engines
Environmental Testing
Ethernet
Evaluation Reports
Executive Aircraft
Explosive Devices
External Commercial and Industrial
   Customers
F/A-18
Filters
Filtration Equipment
Fire Detection/Protection Systems
Flight Controls
Flight Simulators
Flight Test Data
Fluid Power Systems
Freight Air Carriers
Fuel
Fuel Pumps

Fusing Devices
General Aviation Aircraft
Global Support
Ground Support Services
Heavy Equipment
Helicopters
High-Security
High-Technology Ferrous
Hydraulic
Igniter Assemblies
Industrial Applications
Industrial Automation and Control
Industrial Gas Turbine Engines
Industrial Lighting Products
Industrial Machinery
Industrial Use
Inertial Navigation and Guidance
Information Systems Management
Intercomputer Network Communications
Interior Aircraft Equipment
Jet Aircraft Engine Parts
Jet Engines
Laminates
Large Commercial Aircraft
Laser Firing Systems
Latching Devices
Light Machining
Liquid Propellant
Local Area Network
Logistics
Logistic Support Analyses
Major Aircraft Manufacturers
Manufacturing Methods
Manufacturing Support Services

Marine Systems
Measuring Methods
Mechanical Separation Devices
Medical Supplies
Medical Systems and Equipment
Microcircuits
Microelectronics
Microprocessor-Based Electronic
 Sequencers
Military Aircraft
Military Missiles
Military Planes
Missile Systems
Missiles
Molecular Biology Research Items
Nacelle Systems and Components
Navigation Control Systems
Navigational Instruments
Network Topologies
Networking Products
Nonferrous Castings
Operations Research
Optical Equipment
Optical Pick-Offs
Orbiting Satellites
Ordnance-Related Products
Panel Meters
Passenger Air Carriers
Passenger Control Units
Passenger Video Entertainment Systems
Performance Polymers
Plastics
Pneumatic Component Parts
Policies

Positioning Instruments
Power Cartridges
Power Systems
Precision Fastening Systems
Precision Measuring Scales
Precision Patterned Glass and Metal
 Products
Pressure Regulators
Pressure Transducers
Procedures
Processes
Product Development
Programming Experience
Pumps
Quality Assurance
Quality Control
Radar Equipment
Radio and Television Transmitters for
 Aircraft
Remote Network Access
 Communications
Repair Services
Replacement Parts
Resistors
Rocket Engines
Rotary and Linear Optical Incremental
 Encoders
Satellite Guidance Systems
Satellite-Based Communications
 Systems
Scientific Applications
Sensors
Service Accessories
Servovalves

Shared Services
Sheetmetal
Silicones
Simulation-Based Devices
Simulator-Related Training Services
Small-Launch Vehicles
Software Systems
Solid Rocket Motors
Sophisticated Aerospace Equipment
Sounding Rockets
Space
Space and Aviation Systems
Space and Communications
Space and Missile Systems Center (SMC)
Space Applications
Space Systems Architecture
Space Vehicles
Specialty Insurance
Speed
Strategic Missile Systems
Strategic Weapon Systems
Superabrasives
Systems Analysis
Systems Engineering
Systems Management
Tactical Air Defense Systems
Tactical Missile Systems
Tactical Weapon Systems
Technical Guidance
Technical Products
Testing
Token Ring
Training Devices
Training Services

Transmission	Turbine Engines	Waterjet Propulsion Systems
Transportation Systems Products	Valves	Weapon Systems
Troubleshooting	Vibration (Random/Sine) Testing	Wiring Systems

Apparel, Fashion, and Textiles

Buzzwords in this industry highlight experience with clothing design, export, and sales; knowledge of current style or style characteristics; or the manufacturing, weaving, and knitting of fabric, yarn, or cloth. This includes work with curtains, drapery, shoes, and sportswear; skill with nonwoven fabrics, textile goods and finishing, and yarn and thread mills; or the buying, handling, shipping, receiving, and selling of such goods.

Resume Buzzwords

Absorbency	Carpet	Department Store Merchandise
Accent	Casual Wear	Design Concepts
Accessories	Catalog Sales	Designer Jeans
Acetate	Chain Stores	Designer Lines
Apparel	Chamois Flannel	Designs
Apparel Design Arena	Children's Sleepwear	Detail
Apparel-Manufacturing Company	Cloth Labels	Die-Casting
Apprenticeship	Clothes	Direct Marketing
Artwork	Clothing Manufacturers	Distribution Centers
Assortment	Coats	Diversified Line
Automotive Distribution	Color	Divisions
Bandages	Comforters	Draperies
Baseball Caps	Commission	Dress Shirts
Bedroom Ensembles	Complete Line	Dresses
Belts	Consumer Markets	Dye-Printing Process
Block and Slopers Development	Convert Fabric	Dyeing
Blouses	Core Products	Elastic Knitting
Brand Names	Cotton	Export
Brands	Cotton-Blend Fibers	Extensive Range
Bridal Gowns	Curtains	Eye Glasses
Care Labels	Daywear	Fabrics
	Denim	Fashion Apparel Products

Fibers

Filament

Finished Home Products

Footwear

Formalwear

Furnishings

General Merchandise Stores

Global Retailer

Goods

Grade Rules

Half Sizes

Hand-Knitting Yarn

High-Quality Fabric

High-End Velvet

High-Spec Industrial Applications

Home Fashion Products

Home Furnishings

Import

Independent Textile Converter

Industrial Distribution

Industrial Hosiery

Industrial Markets

Industrial Processes

Industrial Uniforms

Interior Furnishings

Intimate Apparel

Inventory

Jackets

Jeans

Jersey Fabrics

Junior Sizes

Knit

Knit Healthcare Products

Knitted Fabrics

Knitted Fleece

Knitted Textile Fabrics

Labels

Laces

Leather Apparel

Leisure Shirts

Leisurewear

Licensed Labels

Licenses

Licensing

Loungewear

Luggage

Lycra and Rubber Products

Mail Order Catalogs

Major Discounters

Manmade Fibers

Manufacturers

Manufacturing Plants

Marketing

Markets

Mass Merchants

Mass Volume Retailers

Material

Measurement Charts

Medical Products

Men's Apparel

Merchandise

Metal and Coil Slide Fasteners

Micro-Safe Fiber

Misses Sizes

Narrow Elastic Fibers

National and Regional Chains

Nationally Distributed

Natural and Synthetic Fibers

Neckwear

Nonwovens

Novelties

Nylon Fibers

Nylon Travelers

Outerwear Line

Packaging Products

Pants

Paper-Making Machines

Patternmaking

Patterns

Petite

Petite Dresses

Pillows

Plaids

Plastic Injection Moldings

Polyurethane-Coated Fabrics

Principal Buyers

Printed Fabrics

Printed Items

Private-Label Designer

Private-Label Sleepwear

Private Labels

Private Retail

Processing

Processing Wool

Producing Pattern

Product Development

Production

Products

Purses

Quality Control

Retail Outlets

Retail Sales Prices

Retail Units
Retailers
Robes
Rug Kits
Sale
Sales Category
Samples
Scarves
Sewing Thread
Sheets
Shirts
Shoes
Skirts
Slacks
Special Machinery Spools
Special Occasion Dresses
Specialty Fabrics
Specialty Markets
Specialty Stores
Specialty Weaves
Spinning Cotton
Sportswear
Sportswear Items
Spun Yarns
Stores
Stretch Panties

Styles
Suits
Support Facilities
Synthetic
Synthetic Filament Polyester
Synthetic Thread
Tailored Men's Clothing
Tapes
Textile Outerwear
Textile Products
Textile Products Manufacturing
Textile Wholesaler
Textile Yarns
Textiles
Textured Nylon
Texturing
Towels
Trading
Trimmings
T-Shirts
Twisting
Undergarments
Uniform Shirts
Uniforms
Upholstery
Value-Priced Apparel

Variety
Warp Knit Fabrics
Washable Service Apparel
Watches
Wear
Weaving
Weekend Casual Sportswear
Wide-Warp Knit
Winding
Window Treatments
Women's Apparel
Women's Sheer Hosiery
Woodturnings
Woolen Coats
Worldwide
Woven
Woven Finished Fabrics
Woven Greige Fabrics
Woven Synthetics
Woven Velvets
Wrinkle-Free Cotton Fabrics
Yarns
Young Ladies'
Young Men's Apparel
Youth Market

Architecture, Construction, and Engineering

In these fields, effective buzzwords highlight one's experience with applying scientific and mathematical principles to the design, layout, and construction of machines, structures, buildings, and systems. This includes planning the physical composure of a bridge, house, or monument; graphically conceptualizing the mathematical dynamics of huge land structures; and physically preparing, assembling, or renovating pre-existing architecture.

Resume Buzzwords

Accident Reconstruction
Accident Statistical Data Analysis
Aggregates
Air Conditioning Systems
Airfield Lighting Power Distribution
Airfields
Airports
Architectural Planning
Architectural/Engineering Services
Asphalt Felt–Based Linoleum
Asphalt Paving
Aviation
Banks
Biomechanics
Brick Masonry
Bridge Inspection
Bridges
Budget Development
Builders
Building Entrances
Building Materials
Building Plans
Building Products
Building Restoration
Buildings
Business Support Services
Cabinets
Carpet Base
Chemicals
Civic Centers
Civil Disciplines
Civil Engineering
Coal

Coal Production
Code Compliance
Commercial Architecture
Commercial Construction
Commercial Industries
Commercial Services
Compressor/Vacuum Pump Products
Computer-Aided Design (CAD)
Conceptual Design
Concrete Repair
Condominiums
Construction
Construction and Renovation Projects
Construction Base
Construction Drawings
Construction Forensic Services
Construction Maintenance
Construction Management
Construction Management Firm
Construction Management Services
Construction Services
Construction Site
Construction Support
Construction/Structural Engineering
Consulting Services
Contract Documents
Contract Drawings Development
Contractor Submittals
Contractors
Cost Control
Cost Estimates
Cost Estimation
Crushing Operation
Curtainwall Systems

Defense Industry
Design
Design and Construction Phases
Design Calculations
Design Drawings
Design Reports
Design Tasks
Document Review
Doors
Drafting Team
Drainage
Drainage and Flood Control
Drawing Review
Earthwork Volume
Educational Facilities
Electrical Construction
Electrical Subcontracting
Electricity
Electronic Security System Projects
Energy
Energy Industry
Energy Management
Engineering
Engineering Consulting
Engineering Design
Environmental Assessments
Environmental Consulting
Environmental Engineering
Environmental Studies
Equipment Management
Equipment Rental Sales and Service
Estimates
Extensive Variety
Exterior Finishing Materials

Fabricated Products

Facilities and Transportation

Facings

Feasibility Studies

Federal Programs

Field Crews

Field Engineering and Inspection

Field Experience

Field Reports

Field Responsibilities

Financing Operations

Fire/Life Safety Design

Fittings

Floor Adhesives

Flooring

Flooring Products

Frame Parts

General Contracting Firm

General Contractor

Geotechnical Investigation

Geotechnical Services

Global Services

Government Bases

Graphics

Hard Floor Coverings

Hazardous Waste Assessment and
   Remediation

Heating and Air Conditioning
   Equipment

Heating Systems

Heavy Construction

Heavy Industrial Construction

Heavy Rail

Heavy-Civil Contractor

Highway Capacity

Highway Contractor

Highways

Homebuilders

Hospitality Projects

Hotels

Industrial Complexes

Industrial Facilities

Infrastructure Systems

Interior Design Services

Job Site Management Team

Labor Units

Laboratories

Land Planning

Lateral and Axial Pile Analyses
   Programs

Lav-Tops

Layout

Leading Mortgage Finance Company

Lighting Control and Monitoring
   System

Lighting Products

Loss-Control Services

Maintenance Services

Major Bridges

Major Cargo Airports

Management Consulting

Manufacturing Industry

Marine Facilities

Marine Investigations

Material Take-Off

Materials and Product Testing

Mechanical Contracting

Mechanical Design Drawings

Mechanical Estimates

Mechanical Subcontracting

Metal Fabrication Services

Metal Siding

Metals

Minerals

Monitor Panels

Multidisciplinary Approach

Multifaceted Construction Firm

Multifamily Apartment Complexes

Nonresidential Architectural Building
   Products

Nuclear Fuel

Occupancies

Office Buildings

Operating Groups

Operation and Construction Management Services

Pavement

Petrochemical Industry

Petroleum Refining

Pharmaceuticals and Biotechnologies
   Industries

Piping Pricing

Piping Takeoffs

Planning

Plumbing

Plumbing Supplies

Policyholders

Pollution Control

Polymers

Power Distribution

Precast Concrete

Prevention of Accidents and Failures

Private Sectors

Probable Risk Assessment

Procurement

Procurement Management

Professional Services Organization

Programming

Project Conception

Project Planning

Project Team

Properties

Protection of Traffic Plan
  Development

Public Facilities

Public Sectors

Public Works

Pulp

Quality Control

Quantity Estimates

Quantity Takeoff Calculations

Railroads

Railway Signal Engineering Designs

Range Hoods

Ready-Mixed Concrete

Real Estate Agencies

Refrigeration Contractor

Related Mobile Home Products

Relevant Codes

Remediation Services

Remote Site Camps

Renovation

Research Laboratories

Residential

Residential Building Maintenance
  Services

Restoration

Risk Prevention/Mitigation

Road/Highway

Roof Domes

Roof Vents

Roofing

Safeguard the Environment

Semiconductor

Sheet Metal Fabrication

Siding

Single-Family Homes

Slope Stability Modeling Programs

Solar Energy Components

Solid Waste

Spatial and Statistical Analysis

Specialists

Specialty Construction Services

Specialty Sheets of Foam

Specifications

Sports Facilities

Sprinkler and Irrigation Products

Steel Industry

Storefronts

Streets

Structural Concrete Construction

Structural Engineering

Structural Projects

Stucco

Subcontractors

Suppliers

Surety Claim Services

Surveying

System Safety and Reliability

Task Areas

Technical Consulting

Technical Presentations of Proposals

Tenant Improvements

Tile

Toplights

Total Engineering

Traffic

Traffic Signal Design and Maintenance

Training

Transition Strip Accessories

Transportation

Transportation Markets

Transportation Model Network Coding

Transportation Related

Tunnels

Value Management

Valves

Ventilation

Warning and Labeling Issues

Waste Management

Wastewater Collection

Wastewater Reuse

Wastewater Treatment

Water Management

Water Resources

Water Treatment and Distribution

Water/Wastewater Services

Waterfront Facility

Wide-Ranging Climates

Window Framing

Arts, Entertainment, Sports, and Recreation

These buzzwords are just some of those from the often glamorous worlds of entertainment, sports, and arts; each individual field within these industries will have many more specific terms that might be used to demonstrate your knowledge and experience. Arts-resume buzzwords display experience with production or arrangement of sounds, colors, forms, movements, or other visual elements. Entertainment-industry buzzwords exhibit experience-producing performances or shows to amuse, please, or divert an audience's attention. Entertainment buzzwords also display experience working for studios, networks, production companies, record companies, and radio stations. Sports and recreation buzzwords highlight experience with both competitive and relaxing activities such as games and matches.

Resume Buzzwords

360-Degree Theater Systems
Action/Adventure Films
Actor Management
Amusement Park
Ancient Art
Animation
Arcade
Art Department
Art Media
Awards Shows
Background
Ballets
Banquet Facilities
Botanic Gardens
Broadcasting
Broadway Theaters
Cable Television Networks
Casinos
CD Manufacturing and Distribution Facility
CD-audio and CD-ROM Mastering and Replication

Children's Cartoons
Circus
Coaching Staff
Comedic Theater
Comedy Films
Concerts
Concession Facilities
Conservation and Curatorial Departments
Contracted Artists
Convention and Meeting Facility
Dance
Digital Effects
Digital Images
Director Management
Discovery Labs
Documentary
Editing, Design, Sound, and Related Services
Education Services
Educational and Research Programs
Entertainment
Entertainment Production Company

Event Television
Exercise Programs
Exhibition Halls
Family Audiences
Fashion
Feature-Length Motion Pictures
Fellowships
Film Development
Film Distribution Company
Film-to-Tape and Tape-to-Film Transfer
Finishing
First-Run Syndication
Fitness and Aerobic Classes
Fitness Center
Foreign Television Networks
Free Television
Fulfillment Services
Full-Service Health and Fitness Club
Giant Screen
Guest Hotel Facilities
Hair
Harness Racing Facility

Hiking Trails
Historic Artifacts
Historical Interpretation
History Museum
Home Video
Horseracing Tracks
Independent Multimedia
    Manufacturing
Integrated Merchandising
Intellectual Property Rights
Interactive Games
Interactive Media
Internships
Laser Disc Licensees and Distributors
Laser Video Disc Recording
Layout
Lectures
Leisure and Entertainment Company
Libraries
Licensing
Live Animals
Live Entertainment
Low-Budget Theatrical Motion
    Pictures
Made-for-TV Movies
Magazines
Makeup
Manuscripts
Media Company
Meets
Merchandising
Miniseries
Modern Art
Motion Picture Business

Motion Picture Film Processing
Motion Pictures
Museums
Music Production
National and International Tours
National Basketball Association (NBA)
National Football League (NFL)
National Hockey League (NHL)
Major League Baseball (MLB)
Nature Center
Newspapers
Nonprofit Art Gallery
Nonprofit Arts Showcase
Nonprofit Cultural Organization
Nonprofit Performing Arts Theater
Off-Broadway
Off-Line and Online Video Editing
On-Broadway
Online Services
Opera
Opera House
Orchestra
Outdoor Activity Programs
Packaging
Paddle Boats
Parks
Pay Television
Performing Arts Facility
Personal Training
Photo Finishing
Pipeline
Political Satire
Popular and Classical Records
Portable Simulator

Practice
Preservation of Buildings and Ships
Production Planning
Professional Hockey
Professional Resident Theater
    Company
Professional Sports Teams
Prospecting
Publications and Reproductions
Publishing
Puppetry
Recreation Program
Regional Cable Television Sports
    Networks
Research Library
Revisualization Sequences
Rights to Films
Roller Skating Rink
Satellite Transmission Uplinking
    Services
Schedules
Set Dressing
Shakespearean Productions
Sitcoms
Snack Bar
Special Effects
Special Interest Programming
Special Productions
Sports Highlights
Stakes Races
State-of-the-Art Theaters
Student Art Exhibitions
Studio Facilities and Technology
Syndicates

Talent and Literary Agency
Talk Shows
Tanning
Television Programs
Theatrical Exhibitions
Theatrical Performances
Toy Design
Type Design
Uniforms

Vaudeville
Venues
Video and Film Duplication
Video Post-Production Services
Video Theater
Videocassette and Audiocassette
    Duplication
Virtual Reality Theater Systems
Visual Arts Museum

Warehousing
Water Theme Park
Websites
Weights
Women's National Basketball Asso-
    ciation (WNBA)
Women Viewers

Automotive

Buzzwords for the automotive industry highlight experience in repair shops and with producing automotive equipment and knowledge of auto sales and services.

Resume Buzzwords

Accessories
Air Conditioners
Air Filters
Air Injection
Airbag Electronics
Airbags
Alignment
Alloy Wheels
All-Wheel Drive
Aluminum Bodies
Antilock Braking Systems (ABS)
Antilock Brakes
Assemblies
Assembly Services
Auctions
Auto Body Parts
Auto Reconditioning

Automatic
Automobile Doorframes
Automobile Parts
Automotive
Automotive Aftermarket
Automotive Design
Automotive Electronic Controls
Automotive Electronics
Automotive Glass
Automotive Occupant Restraint
    Systems
Automotive Parts
Automotive Regulators
Automotive Roll Form Products
Automotive Seating Systems and
    Components
Automotive Service
Automotive Starting Systems

Automotive-Original Equipment
Axles
Ball Bearings
Bimodal Vehicles
Blow Moldings
Body Stampings
Book Value
Brake Linings
Brake Pads
Brakes
Brazed Assemblies
Bus Specialty
Bushings
Caliper
Camping Trailers
Car Stereos
Cars
Certified Automotive Parts Supplier

Chassis

Chemicals

Child and Infant Seats

Climate-Control Systems

Clutch

Clutch Plates

Coatings

Coils

Combined Markets

Combustion Chamber

Commercial Vehicles

Compressor

Connecting Rod

Continuous-Strand Fiberglass

Contract Manufacturing Services
    Solutions

Conversion Facility

Conversion Van

Convertible Systems

Coolant

Coolant Systems Pressure Gauges

Custom Vehicles

Custom-Designed

Customers

Customizes

Cylinder Head

Cylindrical

Dealers

Decorative Laminates

Delivery Vehicles

Design

Development

Diesel Engines

Differential

Displays

Distributor

Domestic

Door Systems

Driveshaft

Drivetrain Components and Systems

Dry Freight Vans

Electric Automotive Switches

Electric Motors

Electrical

Electrical Automotive Equipment

Electrical Power Distribution
    Equipment

Electronic Controls

Electroplating

Engine Components

Engine Mounts

Engine Parts

Engineering Services

Exhaust

Exhaust Systems

Exterior Automobile Mirrors

Exterior Enhancement Programs

Extruded Plastic Materials

Fabricated Glass

Factory Equipment

Fifth Wheels

Financing

Flat Glass Products

Flat Tire

Flatbed Trailers

Floor Consoles

Fluid Connectors

Fluid Power

Fluid Systems Components

Four-Wheel Drive

Frames

Franchised Auto Dealerships

Franchised Automotive Service
    Locations

Front-Wheel Drive

Fuel Filters

Fuel Injection

Fuel Injectors

Fuel Pumps

Fuel Systems

Fuel-Carrying Systems

Fuel-Handling Products

Full-Line Vehicle Manufacturers

Full-Size Vans

Fully Loaded

Gaskets

Generating Systems

Halogen Headlamp

Headlights

Heaters

Heavy Truck Chassis

Heavy Trucks

Heavy Vehicle Systems

Heavy-Duty Trucks

Hoses

Hydraulic Power Units

Hydraulic Products

Hydraulic Pumps

Ignition Systems

Import

Independent Supplier

Independent Suspension

Industrial Products
Inflatable Restraints
Information Technology
Injection Moldings
Inspections
Instrument Clusters
Instrument Panel Components
Interior Automotive Products
Interior Trim
Iron Castings
Latch Assemblies
Light Truck Seating Systems and
    Components
Light Trucks
Light Vehicle Aftermarket
Light Vehicle Systems
Lighting Products
Lighting Systems
Limited Slip Differential
Maintenance
Manual
Manufactured Goods
Mass Transit
Metal Automobile Components
Metal Stampings
Midrange Diesel Engines
Midsize/Luxury Car Group
Mini Motor Homes
Minivans
Miscellaneous Automobile Parts
Molded Materials
Molded Plastics
Motor Coaches
Motorhomes

Motors Insurance
Octane Reading
Off-Road Machinery
Oil Caps
Oil Changes
Oil Filters
Options
Original Equipment Manufacturers
    (OEM)
Overdrive
Overhead System Components
Oxygen Sensors
Park Models
Parts
Passenger Cars
Pickup Truck Bedliners
Pickup Trucks
Pinion Steering Gears
Pistons
Piston Rings
Plastic Fasteners and Clips
Plastic Injection Molding
Plastic Interior Items
Plastic Products
Plastics
Pneumatic Products
Ports
Power Rack
Power Units
Powertrain
Powertrain Components
Powertrain Systems
Precision Parts
Precision Stamping

Product Design
Production Facilities
Push Rod
Quarter Panel
Radiator Pumps
Radiator Valves
Radiators
Recreational Vehicle Manufacturers
Recreational Vehicles
Refined Motor Cars
Refrigerated Trailers
Related Components
Rental
Replacement Parts
Replacement Parts Distribution
Research and Development (R&D)
Residual
Resins
Resonator
Ride-Control Products
RV
Safety Restraint Products
Sale
Sales/Service Groups
Sales-Automotive Aftermarket
Sealing
Seals
Seat Belts
Seats
Sectors
Sedans
Sensors
Service Centers
Service Operations

Shims

Sleeve Bearings

Small Car Group

Specialized Applications

Specialized Fibers

Specialized Truck Bodies

Spoilers

Sport-Utility Vehicles (SUV)

Standard Transmission

Steering Linkage

Strut

Sun Visors

Sunroofs

Supplies

Suspension

Suspension Ball Joints

Suspension Parts

Suspension Systems

Tail Lamps

Tapered Roller Bearings

Test Drive

Testing

Thrust Washers

Tier One Supplier

Tier Two Supplier

Timing

Tinted Glass Products

Tires

Tool-Building Services

Tooling Applications

Torque

Traction Control

Tractors

Trailer Hitches

Transmission Bands

Transmission Parts

Transportation Manufacturing Firm

Travel Trailers

Trimming

Truck Bodies

Truck Campers

Truck Doorframes

Truck Drivetrain Systems

Truck Group

Trucks

Tune Up

Turbocharger

Universal Joint

Upscale Model

Used Cars

Valve Train

Valves

Van Bodies

Van Campers

Vehicle Development Groups

Vehicle Leasing

Vehicle Parts

Vehicle Transport Services

Vehicular Lighting Products

Vibration Control Parts and Systems

Washers

Welded Assemblies

Wheel Base

Wheels

Wholesale Distribution

Wholesale Value

Windows

Worldwide Markets

Biotechnology and Pharmaceuticals

The buzzwords in these industries are often highly technical, and they exhibit a science background with in-depth familiarity of biology and chemistry. Resumes may demonstrate experience with cellular biology, vaccine research, prescription drugs, over-the-counter medicines, chemical compounds used in pharmaceuticals, and tools used to diagnose diseases. Relevant experience includes synthesizing new drugs, testing of drugs, determination of dosages and delivery forms (such as liquid or tablets), calculating cost-effectiveness of a proposed drug, and selling/marketing of pharmaceuticals.

Resume Buzzwords

Advanced Cellular and Molecular Biology

Agricultural Biotechnology

Allergies

Analytical Tools

Anemia

Antibodies

Antiviral

Aqueous-Based Synthetic Solutions

Aseptic Processing Design

Assay (ELISA) Test Kits

Autoimmune

Bioinformatics

Biomedical Research

Biopharmaceutical Development

Biopharmaceutical Fermentation

Biosciences

Biostatistics

Biotechnology

Blood Management Systems

Blood Tests

Bone Marrow Transplantation

Breakthrough Drug

Calibration Programs

Cancer Research

Cardiovascular Disease

Cell Biology

Cell Lines

Cell-Based Functional Secondary and Tertiary Assays

Centrifuges

Chemical Manufacturing

Chemotherapeutic Pharmaceuticals

Clean Room Certification

Clinical Laboratories

Clinical Laboratory Services

Clinical Trials

Clinics

Cohort Studies

Compliance

Compound Screening

Computer Validation

Computerized System Validation

Contract Research Organization (CRO)

Contract Sales Organization (CSO)

Critical Care Products

Cultured Primary Cells

Data Analysis

Data Processing Software

Data Sets

Dermatology

Detection and Measurement Equipment

Development and Consulting

Diabetes

Diagnostic Analysis

Diagnostic Imaging

Diagnostic Medical Devices

Diagnostic Tests

Dialysis Centers

Direct-to-Consumer (DTC) Marketing

DNA Synthesizers

Donor Center

Dosing

Double-Blind

Drug Delivery Systems and Technologies

Drug Discovery

Drug Optimization Programs

Drug Strategies

Education

Electrophoresis Systems

Engineering Sciences

Environmental Monitoring Programs

Environmental Testing

Enzymatically Dissolved Hair Samples

Enzyme-Linked Immunosorbent

Epidemiological Issues

Epidemiological Research

Epidural Anesthesia

Ethical Pharmaceuticals

FDA Approval

FDA Compliance Strategies

Formulary

Gas Chromatography/Mass Spectrometry

Gene Therapies

General Chemical Systems

Generic Drug

Genetics

Genomics

Gerontological Studies

GMP Audits

Good Manufacturing Practices (GMP)

Government and Private Industry Research

Grant Proposals

Growth Deficiency Treatment

Health and State Policy

Healthcare Policy

Health Inequalities and Disparities

Health Insurance
Hematology
Hormones
Human Genetic Information
Human Therapeutics
Humanized and Human Monoclonal
  Antibodies
IC50/ED50 Values
Immunoassays
Immunodiagnostic Products
Immunological Reagents
Immunology
Impact Research Programs
In Vitro
In Vitro Pharmacology Assays
In Vivo
Industrial Microbiology
Infectious Diseases
Intravenous Systems and Solutions
Inventory Management
Investigational New Drug (IND)
  Application
IQ, OQ, and PQ Protocols
IV Accessories
Laboratories
Large-Scale Surveys
Life Science Systems
Life Sciences
Longitudinal Analysis
Manufacturing Regulations
Measurement and Analysis of Physi-
  ologic Data
Medical Affairs
Medical Conditions

Medical Immunodiagnostic Test Kits
Metabolic Diseases
Metabolism
Metabolites
Multidisciplinary Research
Natural Growth Conditions
New Drug Application (NDA)
Observational Studies
Ophthalmic Pharmaceuticals
Ophthalmology
Organ Preservation Solutions
Organ Transplantation
Outsourcing Services
Over-the-Counter (OTC) Drugs
Patented Drugs
Patient Care
Patient-Specific Intravenous Drugs
Pharmaceutical Companies
Pharmaceutical Devices
Pharmaceutical Discovery
Pharmaceutical Products
Pharmaceuticals
Pharmacy Services
Phase I
Phase II
Phase III
Pipeline
Placebo-Controlled Protocol
Plasma Exchange
Plasma Expanders
Preclinical Stage Programs
Public Health Research
Quality Control/Quality Assurance
  (QC/QA)

Quantitative Analysis
Reagents
Recombinant DNA
Regulatory Affairs
Regulatory Issues
Reproductive Disorders
Research and Clinical Applications
Research Methodologies
Retrospective Studies
Robotic Workstations
Scientific Instruments
Side Effects
Social Determinants of Illness
Social Research
Specialty Chemical Systems
Sterilization Processes
Surveillance
Testing for Acute and Chronic Human
  Illnesses
Therapeutic Systems
Thyroid Disorders
Tissue and Organ Replacement
Treatment for Life-Threatening
  Diseases
U.S. Food and Drug Administration
  (FDA)
Urine Tests
Urology/Gynecology Studies
Vaccines
Validation
Veterinary Applications

Communications

Industry buzzwords in the area of communications highlight writing, graphics, public relations, publicity, and promotions skills and experience. This includes activities associated with creating, distributing, and transmitting text and graphic information via varied print, video, audio, computer, and web-based media. Some of the buzzwords below concerning editing and writing would also be useful for those applying for positions in publishing.

Resume Buzzwords

Acquisition of Titles
Administrative Skills
Advertising
Annual Fact Book
Antenna Designs and Measurements
Art and Production Elements
Arts and Entertainment
Articles
Assignments
Asynchronous Transfer Mode (ATM)
Audio Production
Authors
Automatic Call Distributors
Automation Solutions
Backlist
Blemishes
Book Production
Booklets
Broadcasting Operations
Business Presentations
Cable Television
Call Center Management
Call Centers
Camera Operation
Campaign Letters

Casting Contracts
Catalogs
CDs
Cellular Phones
Circulation Records
Classified Advertisings
Collaboration
Columns
Commercials
Communications Intelligence
    Collection
Communications Management
Communications Service Provider
Communications Systems
Computer-Telephony Integration
    Solutions
Consumer Markets
Content
Content Development
Contributing Writers
Copyedit
Corporate Imaging
Cover Story
Creative Writing
Darkroom Procedures
Data Communications Equipment

Data Communications Services
Data Management
Data Services
Data Systems
Deadlines
Design
Desktop Publishing
Digital Music Service
Direct Mail
DSL Products
Editing
Editorial Changes
Editorial Committee
Editorial Direction
Educational Programs
Electronic Telecommunications Test
    Equipment
e-Mail Systems
Facsimile Systems
Fact Checking
Federal Agencies
Fiber-Optics
Films
Formatting
Frame Relay
Freelance Projects

Fundraising

Galleys

General Interest Topics

General Trade Reference Titles

Government Network Solutions

Grammar

Grant Proposals

HDTV

Healthcare Communications Systems

High-Bit-Rate Digital Subscriber Line (HDSL)

High-Speed Data

Historical Articles

Independent Telephone Operating Companies

In-Depth Features

Industrial Films

Institutional

Integrated Microwave Antenna Subassemblies

Interconnect Carriers

International Newsletter

Internet

Internet Access

Internet Equipment

Interview

LAN Internetworking

Layout

Ledger

Lighting and Broadcasting System

List Building

Local and National Affiliates

Locator Systems

Low-Radar Cross-Section

Manuscripts

Marketing

Marketing Proposals

Media Lists

Media Relations

Media Tours

Medical Journal

Monograph

Monthly Newspaper

Multimedia Group

Negotiated Contracts

Network and Data Services

Network Architectures

Network Operations

Network-Affiliated

News

News Briefs

News Casting

Newscasts

Newsletters

News Media

Newspapers

On-Air

Order Filling

PageMaker

Pamphlets

Paste-Up/Mechanicals

People Skills

Periodical Publishing

Planning and Forecasting Packages

Poetry

Press Kits

Press Releases

Printers

Private Communications Networks

Private Network Managers

Problem Analysis

Production

Production Details

Program Hosting

Promotions

Proofread

Props

Prototype

Public Carrier Providers

Public Relations

Public Service Announcements

Publication

Publication Process

Publicity

Publicity Files

Publishing Process

Radio Broadcasting

Record Maintenance

Recruitment Experience

References

Reporting Software

Reports

Reproduction

Research Findings

Research Papers

Research Papers and Reports

Residential Local and Long Distance Telephone Services

Review

Satellites

Schedules

Scholars

Scripts
Signal Reconnaissance Equipment
Skin
Social and Political Issues
Specialized Publications
Speeches
Stage Design
Standards and Procedures
Story Development
Story Ideas
Style Criteria
Subscribers
Subscription Orders
Subscriptions
Surface Flaws
Surveys

Switched Multimegabit Data Service
Tape Recording
Technical/Engineering
Telecommunications Signals
Telephone Equipment
Telephone Systems
TelePrompter
Television
Television Commercials
Text
Textbooks
Touchtone Telephone
Trade Magazines
Trade Newspaper
Trends
Updates

Video and Voice Applications
Videoconferencing
Voice Messaging
Voice Systems
Voicemail
Voice-Processing
Volunteer
Wardrobe Arrangements
Wide Area Network (WAN)
Wireless Access Network
Wireless Service Plans
Word Process
Workflow Systems
Writing

Computers and Mathematics

For positions in the computer industry, buzzwords are highly technical and change fairly rapidly. Effective buzzwords highlight experience with defining, analyzing, and resolving business problems and utilizing knowledge of computer systems to examine problems and design solutions. Important skills and experience include planning new computer systems or devising ways to apply existing systems to operations that are still done manually.

Resumes for positions in mathematics should spotlight activities ranging from the creation of new theories and techniques to the translation of economic, scientific, engineering, and managerial problems into mathematical terms.

Resume Buzzwords

Accounts Payable
Accounts Receivable
Administrative Tasks
Algorithms
Alternative Concept Development

Applications
Architecture
Architecture Requirements and
    Capabilities
Backup and Multiplatform Connectivity Systems

Batch System
Billing Systems
Bookkeeping
Bugs
Business Problems
Business Re-Engineering

C++

Client Database

Client Support Services

Client/Server Technology

CMS-2

COBOL Programming

Coding

Communications Technology

Computer Information Systems

Computer Interface Circuitry

Computer Program Requirements

Computer Programming Languages

Computer Reselling

Computer Science

Computer Software

Computer Systems

Conversion Products

Customer Needs

Customer Requirements

Customer Service System Consulting

Data Acquisition

Data Communication Systems

Data Communications

Data Entry

Data Migration

Data Processing

Data System Design and
   Implementation

Database Management

Database Repair/Troubleshooting

Database Systems

Deadlines

Design and Implementation

Developmental Math

Device Driver

Differential Equations

Digital Audio and Video Tools

Disk System

Documentation

DOD Telecommunications Technology,
   Architecture, Policy, and Standards

DOS Batch Files

Drivers

Dynamical Systems Analysis

Electronic Components

Engineering Projects

Engineering Solutions

Failure and Analysis Reports

Fault Tolerant Signal Generation
   Software

File Structure

Financial Reporting Systems

Fixed Storage Space

Flowcharts

Hardware Products

Host Users

Information Architecture

Instructions and Guidelines

Integration

Internet Sales Systems

IT Planning

LAN Management

Large-Scale Networking
   Environments

Logical/Manageable Components

Mainframe Production Environment

Management and Technology
   Consulting

Manufacturing Efficiency

Manufacturing Test Systems

Membership Records

Memory Upgrades

Microcomputer

Mini Computers

MIS

Monitor Networks

Multiuser Database

Multivariable Calculus

Network-Based Applications

Network Configuration

Network Installation

Network Interface Cards

Network Management

Network Tools

Networking Solutions

Noncompliant Issues

Online Message System

Open Systems

Open Systems Migration

Operating Efficiencies

Operating Systems

Operational Procedures

Optical Disks

Parallel Architectures

PC Products

PC Software

Performance Standards

Peripheral Manufacturers

Preproduction Testing

Process Control

Process Time

Product Demos

Product Presentations

Products and Components

Programming Skills

Project Cost Effectiveness

Prototype

Real-Time Computer Programs

Real-Time Embedded Software
Design

Real-Time Interactive Visual
Communications

Real-Time Simulation

Record Compilation

Reliability

Reporting Systems

SAS Programming

Server Machines

SGI Workstation

Shared Storage Systems

Software

Software Design

Software Development

Software Guide

Software Implementation

Software Testing

Software Upgrades

Source Code

Specifications

Statistical Knowledge

Strategic Planning

Subassemblies

System and Subsystem Interface

System Design Engineering

System Enhancements

System Safety

System Testing

Systems Configuration

Systems Engineering

Systems Test and Integration

T1 Connection

Technical Directions

Technical Notes

Technical Reports

Technical Solutions

Technology Integration

Terminal Servers

Test Data

Test Networks

Test Plan

Test Procedures

Test Software/Hardware

Troubleshooting

Uninterrupted Transmissions

UNIX Market

User Manuals

Utilities

Video Communications

Video Images

Visual Basic

Visual Programming Languages

Voice Communications

VxWorks

Warehouse Development Tools

Whitepapers

Windows

Workstation Configuration

Workstation Maintenance

Workstations

Education and Library Sciences

Education buzzwords display a familiarity with child development, kindergarten and elementary school education (including math, language, science, and social studies), private and public preschools, elementary schools, middle and secondary schools, colleges and universities, as well as tutorial operations. Library science buzzwords highlight experience related to the collection and cataloging of library materials and direct information programs for the public.

Resume Buzzwords

Absent
Academic Development
Academic Schedule
Accountability
Accreditation
Administrative Problems
Advertising
Aesthetics
After-School Programs
Age Appropriate
ALA Filing Rules
Alertness and Coordination
Algebra I & II
Algorithm
Alumni Relations
Appreciation
Art
Artistic Skills
Audiovisual
Authentic Assessment
Author
AV Equipment
Balanced Development of Children
Balanced Reading
Basic Academic Skills
Behavioral Problems
Behavioral Strategies
Bibliographic Data
Bibliographies
Block Scheduling
Books
Bookstore Operations
Brain-Based Learning

Budget Planning
Building Self-Esteem
Bus Stops
Business Math
Card Catalog
Cataloging
Certification
Chair Meetings
Charter Schools
Child Development
Child-Centered Teaching
Chronically/Terminally Ill Children
Circulation Desk
Class Trips
Classroom Safety
Classroom Supervision
Classrooms
Coach
Cognitive Development
Cognitive Skills
Collaboration Skills
Collaborative Projects
College Archives
College-Level Courses
Committees
Computer Curriculum
Computer Lab
Computers for Classroom
  Management
Consensus
Content Areas
Copyright Policies
Course Descriptions
Crafts Instruction

Creative Expression
Creativity
Critical Thinking
Cultural and Recreational Activities
Curricula Methods
Curriculum
Curriculum Development
Curriculum Plans
Daily Lesson Plans
Daily Operations
Day Camp
Debater
Decode
Department of Education
Department of Social Services (DSS)
Department of Youth Services (DYS)
Departmental Text
Detention
Development of Initiative and
  Self-Reliance
Dexterity
Direct Mail
Direction
Disabled Students
Discovery Learning
Donor Gifts
Drilling
Dues
Education
Education Expeditions
Education Institutions
Education Plans
Education Reform
Education Reinforcement

Educational and Psychological Testing

Educational and Recreational
Activities

Educational Committees

Educational Requirements

Elementary Education

Elementary School

Emotional Methods

Emotionally Disturbed Class

English

Environmental Simulation

Evaluation

Exercises

Faculty and Staff Counsel

Food Service Management

Fundraising

Geometry

Grades 9–12

Grades K–8

Grades/Marks

Group Counseling

Group Presentation

Group Study

Guidance Counselor

Half-Time

Handbook

Handicaps

High School

Higher-Order Thinking

History

Honors

Index Tools

Indexes

Individual IEP's

Individual Lesson Plans

Individualized Treatment/Education
Plans

Infant Care

Intellectual Methods

Interpreter/Translator

Journals

Junior High

Language

Language Arts

Language/Learning Disabilities

Leadership Training

Learning Aids

Learning Disability Class

Learning Through Play

Lectures/Seminars

Letter Sounds

Library Services

Life and Career Skills

Lifelong Learning

Literacy and Numeracy Skills

Mass Media Communications

Mathematics

Media Releases

Microfiche

Microfilm

Monograph Collection

Montessori Method

Multicultural Populations

Multiculturalism

Multioffice Communication

Multiple Intelligences

Museum Trips

Music Lessons

Negotiator

New Book Orders

Newsprint Publications

NLM Classification System

Nonprofit Service Organization

Numerical Ability

Observation Skills

One-to-One Instruction

Onsite Visitation

Oral Language Skills

Orientation Programs

Outcome-Based Education

Outings

Parent Involvement Committee

Parent Relations

Parent Teacher Association (PTA)

Parent-Teacher Conferences

Peer Tutoring

Performance Standards

Periodicals

Personal Care and Play

Phonics

Photo Indexing

Photocopy

Photocopy Policies

Physical Development

Physical Skills

Physical Therapy

Portfolio Assessment

Positive Behavior Modification
Techniques

Pre-Calculus

Preparation

Preschool/Daycare Setting

Press Releases

Private School

Procedures

Program Coordination

Progress Reports

Project Approach

PTSA

Public Relations

Public School

Public Service

Public Speaking

Publishing

Pupil-Led Play

Reading

Reconstitution

Recreational Activities

Recruiting

Reference and Search Files

Reference Questions

Reference Services

Religion

Remedial Math

Remedial Reading

Research

Residence Halls

Retrospective Conversion

Role Model

Rote Learning

SAT Preparation

Scholarships

School Administration

School Board

School Policies

School Year

Science

Secondary School

Secretary of Education

Severe Emotional Disabilities
   Classroom

Sign Language

Social Studies

Special Education

Speech Pathology

Spelling

Staff Meetings

State Standards

State-Certified

Statistics

Student Accomplishments

Student Activities

Student Affairs Calendar

Student Assessment

Student Athletes

Student Evaluation

Student Groups

Student Performance

Student Relations

Substitute

Success-Oriented Group

Summer School

Superintendent

Superintendent of Public Instruction

Systems

Tardy

Teacher Dues

Teacher Evaluation

Teacher Recruitment

Teacher Union

Teacher-in-Service Training

Teaching Aids

Teaching Methods

Teaching Skills

Teaching to the Test

Teaching/Training

Terminals

Textbooks

Therapeutic Group Services

Traditional Teaching Mode

Training

Trigonometry

Troubleshooting Skills

University

University Students

Vocational Counseling

Vocational Interest

Voucher

Weekly Meetings

Whole Child Development

Whole Language

Workshops

Writing

Engineering

Buzzwords from the various fields of engineering demonstrate experience with the theories and principles of science and mathematics and with designing machinery, products, systems, and processes for efficient and economical performance. This includes designing industrial machinery and equipment for manufacturing goods, defense systems, and weapons for the armed forces. Other important skills and experience include planning and supervising the construction of buildings, highways, and rapid transit systems; and designing and developing consumer products and systems for control and automation of manufacturing, business, and management processes.

Resume Buzzwords

3D Modeling
Acoustic Testing
Aerodynamics
Allocation
Analog Electronics
Architecture Enhancements
Assembly Design
Assembly Modification
Bid and Cost Plus Work
Bid Sheets
Bidder Lists
Board of Safety Standards
Buildings
C Programming
C4 Navigation and Intelligence
Cable Products
Capital Equipment
Ceramic Capacitors
Chemical Engineering
Chemistry
Circuitry
Civil Engineering
Commercial Projects
Competitive Analysis

Complex Electromechanical Systems
Component Evaluation
Components and Assemblies
Compression Tests
Computer Product Design
Computer Programming
Computer Software Packages
Computer-Based Transducers and
    Loudspeaker System Measurement
Conceptualization
Conflicts Resolution
Consistency and Compatibility
Construction Coordination
Construction Estimates
Construction Industries
Contract Engineering
Cost Reduction
Creep Tests
Customized Security
Data Collection and Analysis
Data Performance Characteristics
Design and Construction of RF
    Equipment
Design Methodologies
Design Verification Testing

Detailed Models
Development Environment
Digital Electronics
Documentation
Dynamic Systems
Economical Solution
Efficiency Control
Electrical Analysis
Electrical Design
Electrical Engineering
Electronic Design
Electronic Equipment
Electrostatic Discharge
Emissions Testing
Engineering Estimates
Engineering Field Supervision
Engineering Management
Environmental Engineering
Environmental Problems
Environmental Regulations
Environmental Testing
Equipment Maintenance
Exploration of Mines
Fabrication Methodologies
Facilities

Facilities Engineering

Facilities Inspections

Flow Patterns

Fluid Compression

Fluid Mechanics

Fluid Systems

Functional Flows

Functionality

Geological Formations

Global Marketing

Government Markets

Hardware Evaluation

High-Density Surface Mount Printed
   Circuit/Wiring Board (PWB)

High-Speed Applications

High-Temperature Environments

Highways

Hydraulic Systems

Hydrologic Surveys

Industrial Engineering

Industrial Projects

Information-Based Systems

Injection Molding Design

Inorganic Chemistry

Integrated Solutions and Services

Integrated Systems

Interdisciplinary Requirements

Internal Controls

Justification Studies

Land Surveying Services

Line Balancing

Load Monitors

Logical Performance Characteristics

Logistics

Machinery

Machinery Maintenance

Maintenance Documentation

Management Processes

Manufacturing

Manufacturing Problem Resolution

Manufacturing Processes

Marine Engineering

Master Specifications

Mathematical Models

Mathematics

Mechanical and Control Systems

Mechanical Design

Mechanical Design Integrity

Mechanical Engineering

Mechanism Design

Microscopic Analysis

Mission-Critical Programs

Motion Control

Mounting

Networked Systems

Networking Functionality

New Product Development
   Environment

OEM

Operations Manual

Part Tolerance

Parts Modeling

Performance Characteristics

Petroleum Accumulation

Petroleum Generation

Petroleum Migration

Phase Separation

Physical Performance Characteristics

Planning

Polishing

Powder and Bulk Solids Handling

Power Supply Test

Preproduction Engineering Prototypes

Preventive Maintenance Programs

Principles

Problem-Solving Skills

Procedures

Process and Procedure Development

Process and Project Documentation

Process Control

Process Development

Process Improvements

Process Methods

Process Sheets

Product Development

Productivity

Professional Consulting

Programmable Logic

Project Cost

Project Engineering

Project Management

Project Specifications

Project Start-Up

Prototypes

PWB Fabrication

Qualitative Analysis

Quality Assurance

Quality Assurance Tests

Quality Control

Quantitative Analysis

Radiation Monitoring Equipment

Radiological Controls

Reactor Design
Reactor Maintenance
Reconnaissance
Regulatory Compliance
Regulatory Requirements
Reliability
Reliability and Quality Assurance
Reliability Life Testing
Research and Development (R&D)
Safety Regulations
Scheduling
Science
Scientific Discovery
Sheet Metal Design
Space Platforms
Space Systems and Electronics
Specifications
Statistical Analysis
Statistical Process Controls

Stress Analysis
Structural Design
Subsystems
Surveillance
Susceptibility Testing
System Analysis
System Baselines
System Characterization and Test
System Dynamics
Systems Analysis
Systems Dynamics
Systems Maintenance
Technical Files
Technical Guidelines
Technical Guides
Technical Support
Technical Writing
Tensile Tests
Test Planning and Field Operations

Test Plans
Test Processes
Test Specimens
Testability and Verifiability of
    Requirements
Testing Policies
Testing Standards
Theories
Thermodynamics
Thermoforming Design
Timing Violations
Tooling
Top-Level System Architecture
Vendor and Partner Technology
    Relationships
Weight and Distribution Properties
Worst-Case Scenarios
Written Specifications

Executive and Managerial

Executive and managerial positions exist in all types of businesses. Executive buzzwords should highlight experience ranging from general supervisory duties to running an entire company. Relevant skills include management of individual departments within a larger corporate structure, motivating workers to achieve their goals as rapidly and economically as possible, budgeting and directing projects, and evaluating company processes and methods to determine cost-effective plans.

Resume Buzzwords
Account Management
Account Retention
Accounting
Accounts Payable

Accounts Receivable
Administration
Administrative Detail
Advertising
Allocation

Annual Sales
Appointment Generation
Asset Base
Asset Management
Auditing

Audits
Banking Objectives
Banking Operations
Banking Transactions
Benefit Eligibility
Benefits Coordination
Bookkeeping
Branch Consolidation
Branch Management
Budget
Budget Development
Budget Planning
Budgeting
Budgets
Business Contacts
Business Development
Business Software
Business Strategies
Capability
Cash Administration
Cash Disbursement
Cash Flow
Certified Public Accountant (CPA)
Check Processing
Claim Errors
Claims
Claims Adjustments
Claims Processing
Client Base
Client Relations
Cold Calling
Commercial Balances
Commercial Financing Enterprise
Commercial Loans

Commercial Paper Transactions
Commercial Real Estate
Commissions
Communications
Company Programs
Compatible
Competitive Analysis
Complaint Activity
Compliance
Consultation
Consulting
Contingency
Contract Management
Contractual Agreements
Contractual Modifications
Corporate Clients
Corporate Mission
Corporate Planning
Corporate Returns
Corporate Strategy
Correspondences
Cost Reports
Credit Lines
Custom and Importing Regulations
Customer Education
Customer Relations
Customer Service
Data Processing
Database
Database Management
Day-to-Day Operations
Direct Mail
Direct Response Agencies
Domestic Letters of Credit

Efficient Operations
Employee Morale
Employee Training
Equipment
Evaluation
Expense Control
Expenses
Facilities
Facility Coordination
Fiduciary Income
Finance
Financial Controls
Financial Management
Financial Reports
Financial Statements
Financial Transactions
Franchise Management
General Ledgers
Hardware
High-Dollar Contracts
Hiring
Import/Export Shipments
Incremental
Individual Returns
Insurance
International Letters of Credit
Inventory
Inventory Control
Invoices
Lead Development
Leasing
Lending
Logistics
Long-Term Goals

Loss Prevention
Maintenance
Major Accounts
Management
Manpower
Marketing
Marketing Activities
Markets
Merchandising
Mobility
Motivation
Negotiation
New Business Development
New Products
Objectives
Operational Objectives
Operations
Outside Sales and Support Staff
P&L Management
Payables
Payroll
Personnel Management
Personnel Relations
Policies and Procedures
Product Awareness

Profit Loss
Profit Margin
Progressive Organization
Projection
Promotions
Property Management
Prospects
Provider/Client Communication
Public Relations
Purchasing Process
Purchasing Systems
Quality Control
Receivables
Records
Referrals
Regulatory Requirements
Relationship Management
Reorganization
Reports
Restaurants
Retail Banking
Retail Sales
Revenue
Revenue Development
Sales Experience

Sales Expertise
Sales Objectives
Sales Presentations
Sales Support
Sales Techniques
Scenarios
Scheduling
Service Contracts
Service Operations
Small Business
Staff Supervision
Statistics
Store Operations
Supervision
Supervisory Experience
Tax Issues
Team Management
Technical Support
Third-Generation
Time-Phase
Training
Transitional
Troubleshooting
Yearly Transactions

Food and Beverages/Agriculture

Industry buzzwords for these fields highlight experience with growing, processing, packaging, shipping, receiving, storing, preparing, and selling consumable products. This includes farming (whether it be animal, fruit, or vegetable); transport and delivery of products between farms, processing plants, and vendors; scientific research and development of products to ensure quality and safety of foods; and export and sale, both foreign and domestic.

Resume Buzzwords

Advanced Breeding

Advertising Claims

Agricultural

Agricultural Chemicals

Agricultural Commodities

Agricultural Products

Agricultural Trade Association

Animal Feed Ingredients

Animal Oils

Baby Food

Baked Products

Baking Breads

Basic Ingredients

Beef

Beer

Beer Brands

Beer, Wine, and Spirits Distributor

Beverage Vending Company

Beverages

Biotechniques

Bottled Water

Bottling Facility

Brands

Brewing

Business Efforts

Cabernet Sauvignon

Cakes

Candy

Canned Beans

Canned Fruits and Vegetables

Canned Meat Products

Canola

Cans

Cash Advances

Cattle Feeding Procedures

Cereals

Chardonnay

Cheese

Chemical Dispensing Equipment

Citrus Growing and Processing Firm

Coin-Operated Vending Machines

Commercial Soups

Commodities

Commodity Trading

Competitive Prices

Competitively Priced

Condiments

Confections

Consumers

Convenience Food

Cookies

Cooking Oil

Corn

Corn Refining Process

Corrugating

Costing

Cotton

Cottonseed Flour Products

Creative Solutions

Crop Areas

Crop Growth

Crop Insurance

Crop Nutrients

Culinary Background

Dairy Dessert Products

Dairy Products

Define Problems

Dehydrator

Dessert Products

Diet Soft Drinks

Dips

Distribution

Diversified

Diversified Livestock Company

Doughnuts

Drinking Water

Dry Bulk Warehousing

Edible and Industrial Plant Oils

Eggnog

Erythritol

Ethanol

Farm

Farm Products

Farmers

Farming

Feed

Feed Ingredient Trading

Feedlot

Fermentation Lab

Fermentation Products

Fermentor Systems

Fertilizers

Financial Markets Division (FMD)

Flavoring Products

Food and Consumer Products

Food and Cosmetic Product
   Regulations

Food and Seed Industries

Food Industry

Food Processing Businesses

Food Production

Food Products
Food Safety
Food Safety Systems
Food Service Disposables
Food Service Experience
Formulas
Freight Management
Fresh and Frozen Fish Products
Frozen Foods
Frozen Meats
Frozen Potato Products
Fruits
Fuel
Functional Foods Markets
Genetic Engineering
Genetically Engineered Plants
Government Regulations
Grain Merchandising
Grain-Based Foods
Grains
Greenhouse
Groceries
Growers
Ham
Handling
Harvesting
Herbs
High-Fructose Corn Syrup
High-Quality
Horticulture
Hybrids
Ice Cream Manufacturer
Imports
Incremental Break Boxes

Industrial-Grade Starches
Ingredients
Institutions
Inventory Management
Irrigation
Juices
Ketchup
Labels
Lamb
Livestock Marketing
Livestock Production
Livestock Quality
Local Vineyards
Luncheon Meats
Major Producer
Major Trader
Malt Beverages
Manufacturer
Manufacturing
Margarine
Market
Market Conditions
Meat Products
Merchandising
Military Markets
Milk
Minerals
Mines
Nationally Distributed Food Products
Natural Ingredients
Nonagricultural
Nutritional Products
Oilseeds
Order Placement

Order Selection
Packaged Food Companies
Packaging
Pasta Products
Pasta Sauces
Pest Control
Pet Food
Pharmaceutical
Phosphates
Pickles
Pinot Noir
Plant Breeding
Plant Products
Planting
Pork
Portion Control
Potash
Premium Line
Premium White and Red Varietal
    Table Wines
Premium Wines
Prepared Feeds
Processed Consumables
Procurement
Product Specifications
Protein Powders
Proteins
Public Stockyards
Pudding
Purchasing
Quality Control
Quality Raw Materials
Quick-Service Restaurants
Raising Livestock

Ready-to-Eat Cereals
Recognized Brand Names
Reconditioning
Refrigerated
Rent
Repackaging
Replenishment
Restaurants
Retail Food Markets
Retail Food Stores
Retail Locations
Rice
Risk Management
Rolls
Salad Dressings
Salt Products
Sauces
Sauvignon Blanc
Seafood
Seasoning Blends
Seasoning Mixes
Seasonings

Seed
Seed Varieties
Smoked Salmon Ravioli
Snack Foods
Soft Drinks
Sour Cream
Soy Flour
Soy Isolates
Soy Milk
Soy Protein
Soybeans
Spaghetti Sauces
Specialty Food Company
Specialty Food Items
Specialty Ingredient
Spices
Sports Beverages
Starches
Sterility Control
Storing
Strain Management
Sweeteners

Temperature Controlled
Tomato Sauces
Tomato-Based Products
Transporting
Tryptophan
TVP
Veal
Vegetable Oil Refinement
Vegetable Oils
Vegetable Products
Vegetables
Vendors
Vitamin C
Vitamin E
Vitamins
Wheat
Wholesale Food Distributors
Wholesale Outlets
Wholesaler
Yogurt

Government

For those interested in positions in politics and government, buzzwords highlight experience in executive, legislative, judicial, or general government agencies as well as with public agencies, such as firefighting, military, police work, or the United States Postal Service. This includes researching and evaluating military materials; cleaning, maintenance, and general service for public works; participating in political campaigns by networking, fundraising, or organizing; and working to control narcotic and dangerous drug use through prevention and law enforcement. It also includes mail pickup and delivery experience, public relations and press work, and public outreach activities.

Resume Buzzwords

Administration

Administrative Offices

Administrative Services

Advanced Development Programs

Agency

Agency Management

Agricultural Production

Agriculture

Air and Water Pollution

Air Quality

Annex Building

Area-Wide Governmental Organization

Assistance Services

Bank Holding Companies

Borrowing Transactions

Briefing Reports

Broadly Based Exploratory Programs

Building Activities

Bureau

Business Administration

Business Interests

Business Relationship

Central Headquarters

Central Management Agencies

Chamber of Commerce

Citizens

City Council Offices

City Departments

City Highways

City Manager

City Transportation Department

Classification Compliance Audits

Coastal Waters

Committee

Community Service Jobs

Complete Range of Mail Pickup and
    Delivery Services

Computerized Procurement Systems

Constitutional Officer

Consumer Rights

Consumers and Businesses

Control Audits

Coordinating Food Protection
    Programs

Debate

Debt Management

Defense Contract Management

Democratic Party

Department of Industrial Accidents

Department of Labor and Workforce
    Development

Dependents

Developing Countries

Diplomatic Capabilities

Disaster Management

Disaster Prevention

District Court

Domestic Disputes

Econometrics

Economic and Educational Support

Economic Conditions

Economic Development

Economic Growth

Economy

Education

Educational Issues

Educational Programs

Elections

Emergency Situations

Energy

Enforcement

Engineering

Environmental Protection

Environmental Quality

Environmental Sciences

Environmental Studies

Exchange Rate Management

Executive Branch

Export Counseling

Federal Bank

Federal Benefits

Federal Campaigning Activities

Federal Environmental Laws

Federal Government

Federal Government Agency

Federal Labor-Management Relations

Federal Planning

Federal Records

Federal Reserve Notes

Federal Space Exploration Program

Field Locations

Field Offices

Finance

Financial Institutions

Fire Prevention

Fish and Wildlife

Food Protection Program

Food Stamps

Foreign Intelligence

Functional Divisions

Funding

General Services
Generating Electricity
Government Assistance
Government Offices
Government Organization
Government Program Applications
Government Registration Activities
Governmental Organization
Government-Owned Facilities
Government-Run
Governor
Grant
Guidelines
Health and Human Services Facility
Highway Maintenance
Human Health Protection
Impact of Trade
Import
Inadequate Housing
Income Distribution
Income Tax Returns
Independent Auditor
Information Services
Information Technology
In-House Research
Institutional Issues
International Agency
International Aid
International Companies
International Lending Agency
International Trade
Issuance of Licenses
Job Market
Job Placement

Job Seekers
Justice
Labor Unions
Land Use
Law
Law Enforcement Services
Legal Cases
Legal Determinations
Legal Services
Legislative Branch
Legislative Requests
Legislators
Lending to Third World Nations
Local Businesses
Local Government Agency
Local Office
Long-Term Economic Growth
Macroeconomics
Maintenance and Improvement
Mandate
Manufacturing Quotas
Mayor's Office
Medicaid Services
Medical Devices
Medical Emergencies
Medico-Public Health Laboratory
Metro
Metropolitan Development
Missions
Monetary Policy
Monetary Theory
Multidisciplinary Support
National Cemeteries
National Headquarters

National Health Programs
National Law Enforcement Agency
National Parks
Nationwide Healthcare Programs
Natural Resources
Nature and Wildlife Preservation
Naval Warfare Centers
Navy Needs
Nonprofit
Nuclear Materials
Nuclear Power
Objective Trade Expertise
Operations
Organization Analysis
Passport Acceptance
Patent
Patrols
Physical Sciences
Police Department
Policies
Political and Legislative Support
    Functions
Political Economy
Productivity of Natural Resources
Public Buildings
Public Expenditure
Public Finance
Public Order
Public Use
Public Works
Purify City Water
Quality Health Care
Quality of the Environment
Radiation Emitting Products

Recreation Areas
Rectifying Disputes
Recycling Services
Reducing Manufacturing Costs
Regional Offices
Regional Planning Agency
Regional Problems
Regional Training Institutes
Regulation of Companies
Regulatory Agency
Regulatory Commission
Renewable Energy
Repair Services
Republican Party
Roads and Highways
Safe Living Conditions
Sale of Consumer Products
Securities Market
Security Documents

Security Products
Seminars
Senior Services
Significant Economic Changes
Small Business
Snow Plowing
Space Systems Technology
Special Investigations
Standards
State Entities
State Government
State Parks and Reservations
State Representation
State Tax Information
State-Run Agencies and Universities
Statewide Financial and Compliance
   Audits
Statistical Material
Statistical Methodologies

Statutory Filings
Street Repairs
Tax Forms
Tax Publications
Trade Actions
Trade Association
Trade Seminars
Traffic Congestion
Transportation Planning
U.S. Industries
U.S. Paper Currency
U.S. Policy
Urban Development
Utility Companies
Volunteers
Water Supply
Welfare Office
Work Force Conditions
Workers' Compensation Claims

Health and Medical

Buzzwords from the vital health and medical fields demonstrate experience with illness, working toward achieving and maintaining healthy lifestyles, and helping to address and resolve related issues, such as insurance and medical claim forms. This includes working directly with patients and their families in dealing with health problems; assisting patients by providing medical advice regarding prescriptions, insurance claim forms, and related issues; and researching medical treatments and techniques.

Resume Buzzwords
Acute and Chronic Patients
Agency Staff
AIDS
Ambulatory Services

Anatomy/Physiology
Anesthesia Operations
Angioplasty
Appointments
Behavioral Programs

Biochemistry
Blood Chemistry
Blood Draws
Bone Fractures
Budget Preparation

Budget Responsibilities

Burn Patients

Business Management Activities

Calisthenics

Cardiac Anatomy

Cardiac Catheterization

Cardiac Patients

Case Management

Childbirth

Chronic Pain

Chronically Ill

Clerical Support

Client Eligibility

Clinical Cardiology

Clinical Instruction

Clinical Operations

Communication Disorders

Community Hospitals

Comprehensive Care

Computer Literacy

Conduct Disorders

Conferences and Lectures

CPR

Crisis Intervention

Crowns

Daycare Centers

DEA Regulations

Dental Impressions

Dental Laboratory

Dental Materials

Dentures

Department Budgets

Departmental Meetings

Diet Aides

Dietetic Technicians

Discharge Planning

Disease Research

Drills

Drug and Alcohol Abuse

Drug Delivery

Echocardiography

Educational Counseling

Educational Videos

EKG

Electric Stimulation

Emergency Care

Emergency Medical Procedures

Emergency Services

Emergency Treatment

Exercise Classes

Family Conferences

Filing Systems

First Aid

Follow-Up Medical Treatments

Formal Education Programs

Front Desk Procedures

Gastroenterology

Government-Funded Food Programs

Grinders

Health/Recreation Clubs

Heimlich Methods of Resuscitation

Hematology and Serology Testing

Historic Research

HMOs

Home Care

Home Care Agencies

Home Health Agencies

Hospital Policies

Hospital, State, and Federal
  Guidelines

Human Services

ICU

Individualized Treatments

Infusion Therapy Services

Inhalation Therapy

Injured Patients

Inlays

In-Patient and Outpatient Care

In-Service Consultation

Instrument Set-Ups

Insurance Companies

Intensive Aerobics

Intravenous Therapy

IV Antibiotic Therapy

Lab Procedures

Lab Results

Laboratory Operations

Lathes

Manic Depression

Massage Therapy

Medical Equipment

Medical Management

Medical Photography

Medical Records

Medical Research

Methodology

Metropolitan Hospitals

Modalities

Motivational Skills

MRI Department

Multidisciplined Practice

New Medications

Nursing Home Placement
Nursing Practice Standards
Nursing Services
Nutrients
Nutrition
Nutritional Care Plans
Order Entry
Outpatient
Parenteral and Enteral Nutrition
Pathology
Patient Care
Patient Charts
Patient Records
Patient Relations
Patient Services
Patients
Pediatric Patients
Pediatric/Emergency Medicine
Personality Disorders
Pet Food Products
Pet Nutrition
Pharmaceutical Companies
Pharmaceuticals
Pharmacology
Pharmacology and Behavioral Modifi-
    cation Methods
Physical and Psychosocial Needs
Physical Standards
Physical Therapy Standards
Policy and Procedures Development
Polishers
Post-Op Care
Postoperative Care

Preliminary Diagnoses
Preoperative Care
Prescription Reimbursement Claims
Prescriptions
Primary Nursing Care
Private Practice
Psychiatric Care
Psychology
Psycho-Social Assessments
QA Monitoring
Qualitative Research
Quality Assurance
Quantitative Research
Radiology
Referring Physicians
Respiratory Therapy
Service-Related Incidents
Severely Ill Patients
Side Effects
Skilled Nursing Assessment
Social Services
Specialized Nursing and Medical Care
Staffing Issues
State-Funded Programs
Statistical Reports
Strength and Stamina
Stretching
Stretching/Strengthening Exercises
Strokes
Substance Abuse
Surgical Procedures
Teaching
Therapy

Tracheotomy Care
Ultrasound
Unit Doses
Urinalysis
Ventilators
Veterinary Medicine
Vital Signs
Word Processing
Work-Related Injuries
Workshops
X-Ray Department
X-Ray Procedures
Yoga

Hotels and Restaurants

In these service industries, buzzwords reflect experience and familiarity with restaurant management, food services, banquets and conventions, guest/customer service, and promotions. Other valuable skills include culinary, business/accounting, interpersonal communication, and facilities management. Many of these buzzwords would also apply for many positions in the travel industry.

Resume Buzzwords

ACF (CEC) Certification
ACF Apprenticeship
Administrative
Amusement Facilities
Audio Equipment
Bakeries
Bakery and Confectionery
Banquet Activities
Banquet Equipment
Banquet/Meeting Facilities
Bar Set-Up and Breakdown
Beauty Culture
Bookkeeping
Budgeted Food Costs
Buffet and Restaurant Displays
Buffing Wheel
Burnishing Machine Tumble
Cafes
Cash Control
Cash Handling Procedures
Casual-Dining Restaurants
Catering
China, Glass, and Silver Service
    Inventory
Cleanliness
Cleanup of All Banquet Functions

Cocktails
Company Standards
Conference Center
Cookery Craft
Coolers/Storerooms
Country Clubs
Culinary Arts
Culinary Management
Culinary School
Cultural Centers
Customer Satisfaction
Daily Quality Checks
Deluxe Hotels
Dinnerware
Dishwashing Machine
DJs
Drive-Thru Restaurants
Eating Venues
Employee Relations
Ethnic Cuisine
Excess Production
Exclusive Health Clubs
Family-Oriented Restaurants
Fast-Food Restaurants
Federal, State, Local Safety and
    Health Regulations
Fine Dining

Floor and Capacity Charts
Flow of Guests
Food and Facilities Management Ser-
    vices Company
Food and/or Beverage Orders
Food Preparation and Presentation
Food Preservation
Food Production Management
Food Retailing
Food Service Companies
Food Service Facilities
Food Service Handlers Certification
Foreign Hotel Institutions
Franchises
Fresh Products
Front Office Operation
Glassware
Global Sales
Groundskeeping
Guest Occupancy
Guest Services
HACCP Standards
Health Department Rules
Hiring
Home Science
Hospitality Management
Hotel Accounting

Hotel Management

Hotel Standards

Housekeeping

Ingredients

Integrated Facilities Management

International Hospitality

Inventory and Food Costs

JCAHO Knowledge

Kitchen

Leisure and Tourism

Leisure Attractions

Licensed House Management

Liquor and Wines

Live Entertainment

Luxury Hotel

Management Experience

Meat Blocks

Meeting Rooms

Menu

Menu Development

Menu Planning for Various Disease
   States

Nightclub Promotions

Nutritional Requirements

Nutritional Screening and
   Assessment

Online Reservations

Organizational Functions

Orientation

Outsourcing Solutions

Personality

Pizzeria

Plant Operations and Maintenance

Plating and Presentation

Portion Sizes

Pots, Pans, and Trays

Presentation

Pre-Shift and Regularly Scheduled
   Meetings

Prices

Problem-Solving Capabilities

Promotions

Proper Food Handling

Public Recreation Facilities

Quality Standards

Reception

Recruiting Efforts

Refrigerators

Reservation

Resorts

Restaurants

Roadside Lodges

Room Set-Ups

Safety Procedures

Sales Figures

Sanitation Practices

Scheduling

Server Stations

Special Packages and Promotions

Spoilage

Squirrel POS System

Staff Development

Staffing

Tables

Techniques and Standards

TIPS Certification

Tourism

Training

Trash and Garbage Removal

Travel

Vendor and Distributor Relations

Vocational Training

Weddings

Weekly and Monthly Inventories

Worktables

Human Resources

Human resources buzzwords display experience recruiting, interviewing, and hiring employees according to their qualifications and suitability to the organization. Additional responsibilities often include encouraging a productive company culture by effectively utilizing employee skills and fostering job satisfaction; handling employee health and pension plans; and maintaining and articulating knowledge of government regulations regarding labor and employee benefit regulations.

Resume Buzzwords

Accounts Payable System
Accounts Receivable System
Ad Management
ADA
Administration
Affirmative Action
Background Checks
Behavioral Sciences
Benchmarking
Benefit Checks
Benefit Consulting
Benefits
Benefits Administration
Blended Learning Solutions
Business Results
Business Value
Candidate Pool
Candidate Screening
Career Counseling
Career Development
Career Fairs
Claim Adjudication
Client Management
Coached Learning Solutions
Coaching

College Programs
Compensation and Payroll Functions
Compensation Consulting
Compensation Data
Compensation System
Competencies
Confidential Personnel Records
Consultative Skills
Content Assessment
Contract Negotiations
Contracts
Corporate Communication
Corporate Learning
Corporate Performance
Corporate Philosophy
Creation of Reports and
    Correspondences
Current Trends
Customer Service
Delivery Assessment
Departmental Contacts
Departmental Expenditures
Development Initiatives
Direct Mail
EEO/AA Compliance
e-Learning

Electronic Learning Solutions
Employee Counseling
Employee Effectiveness
Employee Records
Employee Relations
Employee Relationship Management
    Solution
Employee Status Forms
Employees
Employment
Entitlement
Evaluation Process
Executive Bonus Plan
Executive Search Companies
Exempt Positions
Federal and State Laws
General Ledger
Global Leadership Attributes
Grievance Interviews
Grievance Procedures
Gross Sales Reconciliation
Hard-Core Unemployed
Health Care and Group Benefits
HRIS Technologies
HRMS Products/Solutions
Human Capital Strategy

Induction Programs
Industry Trends
Insurance Payments
Integrated Development Approach
Internal and External Resources
Internal Staffing
Interview Process
Invoice Processing
Job Descriptions
Job Requirements
Key Business Outcomes
Key Competencies and Deliverables
Labor Disputes
Labor Management
Labor Relations
Leader Effectiveness
Leadership Assessment Tools
Leadership Development Programs
Leadership Responsibilities
Maintenance Bills
Management
Management Techniques
Maternity Leave
Measurement
Meetings
Mentor
Merit Budget Recommendations
Methodologies
Modularized Learning Solutions
Needs Analysis
Networking Activities
Non-Exempt Positions
Office Interviews
Office Supply Maintenance

Open Enrollments
Open Positions
Organizational Development
Organizational Learning
Organizational Objectives
Outplacement Services
Payroll Database
Payroll Transmissions
Pension/Health and Welfare Reports
People Development
Performance Development
Performance Management
Performance Measurement and
    Rewards
Permanent Personnel Actions
Permanent Positions
Personnel
Personnel Policies
Placement
Portfolio Assessment
Position Analysis
Potential Candidates
Prescreening
Pricing Information
Private Sector
Productivity
Professional Associations
Professional Development
Professional Staffing Costs
Program Delivery
Progressive Human Processes
Prospective Employees
Qualified Professionals
Real-Time Information

Recruiting Resources
Recruitment
Recruitment Sources
Reference Checks
Referrals
Regulations
Regulatory Agencies: EOHS, OER,
    DPA, PERA
Reinsurance Carrier
Request for Proposals (RFP)
Resume Preparation
Retirement Consulting
Return on Investment (ROI)
Salaried Jobs
Salary Administration
Salary Reviews
Salary Surveys
Self-Directed Learning Solutions
Skills Testing
Staffing
Statistical Records
Strategic Human Resource Planning
Team Development
Team Performance
Team-Based Environment
Telemarketing
Temporary Assignments
Termination
Time and Labor Solutions
Training
Tutoring
Unclaimed Wages
Unemployed Youth
Unemployment Insurance

Unions

Unskilled

Vacation Schedules

Vendor Selection

Visitors

Wages

Web-Based Enterprise Applications

Website Job Postings

Workers' Compensation

Workflow

Workplace Laws

Workplace Stress

Insurance

For the insurance industry, appropriate buzzwords highlight experience with contracts, claims, personal injury, workers' compensation, and assets. This includes knowledge of different areas of insurance, such as fire, theft, automotive, property, business, health, and disability. Familiarity with premiums, appraisals, policies, financial planning services, and insurance sales should also be included.

Resume Buzzwords

Accident

Accountability

Accounts Receivable

Act of God

Adhesion

Adjust

Adjustment

Advance

Agency

Agents

Aggregate

Aid

Amendment

Annuities

Annuity Plans

Annuity Products

Appraisal

Asset Accumulation

Asset-Based Lending/Financing

Assets

Attorneys

Audit

Auto Insurance Claims

Automobile Accident

Automobile Dealers

Automobile Insurance

Automotive

Basic Coverage

Benefits

Binding Agreement

Book Value

Borderline Risk

Branch Offices

Broad-Based Customer Group

Brokerage

Building Code

Capacity

Capital

Captive Agents

Care Plan

Carrier

Caseload

Cash Value

Casualty

Certificate

Charitable Health Care Corporation

Charter

Claims

Claims Management Services

Class

Clause

Clients

Closing Services

Collision

Commercial and Individual Financial
   Services

Commercial Clients

Commercial Insurance

Commission

Common Law

Compensation

Consolidation

Contingency

Contract

Convention

Convergence

Conversion

Countersignature

Coverage

Covered Loss

Credit Associations

Credit Insurance

Credit Life Insurance

Credit Report

Customers

Daily Report

Damage

Deductible

Dental Care Services

Dental Insurance Firm

Dependents

Descendent

Disability Coverage

Disability Income Insurance

Earned

Emergency Coverage

Endorsement

Enterprise

Equity

Escrow

Estate

Estate Planning

Exclusion

Expense

Extended

Fee

Field

Financial and Insurance Operations

Financial Services Group

Firm

First Party

Flat

Gain

Geographical Location

Gross

Group Health

Group Life

Group Pension

Guiding Principle

Hazard

Healthcare Delivery

Health Maintenance Organizations
  (HMO)

Health Plan Coverage

High-Exposure Claims

Holding Company

Homebuyers

Homeowners

Indemnity Medical

Individual Life

Inevitable Accident

Injury

Inspection

Institutional Investments

Insurance Carrier

Insurance Products

Insurance Provider

Insurance Risks

Interest Rate

Investigation

Investment

Investment Planning

Investment Planning Company

Joint Coverage

Jurisdictions

Leaseholder

Lenders

Lending Organizations

Liabilities

License

Life Insurance

Limitations

Liquidation

Loss

Loss Prevention

Major Disasters

Malpractice Insurance

Market Value

Members

Mortgage

Multiline Financial Services

Multiperil

Multiple-Line

Mutual Funds

Mutualization

Natural Death

Negligence

Net Loss

Noninsurable Risk

Nonrenewal

Offices

Outsource Vendor

Overrides

Ownership

Payee
Pension
Pension Planning Markets
Performance Reports
Permanent Insurance
Personal Automobiles
Personal Injury
Personal Insurance
Personal Lines of Insurance
Policies
Policy Cancellation
Policy Writing
Policyholders
Portfolio
Power of Attorney
Premium Rate
Premiums
Prevention

Primary Coverage
Primary Insurers
Procedures
Product Portfolio
Professional Liability Insurance
Professional Medical Services
Proof of Loss
Property
Property and Casualty Reinsurance
Provider Reimbursement
Providers
Quota
Rates
Real Estate Brokers
Real Estate Transactions
Rebate
Records

Regional and Specialty Property and
  Casualty Insurers
Reinsurance Intermediary Facilities
Renewal
Retirement Planning
Risk Management Programs
Risks
Search and Examination Services
Securities
Selling
Services
Settlement
Severity
Special Accounts
Sum
Surety
Title Insurance

Legal and Protective Services

In these fields, buzzwords highlight experience with interpreting and enforcing the laws. This includes supporting the legal system; patrolling and inspecting property to protect against theft, vandalism, and illegal entry; and ensuring the safety and security of persons who have been arrested, are awaiting trial, or who have been convicted of a crime and sentenced to serve time in a correctional institution. It also includes maintaining order, enforcing rules and regulations, and supplementing counseling.

Resume Buzzwords

Administrative Hearings
Administrative Support Services
Advisory Committees
Advisory Opinions
Alarms

Ambulance
Antitheft System
Appeals Court
Appellate Briefs
Appellate Litigation
Applicants

Appointments
Appropriate Parties
Arbitrators
Arraignment
Assigned Areas
Attorney Appearance Records

Attorney-Client Conferences

Bail Agreements

Bail Motions

Bankruptcy

Bankruptcy Trustees

Brief

Budgeting

Building Security

Burglar Alarms

Bylaws

Camera Surveillance System

Campaign Activities

Capital Projected Costs

Care and Protection Cases

Case Files

Case Management Project

Case Research

Cell Checks

Citations

City Property

Civil Action

Civil Litigation

Civil Motions

Civil Pleadings

Civil Probate Court

Civil Proceedings

Civil Rights

Clerical Support

Client Forms

Client Needs

Client Scheduling

Client Service Plans

Clients

Client's Suit

Co-Counsel

Codes

Collective Bargaining Issues

Commercial Accounts

Commercial Law Department

Commissions

Committee Hearings

Communication Law

Community Outreach

Community Relations

Community Resources

Complaints

Complex Litigation

Computerized Information System

Conciliations

Conclusion of Law

Confidential Reports

Constituents

Contract Administration

Contract Law

Contractual Support

Copyright Registration and Licensing

Corporate Acquisitions

Corporate Compliance

Corporate Data

Corporate Documents

Corporate Financing

Corporate Law

Corporate Tax Standing

Corporate Votes

Correctional Institutions

Correspondence

Cost Analysis

Cost Records

Court

Court Proceedings

Court Reporter

Court Scheduling

Court Sessions

Court Transcripts

Courthouses

Courtroom

Courtroom Activity

CPR/First Aid

Crime Deterrence

Crime Prevention

Crime Zones

Criminal Action

Criminal Arrest Citations

Criminal Cases

Criminal Investigations

Criminal Law

Criminal Motions

Criminal Proceedings

Criminal Situations

Crisis Intervention

Custody/Traffic Direction Processes

Deadlines

Debtors

Defamation Claims

Defendants

Defense Attorney

Delegation of Tasks

Department of Corrections

Department Procedure

Departmental Goals and Direction

Deposition

Deposition Hearings

Discharge

Discharge Petitions

Discovery

Discovery Motions

Dissolution Plans

District Attorney's Office

District Court

Drafting Wills

Drafts

Elective Offices

Emergency

Emergency Situations

Emergency Transportation

Emotional Status

Energy Maintenance Program

Enlistment

Environmental Arenas

Environmental Litigation

Environmental Programs

Environmental Status

Evaluation

Evidence Information

Execution of Duties

Extensive Corporate Dealings

Facilities

Fact

False Advertising

False Claims

Final Payments

Final Settlement Statement

Financial Institutions

Financing Statements

Fingerprints

Fire Academy

Fire Fighting

Fire Prevention

Firearms

Firearms Qualified

Foot Patrols

Forensic Fire Photography

General Business Litigation

General Laws

General Patrol Responsibilities

General Practice

General Practice Law Firm

General Public

General Security Proceedings

Good Will

Government

Government Agencies

Governmental Communications

Grand Jury Testimony

Guard Forces

Guardianship

Guidance

Hearing Practice

High-Crime Area

High-Pressure Arenas

Hospital Transportation

Housing Area

Human Services

Immigration Case Conferences

In Custody

Incentive Programs

Incident Reports

Inmate Population

Inpatient Facilities

Inquiry Recording System

Insurance Claims

Insurance Companies

Intellectual Property Law

Interviewing of Witnesses

Investigation of Losses

Investigations

Involved Parties

Judicial Arenas

Judicial Lobbies

Justices

Juvenile Court

K-9 Handler

Labor Law

Labor Litigation

Labor Relation Issues

Larceny

Law

Law Enforcement

Law Enforcement Agencies

Law Firm

Law Office Accounts

Law Schools

Legal Counsel

Legal Opinions

Legal Research

Legislation

Legislative Bills

Legislatively Mandated Advisory
   Committee

Library Research

Licensing

Liens

Liquidation

Litigation Experience

Litigation of False Advertising

Loan Documents

Lobby

Local Agencies

Long-Term-Care Issues

Loss Prevention

Maintenance Contracts

Major Felony Cases

Management Inspection

Management Labor Relations

Marriage Certificates

Material Handling

Media Relations

Mediations

Medical Documentation

Medium-Sized Law Firm

Memoranda

Memorandums of Law

Mental Health Law

Mentally Handicapped Clients

Misdemeanors

Modernization of Office Procedures

Money Orders

Monthly Logs

Mortgage Payment

Motions

Motor Vehicle Fraud

Municipal Buildings Security

Municipal Lien Certificates

Municipal Public Safety

Municipalities

Negotiation Strategies

Notarizing Legal Documents

Notice System

Official Records

On Foot

Outside Hospital Guard

Paralegal Services

Patients

Patrol

Peace

Perjury

Permitting Processes

Personal Effects

Physical Status

Plaintiffs

Plea Agreements

Policies and Procedures

Policing Functions

Polygraph Techniques

Population Counts

Post-Closing Functions

Powers of Arrest

Practice

Precedent Information

Predisposition Conferences

Preparation of Cases

Pretrial Conference

Prioritize Assignments

Prisoner Visitation

Prisoners

Private Interests

Private Sector

Procedural Issues

Proceedings

Procurement Inspection

Production

Proper Operation

Properties

Property Cases

Property Matters

Proposed Findings

Prosecute

Protection

Provision of Security

Public Agency

Public Interests

Public Relations

Public Safety

Public Traffic

Public Utility Litigation

Purchasing Agent

Real Estate Law

Record Filing

Recording System

Records

Recruiting Efforts

Registration

Registration Process

Registry of Motor Vehicles

Repair Contracts

Reports

Requirements

Resident and Building Security

Respond to Alarms

Restructuring Transactions

Routine Patrol

Safety

Safety and Crime Prevention

Safety of Students

Safety Program

Safety/Self-Protection

School Security
Searches
Security
Security Programs
Security Supervision
Seminars
Service Contracts
Settlement
Small Claims Settlements
Social Trends
Special Prisoners
Special Projects
Special Radar Program
Specifications
State Agencies
State Enabling Statute
State Revenue Sharing
State Tax Liens
Statewide Moratorium
Strategy Planning

Subcontract
Substance Abuse Treatment Centers
Substantive Issues
Superior Court
Support System
Supporting Documents
Supreme Court Arenas
Supreme Court Decisions
Surveillance
Tax Bills
Testify
Third-Party
Title Insurance Forms
Title Searches
Titles
Trademark Licensing
Training Drills
Training Workshops
Transactional Experience
Transactions

Transfer
Treatment Programs
Trial
Trial Attorney
Trial Papers
Trial Preparation
Trial Proceedings
Uniformed Commercial Code
Union Members
Vandalism and Theft Deterrence
Vendors
Victims
Violating the Law
Volunteers
Weaponry Training
Witnesses
Work Schedules
Workload
Work-Study
Writing Skills

Marketing and Sales

Buzzwords for positions in the fields of marketing and sales highlight experience with attracting customers, promoting businesses and increasing their public profiles, and closing deals. For these results-oriented positions, specific references to measurable accomplishments are most effective.

Resume Buzzwords

4-Color Process
Account Acquisition
Account Balances
Account Locations
Account Performance

Accountable Documents
Accounting Noting Systems
Accounting Operations
Accounting Reports
Accounts
Accounts Receivables

Acquisition
Additional Business
Additional Sales
Adjusters
Adjustments

Administrative and Marketing
  Responsibilities
Administrative Policies
Administrative Procedures
Advertisement Placement
Advertisements
Advertising
Advertising Budget
Advertising Campaigns
Advertising Lineage
Advertising Positioning
Advertising Space
Advertising Strategy
Advertorials
After-Market Volume
After-Sales Support
Aggressive Workflow Management
Analysis
Analysis of Current Accounts
Analysis of Old Accounts
Annual Ad Placements
Annual Division Sales
Annual Marketing Budget
Annual Purchases
Annual Sales
Annual Volume
Appointments
Area Trade
Assets
Assigned Sales Quotas
Average Annual Sales
Average Unit Sales
Awareness
Banking

Bank-Wide Advertising
Basement Store
Behavior-Based Research Projects
Benefits Administration Software
Biannual Sales Conferences
Billboard
Billing
Booking
Booking Agency
Booths
Branch Profits
Brand Initiative
Brochure Production
Brochures
Broker Accounts
Brokerage Concerns
Budget Controls
Budget Management
Budget Recommendation
Budgets
Business Accounts
Business Contacts
Business Expansion
Business Plan
Business Protocols
Business Relationships
Business Reviews
Business-to-Business Services
Buyers
Buying Trips
Camera-Ready Ads
Cash Transactions
Catalogues
Centralized Reporting System

Claim Settlements
Claims Handling
Claims Service
Classified Advertising
Client Base
Client Confidence
Client Needs
Client Relations
Client Service
Clients
Closing
Closing Capabilities
Cluster Analysis
Cold-Call Sales-Generation Centers
Cold Calling
Collateral Materials
Collection
Color Brochures
Commerce
Commercial Products
Commercial Properties
Commission Checks
Commissions
Communication Audits
Communication Network
Company Development
Company Distribution Center
Company Management Structure
Company Procedures
Company Purchase Agreements
Company/Customer Personnel
Competitive Pricing
Competitive Ranking
Comprehensive Expertise

Computer Estimating Software Package
Concept Testing
Confidential Reports
Constituency Relations
Consulting Firms
Consumer Behavior Models
Consumer Goods
Consumer Oriented
Consumer Products
Contract Negotiations
Contract Options
Contracted Vendors
Contracts
Contractual Reversions
Controller
Cooperative Sales Strategy
Core Products
Corporate Accounts
Corporate Chain
Corporate Clients
Corporate Contacts
Corporate Field Contact
Corporate Financial Management
Corporate Objectives
Corporate Plans
Corporate Position
Correspondence
Cost Parameters
Cost-of-Lead
Counters
Creative Concept
Creative Ideas
Creative Services

Credit Checks
Current Pricing
Customer Base
Customer Buying Policies
Customer Follow-Up
Customer Inquiries
Customer Needs
Customer Package Specifications
Customer Relations
Customer Reservation Specification
Customer Satisfaction
Customer Satisfaction Measurement
Customer Service
Customer Service Procedures
Customer Service Techniques
Customer Specification
Customer Studies
Cycles
Daily Calendar History
Daily Deposits
Daily Interface With Clients
Daily Operations
Daily Reports
Daily Tax Title Receipts
Dealer Channels
Dealer Commission
Dealer Locations
Dealer Promotions
Decision-Making Process
Deep Discount Stores
Department Procedures
Department Standards
Departmental Contracts
Design Concepts

Detailed Sales Forecasts
Determination of Costs
Development Projects
Direct Calls
Direct Claims Handling
Direct Liaison
Direct-Mail Brochures
Direct-Mail Promotions
Direct-Mail Schedule
Direct-Mail Strategy
Direct Marketing
Direct Sales
Display Techniques
Displays
Distribution
Distribution Disagreements
Diverse Specifications
Divisional Business Plan
Documentation
Dollar Volume
Domestic Calling Needs
Domestic Fares
Education Accounts
Elicit Interest
Employee Studies
Employee Training and Effectiveness Program
End-User Software
Engineering Solutions
Engineering Staff
Equipment Installation
Events Planning
Executive Relocations
Exhibit

Exhibit Posters

Exhibitions

Existing Accounts

Expense Account

Fabrication

Facilitate Sales

Factory Authorized Dealers

Field Coordination

Field Sales

Field Surveys

Final Itineraries

Finance

Financers

Financial Account

Financial Institutions

Financial Packages

Financial Statements

Financial Support Services

First-Time Buyers

Flyers

Focus Group

Follow-Through

Follow-Up

Forecast

Foreclosure Sales

Foreign Customs

Freelance Models

Fundraising Capabilities

Future Action

Future Sales

General Accounting Functions

General Management

General Supplies Purchasing

Goals

Government Allotments

Government Contractor

Gross Sales

High Exposure Claims

High Motivational Level

High-End Sales

Historical Data Planbook

Immediate Goals

Incentive Programs

Incoming Calls

Incoming Invoices

Increase Sales

In-Depth Questionnaires

In-Depth Sales Training

Individual Sales Leads

Industry Knowledge

Industry Research

Industry Trends

Information Requests

In-House Promotions

Initial Business Plan

Innovative Techniques

In-Print Advertising Campaigns

In-Print Marketing Campaigns

Installation of Systems

Installed Accounts

Instrument Development

Intake Forms

Interior Displays

Internal Strategic Planning

International Calling Needs

International Distributors

International Fares

Interviewing Techniques

Inventory

Inventory Control System

Inventory Products

Investment Properties

Involved Parties

Key Account Relations

Key Account Sales

Key Accounts

Large-Scale Development

Large-Scale Investments

Lead Analysis

Leads

Leasing

Legal Documents

Legal Requirements

Leisure Accounts

Letters of Intent

License Regulatory Issues

Licensees

Lines of Merchandise

Local Franchises

Local Promotions

Long-Range Business Planning

Long-Term Contracts

Long-Term Goals

Loss Performance

Loss Prevention Programs

Loss Report Reviews

Low Turnover Rate

Major Accounts

Major Manufacturers

Major Wholesalers

Management Reports

Management Systems

Manufacturing Requests

Market Analysis

Market Conditions

Market Enthusiasm

Market Opportunities

Market Research

Market Segment

Market Share

Market Trends

Marketing

Marketing Campaigns

Marketing Effort

Marketing Expenses

Marketing Information

Marketing Materials

Marketing Plans

Marketing Promotions

Marketing Research and Analysis

Marketing Research Needs

Marketing Segmentation

Marketing Strategies

Marketing Support Operations

Marketing Technology

Mass Marketing

Mass Merchandising

Maximize Sales

Media Contracts

Media Coverage

Media Department

Media Events

Media Files

Merchandising

Merchandising Concepts

Merchandising Functions

Merchandising Materials

Merchandising Products

Merchants

Mid-Size Companies

Monthly Claims Quota

Monthly Communications Packages

Monthly Forecast

Monthly Planbook

Monthly Sales Plan

Multiethnic Population

Multimillion-Dollar Negotiations

Multivariate Techniques

Name/Logo Testing

National Account

National Probability Survey

National Sales Strategy

Nationwide Network

Negotiate

Net Operating Profit

Net Profit Margins

New Business Development

New Business Technology

New Clients

New Product

New Product Launch

New Product Research

Newsletters

Newspaper Ad System

Newspaper Inserts

Nonprofit Accounts

Ongoing Customer Relationships

Onsite Survey Groups

Open-Order Status Reports

Operating Plans

Operational Budgets

Operational Deadlines

Operational Procedures

Order Accuracy

Order Placement

Order Processing

Orders

Outlet Sales

Outside Sales

Outstanding Performance

Overall Market Strategy

Overall Sales Efforts

Parallel Exporting

Parallel Processing

Percentages

Performance

Performance Evaluations

Performance Incentives

Periodic Claims Reviews

Personal Account Information

Personal Relations

Pertinent Materials

Petitions of Foreclosure

Placement

Point-of-Sale Forecasting

Policy

Portfolio Objectives

Portfolios

Positioning

Positive Company Image

Post-Installation Analysis

Posters

Potential Business Applications

Potential Clients

Prebooked Sales

Prequalification

Press Clippings

Press Kits

Press Releases

Price

Price Selections

Pricing Data

Primary Emphasis

Print Licenses

Print Marketing

Print Production

Private Investors

Procedures

Procurement Negotiation

Product Awareness

Product Development Operations

Product Enhancements

Product Knowledge

Product Line Presentation

Product Merchandising

Product Packages

Product Presentations

Product Recognition

Product Requirements

Product Sales

Product Training

Product Usage

Production

Production Schedules

Professional Growth

Professional Sales

Profit Estimates

Profitable Line

Profitable Relationships

Program Commitment

Program Performance

Project Specification

Promotional Agencies

Promotional Concept

Promotional Copy

Promotional Events

Promotional Material

Promotional Strategies

Promotional Work

Promotions

Proof

Proposal Preparation

Proposals

Prospect Identification

Prospecting

Prospective Clients

Provision-of-Sales Services

Public Relations

Publicity Opportunities

Purchaser/User Studies

Qualified Clients

Qualified Prospects

Quality Performance

Quality Product

Quantitative Research Projects

Quarterly Budget Reports

Quarterly Forecasts

Quota Assignment

Quota Expectations

Quoting System

Radio Marketing

Rapid-Growth Organization

Rate Structure

Ratebook

Reactivation of Dormant Accounts

Real Estate Companies

Real Estate Development Division

Real Estate Sales

Real-Time Market Data

Recurring Revenue Agreements

Referral

Registration Data

Releases

Remote Market Information

Remote Markets

Remote Territory

Rental Contracts

Rentals

Research Laboratories

Resellers

Residential Consumers

Retail Buying

Retail Outlets

Retail Sales

Retailing

Revenue Streams

Roundtable Discussions

Salary Reviews

Sales Aids

Sales Appointments

Sales Campaigns

Sales Candidate

Sales Collateral

Sales Conventions

Sales Efforts

Sales Goals

Sales Objective
Sales Per Year
Sales Plan
Sales Presentations
Sales Priorities
Sales Production
Sales Productivity
Sales Programs
Sales Projections
Sales Promotions
Sales Results
Sales Scripts
Sales Services
Sales Support
Sales Techniques
Sales Volume
Sales/Marketing Copy
Sample Development
Seasonal Merchandise
Seasonal Planbook
Seasonal Planning
Selling Reports
Seminars
Service Accounts
Short-Range Business Planning
Software Vendor
Source Selections
Space Ads
Special Advertising
Special Assignment
Special Events
Special Ordering
Special Requests
Special Seasonal Sales

Specialty Book Club Licenses
Sponsor Relations
Stock
Stock Areas
Stock Control
Stock Levels
Store Chains
Strategic Planning
Subcontractors
Subsidiary Rights Contracts
Subsidiary Rights Licenses
Subsidiary Rights Monies
Supplement Program
Support Networks
Support Services
Tally Sheets
Tapes
Target Accounts
Target Grids
Target Market
Technical and Cost Proposals
Technical Presentations
Technical Sales
Technical Sales Support
Tele-Interviewing
Telemarketing
Telemarketing Scripts
Telephone Techniques
Terms
Territory
Third-Party Distribution Channels
Timely Merchandising Delivery
Top Account Executives
Top Sales Performer

Total Client Satisfaction
Total Quality Implementation
Total Volume
Tour Schedules
Track Record
Trade Shows
Training Record
Transaction Data
Travel Orders
Union Labor
Unit Pricing
Unmarked Territory
Upwardly Mobile Buyers
User-Friendly
Valuable Application
Value of Claim
Vendor Programs
Vendors
Verbal Sales Skills
Vertical Market Framework
Viable Network
Visual Appeal
Volume Increase
Warehouse
Warehouse Accountability
Warehouse Administration
Weekly Planbook
Well-Traveled
Well-Established
Wide Range
Window Displays
Wire Trades
Working Knowledge
Working Relationships

Worksheet Program

Workstations

Yearly Sales Activity

Workshops

Written Communication Skills

Year-to-Date Sales

Printing and Publishing

Printing and publishing buzzwords display experience and familiarity with content management, book and magazine production, printing environments, and applicable technologies and systems.

Resume Buzzwords

Academia

Academic Books

Acquiring Authors

Acquiring Books

Adult Secondary and Primary Material

Advance

Advertising Specialties

Agents

Animation

Announcements

Annual Reports

Aptitude Tests

Art Design

Artwork Services

Authoring Process

Authors

Backlist

Billing and Payment

Billing Orders

Binders

Bindery Equipment

Binding

Block Printing

Boiler Plate

Book Manufacturing

Book Production

Brochures

Bundling

Business Forms

Business Stationery

Cable Television

Calligraphy

Camera-Ready Graphics

Catalog Copy

Catalogs

Character

Children's Books

Circulation

Color Correction

Color Forms

Commercial Printing

Communications Firm

Communications Systems

Consumer Magazine Publishing

Content Editing

Contract

Converting Process

Copyediting

Corporate Printing

Corporate Publishing System

Counting

Course Needs

Cover Copy

Custom Publishing

Customer Accounts

Customer Needs

Daily Newspapers

Data Entry

Data Manipulation Services

Database Development

Deal Sheet

Design

Detail-Oriented

Developing Books

Dictionaries

Digital Color

Digital Fonts

Digital Media Input

Direct Mailing

Directories

Distribution

Distribution Technology

Document Library Services

Document Management

Documentation Services
EDI (Electronic Data Interchange)
Editing
Editorial Calendar
Editorial Literary Services
Editorial Materials
Editorial Process
Editorial Vision
Educational Material
Electronic Archiving
Electronic Printer
Electronic Production
Electronic Publishing
Electronic Storage and Retrieval
    Systems
Electrotype
Encyclopedias
Engraved Plate
Engraved Rollers
Fiction
Fiction Book Publisher
Film
Financial Printing
Formats
Formatting
Fulfillment Services
Full-Color Process
Galleys
Guides
Handbills
Hardcover
High-Production Environment
High-Speed Digital Printers
High-Volume Photocopying

Illustrations
Imaging
Impression
Imprints
Independent Publishers
Information Management
Information Services
Informational Publications
Ink
Ink Jetting
Inked Type
Instructional Materials
Integrated Circulation Services
Internet Content Publishing
Inventory Management
ISO9002 Certification
Ivory Black
Laminating
Lampblack
Large Format
Laser Imaging
Layout
Legal Printing
Lettering
Libraries
Library Information Science
List Acquisition
List Management
Literary Fiction
Literary Manuscripts
Lithographic Stone
Local Distribution
Logos
Magazines

Mailing
Manuals
Market Research
Market Share Analysis
Market Studies
Marketing Collateral
Marketing Services Company
Markings
Mass Market Paperback
Matter
Media
Media Buying
Media Planning
Medical Books and Journals
Mission-Critical Data
Movie
Multimedia Products
Multiple Machine Environments
Musical Piece
Negatives
Network-Affiliated TV Stations
New Title Development
News-Gathering
Newsletters
Newswire Service
Nonfiction
Nonfiction Book Publishers
Offset
Online Library
Online Sports Information
Outside Vendors
Package
Packaging and Finishing
Pagination

Pamphlets

Parcel Fulfillment

Perfect Bind

Periodicals

Photo Retouching

Photographic Image

Photography

Photosensitive Surface

Pickup and Delivery

Plates

Poems

Poetry

Post Press

PostScript Files

Presentations

Press

Presswork

Primary Source Material

Printed Material

Printing

Printing Frame

Printing House

Printing Ink

Printing Paper

Printing Press

Printing Wheel

Print-on-Demand

Print-Production

Production Costs

Production Environment

Production Process

Professional Production Services

Professional Testing Products and
  Services

Project Costs

Project Management Experience

Promotional Activities

Promotional and Premium Copies

Promotional Copy

Prose

Public Attention

Public Contact

Public Distribution

Publication Layout

Publicity

Published Work

Publisher

Quick Conversion

Quote Generation

Radio Data Terminals

Real-Time Financial Market Data

Replication Services

Reprints

Reproduction Process

Research

Retouching

Roll Systems

Royalties

Scanning

Schedules and Quality Guidelines

Scholarly Books

Science Textbooks

Seal

Sensitized Paper

Short-Run Books

Single-Source Marketing Organization

Small Press Publishers

Software Packaging

Sorting

Specialty Publishers

Specs

Stacking

Stamp

Statistical Information

Stereotype

Subscriptions

Subsidiary Ledgers

Supplements

Targeting Strategies

Technical and Reference Books

Technical Manuals

Textbooks

Text Capture Services

The Press

Third-Party Publishers

Titles

Trade Publications

Trucking

Turnaround Time

TV Broadcasting Services

Typesetting

Typing Ability

Typography

University Presses

Verses

Warehousing Books

Web Publishers

Weeklies

Wire-O Books

Wood Block

Workflow

Yearbooks

Real Estate

Buzzwords for positions in this field highlight experience acting as a medium for transactions between homebuyers and sellers. They should show knowledge in evaluating the construction of a home in order to estimate its market value; contacting individuals by phone, mail, or in person to interview and assist them in completing various forms; and verifying the information obtained and performing various processing tasks. This often includes knowledge of leasing laws, contracts, and mortgages.

Resume Buzzwords

Abandonment
Acquisitions
Active Adult Communities
Adjustable Rate
Adjustment
Adult Retirement Communities
Advisory Services
Agency
Agreement
Apartment Buildings
Apartment Communities
Apartment Sales
Apartments
Applications
Applications Processing
Appraisals
Approvals
Asking Price
Asset Management Services
Asset Value
Assets
Assignment
Assisted Living Centers
Audits
Balance

Bankruptcy
Base Salary
Beneficiary
Bill of Sale
Binder
Blanket Mortgage
Bonds
Breach
Brokerage
Budget Forecasts
Buffer Zone
Building Code
Buying
By Owner
Capital Gain
Certificate of Title
Clause
Clients
Closing
Code of Ethics
Collateral
Colonial
Commercial
Commercial Office Space
Commission
Common Law

Company Policy
Complexes
Condominiums
Construction
Contingency
Contract
Conveyance
Corporate Investors
Corporate Office Buildings
Corporate Relocation Markets
Corporate Relocation Services
Corporation
Covenants
Credit
Credit History
Credit Report
Debt
Debt Structures
Deed
Deed in Lieu of Foreclosure
Default
Department Stores
Deposit
Design
Development
Direct Sales

Documents

Down Payment

Easement

Eminent Domain

Encroachment

Equity

Escrow

Estate

Ethics

Eviction

Exclusive Listing

Existing Properties

Fair Market Value

Financing

Firm

Fixed Rate

Fixture

Foreclosure

Full-Service Real Estate Development
   Firm

Fully Furnished

Gas Stations

Good Faith

Government Loan

Greater Area

Grocery Stores

Healthcare Facilities

Heir

Holding Company

Home Sales Transactions

Hotels

House

Housing Builder

Individual Investment

Industrial

Inflation

Installment Sales Contacts

Institutional Buildings

Institutional Investors

Insurance

Insurance Claims

Integrated

Interest

Interest Rate

Investment Trust

Investments

Joint Tenancy

Land

Lease

Lease-Up

Leasing

Leasing Goals

Leasing Operation

Lessee

Lessor

Leverage

License

Liens

Listing

Loans

Locations

Loft

Long-Term

Long-Term-Care Services

Luxury Housing

Maintenance

Major Metropolitan Area

Management Firm

Market Research

Market Value

Marketing

Markets

Master Planning

Metropolitan

Mid-Priced Single-Family Homes

Mobile Homes

Mortgage

Mortgage Loans

Motels

Move-Ins

Multifamily Properties

Multifamily Property Management

Multitenanted Property

Notes

Nursing Homes

Office

Office Buildings

Open House

Owner Financing

Partial Payment

Performance Reviews

Personal Property

Plazas

Point

Power of Attorney

Preapproval

Prepayment

Prequalification

Prime Rate

Principal

Private Investors

Project Development

Promissory Note	Rent Rolls	Shopping Centers
Properties	Rental Units	Site Reporting
Property Acquisitions	Rentals	Specializes
Property Management	Repayment Plan	Structural Integrity
Property Service Records	Resident Files	Studio
Prospective Resident	Residential	Subacute
Purchase Agreement	Residential Properties	Subdivision
Purchases	Residential Real Estate	Subsidiaries
Ranch	Residential Real Estate Consumers	Tax Credit
Rate Lock	Residential Relations	Taxes
Real Estate Brokerage	Resort Properties	Tenancy
Real Estate Developer	Resorts	Tenancy-at-Will
Real Estate Firm	Restaurants	Third-Party Property Owners
Real Estate Investment Trust	Retail	Title
Real Estate Rentals	Reviews	Title Insurance
Real Estate Sales	Sales	Trailer Parks
Realty	Secured Loan	Transactions
Refinance Transaction	Securities Portfolio Management	Turnover
Refinancing	Security	Unit
Related Services	Security Deposit	Vacancies
Relocation Services	Self-Administered	Vendor Relations
Remaining Balance	Self-Managed	Work Orders
Rent	Selling	
Rent Collection	Services	

Retail

Retail industry buzzwords demonstrate experience in the sale of clothing, goods, or appliances, either directly to consumers or to the retail stores, or the buying of such products for sale in stores. They also demonstrate knowledge of customer service; handling transactions, complaints, and returns; and the management of a retail environment.

Resume Buzzwords

Accessories
Accounts Receivable
Advertising
Advertising Programs
American Designers
Annual Circulation
Antiques
Apparel
Appliances
Art
Assortments
Audio Equipment
Automobiles
Automotive
Automotive Aftermarket Products
Automotive Manufacturers
Back Order
Baking Facilities
Barcode
Beauty Care Products
Bedroom Sets
Book Titles
Bookstores
Boutique
Branch
Brand Names
Building Materials
Buyback
Call Recording Devices
Camera Shop
Car Audio Systems
Cash on Delivery
Cash Register

Cash Register Tape
Cash Transaction
Casual Apparel
Catalog Retailer
Cataloger
Categories
Cellular Phones
Children
Children's Activewear
Children's Products
Christmas Products
City-Style Apparel
Classic Apparel
Clearance Sale
Clothing
Coatings
Collegiate Department Store
Company-Owned
Computers
Consumer
Consumer Advocate
Cookware
Co-Operative
Copy Center
Cost
Credit Card Transactions
Customers
Daily Sales Audit
Decorative Products
Delicatessen
Demo
Department Store
Department Store Merchandise
Design

Design Professionals
Desks
Dining Room Sets
Direct-Mail Software
Direct Marketing
Direct Selling
Discount Bookstore Chain
Discount Drugs
Discount Office Products
Discount Outlet
Discounted Prices
Distressed Goods
Doors and Windows
Dresses
Drug Store Products
Drugstores
Dry Cleaning
Electrical Supplies
Electronic Funds Transfer
Electronic Products
Electronics
End Caps
Exchange Policy
Exchanges
Fabric Retailer
Factory-Direct
Fad
Family Apparel
Fashion
Fashion Jewelry
Features
Floor Model
Focused Selection
Food Retailers

Food Service Distribution Businesses

Food Services

Footwear

Fragrances

Franchisees

Full-Line

Full-Line Department Store

Full-Price Stores

Furniture

Furniture Manufacturers

Gardening Products

Gas Stations

General Merchandise

Gift Certificate

Gift Products

Gift Receipt

Gifts

Global Retailer

Grocery Chains

Gross Margin

Hang Tag

Hardware

Headsets

Health and Fitness

High-Volume

Home and Safety

Home Audio Systems

Home Furnishings

Home Improvement Centers

Home Office Systems

Home Theater Speakers

Hosiery

Household Products

Housewares

Ice Cream

Ice Cream Manufacturer

Independent Dealers

Independent Operators

Independent Sales Representatives

Independently Owned

Industrial Maintenance Market

Initial Markup

International Designers

Inventory

Item Price Marking

Kiosk

Kitchen Furniture

Knitted Fabrics

Label

Layaway

Leading Retailer

Leased

Leisurewear

Licensed Franchises

Limited Warranty

Line Switches

Lingerie

Living Room Sets

Locations

Loss Prevention

Lumber

Mail-Order Retailing

Mail-Order Apparel

Mall

Mall-Based Retail Outlets

Management Support Designed

Mannequin

Manufactures

Markdown

Marketing

Marketing Research

Markets

Markup

Mass Merchandisers

Material

Meat Processing

Member-Owned

Men

Merchandise

Merchandising

Milk Processing Plant

Moderately Priced Merchandise

Music

Music Departments

National Direct Sales Company

Nationally Recognized Brands

Network

No Frills

Office Products

Off-Price Outlet Stores

Off-Price Retail

Online Sales

Original Equipment Manufacturers
(OEM)

Outdoor and Garden Merchandise

Paint

Percentage

Personal Care Products

Photo Development Services

Photographic Equipment

Plumbing Supplies

Price Marketing

Price War
Prints
Private Labels
Product Line
Products
Promotion
Promotional Advertising
Promotional Discount
Quantity Discount
Ready-to-Assemble
Receipt
Refund
Related Support Facilities
Reserve Stock
Retail Chain
Retail Convenience Stores
Retail Drug Stores
Retail Fabric Stores
Retail Furniture Stores
Retail Locations
Retail Price
Retail Units
Retail Warehouse Stores
Retailer
Returns
Sales Forecasting
Sales Promotion
Seasonal Discount
Selected Home Furnishings
Serving Equipment
Shoe Departments
Site Location
Soft-Goods Products

Software
Specialty Catalog Retailer
Specialty Catalogs
Specialty Clothing
Specialty Fashion Store
Specialty Menswear
Specialty Paint and Wall Covering
   Stores
Specialty Retailer
Specialty Women's Clothing Retailer
Sportswear
Stereo
Store Chain
Store Credit
Store Items
Suggestive Selling
Super Drug Stores
Supermarket Chain
Superstores
Swimwear
Target Market
Telephone Productivity Items
Telephones
Televisions
Toys
Trade
Traffic Paint Market
Travel and Luggage
Trend
Tuxedo
Unit-of-Sale Method
Universal Product Code (UPC)
Used

Value-Priced
Various Industries
Video Rental
Videos
Warehouse Foods
Warehouses
Warranty
Wholesale
Wholly Owned Subsidiaries
Wide Assortments
Wide Variety
Women's Apparel
Women's Intimate Apparel
Work Clothing
Woven Fabrics

Science

For scientific positions, each particular field will have many specialized technical terms aside from those listed here. Science industry buzzwords, in general, display experience with research and development. This includes research to develop new medicines; increase crop yield; improve the environment; study farm crops, animals, and living organisms; and explore practical use and knowledge of chemicals, as well as the atmosphere's physical characteristics, motions, and processes.

Resume Buzzwords

Aberrations

Absolute Molecular Weight

Acreage Evaluation

Agrarian-Based Industries

Agriculture

Air Pollution

Algal Organisms

Amphibious Surveying Operation

Analysis

Animal Care

Animal Health Practices

Animal Husbandry

Animals

Annual Operating Budget

Aquaculture Projects

Arborists

Artificial Insemination Considerations

Assisted Animals

Bacteria

Bale

Beef

Bid Documents

Binary Stars

Biochemical Procedures

Biochemistry

Biological Research

Biological Sources

Blood Banking Procedures

Blood Components

Blood Products

Branching Data

Breeding

Briefing Papers

Briefings

Brillouin Scattering

Briquetting

Cadmium Telluride Gamma Ray
   Detector

Calculations

Carcinogenic Analysis

Cellular Structure

Ceramics

Chemical Synthetic Procedures

Chemicals

Chemistry

Classroom-Style Lectures

Cleanup Procedures

Coastline

Common Illnesses

Compositions

Comprehensive Management Plan

Computer Record Maintenance

Computerized Assays

Continuous Viscometer Detector

Contractual Services

Courses

Cows

Crop

Crossbreeding

Culture Facility

Cultures

Curation

Custom Instrumentation

Custom Test Equipment

Cutting

Daily Temperature

Dairy Cows

Dairy Produce

Dairy Production

Data

Deadline Pressure

Dental X-Ray Calibration

Designated Forecasts

Detailed Reports

Digital Equipment

Digital Recording

Dilutor System Analyses

Disciplines
DNA Research
DNA Sequence Analysis
Drainage
Dredge Materials
Dressage
Drilling Fluids
Ecological Sources
Ecosystem
Education
Effluents
Eggs
Electron Microscopy
Electronic Repair
Elementary Level
ELISA (Enzyme-Linked Immunosor-
    bent Assay)
Environmental Issues
Environmental Protection
Environmental Science
Epithelial Cellines
Equipment
Expected Inherited Traits
Experimental Research
Experiments
Expertise
Exploration
Fabry-Perot Interferometer
Farm Equipment
Feed
Fermentor Microcarrier Cultures
Fertilization
Fibrinogens
Fibroblast

Field Support
Field Surveys
Findings
Fire Prevention
Firefighting Techniques
Fish
Fish Ponds
Fisheries
Flood Protection
Foaling
Forecasting Weather
Forecasts
Forestry
Forests
Fungal Cell Metabolism
Funnel Extractions
Gel Permeation Chromatography
Genetic Factors
Genetic Research
Genetics
Geological Aspects
Geological Background
Geophysical Crew
Geophysical Exploration Programs
Glacial Deposits
Grant Tracking Support
Grooming
Ground Water
Growth Parameters
Hay
Heat Treatment
Heavy Mineral Separation
Helium Neon Laser
Herbicides

Hormonal Assays
Horticultural Planting
Horticulture
Hospital Laboratories
Hubble Telescope
Humidity
Hurricanes
Industrial Wastes
Instrument Automation
Instrumentation
Inventory
Invertebrate
Irrigation
Isolation Schemes
Lab
Lab Samples
Labeling
Labor
Laboratories
Laboratory Inventory
Laboratory Operations
Laboratory Setting
Lamb
Lambing Season
Large-Scale Fermentation
Light Mineral Separation
Lightweight Aggregates
Lime Manufacturer
Livestock
Local Dairies
Lumber Projects
Magnitude
Mainframe System
Maintenance Schedules

Malformations

Manual Assays

Manufacture

Maps

Mares

Market

Materials

Materials Research

Mathematics Text

Mating Procedures

Mating Season

Measurements

Meat Processing Industry

Metals

Methodology

Microbiology Classes

Microcomputer Systems

Microprocessors

Mill Contractors

Mineral Content

Mineralogical

Minicomputers

Miniprep DNA Purification

Molecular Biological Problems

Molecular Biology

Monitoring Survey

Moon

Municipal Records

Mutations

National Chemistry Convention

Natural Disasters

Natural Habitat

Newborn Foal Diseases

Nonlinear Optics

Nucleic Acid Hybridization

Nucleotides

Oceanic Research

Oil Company Consortium

Old Stars

Organic Extractions

Organic Liquid Crystals

Organic Pigment

Organic Synthesis

Palletizing

Park Collection

Park Records

Particle-Size Instruments

Patented Design

PCB

Perfusion System

Pest Control

Pest Control Program

Pesticides

Petrographic Technique

Petroleum Monitoring Programs

pH Adjustments

Physicians

Physics Labs

Pilot Plant Equipment

Planetary Surface Research

Planets

Plant Acquisition

Plant Alkaloids

Plants

Plasmid Constructions

Plasmid DNA Purification

Positron Annihilation Spectroscopy

Precipitation Level

Preparing Media

Private Sectors

Privately Funded Organizations

Process Experimentation

Produce

Produce Farm

Production Basis

Production Handling

Proper Calibration

Protein Assays

Protein Purification

Proteins

Pruning

Q-Switched Ruby Laser

Quality Control Systems

Radar

Radiosonic Equipment

Raw Material

Recombinant DNA Technology

Research and Development

Research Papers

Research Problems

Research Reports

Research Techniques

Ribosome Structure

RNA Component

Sanitation Procedures

Satellites

Science Texts

Scientific Crew

Scientific Seminars

Sea Transportation

Seasonal Climate Conditions

Seeds

Semiconductor Neutron Detector

Semiconductors

SI Mapping

Slides

Soil Samples

Soil Testing

Special Forecasts

Specialized Instrumentation

Specialized Test Equipment

Stars' Magnitudes

Steroids

Stimulated Sound Scattering

Studs

Study Subjects

Subsurface

Supernovae

Surface Stations

Surrogate Solutions

Surveying

Technical Applications

Technical Data

Technical Writing

Telescope

Temperature

Territorial Logging

Test Results

Tests

Textbook

T-Flasks

Thoroughbreds

Tilapia

Timber

Tissue Culture Glassware

Tissue Experiment

Total Maintenance Program

Toxicity Tests

Trace Organic Analysis

Traces

Transfusion

Tree Acquisition

Trees

Turf Management

U.S. Wildlife Department

Upper-Air Data

Upper-Air Stations

USDA Regulations

Vaccination Schedules

Vegetation

Veterinary Medicine

Viral Immunology Testing

Vitamins

Waste Disposal

Wastewater

Water Supply

Weather Balloon

Weather Conditions

Weed Control

Well Logging

Wet Chemistry

Wildlife

Wildlife Activities

Winds

Zoo

Service

These service industry buzzwords highlight experience with providing high-quality customer service. This includes positions in food preparation, clerical work, retail, and the like.

Resume Buzzwords

Academic Training

Account Adjustment

Accounting

Accounting Principles

Address Changes

Adjustments

Administrative Policies

Advice

Analysis of Services

Assisting Customers

Attractive Presentations

Automated Solutions

Banquets

Base Salary

Bill Maintenance and Reconciliation

Billing

Billing Process

Bookings

Booth Set-Up

Budget

Budget Worksheets

Business Conventions

Business Management

Business Practices

Business Protocol

Business System Support

Business System Training

Cash Control

Cash Deposits

Cash Intake

Cash Received

Cash Reconciliations

Cash Transactions

Cashiering

Centralized Management Systems

Check-In

Checkout

Client Base

Client Needs

Clientele

Clients

Cold Calling

Commercial Account Installation

Commitment to Excellence

Community Development

Complete and Thorough Service

Confidential Client Files

Conflict Resolution

Consulting with Guests

Consumer Services

Contract Negotiation

Corporate Accounts

Corporate Communication

Corporate Events

Corporate Foundations

Corporate Membership Packages

Correspondence

CPR

Credit Card Transactions

Credits

CRM Systems

Cross-Industry Marketing Efforts

Customer Assistance

Customer Care

Customer Loyalty

Customer Relations

Customer Service

Customer Support Environment

Customers

Daily Reports

Data Entry

Delivery Processes

Department Regulations

Design

Desserts

Develop and Maintain Client
    Relationships

Distributors

Diversity

Diversity of Professionals

Documentation

Drafts

Economies of Scale

Emergency Equipment

Emergency Evacuation Plan

Employee Performance

Employee Relationship Management

Employee Satisfaction

ERP Systems

Establish Rapport

Executive Guidelines

Existing Accounts

Facility Operations

Fast Food Industry

Field Inquiries

Field Support

Filing

Filing Invoices

Filing System

Filling Job Orders

Finance

Financial Experience

Financial Record Keeping

Financial Systems

Front Desk Operations

Frontend Systems

Guest Check-In

Guest Checkout

Guest Complaints

Guest Mail and Faxes

Guestrooms

Guest Services

Guest Survey

Guests' Needs

Guidelines

Hospitality-Oriented

Human Resources
Incoming Calls
Increased Sales
Independent Worker
Instructions
Interpersonal Skills
Inventory
Job Applicants
Job Openings
Job Placement
Light Maintenance
List Management
Mailing Checks and Statements
Managed-Care Industry
Management Reports
Management Systems
Marketing Initiatives
Marketing Office
Marketing Plans
Marketing Report
Marketing Strategies
Materials Costing Processes
Media Relations
Merchandising
Monitor
Monitored Payroll
Monitoring Delivery Personnel
Monthly Menu
Monthly Reports
Monthly Seminars
Multiple Accounts
Multiple Tasks
National Business Convention
New Associate Training Program

New Business Development
Office Operations
Office Responsibilities
Operational Deadlines
Operational Procedures
Operations
Ordering
Organization of Delivery Schedules
Outbound Calls
Overnight Operations
Passenger Boarding
Passenger Manifest
Passenger Safety
Passengers
Patient
Payroll
Performance
Performance Bonus
Personalized Client Interactions
Personnel
Personnel Assistance
Personnel Management
Phone Interaction
Plan Design Features
Plane Reservations
Portioning
Practical Applications
Premium Refund
Prep Work
Preparation
Preselected Client Groups
Presentation
Presentation of Goods
Prioritize Tasks at Hand

Problem Area
Problem Resolution
Problem-Solving
Procedures
Process Payments
Processing Returns
Production
Products
Professional Image
Professional Services Environment
Promotion
Promotional Demonstration Activities
Promotional Efforts
Promotional Events
Promotional Opportunities
Prospective Customers
Proven Track Record
Public Relations
Purchasing
Purchasing Procedures
Quality Control
Quick and Accurate Decisions
Realization of Customer
   Specifications
Receiving
Reconciling
Reconciling Commission Reports
Referral Service
Referrals
Register Control
Registers
Relationship Building
Relationship Building Skills
Rentals

Reporting Tools

Reports

Requisitions

Researching and Resolving Customer
    Inquiries

Reservations

Resolve Customer Complaints

Resolve Guest Grievances/Problems

Restaurants

Retail

Route-Oriented Industry

Sales Goals

Sales Programs

Sales Staff

Sales Support Services

Sales Territory Development

Sales/Marketing

Schedule of Shows

Scheduling

Seating Allocation

Selection and Referral Process

Seminar

Service Business Systems

Service Distributors

Service Opportunities

Service Procedures

Services

Shift Management

Shift Scheduling

Shipping

Shipping Errors

Shop Management

Show Expenses

Sourcing Network

Sourcing of Vendors

Special Functions

Special Interest Groups

Special Orders

Special Sales

Specialized Training

Staff Motivation

Staff Training

Standardized Processes

Stations

Strong Academic Background

Strong Communication Skills

Supermarkets

Supplies

System Support

Takeout

Team Member

Telemarketing

Telephone Bookings

Telephone Survey

Telex Bookings

Terminations and Commission
    Assignments

Three-Star Hotel

Time and Labor Solutions

Tour Arrangements

Tourist Information

Tracking Demands

Tradeshows

Training Program

Transactions

Transportation Coordination

Travel Problems

Troubleshoot

Typing

Weekly Volume

Weekly Work Schedule

Workflow

Workshops

Social and Human Services

Industry buzzwords for these helping fields highlight experience with improving the emotional well-being of individuals in need; studying human behavior and mental processes to understand, explain, and change people's behavior; developing programs to provide for growth and revitalization of urban, suburban, and rural communities and their regions; and helping local officials make decisions on social, economic, and environmental problems. This also includes work in group homes and halfway houses, correctional, mental retardation, and community mental health centers.

Resume Buzzwords

24-Hour Hotline
Academic Assistance
Achievement Test
Administrative Duties
Admissions
Adoption Purposes
Advocacy
After-School Program
Assessment of Clientele
Assignment of Children
Assisted Living
At-Risk Students
Behavior Modification
Behavioral Programs
Bicultural Experience
Bilingual
Campaign Fund Solicitations
Case Management
Case Presentations
Case Prevention
Case Studies
Child Advocate
Clarification Exercise
Client Need
Client Progress

Clientele
Clients
Clinical
Clinical Practices
Clinical Treatment Plans
Co-Directed
College-Prep Test
Commercial Development
Community Agencies
Community Development Group
Community Group Meetings
Community Mobilization
Community Outreach
Community Residents
Community-Based Agencies
Compliance
Concrete and Supportive Services
Conduct Assessment
Consultant Reports
Contact Development
Content Planning
Cooperative Experience
Counseling
Credit Management
Credit Program
Crisis Intervention

Crisis Situation
Curriculum Development
Curriculum Implementation
Curriculum Recommendations
Daily Living Skills
Department of Social Services (DSS)
Developmental Stimulation
Developmentally Delayed Clients
Diagnostic Evaluation
Difficult-to-Place Clients
Direct Assistance
Direct Patient Care
Discharge Planning
Disciplinary Problems
Discipline
Discussion Groups
Economic Analysis
Economic Development
Editorial Department
Education
Education for Families
Educational Institutes
Educational Testing
Effective Treatment Strategies
Efficient Daily Operations
Emotional Support

Enterprise Project

Evaluation of Mental Status

Extrinsic Motivation

Families at Risk

Families in Crisis

Family Life Education Group

Family Therapy

Feasibility Analysis

Foundation Fundraising

Fundraising

Grant Programs

Grant Proposals

Group Activities

Group Practice

Group Therapy Sessions

Home Studies

Hotline Calls

House Management

Housing Authority

Housing Development

Human Services

Hypothesis Testing

Individual Educational Programs

Individual Psychotherapy Sessions

Individual Social Work

Individualized Academic Instruction

Industrial Expansion

Industrial Retention

Informal Family Therapy

Information Referral

Initial Evaluation

In-Service Education

In-Service Training

Interdisciplinary Team

Intrinsic Motivation

Knowledge Management

Legal Resources

Legislative Documents

Local Organizations

Long-Term Treatment Plans

Maintenance Services

Managed Cases

Management Development

Mass Mailing Programs

Medical Charts

Multidisciplinary Education

Multidisciplinary Team

Negotiation

New Programs

Nonprofit Organization

Nursing Care

On-Call

One-on-One Meetings

One-to-One Basis

Outpatient Clinic

Outpatients

Outreach Clinical Services

Outreach Services

Outside Consulting

Parent Education Groups

Parent-Teacher Conferences

Patient Independence

Personal Practice

Petitions

Placement Services

Play Groups

Policies and Procedures

Policy Development

Position Case Study

Preventive Strategies

Primary Care

Private Agencies

Private Practice

Problem Diagnosis

Procedural Guidelines

Professional Development

Progress Charting

Project Development

Promotional Letters

Proposals

Protective Custody

Psychiatric Admissions

Psychiatric Assessment

Psychological Assistance

Psychological Testing

Public Agencies

Public Relations

Record Keeping System

Records

Recreation

Recruitment

Recruitment of Prospective Parents

Referral Requests

Referral Services

Regression Analysis

Relationship of Trust

Remedial Plans

Residential Program

Residential Treatment Facility

Routine Monitoring

Self-Image Enhancement

Seminars

Service Networks

Shelter

Situation Evaluation

Skill Utilization

Small-Scale Enterprise

Social Assistance

Social Problems

Social Service Arena

Social Service Organization

Social Work

Special Service Network

Specialized Services

Status Reports

Students

Survival Skills

Task Force

Teaching Staff

Technical Assistance

Therapeutic Activities

Therapeutic Intervention

Therapeutic Plans

Treatment

Treatment Plans

Vocational Test

Workflow

Workshops

Youth Programs

Technical

Technical industry buzzwords highlight experience with applying specialized knowledge of technology, systems, engineering, and science. Potential applications for technical skills and experience exist in virtually all industries, including transportation, building design and inspection, engine repair and maintenance, electrical systems design, and communications.

Resume Buzzwords

Administration Lead

Air-Cooled Condenser

Aircraft Maintenance

Aircraft Power

Aircraft Towing

Alignment

Analog

Analytical Attributes

Annual Network Costs

Architectural Development

Architectural Landscape Design

Architectural Landscaping

Architectural Renderings

Architecture

Artistic Illustration

Assemble

Assembly Drawing

Attainment

Baffle Tiles

Battery Connections

Battery Disconnections

Blueprints

Boiler Hookup

Boilers

Bookkeeping

Building Codes

Building Inspection

Building Laws

Bulk Memory Cards

Burners

Cable Drawings

Calcium Silicate Block

Chart

Chimney

Civil Engineering

Codes and Standards

Commercial Buildings

Commercial Wiring

Commercials

Community Production

Completed Framing

Compliance Procedures

Component Drawing

Component Parts

Computer Aided

Computer Aided Design (CAD)

Computer Design Base (CDB)

Computer Product

Computer Programming

Computer Science

Computer Tradeshow

Computer Work Station

Conceptualization Stage

Concrete Design

Condenser

Condenser Head

Configuration Time

Continuing Engineering Functions

Control Chart

Cost Control

Craft Workers

Custom Construction

Custom Style

Customer Housing

Customer Service

Customer Support

Cylinder

Data Testing Standards

Database

Database Management

Datum Structure

Design Development

Development

Diagnostic Test

Digital Concept

Dimensioning System

Dimmer Board

Disassemble

Disk Interface

Distributor

Drafting

Drafting Technology

Drawing

Drawing Development and Detailing

Electrical

Electrical Regulations

Electrical Repairs

Electrical Technology

Electronic

Electronic Illustration

Electronics Technology

Emissions Certificate

Engine Cowl

Engineering

Equipment Application

Estimate

Experience

Exploded View

Exterior

External Credentialing Groups

Extrusions

Fabricated Complex Parts

Fabrication

Facility Justification of Systems and
   Networks

Federal Licensing/Certification

Field Drawing

Field Service

Field Service Engineer

Field Tested

Film Production

Final Inspection

Final Product Design

Final Recommendation

Final Release

Final Report

Fire Brink

Flat Patterns

Flight Officer

Flight-Line Launching

Flight-Line Recoveries

Floating-Point Processors

Floor Framing

Flow Model

Fluid System Design

Footings

Foreman

Fuel Product

General Construction

General Repairs

Grading Safety Laws

Graph

Hand Tools

Hardware

Harnessing

High-Speed Logic Board

Hybrid Microcircuit Design and
   Drawing

Illustration

Image Memory Cards

In Process

Incoming Material

Information Distribution

In-Plant

Inspection

Inspection Area

Inspection Records

Inspection Technique

Insulator Skills

Interfacing
Interior Spaces
Internal Support
Internal Technical Operations
International Broadcasting
International Marketing Tool
Interpret Legal Requirements
Inventory
Landing Gear
Lights
Line Artwork
Lock Repair
Lubrication
Machine and Sheet Metal Parts
    Inspection
Machine Drawing
Machine Language Firmware
Machined
Machinery Support
Mainframe
Maintenance
Manufactured Products
Manufacturing
Mason Skills
Mechanical
Mechanical Aptitude
Mechanical/Electronic Detailing and
    Drawing
Microcomputer Industry
Microprocessor Principles
Military Construction
Military Hardware
Model Assembly
Model Construction

Model Part
Multilocation Companies
Multimedia Product
Network Design
Network Facility
Onsite Research
Operating Systems
Operational Discrepancy Logs
Operations
Overlay Applications
Parts Numbering System
Permanent Building Inspector
Permits
Photo-Typesetting
Piping
Plant Construction
Plumbing Regulations
Precision Inspection
Presentation
Presentation Graphics
Pressure Chamber
Pressure Fuel Oil Tank
Pressure Parts
Preventive Maintenance
Print Specification
Private Sectors
Procedure
Product Development
Product Performance
Product Reliability
Production
Program Logs
Program Management Techniques
Program Sources

Project Leadership
Project Management
Project Scheduling Priority System
Project Superintendent
Promos
Proposal
Prototype System
Public Sectors
Public Service Announcements
Public Works
Pump
Quality Assurance
Quality Workmanship
Radio-Television-Film Technology
Real Estate Development Layout
Reconfiguration
Refueling
Refurbished Technology
Regulations
Regulatory Compliances
Repair
Research
Research Data
Residential Electrical Needs
Residential Heating Needs
Residential Plumbing Needs
Residential Wiring
Retaining Walls
Revision Cycle
Routing Sheet
Sample Part
Sand Casting
Satellite Feeds
Schematic Capture

Scoop Lights

Service Manual

Servicing

Sheet Metal Drawing

Sheet-Metal Layout Inspection

Sheet-Metal Fabrication

Single Location Companies

Site Survey

Software

Software Enhancements

Specifications

Stairway

Standards

State Building Codes

State Rules and Regulations

Station Organization

Strategic Alliance

Streamlined Procedures

Strict Quality Control

Structural Steel Work

Studio Camera

Studio System

Sub-Assembly

Submit Reports

Submittal

Successful Development

Surface Ship Propulsion System

System Design

System Recommendation

System Test

System Test Board

Tactical Research

Technical Drawing

Technical Illustration

Technical Writing

Telecommunications

Television Production

Template

Terminal

Territory Management

Test Date Format

Test Equipment

Test File

Test Results

Testing Program

Testing Time

Topographical Survey

Track Trends

Transmitter Logs

Troubleshooting

Turbines

Variances

Verbal Specification

Video Adjuster Boards

Video Conference

Video Latch Boards

Video Sync Boards

Well Developed

Wing Tips

Wiring

Wiring Lamps

Working Audit

Working Drawing

Workstation Product Lines

Worldwide Television Deregulation

Writing Diagrams

Zoning Laws

Zoning Safety Laws

Transportation and Travel

In the transportation and travel industries, buzzwords highlight experience with conveying passengers or goods, providing or controlling means for transportation, and coordinating or advancing the travel of others. They also include knowledge of various transportation methods, either from the customer service side or the transporting side.

Resume Buzzwords

Air Compressor

Air Express Network

Air Freight

Air Tank

Aircraft

Aircraft Fittings

Airframe Services

Airport Code

Airport Facilities
Airport Transfers
Airports
Alignment
Area School Bus Company
Assembly
Automated Control Systems
Automated Guideway Transit
Automatic Train Control
Average Weekday Traffic
Aviation Industry
Baggage Check
Barges
Berthing Facilities
Boarding Pass
Boxcars
Brake Shoes
Bulk Freight Shipping
Bulk Transportation
Bus Service
Buses
Business Meetings
Business Trips
Cab Signaling Equipment
Cabin Cleaning
Cam Buckles
Canal System
Canopy Platform
Capacity
Capital Asset Financing
Car Maintenance
Car Rental Agreement
Car Repair
Cargo Handling

Cargo Restraint Equipment
Cargo Services
Carrier
Carry-On
Charter Bus Service
Charter Services
Chemicals
City-Funded
Cleaning Planes
Coal Cars
Code System Emulators
Commission
Commission Sales Agents
Commodities
Common Carrier Freight Line
Common Carrier Trucking Firm
Communities
Commuter Train Lines
Complete Packaged Transportation
    Service
Computerized Aircraft Maintenance
    Services
Confirmation
Connecting Flight
Connections
Constituent Agencies
Construction Aggregate
Construction Services
Container Freight Station Operations
Containerized Cargo Distribution
    System
Contracting Services
Control Systems
Corporate Clients

Corporate Rate
Covered Hoppers
Cruise Line
Cruise Speed
Customs Brokerage
Deep-Sea and Coastal Towing
Dinner/Theater Events
Direct Flight
Direct Services
Discount Fairs
Dispatch Computer
Distribution
Districts
Domestic Offices
Domestic Travel
Double Stack Intermodal Facilities
Drop-Off Locations
Dwell Time
Electronic Controls
Elements
Emergency Air and Truck Freight
    Services
Emergency Road Services
Engine Services
Engineering Consulting
Equipment Housings
Equipment Management Services
Executive Travel
Expedited Air and Truck Freight
    Services
Express Services
Express Transportation
Extensive Commuter Passenger Ser-
    vice Railroad Operations

Fare

Flat Rate

Fleet

Fleet Financing

Floor Jack

Foreign Travel

Freight Cars

Freight Forwarding

Freight Handling

Freight Service Railroad Operations

Freight Traffic

Fueling Planes

Full-Service

Global Transportation

Ground-Handling

Group Rate

Guideway

Heavy Rail Transit

High-Speed Rail

Highway Trailers

Highways

Household Goods

Import/Export Brokerage

Inbound Marine Shipping

Independent Contractors

Industrial Development

In-House Capabilities

Inspections

Insurance

Integrated Logistics Programs

Intermodal Cars

Intermodal Distribution Company

International Air and Ocean Freight
    Forwarding Services

International Air Carrier

International Travel

Interstate Freight Carrier

Into-Plane Fueling

Jumper Cables

Land Shippers

Lease Types

Leasing Company

Light Rail Transit

Limousine Transportation Services

Loading Standards

Loading/Unloading

Local Service

Lock-Out Tools

Locomotives

Logistics

Main Lines

Mainline Railways

Maintenance

Major Cities

Major Lessor

Major Markets

Marine Divisions

Marine Towing

Marine Transportation

Maritime Academies

Mass Transportation

Microprocessor-Based Automatic
    Train Control

Mileage

Modification Services

Motor Carrier

Motor Freight Carrier

Motorists

Moving

Moving Company

Nonrail Holding Company

O/C Buckles

Off-Road Divisions

Oil Transportation

Operator Consoles

Original Equipment Products

Outbound Marine Shipping

Overseas Forwarding

Packages

Park-and-Ride

Passenger Car Heating and Air Condi-
    tioning Equipment

Passenger Railroad Operators

Passenger Service

Passing Track

PC-Based Systems

Peak Hour

Peak Period

Peak Season

Petroleum Transport

Pipelines

Plastic Resins

Platform

Positioning Tunnel and Bridge
    Segments

Pressure Differential Cars

Private Customers

Public Benefit Corporation

Public Transportation Firm

Rail Cars

Rail Networks

Rail Signal

Rail Transportation

Railcar Equipment

Railcars

Railroad Industry

Railroad Operations

Railroad Speed Indicating/Pacesetting
 Controls

Railroad Tracks

Railway Freight Cars

Ramp Services

Regulations

Relay-Based Automatic Train Control

Relays

Replacement Products

Reservation

Route System

Routes

Rush Hour

Safety Policies and Procedures

School Bus Contractor

Secondary Main Lines

Self-Propelled Vehicles

Self-Unloading Bulk Carriers

Ship Docking

Shippers

Shipping Agency

Ships

Shoring Beams

Sightseeing Activities

Signals

Spare Parts Inventory

Special Projects

Specialized Transportation Services

Specialty Cars

Standby

Station

Steam Generators

Steel Products

Storage Services

Storage Tanks

Subways

Switch Machines

Switching Track

Tank Cars

Tank Storage Terminals

Terminal

Ticket Broker

Tire Iron

Tow Services

Track

Track Circuits

Tractors

Traditional Freight Forwarding

Transit Rails

Transportation Services

Travel

Travel Agency

Travel Demand

Trips

Trolleys

Truck Rental Company

Truck Transportation

Trucking

Trucking Company

Truckload Transportation Services

Tugs

Turnaround Time

Vacations

Van Transportation Company

Vehicle Leasing Companies

Vehicles

Vital Processors

Vital Timers

Volume

Warehouse Space

Warehousing

Warehousing Facilities

Wayside

Weddings

Wheel Services

Wheels

Winches

Work Equipment

Workstation-Based Systems

Worldwide Supply Chain Solutions

Yachts

Yard Track

Visual and Performing Arts

These buzzwords for the visual and performing arts concentrate on those positions for creative artists. Arts buzzwords highlight experience with creating art and with entertaining an audience through performance art, theater, and music. This includes organizing and designing articles, products, and materials; portraying people, places, and events; communicating ideas, thoughts, and feelings; making words come alive by creating a visual and oral presentation based on written words in a script; expressing ideas, stories, rhythm, and sound; and creating dance interpretations.

Resume Buzzwords

Accessory
Act
Advertising
Airbrush
Album Tour
Apparel
Architectural Design
Artist Shop
Artistic Feasibility
Artwork
Ballet
Black and White
Book Illustration
Bound Printed Material
Broadway
Brochures
Business and Art Professional
Cable Program
Calligraphic Artwork
Camera-Ready Art
Charts
Choreography
Classical Ballet
Classical Piano

Color
Color Film Development
Color Promotional Samples
Comedy Sketch
Commercial Art
Commercials
Computer Art
Contemporary Ballet
Corporate Design
Corporate Portrait
Costume Design
Costumes
Creative Analysis
Creative Dance
Creative Planning
Dance Studio
Dealer Sell Sheets
Debut Album
Departmental Database Network
Design
Design Logos
Diagram
Diagram Maps
Direct Lighting
Display Technique

Drum Technician
Extra
Fabric
Fashion Design
Fashion Show
Fashion Tradeshow
Feature Film
Fine Arts
Flyers
Freestanding Insert Ads
Freehand
Freelance
Front Window Display
Full Color
Gallery Logo
Garment
Hand-Design
Header Cards
Illustration
Improvisational Workshop
In the Round
Independent Record
Interior Design
Interior Finish
Japanese Motif Sketch Design

Jazz

Large-Format View Camera

Laser Printing

Layout and Design

Lighting

Lighting Effects

Lighting Equipment

Location

Location Photography

Mail Marketing Pieces

Major Label

Makeup

Marketing Brochure

Marketing Lists

Material

Mechanical Paste-Up

Mechanical Stages

Mechanicals

Method Style of Acting

Model

Modern Ballet

Modern Dance

Modern Piece

Music Director

Music Format

Musical

Narrative Sketch

New York Stage

Onstage

Operational Deadlines

Orchestra

Orchestral Experience

Oriental Design

Outside Vendor

Pastels

Paste-Up

Pattern

Pattern Making

Performance

Performer

Photo Essay

Photography

Photography Sessions

Playwright's Text

Point-of-Sales Material

Portfolio

Portrait

Positive and Negative Images

Prerelease

Printing

Printing Process

Producer

Production Report

Promotional Campaign

Promotional Event

Promotional Photography

Promotional Pieces

Promotions

Prop

Props and Backgrounds

Proscenium Arch

Prototype Design

Published

Radio Chart

Recital

Reprint Titles

Reproduction Camera

Road Crew

Road Tour

Runway Show

Scene

Script

Seasonal Floor Set

Set

Sew

Shelf Talkers

Showcase

Showcase Club

Sing

Sketch Comprehensives

Slide Materials

Slideshow

Small-Format View Camera

Soft Sheets

Sound

Sound Technician

Sound Work

Special Effects

Special Market Division

Specialized Technology

Stage Direction

Stage Management

Staging

Stand-Up Comedy

Stanislavski Style of Acting

Stat Camera

Structure

Studio Art

Studio Assignment

Stylized Lettering

Superstructure

Tailor

Tap

Teaching

Tear-Off Pads

Technical Art

Technical Report

Theater Production

Theatrical Direction

Three-Color Brochures

Tickets

Top-10 Selling Record

Trade Promotions

Traditional Art and Drawing

Traditional Painting and Drawing

Type Layout

Vendor

Video

Visual Audit

Visual Checklist

Visual Criteria Standardization

Visual Presentation

Wardrobe

Window Display

Window Display Fixture

Worldwide Tour

Commonly Used Action Verbs

Accounting and Finance

Acted
Actuated
Adjusted
Administered
Allocated
Analyzed
Anticipated
Appraised
Assessed
Audited
Balanced
Budgeted
Calculated
Compiled
Completed
Composed
Computed
Conserved
Controlled
Corrected
Created
Determined
Developed
Entered
Established
Estimated
Expanded
Filed
Forecasted
Generated
Implemented

Improved
Maintained
Managed
Marketed
Measured
Monitored
Netted
Oversaw
Passed
Performed
Planned
Posted
Prepared
Programmed
Projected
Provided
Qualified
Reconciled
Recorded
Reduced
Researched
Resolved
Retrieved
Reviewed
Settled
Supported
Utilized
Worked

Administrative

Arranged
Assisted

Budgeted
Collected
Conducted
Coordinated
Created
Designed
Developed
Distributed
Edited
Executed
Facilitated
Filed
Handled
Implemented
Improved
Managed
Monitored
Organized
Performed
Planned
Prepared
Prioritized
Produced
Provided
Recorded
Resolved
Scheduled
Secured
Served
Serviced
Solicited
Sorted

Supervised
Tested
Translated
Utilized

Aerospace

Analyzed
Assisted
Designed
Developed
Engaged
Engineered
Established
Evaluated
Generated
Led
Manufactured
Performed
Planned
Prepared
Production
Provided
Recommended
Researched
Supplied
Tracked
Wrote

Apparel, Fashion, and Textiles

Checked
Created

Designed
Developed
Established
Featured
Finished
Generated
Handled
Licensed
Managed
Manufactured
Oversaw
Printed
Processed
Produced
Purchased
Received
Sold
Supervised
Tailored
Wove

**Architecture,
Construction, and
Engineering**
Built
Completed
Conceptualized
Conducted
Constructed
Controlled
Designed
Drafted
Drew
Generated

Managed
Outlined
Oversaw
Planned
Prepared
Programmed
Proposed
Renovated
Researched
Scheduled
Served
Supervised
Surveyed
Transported

**Arts, Entertainment,
Sports, and Recreation**
Acted
Analyzed
Competed
Conceptualized
Created
Developed
Directed
Managed
Organized
Oversaw
Planned
Produced
Promoted
Provided
Supervised

Automotive
Accessorized
Assessed
Built
Certified
Customized
Diagnosed
Distributed
Drove
Explained
Formed
Improved
Installed
Managed
Manufactured
Ordered
Performed
Produced
Repaired
Replaced
Serviced
Showed
Sold

**Biotechnology and
Pharmaceuticals**
Applied
Compared
Contributed
Coordinated
Designed
Determined
Directed
Discovered

Disseminated
Facilitated
Generated
Guided
Identified
Implemented
Labeled
Leveraged
Maintained
Managed
Performed
Planned
Processed
Provided
Received
Sampled
Tracked
Trained
Utilized

Communications
Acted
Administered
Aided
Assisted
Conducted
Controlled
Coordinated
Created
Developed
Directed
Drafted
Edited
Evaluated

Generated
Identified
Implemented
Interviewed
Managed
Operated
Ordered
Organized
Oversaw
Performed
Planned
Produced
Promoted
Proofread
Publicized
Received
Recommended
Reported
Researched
Resolved
Scheduled
Served
Solicited
Supervised
Typed
Wrote

Computers and Mathematics

Adapted
Analyzed
Assisted
Calculated
Contributed

Controlled
Correlated
Created
Defined
Designed
Developed
Directed
Engineered
Evaluated
Formulated
Functioned
Identified
Implemented
Installed
Instituted
Led
Maintained
Managed
Monitored
Performed
Presented
Processed
Programmed
Provided
Published
Researched
Resolved
Scrutinized
Suggested
Supplied
Supported
Translated
Updated
Upgraded

Wrote

Education and Library Sciences

Administered
Aided
Arranged
Articulated
Assisted
Assumed
Budgeted
Cataloged
Chaired
Compiled
Computerized
Conducted
Coordinated
Created
Designed
Developed
Directed
Ensured
Facilitated
Generated
Handled
Hired
Initiated
Instructed
Interviewed
Managed
Organized
Participated
Performed
Planned

Prepared
Provided
Purchased
Recorded
Recruited
Researched
Reviewed
Scouted
Served
Supervised
Taught
Trained
Transferred
Tutored
Worked
Wrote

Engineering

Analyzed
Applied
Assembled
Assisted
Conducted
Designed
Developed
Directed
Engineered
Established
Evaluated
Initiated
Inspected
Manufactured
Modified
Monitored

Observed
Operated
Oversaw
Participated
Performed
Planned
Prepared
Provided
Represented
Researched
Reviewed
Revised
Scheduled
Served
Supervised
Supported
Trained
Utilized
Worked
Wrote

Executive and Managerial

Administered
Analyzed
Appointed
Approved
Assigned
Attained
Authorized
Chaired
Considered
Consolidated
Contracted
Controlled

Converted
Coordinated
Decided
Delegated
Developed
Directed
Eliminated
Emphasized
Enforced
Enhanced
Established
Executed
Generated
Handled
Headed
Hired
Hosted
Improved
Incorporated
Increased
Initiated
Inspected
Instituted
Led
Managed
Merged
Motivated
Navigated
Obtained
Organized
Originated
Overhauled
Oversaw
Planned

Presided
Prioritized
Produced
Recommended
Reorganized
Replaced
Restored
Reviewed
Scheduled
Secured
Selected
Streamlined
Strengthened
Supervised
Synchronized
Systematized
Terminated

**Food and Beverages/
Agriculture**

Acquired
Bred
Controlled
Developed
Displayed
Distributed
Ensured
Exported
Harvested
Imported
Improved
Managed
Manufactured
Marketed

Organized
Oversaw
Planted
Produced
Researched
Sold
Supplied
Worked

Government

Campaigned
Delegated
Demonstrated
Dispatched
Investigated
Lobbied
Managed
Organized
Participated
Practiced
Processed
Raised
Researched
Served
Settled
Supervised
Supported
Updated
Volunteered

Health and Medical

Acted
Administered
Advised

Alleviated
Allocated
Analyzed
Arranged
Assessed
Assisted
Assumed
Attended
Collaborated
Completed
Conducted
Conferred
Constructed
Consulted
Coordinated
Created
Dealt
Demonstrated
Determined
Developed
Directed
Dispensed
Distributed
Drafted
Educated
Encouraged
Ensured
Established
Evaluated
Facilitated
Fielded
Filled
Formed
Functioned

Geared
Generated
Handled
Hired
Identified
Implemented
Initiated
Instructed
Interviewed
Invited
Lectured
Led
Maintained
Managed
Monitored
Motivated
Observed
Operated
Organized
Oriented
Participated
Performed
Planned
Prepared
Presented
Priced
Produced
Provided
Purchased
Ran
Received
Recommended
Recorded
Redesigned

Required
Requisitioned
Researched
Reviewed
Scheduled
Selected
Served
Serviced
Specialized
Started
Structured
Supervised
Supported
Taught
Trained
Typed
Updated
Used
Utilized
Worked
Wrote

Hotels and Restaurants
Adhered
Assisted
Communicated
Ensured
Escorted
Established
Greeted
Hired
Maintained
Managed
Monitored

Participated
Provided
Recommended
Scheduled
Supervised
Trained
Worked

Human Resources
Administered
Advised
Analyzed
Assign
Assisted
Conducted
Coordinated
Counsel
Delegated
Developed
Entered
Established
Evaluated
Expanded
Facilitated
Handled
Hired
Improved
Interpreted
Interviewed
Investigated
Logged
Maintained
Managed
Monitored

Motivated
Organized
Paid
Participated
Performed
Placed
Prepared
Professionalized
Recommend
Reconciled
Recruited
Reduced
Researched
Resolved
Responded
Reviewed
Revised
Screened
Served
Signed
Solved
Spearheaded
Supervised
Terminated
Trained
Updated
Verified
Insurance
Computed
Created
Delivered
Developed
Estimated
Evaluated

Filed
Implemented
Interacted
Negotiated
Processed
Recorded
Sold
Updated
Worked

Legal and Protective Services
Actuated
Advised
Argued
Conducted
Coordinated
Designed
Directed
Initiated
Interviewed
Negotiated
Patrolled
Practiced
Prepared
Presented
Prosecuted
Protected
Represented
Retained
Served
Supervised
Trained

Marketing and Sales
Coordinated
Created
Designed
Devised
Directed
Edited
Executed
Generated
Implemented
Initiated
Interacted
Maintained
Managed
Operated
Organized
Planned
Prepared
Sold
Supervised
Updated

Printing and Publishing
Acquired
Advertised
Announced
Conceived
Declared
Disclosed
Divulged
Edited
Executed
Issued
Maintained

Negotiated
Prepared
Printed
Proclaimed
Produced
Promulgated
Proofed
Read
Revealed
Trafficked
Wrote

Real Estate
Advised
Appraised
Assessed
Bought
Calculated
Conducted
Contracted
Directed
Explained
Handled
Negotiated
Obtained
Processed
Refinanced
Reviewed
Showed
Sold
Specialized
Toured
Updated
Worked

Retail
Bought
Catalogued
Excelled
Explained
Filled
Helped
Inventoried
Managed
Marketed
Operated
Ordered
Organized
Oversaw
Priced
Scheduled
Served
Shipped
Sold

Science
Built
Completed
Conducted
Designed
Developed
Diagnosed
Ensured
Evaluated
Examined
Filtered
Handled
Monitored
Originated

Performed
Processed
Promoted
Recorded
Researched
Sterilized
Supported
Tested

Service
Arranged
Assisted
Conducted
Demonstrated
Designed
Developed
Ensured
Evaluated
Generated
Handled
Ordered
Performed
Prepared
Provided
Received
Served
Trained
Utilized

Social and Human Services
Administered
Assessed
Assisted

Coordinated
Counseled
Established
Evaluated
Handled
Initiated
Led
Managed
Observed
Organized
Provided
Responded
Reviewed
Served
Specialized
Streamlined
Taught
Treated
Worked

Technical
Assigned
Communicated
Conducted
Created
Designed
Developed
Edited
Evaluated
Interpreted
Modified
Outlined
Programmed
Promoted

Researched
Services
Started
Tested
Trained
Updated
Used
Utilized
Worked

Transportation and Travel
Conducted
Confirmed
Contacted
Coordinated
Drove
Enforced
Filed
Flew
Handled
Instructed
Mapped
Operated
Performed
Planned
Prepared
Programmed
Scheduled
Sold
Transported
Traveled

Visual and Performing Arts

Achieved
Acted
Advertised
Assisted
Built
Choreographed
Communicated
Conceived
Coordinated
Created
Designed
Directed
Drew
Focused
Illustrated
Managed
Organized
Oversaw
Painted
Performed
Planned
Played
Produced
Revised
Sculpted
Served
Sewed
Shot
Staged
Videotaped
Worked
Wrote

Endnote: You now have plenty of action words to invigorate your resume and impress a future employer. Once you have planted all the right words in the right places on both your cover letter and resume, there is nothing left to do but click "attach" and "send." You can't control what happens once these fine-tuned materials leave your hands, but you can rest assured that you gave it your best shot.

Chapter 10

FOLLOWING UP

The *Right* Way

Persistence and communication are key in establishing a positive relationship with a prospective employer or a networking contact. Waiting for the next step in the process is a necessary evil of job hunting, but don't be afraid to break the silence in a productive way using the follow-up checklist in this chapter.

After Telephone Conversation Before an Interview

☐ Thank your contact for the time he has taken to meet, speak, or otherwise communicate with you about the position.

☐ Restate relevant experience, skills, and accomplishments that will contribute to your success in the position.

☐ Express interest in meeting with your contact for an interview.

☐ Express gratitude for your contact's consideration of your candidacy.

After a Job Interview

☐ Thank the interviewer for her time.

☐ Reiterate your interest in the position. It is acceptable to state outright that you would be thrilled to receive an offer.

☐ Briefly restate that your experience will be valuable in accomplishing the duties associated with the position.

🗨 Action Speak

Arranged	Encouraged
Contacted	Expressed
Counseled	Facilitated
Cultivated	Inventoried
Directed	Mitigated

☐ Notify your interviewer that you will check on the status of the decision-making process (if appropriate).

☐ Express your enthusiasm and end the letter by thanking your interviewer again for her time and consideration.

For a Good Reference

☐ Thank your reference for his willingness to offer support for your candidacy.

☐ Inform your reference of the outcome (hopefully positive!) of the interview.

☐ Extend an offer to return the favor if your reference ever needs your help.

☐ Thank your reference again for advocating on your behalf.

For a Letter of Recommendation

☐ Thank your contact for providing her recommendation.

☐ Notify your contact that her letter resulted in an offer being made, and that you've happily accepted it.

☐ Restate your gratitude and offer to help your contact in a similar manner should the situation arise.

For a Referral

☐ Announce your acceptance of the position for which you applied.

☐ Thank your contact for referring you for the position and putting you in touch with the appropriate person.

☐ Express your willingness to return the favor if the opportunity arises in the future.

☐ State your enthusiasm to begin your new job and thank your contact once again for his help.

After an Informational Interview

☐ Thank your interview for her time.

☐ Briefly state how the meeting influenced your pursuit of a particular position or career path. (For example, perhaps you will apply for acceptance into a specific educational program or contact a company about future employment.)

☐ Offer to keep your contact up to date on your progress.

☐ Inquire about any additional suggestions, referrals, or contact names that may assist you in the process.

> **Green Light** The more care you take to personalize your follow-up communication, the greater impact it will have on your recipient.

☐ Thank your contact again for her time.

Resurrection Letter

☐ Mention your resume is currently under review, and provide the name of your contact at the company who indicated so.

☐ Direct recipient's attention to attached (if e-mailed) or enclosed (if mailed) resume and restate your continued interest.

☐ Briefly describe relevant experience related to the position and state your interest in arranging an interview.

☐ Thank recipient for her continued consideration.

Response to a Rejection

☐ Thank your contact for giving you the opportunity to interview.

☐ Express gratitude for having been given the chance to meet him and learn more about the company.

☐ State your interest in future openings and, if applicable, freelance or contract-based assignments as well as special projects.

☐ Thank your contact again for his consideration.

Withdrawal from Consideration

☐ Remind your contact that you have submitted your resume and/or application for consideration.

☐ Notify contact of your reason for withdrawing your interest.

☐ Thank your contact for her time spent reviewing your application.

☐ Express a continued interest in the company and keep lines of communication open.

Rejection of an Offer

☐ Thank your contact for the offer of employment.

☐ Briefly explain reason for rejecting offer.

☐ Offer apologies for any inconvenience or issues that arise as a result of your rejection.

☐ Express sincere thanks for your contact's confidence in your abilities, and state that your interest in the position was sincere.

☐ Ask your contact to extend your gratitude to his colleagues for their time and consideration.

Acceptance Letter

☐ Acknowledge receipt of offer letter and state your acceptance.

☐ Express enthusiasm for the position.

☐ Confirm start date and resignation with current employer.

☐ Provide an e-mail address or phone number should contact be necessary prior to your start date.

☐ Reiterate your enthusiasm to join the company.

Address or Phone Number Change

☐ Notify your contact of the change in information.

☐ Direct attention to updated resume (whether attached or enclosed).

☐ State your interest in the position and your hopes to arrange an interview.

☐ Express gratitude for consideration of your candidacy.

Resignation Letter

☐ State, with regret, your resignation and effective date.

☐ Briefly describe your reason for resigning.

☐ Inquire about formal steps to take in order to complete any projects in progress.

☐ Inquire about necessary documentation from Human Resources.

☐ Thank current employer for the experience.

☐ Offer to be as involved in the transition process as possible.

☐ State your desire to continue a professional relationship with your employer.

☐ Express gratitude again for the opportunity to have worked there.

Endnote: As you've learned, following up is one more way to establish a healthy level of accountability between you and your prospective employer. With a graceful turn of phrase, you can open doors for yourself. Keep the communication lines open on your end and you will invite them to communicate as well.

PART III

Interviewing Phrases That Close the Deal

TALKING THE WALK

Chapter 11

Interview Preparation

When you become one of the small pool of top applicants who are asked to interview for a position, you know you're doing something right. Your cover letter and resume have effectively conveyed you as a prized employee and a skilled professional. Now it's time to show them that you *are* in fact as good as you sound on paper. Every interview is different—mostly because every interviewer has a different idea of the types of questions they'll ask you. Some may focus on your past work experience without getting into personal details, and others may rely on personal questions to help them figure out if you're a good fit for the company. You need to be ready for any type of question that comes your way. This chapter reviews basic etiquette and helps you begin to develop your interview persona. You can use the language in this section during interviews or even apply it to your resume.

Use the advice that follows to prepare and practice—and ultimately get the job!

Preparing to Answer Questions

You will be asked a variety of questions on a job interview. These questions will pertain to your skills and abilities, accomplishments, education, and work history. You will also be asked questions about your strengths and weaknesses, your interests and hobbies, and your likes and dislikes, all of which will allow the employer to learn about your personal traits or characteristics.

In the chapters that follow, you will find answers and key phrases to use when responding to questions you might encounter on a job interview. Use them as a guideline. While you should not go into a job interview with a memorized script, you should have an idea of how you will answer most questions that will come your way. Chapter 19 gives you ideas for the types of questions you should ask the interviewer. Use these questions in the same way—as a guideline to be adapted to your particular situation and the company and industry you are interviewing with.

Be Specific

On a job interview, you will be asked questions about your skills, for example. Of course, you know what skills you have, but can you discuss how you acquired them? What if you're asked about your accomplishments? You've no doubt accomplished a lot at work, but can you recall specifics? You need anecdotes that clearly back up your claims, so it is imperative that you prepare in advance and have some good examples of your strengths ready when the subject comes up.

Take Time to Rehearse

In preparing for job interviews it is important that you do some practice interviewing, both alone and with others. Rehearsing for interviews will allow you to work on any problems that may be viewed as negatives by the interviewer. Rehearsing will also allow you to become more comfortable with the interview process. By the time you go on an interview, you will have no problem confidently answering questions.

The First Defining Moments

The first minute or two of any interview is the most crucial. As the saying goes, you only get one chance to make a great first impression, and this is when you want to do just that. Your goal is to wow the interviewer and make a favorable impression that will give you an edge over some of your rivals and open the door to an offer of employment.

Introducing Yourself

When the interviewer arrives, it's show time. If you appear shy or intimidated, an interviewer may not want to dig too deep and embarrass you; that said, she will not ask you the really difficult questions—the questions that get you the job. It's human nature to judge a person by their first impression; it's that first impression that hooks many of us when we fall in love. You and your interviewer do not need to fall in love, but you do need to fall "in like." It shouldn't be difficult to do this, as long as you know what the interviewer is looking for.

Maintaining Eye Contact

When the time for your interview arrives and you get the chance to meet the person who will be grilling you for the next hour or so, stand up and greet him with a warm smile and maintain constant eye contact during your articulate introduction. Establishing eye contact is probably one of the most important parts of your introduction. You want to make sure that you look the interviewer directly in the eye as you are being introduced and/or shake hands. At the same time, you don't want to make him uncomfortable, so be sure not to stare.

Have a Firm Handshake

Similar limitations are placed on the handshake; while you don't want your handshake to be so light that the interviewer is forced to check for a pulse, you also don't want to be so enthusiastic that she winds up in the emergency room with a fracture. In your preinterview sessions with a friend, practice your handshake so that you will be able to offer up a firm grip with a quick shake or two of the hand. Then, don't hold on for dear life; let go.

Starting Off on the Right Foot

Before getting down to the important stuff—like why you would do well with this company—it is likely that the interviewer will engage you in a bit of small talk to get the conversation flowing. Prepare for these questions as well. Don't mistake, for example, "How was your ride in?" or "Did you have any problem finding us?" for anything other than small talk. The interview really is not interested in whether or not you hit any traffic or encountered any accidents on your way to the office. If you anticipate simple questions like these, you can be better prepared to answer them without bogging down the flow of conversation.

All too often, job seekers make the mistake of launching into a huge dialogue about how long it took them to get to the office, how they found a great short cut, and so on. The last thing an interviewer wants—or needs—in response to these initial questions is anything longer than "Great," "Fine," or "No problem!" Also, regardless of how nervous you may be, don't let small-talk questions like these dumbfound you. After all, if you have trouble answering a simple question about the weather, how are you going to help this company come up with a winning marketing strategy?

 RED FLAG!
DON'T BE VERBOSE. It can cause the interviewer to question your suitability to the company immediately.

Upon arriving at the interviewer's office or area of your destination, wait until the interviewer tells you to be seated before sitting, then sit (don't plunk) on the designated chair or sofa. Stick with that chair or sofa even if it proves to be uncomfortable. In fact, you don't want to be too comfortable. You want to keep alert, not doze off!

Be on your best behavior. The traditional rules of etiquette should be observed at all times during a job interview. Don't yawn, chew gum, or fidget. A few more things could be added to this list:

- Don't mimic the body language or mannerisms of the interviewer. (This can happen when you get nervous.)

- Don't keep looking at your watch.

- Don't be negative.

- Don't talk too much.

- Don't ask about money, perks, or things that are unrelated to the job or company at hand.

- Don't move or touch anything on the interviewer's desk. This office is his "home," and you wouldn't want a stranger to touch things in your home.

If your interview is going well and you are sure this is a job you want, don't be afraid to say so. Sometimes candidates who seem to be perfect for the job are passed over simply because they never let the interviewer know they wanted it.

Don't let this happen to you. Don't be afraid to be proactive, and don't be bashful. Wrap up your interview by giving some of the reasons you like the company before asking about your prospects. Make it clear that you think this job was made for you and vice versa.

Set a Tone

The tone of the meeting depends on the personality of the interviewer. He may ask a straight line of professional questions, or he may be more lighthearted and laid back. Regardless of the manner of the interviewer, you should always prepare your answers in a very professional way.

One mistake that candidates often make is to prepare for each question by brainstorming the "perfect" answer. They think about the kind of answer the perfect candidate would give and use that. In most of these instances, the job seeker is wasting the company's time. Trying to project the perfect image can only result in disaster because often the interviewer sees right through it. On the other hand, if the interviewer buys into the candidate's perfect persona, she may be surprised when—once hired—the candidate does not perform as perfectly as expected.

💬 Action Speak

Authorized	Piloted
Conducted	Projected
Diagnosed	Routed
Established	Standardized
Innovated	Surpassed

Though you shouldn't highlight your faults to the employer, neither should you pretend to be someone or something you are not. Many career experts think that the best way to set and maintain a professional tone throughout an interview is to create a sort of job interview persona. Think about the many personal traits a job interviewer would be interested in and be sure to project those characteristics. Which of your traits would make you a strong candidate and set you apart from the rest of the candidates? Think about the many successful people you know or have heard about and the personality traits that make them good leaders. How can you convey to the interviewer that these qualifications are part of your own professional nature?

Think of yourself as a calm, cool, and collected individual. With any luck, your research has provided you with an understanding of the company's vision. If you can link this vision to your own personal vision for your career, you should make a strong impression on your interviewer.

Remember, however, that in the end you have no control over the outcome of an interview; you do not decide whether or not you get the job. In many cases, you could conduct yourself perfectly throughout the interview and still not get the job. On the other hand, you could feel like you've botched the entire interview and still receive an offer.

The only thing you do have control over during the interview is what you do and say while you're there. Always keep the following key qualities an interviewer is looking for in the back of your mind and be sure to convey your aptitude in each of them:

- Adaptability
- Competence
- Confidence
- Creativity
- Dedication
- Dependability
- Easygoing nature
- Enthusiasm
- Leadership ability
- Motivation
- Problem-solving ability
- Resourcefulness

Endnote: Think of these qualities in every answer you give and everything you say, and you should have no problem projecting the image of a confident and competent candidate.

Chapter 12

SPEAKING WITH CONFIDENCE

...About Your Achievements

A prospective employer wants to know, first and foremost, that you will have a positive impact on his company. Your job in the interview is to prove this to him by speaking about your professional achievements. This takes practice and careful wording: Prepare a list of your accomplishments prior to your job interview and use the power phrases and action words recommended in this chapter. The accomplishments you choose to highlight should demonstrate skills and abilities that are most relevant to the job at hand. They should also be realistic and verifiable. Don't be afraid to brag, but overall you should aim for confidence, not cockiness.

One good rule of thumb is this: Use actual numbers or percentages when you are discussing anything that can be expressed in quantifiable terms, such as increases in profits or decreases in costs. Being able to say that you increased sales by 20 percent or cut your department's costs by 35 percent is much better than saying "I increased sales a lot" or "I cut costs greatly."

Be selective. The key to success in discussing achievements is to focus on two or three that clearly demonstrate the skills your prospective employer is seeking. The best thing about accomplishments is that they can be examples from your professional career, academic years, or personal experiences. Use the following examples to highlight your achievements.

Professional and Personal Accomplishments

Q: Tell me about a major accomplishment in your life.

How to phrase it: *As the publicity director of a tiny, alternative publishing house, it can be difficult to get major sources to review our books. Because the subjects we cover are often far from the mainstream, many television shows and review publications find our topics a bit too controversial. Last year, we published a book that I really thought could be a number one bestseller. Though* **I always put forth a lot of effort** *to publicize all of the books we published, I was particularly interested in seeing this little gem find its way from obscurity to popularity.* **Because of my efforts**, *coverage of this book was astronomical, and the book became a New York Times bestseller, with both the author and the book becoming household names.*

RED FLAG!
DON'T STRETCH THE TRUTH, as interviewers have ways of finding out whether your story is true.

Talk to the interviewer about an accomplishment in your life that you are most proud of. The accomplishment should be work related, but it doesn't have to be. Be honest and be specific. Don't just throw out a general statement ("I won an award"); describe the steps you took to accomplish this goal and how all your hard work paid off in the end. One job seeker brought along a picture of herself receiving a prestigious award from a well-known celebrity at an industry awards dinner. It stimulated conversation and made an impression on the interviewer, who would be likely to remember the candidate after the interview was over. Don't be long-winded; instead, focus on your actual accomplishments and the steps leading up to them. The interviewer wants to know whether you will be able to contribute something to this company; this is a great opportunity to prove that you can.

Q: Tell me about a project you completed ahead of schedule.

How to phrase it: *I* **was in charge of** *a new product rollout. In general we completed each phase without a major setback—which was partially luck—but I also systematically called* **two days ahead of every deadline** *to check the status with all groups involved. I believe that is what made the real difference. The launch took place* **two weeks ahead of plan**—*a very significant period of time in our industry, where shelf life for products is generally less than one year.*

In discussing how you were able to complete a project ahead of schedule, make sure that you are not forcing the interviewer to question the integrity of the project, or the attention to detail you displayed while working on it. Focus on how you set goals and schedules, measured results, and championed the outcome of a project. This question is aimed at your diligence in accomplishing tasks and, assuming the project required group effort, at your leadership skills.

Q: Can you tell me about your greatest accomplishment at work?

How to phrase it: *I'm particularly proud of the mentoring program I started about five years ago. I noticed that new employees were having trouble getting acclimated to the company, causing a very high turnover rate during the first year of employment. I developed a program that allowed us to assign each new employee to an employee who had been with the company for at least three years. This allowed new hires to make a smoother transition. Now, 90 percent of new employees are still with us after their one-year anniversaries, up from 50 percent before we started the mentorship program.*

The interviewee provides a specific example in response to this question. She also highlights the fact that she took initiative in developing it; she saw a problem and found a solution. She also shows the result of her efforts with actual numbers.

Q: Describe how you accomplished a work-related goal.

How to phrase it: *When I started working for Daylight Publications, I discovered that I had inherited a huge file cabinet full of photographs. We used photographs in our magazine but usually wound up purchasing stock photos, because our own collection was so disorganized it was impossible to find anything. I designed a filing system and set about putting things in order. I set aside fifteen minutes each day and was able to work my way through the whole collection in about seven months.*

This answer demonstrates how the interviewee took the initiative to set a goal in order to save her employer

money. She then talks about how she went about reaching that goal by using her organization and time management skills.

Q: Can you describe how you accomplished a personal goal?

How to phrase it: *I wrote a short story and my goal was to get it published. I went to the library and researched which magazines accepted short-story submissions. Then I sent my story to the magazines that published stories in the same genre as mine. My story was accepted by one of them and was finally published a little over a year ago.*

This candidate talks about the steps he took to reach his personal goal. He used his research skills to find out where to send his story.

Q: What has been your greatest accomplishment as part of a team?

How to phrase it: *I worked on a team that developed a program for children who were going home to an empty house after school because their parents worked. We had volunteers who would help the kids with their homework and give them time to just burn off energy after sitting in a classroom all day. By the time we actually opened the center, we had seventy-five children enrolled. That told us we were providing a service that was clearly needed.*

This candidate describes in detail the project she considers her greatest accomplishment as part of a team. She talks about what was needed, what they did to fill that need, and what the end result was.

Q: Name the two work-related accomplishments that you are the proudest of.

How to phrase it: *I **converted** a manual payroll system to a computerized system, which **cut down the amount of time** we spent on payroll each week. I **wrote a manual** that explained all bookkeeping department procedures in our company. New employees receive a copy of this manual, which **helps them learn their job faster**.*

Each of the accomplishments this candidate discusses has had a positive result on the company and highlights his many skills.

Q: Tell me about the personal accomplishment that you are the proudest of.

How to phrase it: *Last year I **ran a marathon for the first time**. I've been a runner for years, but I never ran more than four miles at a time. I began training four months before the big day. **It was hard, but I kept going** and I ended up finishing in just over four hours, which I've heard is pretty good for a first-time marathoner.*

By discussing running a marathon, this candidate demonstrates that she will work hard to reach her goals. She also shows that she is not afraid of a challenge, something her prospective employer should appreciate.

Green Light Phrases

Increase in profits	Growth of sales
Ahead of schedule	Developed a program
Designed a system	Took the initiative
Set my goal	Filled a need
Go the extra mile	Decrease costs

Q: What accomplishments have you made so far in reaching your long-range goals?

How to phrase it: ***My long-range goal is** to be a school principal. I've been teaching for ten years, first at PS 118 and then at PS 114. **After five years of teaching** second grade at PS 114, **I was asked to be grade leader**. My experience working with faculty and developing new programs for students has prepared me for the position of assistant principal. I look forward to using my skills to work on some of the projects we discussed earlier.*

This candidate has demonstrated how he has taken steps to reach his goal and plans to continue to do so. He also makes a point of talking about the contributions he plans to make in the job that he's interviewing for.

Q: What motivates you to go above and beyond the call of duty?

How to phrase it: *Honestly, I don't have a sense of what is above and beyond the call of duty. It's not like I can just do enough to get by and then stop. When I work on a project, **I do my very best, always.***

This statement shows that this job candidate is truly a hard worker who cares about her work. It's more than just a job to her. She can't justify giving less than her best effort to any project entrusted to her.

Q: Have you ever been asked to take on a project because of your unique skill or ability?

How to phrase it: *Our senior developer regularly asks me to troubleshoot new programs. I've been **very**

successful at figuring out *why programs aren't working properly, and I can usually do it pretty quickly,* ***allowing the team to move forward***.

This candidate chose to talk about a skill that will be as valuable to his prospective employer as it is to his current one.

Contributions You've Made

Q: Tell me about a contribution you've made to a team accomplishment.

How to phrase it: ***In my current company, all projects are group projects***. *My last work group was made up of five very intelligent and very creative people. However, the overall technical skills were a bit lacking. People knew how they wanted our presentation to look, but they didn't know how to go about achieving it. I am an* ***avid computer user*** *and* ***have taken several classes in*** *graphic design. I think our group's final product was a good mix of creativity and technology.* ***I used my computer skills to help our team come up with a fantastic presentation that the client accepted without hesitation.***

Even if you spend most of your time working independently—or work independently because you choose to—the interviewer wants to be reassured that you deal with other people well. When placed within a group setting, do you immediately try to take control or do you offer up a certain expertise? Think about the kinds of tasks you've performed before in group settings and the skills that you have mastered. What would the other members of your team say about your contributions?

Would they want to work with you again? Would they consider your skills vital to the team's success? Offer proof, using specific examples, that you delivered more than the team expected and that the team would compliment your contributions to the group's efforts.

💬 Action Speak

Combined	Learned
Fixed	Proved
Formed	Spoke
Indexed	Taught
Interpreted	Validated

Q: Are there any special contributions you feel you've made to your employer?

How to phrase it: *For the past four years, I have run a Walk for Hunger campaign at my company as part of our corporate social responsibility program. I believe that it is a very important cause, and I know* ***it can be difficult for a company to find volunteers, so I stepped in to help***. *Each year has been more successful than the last, and coworkers have told me it's one of the things they look forward to most throughout the course of the year, which obviously makes me very happy.*

Convince the interviewer that you are ready to go the extra mile for your employer. Tell her about a specific time when you delivered more than the employer expected. If you were hired, what situations would you handle especially well? What unique contributions can you make to the organization? How would you go the extra mile?

Q: Tell me about a quantifiable outcome of one of your efforts.

How to phrase it: *I **reorganized** inventory planning and **was able to** automate the inventory-recorder function. **A task that used to take forty hours to complete now only takes five**!*

One truth—in business, especially—is that numbers don't lie. One of the easiest way to showcase your accomplishments is to quantify them. But remember, unless you're talking about sales dollars or company profits, don't talk dollar amounts or the earnings of colleagues. Describe a specific accomplishment that produced a clear benefit. Offer proof, using real examples, that you deliver more than what's expected.

Q: Tell me how you were of value to your previous employer.

How to phrase it: *My previous employer valued my ability to deal with difficult clients. **Whenever we had a client who was very demanding, my boss would ask me to be the one to work with him**. She said she knew I was so levelheaded that I would always stay calm, even when a client was really trying my patience.*

With this answer the candidate not only says why he thinks his boss values him, he talks about it from her perspective. He presents a skill that will be valuable to this employer as well.

Q: Have you ever had to take over an assignment at the last minute?

How to phrase it: *I've had to do that more than once—actually several times. The most recent was when a colleague was scheduled to attend a meeting out of town and came down with the flu two days before he was supposed to leave. **My boss asked me if I could attend the meeting and make the presentation my colleague was supposed to make**. I had two days to learn everything about the project. I went over pages and pages of notes and put together a presentation of my own, incorporating input from my colleague, who I spoke to on the phone several times a day.*

Not only does this interviewee say he has taken over an assignment at the last minute, he talks about a specific case. He shows how he stepped in and learned what he needed to learn to make a successful presentation.

Q: If I asked your current employer to tell us about your accomplishments, what do you think she would say?

How to phrase it: *She would probably talk about the time **she asked me to present** a new marketing campaign to one of our more difficult clients. **I spent over a week preparing** for that presentation. Since I knew this client was hard to please, I had to make sure I anticipated every objection he might have. He actually loved the presentation, and **the campaign increased sales by 50 percent**.*

This question gives the candidate a chance to talk about an accomplishment he is proud of. He talks about anticipating possible difficulties and the end result, an increase in sales.

Q: If I asked a college professor about one of your accomplishments, what would he or she say?

How to phrase it: *I **worked on a major research project** under the supervision of my psychology professor. We collected data **over the course of a year** and after ana-lyzing the data, we wrote up the results as an article that we submitted to the Journal of Kangaroo Psychology. **It was accepted, and it was published** a month before I graduated.*

This candidate chose to talk about something that had a tangible result—publication in a professional journal.

Q: Have you ever come up with new ways to solve a problem?

How to phrase it: *Yes, I have. **We had a problem with** dismissal from our after-school program. Too many children were leaving at once, causing a bit of chaos in our parking lot. I **developed a system for** releasing children alphabetically so that parents could pick up siblings in different grades at the same time. If we had released children by grade, parents would have had to wait around for children who were in different grade lev-els. That would have added to the chaos.*

The candidate states a specific problem and then dis-cusses the steps she took to solve it. She even mentions how she anticipated and then prevented a potential problem.

Q: What situations do your colleagues rely on you to handle?

How to phrase it: *Whenever we're faced with a difficult or dissatisfied client, **my coworkers come to me**. Unlike some of my coworkers, I never lose my temper in front of customers. **My ability to remain objective has proven extremely important**, especially when dealing with an irate client.*

Even within a strictly team setting, there are obviously situations that you are better at handling than your col-leagues are. Even though you may not be singled out to deal with each of these situations, tell the interviewer about the situations that you excel in. Which situations are you more qualified for (or better at handling) than your peers? This question provides a good opportunity for you to showcase your dependability, strength of character, and professionalism.

Q: Have you ever "saved the day" for your employer?

How to phrase it: *Yes, I have. It was the afternoon before our company was hosting a big luncheon. We called the caterer to confirm some of the details, but her number had been disconnected. We found out she had gone out of business and didn't bother to let us know. I called some friends at other companies and got a list of cater-ers together, called them, and got someone to do the job. **My boss couldn't believe I managed to hire some-one on such short notice.***

The interviewee, by giving this example, shows how her resourcefulness helped her solve her employer's problem.

Q: Have you ever done something that directly helped your employer either increase profits or decrease costs?

How to phrase it: *I recently **found a way to help my employer save money** on office supplies. For years, they bought office supplies from the same place. It was several blocks away, so it was pretty convenient. I have found that shopping online is almost always less expensive than shopping in a store, so **I did a little comparison shopping** and I found an online source for our office supplies at a **savings of 40 percent** from what we were paying for the same items. Plus, the items are delivered, which is even more convenient. As long as we order several items at once, delivery is free.*

This interviewee's answer illustrates how she looks out for her employer's best interests.

Challenges You've Overcome

Q: Tell me about an accomplishment you had a difficult time achieving.

How to phrase it: *Years ago, when I first began working for my current company, part of my job required meeting with our technical support staff once a week to find out about any technical problems or issues we faced. As part of the human resources team, **it was my duty to** voice any concerns to the right people and get the problems fixed. I didn't have very much experience with computers. For the most part, I didn't understand their complaints. Back then, I didn't even know what a modem was, and I certainly didn't know how to increase the speed of one.*

*I decided that **to do a great job, I would need to learn more** about what it was that each of our departments did. Whenever I could find the time, I would go down to the technical department and sit in for a while. When I had questions, I would ask them. The staff was always very happy to answer and seemed pleased that I had taken so much interest in learning more about their job. Although I definitely **struggled for the first month** or so, **I now make a consistent effort to keep pace with new technology** because I have seen first hand how it impacts employee satisfaction and overall productivity.*

Be careful what you are implying when you answer this question. Citing an instance in which the problem was a coworker can make you sound as though you're not much of a team player, a bit of a know-it-all, or worse, a dinosaur who won't change with the times. Talk to the interviewer about a time when you accomplished something despite obstacles, lack of training, or inadequate experience. Focus on your ability to overcome this problem and achieve successful results. Express your willingness to accept challenges and triumph over them.

Q: Tell me about something you accomplished that required strict discipline.

How to phrase it: *When I was a full-time graduate student, my one goal was to avoid accruing any more student loan debt. In addition to working toward an advanced degree in journalism, I spent twenty hours a week as an intern at a local magazine and another twenty-five hours a week as a waitress. **Juggling these three hectic, very demanding schedules was certainly*** *a challenge, but it makes me appreciate all that I have achieved*.

Here's another opportunity for you to discuss a skill you have had to work hard to develop and have been successful doing. This is also an opportunity to discuss a time when the amount of work you had and the time you needed to finish it were a challenge. Discuss your strong time management skills and how you are able to prioritize to accomplish your goal. How did you remain focused? What were the results? What did you learn from the experience?

Q: Tell me about the most difficult work or personal experience you've ever had to face.

How to phrase it: *A coworker with whom I was very close was going through a very difficult time and had begun to abuse drugs and alcohol. With our firm's support, he decided that the best thing for him was to attend a rehabilitation center.* **For the next six months, I had to take on much of this person's work in addition to my own**. *While the long hours and added pressure were not the ideal situation, I know that he would have done the same for me, so I never once regretted my decision. It's very important to me to have that kind of trust among the members of my work group, and I am* **glad that I was able to help a friend in need**. *It is certainly something I will always be* **proud of**.

The ultimate goal of this question is to find out how well you handle pressure. Ideally, you want to describe a situation—personal or professional—that involved a great deal of conflict and challenge and, as a result, placed you under an unusual amount of stress. Explain,

specifically, what the problems were and what you did to resolve them. What was the result? Is it something you would do again?

Q: How have you handled criticism of your work in the past?

How to answer it: *The first time I ever had a client complain to me, I was devastated. The client was upset about the downtime in ATM machines. Though her complaint had nothing to do with my professional service of the account, I did take it a bit personally. However, rather than dwell on my own disappointment,* **I began to work very closely with this client to see whether there was something I could do about her suggestion**. *While I couldn't change our ATM system, I was able to learn a lot from the experience. I learned that showing empathy usually calms an unpleasant situation. I also learned that no client is going to be happy with everything, even if that client's overall experience is positive. I know that I should not take things personally and, instead, focus on initiatives that will* **yield customer satisfaction without distracting from my core duties**.

The interviewer is trying to learn something about your accountability and professional character. Talk about a time when you were engaged in a specific project or work habit that caused you a problem. Then discuss how you finally faced up to the problem and overcame it. Alternatively, you might describe a time you responded objectively and professionally to particularly harsh or unreasonable criticism of your work. In either case, finish the comment by talking about what you learned from this experience. Remember: Always keep things positive, and refrain from complaining or slandering any past work associates.

RED FLAG!

DON'T PRETEND TO BE PERFECT. "I can't think of anything I've ever failed at" or "I've never had a project that failed" are poor answers to an interview question about failure. Everyone has failed at one time or another, and it's okay to admit it.

Q: Tell me about one of your projects that failed.

How to phrase it: *I've always been somewhat of a work-aholic and have the attitude that I can tackle anything and achieve good results. After a rather destructive hurricane, my insurance company was inundated with claims. I really believed that I was completely capable of handling all the claims in my area and **dove right into a series of eighteen-hour workdays**. Even when others in the office would offer to help, I reassured them that I had it all under control. After about a week and a half, I realized that there was no way I could complete all of the claims on time and on my own. I had to begin **delegating** some of the responsibility to my investigators. **What I learned was that no matter how efficient and competent you are, there are always situations in which you need to ask for help from others**.*

Make sure that you demonstrate the ability to be humble when answering this type of question. Show the employer how much you can learn from your mistakes. In hindsight, what do you think you could have and should have done differently? How have you altered your leadership or professional style as a result of this experience?

Q: Tell me about a time when you had a real problem getting along with one of your work associates.

How to phrase it: *I have always thought of myself as an **easygoing** person; **I tend to get along with most people**. However, I do remember one time when we brought in a new associate who was very bossy—bossy to the point where his attitude really offended one of our interns. As this was not the type of management style that our employees were used to, I took it upon myself to pull the new associate aside and explain that **I found it more productive to ask people for help than to give orders**. Unfortunately, he seemed more offended by my concern for our employees and about the sour relationship he was beginning to form with them than pleased with or grateful for my attempt to help him. The advice didn't change anything with his attitude, but we were much more careful with our hiring process after that experience.*

The best way to answer this question is to discuss a difference in work ethic between you and an associate, not an all-out hatred for each other. Avoid discussing a personality clash between you and a coworker. Instead, speak about a situation with which the interviewer is likely to empathize. For example, you might describe someone whose standards of excellence were perhaps less stringent than yours. Be sure to talk about the steps you took to mend this problem and the end result.

Q: Have you ever had to work with a manager who you thought was unfair to you or who was just plain difficult to get along with?

How to phrase it: *Fortunately, I've never really run into that problem. Of course, my current boss has to work under time constraints—just like everyone else—and she sometimes has a tendency to phrase things rather bluntly to push our department to meet its goals. But I've never considered that unfair or hard to handle; it's just part of the job.* **My supervisors and I have always gotten along quite well.**

Again, no matter how many times an interviewer gives you the opportunity to do so, never criticize a current or former employer! The interviewer is not really interested in finding out whether or not you have worked for difficult people in the past—we all have. What he is trying to discover is whether or not (and how easily) you are willing to badmouth these people.

Q: How do you handle tension with your boss?

How to phrase it: *The only tension I've ever felt occurred only once, when we both got too busy to keep each other informed. My boss overcommitted me with a short deadline, not knowing I was bogged down with another client problem.* **I believe firmly in the importance of staff meetings** *to keep coworkers aware and* **respectful** *of the demands on each other's time, and I* **worked closely with my boss** *to develop a formalized meeting schedule.*

Though the question itself is set in the present tense, your best bet in answering it is to use the past tense. The safest ground here is to describe an example of a miscommunication in your early relationship with a boss and how you resolved it. Talk about the problem itself, but focus more on how the two of you handled the problem. Describe the steps you have taken since that incident to ensure that a similar problem does not reoccur.

Recognition and Rewards You've Received

Q: Have you ever received formal recognition for something you accomplished?

How to phrase it: *Yes.* **I won Salesperson of the Month four times** *when I was working for Ace Stereo. Those with* **the largest increase in sales** *over the previous month were rewarded in this way.*

This candidate chose to discuss being rewarded for something that would be valued by any company—high sales volume.

Q: How has your employer rewarded your accomplishments?

How to phrase it: *My employer initially rewarded me by trusting me enough to give me additional responsibility. This gave me a chance to* **prove myself***, and I was ultimately* **rewarded with a big promotion***.*

This candidate discusses how at first his reward was simply being asked to do more. Did he object to that? No. It only gave him the opportunity to further prove himself so that he received the reward of a promotion.

Q: You seem to have accomplished a lot in your current job. Do you know why you weren't promoted?

How to phrase it: *I wasn't promoted because unfortunately there wasn't a position to promote me to*. JFR was a very small family-owned firm. The boss's two sons held the top positions, which were right above my position.

The candidate explains why he couldn't move beyond his current position in spite of his accomplishments. He doesn't seem resentful, but rather accepts this fact.

Endnote: In an interview situation, your achievements are the best indicator of your value. If you prepare yourself to speak about them with confidence and clarity and make use of the key phrases provided, you should have no problem convincing the interviewer of your worth.

Chapter 13

SPEAKING WITH AUTHORITY

... About Your Skills and Experience

You've learned how to build confidence in your interviewer that you have a record of success. This chapter will deepen your interviewing skills with a focus on key phrases to utilize when questioned about your specific skills, work experience, and personal interests. Employers are looking for two different branches of skills. First, they want to ensure that you have the hard skills, or technical skills, that the job requires. Your interview responses need to demonstrate proficiency in these skills by drawing on specific examples of how you used them in the past. Work-place skills, also called soft skills, are also important to them. Do you have the people skills to deal with various clients? Do you know how to work without constant supervision? How are your decision-making and problem-solving abilities, and can you work on a team? By the end of the interview, you'll want the interviewer to have placed a mental checkmark next to each of these categories. With the right interview persona and a careful choice of words, you'll prove that you're the best candidate for the job.

Key Skills and Abilities

Q: What are your key skills?

How to phrase it: *After spending the past six years as a senior systems analyst, I've developed **a number of important skills, including** business modeling, process re-engineering, software-package evaluation, and advanced programming capabilities in UNIX and C environments. **I was very pleased to discover that these are the skills you are seeking**. Would you like to hear about specific examples of my work?*

Talk about your key skills and how you'll use them in this job. Avoid using clichés or generalities. Offer specific evidence, drawing parallels between your current or previous job and the job you're interviewing for.

> **Green Light** Don't be afraid to ask a question in your interview answer such as, "Would you like more specific examples?"

Q: What skills do you think are most critical to this job?

How to phrase it: *As technology is ever changing, I think that it is important to keep up with the latest marketing trends. **Knowing what kinds of new technologies exist** and how to go about incorporating them into my own marketing plans is what will **keep me ahead of the competition**. Creativity is also of major importance to the marketing industry; new ideas can quickly become stale and stagnant. A **successful** marketing associate will always be **looking ahead to the next big revolution**.*

If, just a few years ago, I had not been aware of the important role that the web would play in our day-to-day duties, my current company could have been wiped out by the competition.

When describing the skills you feel are most important, make sure that you know how these skills relate to the position at hand. Illustrate how the cited skills have helped you in your current and/or past positions.

Q: If you were to stay in your current job, what kinds of tasks would you spend more time on and why?

How to phrase it: ***If I were to stay at my current job, I'd like to gain more experience in** labor negotiating. **In particular**, I'd like to help negotiate labor contracts, **resolve** grievances at the step-4 level, and prepare grievances for arbitration. Though I have a very **strong background in all areas of** human resources, I believe that a **strong grasp of** labor relations experience will **round out my skills** so that I could have the **opportunity to move up** to a position of department head and possibly vice president.*

In answering this question, think about the aspects of your job that interest you most. What are the areas you would like to strengthen and advance in? What are the areas you need work in so that you could advance? Talk about the current responsibilities that give you the most satisfaction. Talk about the career path you are heading down and how the sharpening of certain skills can help you attain your goals.

> **Green Light** One smart move (and one that will score you points in the motivation department) is to talk about the possibility of advancement.

Q: What skills would you like to develop in this job?

How to phrase it: *I'd like to* **develop** *my negotiating skills. I've had* **considerable experience** *interpreting and implementing large contracts, but I've been limited in negotiating the actual conditions, costs, and standards for a major contract. I believe* **this job will offer me the opportunity to** *be a member of a negotiating team so I can begin* **acquiring the skills necessary to lead the team**.

Make sure you are not inhabiting an imaginary world in your answer to this question! First, your answer should coincide with skills that this job will help you develop. Second, you should have already covered some of the prerequisites to developing the skills you mention. For example, you wouldn't want to apply for a job as a receptionist with the Joffrey Ballet and say that you hope to develop your ballet skills.

Answering this question gives you an opportunity to talk a little bit about all your different skills. Discuss your hard (technical) skills, such as your computer knowledge and customer service skills. It's also important to focus on the soft skills you'd like to develop. Describe your functional skills, such as organizing, problem solving, writing, listening, and communicating, as well as personal skills, such as how well you work with others, whether or not you are able to assert authority, and how well you manage your time.

Q: How well do you write?

How to phrase it: *I would say that my writing skills are* **above average**. *I made a very* **conscious effort to develop these skills** *while I was working toward my MBA. I even took an entrepreneurial class in which the chief assignment was to develop, write, and continually rewrite a business plan. I have* **brought it along if you would like to see it**.

A great way to prepare for an interview is to overprepare. If you anticipate a question such as this one, bring along a sample of your work. For more creative positions (photographer, copywriter, graphic artist, and so on), always be sure to pack your portfolio so that the interviewer can see your work and assess your talent for himself. Even if the job you are applying for is not creative in nature, there may be some writing involved. A sharp set of writing skills is always a great asset.

Q: Could you tell me a little bit about your computer skills?

How to phrase it: *I would consider myself very* **well versed** *when it comes to computers. In my current position, I* **typically use Microsoft Word, PowerPoint, and Excel**. *I am also* **familiar with** *various graphic design programs, including Quark, Photoshop, and Adobe Illustrator. I have some experience with Macintosh systems as well.* **I am a pro when it comes to navigating the Internet** *and have even picked up a bit of knowledge as far as HTML programming goes.*

Computer literacy is a must in today's job market, no matter what the position. A working knowledge of a word processing program such as Microsoft Word is essential, and familiarity with database management or graphics programs is valuable as well. If your computer experience is rather limited, have a friend tutor you in an MS Office Suite application, or visit the local library and try to find your way around some of the most basic word processing programs. These programs are simple to learn and will allow you to avoid having to say that you have very limited or no computer skills. You must be web savvy and have a knowledge of e-mail. Windows remains the dominant platform in the work force, but Macintosh environments are prevalent in creative fields such as advertising, publishing, and design.

Q: How are your presentation skills? How do you prepare for presentations?

How to phrase it: *I didn't always like making presentations, but since I had to make a lot of them on my last two jobs, **I've gotten very good at it**. I do a lot of research before any presentation. **I try to find out as much as possible** about the client, the market they are trying to reach, their competitors, and the industry. Sometimes, **if the budget allows for it**, I hire an expert to help me with the research.*

This candidate answered honestly. He knows it's not that unusual to dislike presentations, so he's not afraid to admit that. It also gives him the opportunity to show off his experience and how it has gotten him over his fear. In addition, he knows the importance of having good information and knows what resources he needs to use to get it.

Q: How do your skills relate to this job?

How to phrase it: *I am very organized, I work well on a team, and I have very good communication skills. **Although I haven't worked in this field before, I know these skills will make me a valuable employee.***

Although this applicant is new to the field, she has some very desirable skills, which she makes a point of letting the interviewer know.

Q: Tell me about a crisis you encountered at work and how you handled it.

How to phrase it: *Last year a virus was causing our computers to send out thousands of e-mail messages to our clients. We were being inundated with angry phone calls before we even knew what was going on. Our technical support person was on vacation, so **I made a few phone calls and found someone to fix the problem**. Then I drafted an apology that was sent out by e-mail to our clients.*

This answer is good because the candidate clearly describes the problem and gives specifics on how she solved it. In addition, the crisis is one that could have caused her boss to lose clients, something that would strike fear into the hearts of most employers, including the one interviewing her.

Q: How do you manage your time?

How to phrase it: *I **prioritize** my work. I figure out what needs to get done first, next, and so on. Then **I calculate how much time I will need to spend on each activity or project. I set a schedule for myself and get going**.*

This applicant has a plan. He knows how to prioritize and apportion the proper amount of time to each activity.

Q: Have you ever had to juggle two or more projects at the same time?

How to phrase it: *That happened all the time on my last job. **Several months ago**, I was in the midst of working on one huge project for one of my bosses when my other boss came to me with another project that needed to be completed in two days. **After evaluating** the second project, **I realized I could** complete it in a day. Since I still had about a week before the deadline for the first project, I **decided** to get started on the second one. I **completed** it by the end of the next day and went back to my first project.*

The interviewer asked for an example and this candidate gave one. He demonstrates how his ability to prioritize helped him.

Q: How do you manage stress in your daily work?

How to phrase it: *Unless I have a ton of work to do that I just can't get away from, I make sure that when I take my lunch hour, I actually leave the office. Just that simple change of scenery, even for a few minutes, is enough to keep me **energized** for the rest of the day.*

This is a simple enough question to answer. The interviewer is interested in whether you have a tendency to crack under pressure. She wants to know how you manage high-pressure situations. If you have a simple daily ritual that helps you maintain your composure, even in stressful situations, tell her about it. But beware of how that stress buster might be perceived. A power nap ritual—even on your lunch hour—could mistakenly be construed as sleeping on the job. It may also be helpful to describe a stressful project you've worked on and the specific actions you took to get it done without losing your head. The key is to talk about how you stay professional when under a lot of pressure.

 RED FLAG!
KEEP IT TO YOURSELF if your stress-management solutions—yelling at those who hold lower positions, taking a two hour walk in the middle of the work day—would be frowned upon by the interviewer.

Q: As assistant to the director of human resources, employees will come to you if they feel their supervisor has discriminated against them in some way. How will you handle these complaints?

How to phrase it: *As an HR professional **I know the importance of** being well versed in the laws that affect the workplace. **First**, I will interview the employee, asking for an explanation of exactly what happened. **Then**, I'll interview the supervisor and get his or her side of the story.*

This candidate will take a balanced look at the situation. He will evaluate it using his knowledge of employment law and then try to solve the problem.

Q: You have many of the skills we're looking for. However, we also need someone with very strong sales skills. I don't see anything on your resume that indicates that you have that kind of experience.

How to phrase it: *It's true that I don't have any formal experience in sales. I do have some informal experience, however.* *I ran the book fair at my son's school for the past few years. I also sold jewelry that a friend made. We rented tables at craft fairs all over the region.*

While a candidate can't make up experience, she should draw on unpaid or volunteer experience that demonstrates her skills.

Q: Are you good at doing research?

How to phrase it: *I haven't done a great deal of research at work, but I do a lot of it on my own.* *Before I make any major purchases, take any medication, or go on vacation, I do a lot of research. I'm very good at it. The librarians at my local library are a great resource, so I make sure to go to them when I need help.*

It would have been nice if this job candidate could have drawn on work experience to highlight her research skills, but since she couldn't, she did the next best thing. She has given examples of what kind of research she has done and how she does it.

Q: I see from your resume this isn't your first job working in a medical office. What skills did you pick up on your two previous jobs that you think would help you on this job?

How to phrase it: *When you described the job to me, you said* *you needed someone who was good with patients. You also said you wanted someone who knows a lot about the different insurance plans. My primary responsibility at both these jobs was billing. I had to deal with insurance companies every day. I found that if I learned how each one worked, it was a lot easier for the doctors in my practice to get paid and for patients to get reimbursed. I also worked at the reception desk at these jobs. Many patients who came in were clearly anxious. I was happy to be able to calm them down and hopefully offer some reassurance.*

This candidate listened to what the employer said and was able to clearly state how her skills would fill this medical practice's needs.

Interpersonal Skills

Q: What personal characteristics do you think add to your overall effectiveness?

How to phrase it: *I think that I have a strong ability to create deeper relationships with people than business usually allows for. I am able to know more about a client than just the amount of money she brings to my company each year. I get to know my clients on a more personal level, and I keep them in mind all the time. If I read an article that I know one of my clients might enjoy, I'll send the clip along. In doing so, I find that my phone calls are returned much more quickly—and happily—than the next person's might be.*

What is it about your personal style that makes you unique from the other candidates that the interviewer has met with? What traits do you possess that make you more effective? Without sounding cocky or exploitative, talk about why you think you are able to get cooperation from others.

Q: What type of people do you work with most effectively?

How to phrase it: *My **favorite type of coworker** is someone who is not afraid to voice her opinion. **I love to work with people** who are creative and willing to brainstorm ideas before deciding upon a particular solution. Confidence is always important as well.*

The key here—and in every question, really—is to remain positive. Far too many people answer this question in a way that fails to highlight the positive points they like in their coworkers; instead they drone on and on about the things they hate. A negative attitude is never in a job description, and it's certainly not something you should convey—either intentionally or unintentionally—during an interview. Make sure the company would approve of the characteristics you are describing. For example, if you are a bit of a chatterbox, you might love to have a few other talkative people in your department, but this is not the type of thing you should mention in your interview. Always remember that the interviewer is interested in how well you will fit in with the company's other employees, not how well they'll fit in with you.

Q: Unfortunately every office has personality conflicts. What do you do when you work with someone you don't particularly like?

How to phrase it: *While I know you don't have to be buddies with everyone you work with, **workplaces are more productive if coworkers get along**. I would try to **resolve my differences** with that person. If that wasn't possible, I'd find something about that person I could **admire and respect** and I'd focus on that instead of the things I didn't like.*

This applicant shows she's proactive when she says she would try to work out her differences with her coworker, but realistic when she says that if she can't, she will find something to respect about her coworker—everyone has redeeming qualities.

Q: As a supervisor, what do you do when employees working under you don't get along?

How to phrase it: *I actually **encountered this situation** a few months ago. There were two employees in my department who were both very nice people, but they got off on the wrong foot when one of them transferred into the department. **I called a meeting with them and asked them to try to resolve their differences for the good of the department**. I can't actually say they like each other now, but there is a level of respect between them.*

Nothing is better than a real-life experience. This job candidate was lucky enough to have one he could draw upon. He solved this problem in a very logical way, and was very honest about the outcome.

Q: What would you do if you disagreed with your boss?

How to phrase it: *It would depend on the situation. If I disagreed with her about whether the office is warm or cold, I might not say anything. However, if I disagreed with my boss about whether the new marketing campaign was going to work, I'd **share my thoughts** with her.*

This applicant knows he has to choose his battles wisely. There's a difference between being disagreeable and disagreeing.

Q: What do you expect someone you supervise to do if she disagrees with you?

How to phrase it: *I would expect that person to let me know what she's thinking. It could influence my decision. If she doesn't share her thoughts with me, I won't have **the opportunity to hear her take on things**.*

This job candidate respects her coworkers' opinions. She knows it wouldn't be wise to make decisions without taking their comments into consideration.

Q: Have you ever been in a situation where the majority disagrees with you? What did you do?

How to phrase it: *I **haven't been in that situation, but here's what I would do if I were**: First I would listen to why the majority felt the way they did. Then I'd have to decide whether I needed to reconsider my position. If I still felt strongly about it after hearing their side, I would try to persuade them.*

This candidate knew better than to dismiss the question just because he couldn't draw on his experience to answer it. Rather than make something up, he tells the interviewer what he would do if he were in that situation. His answer shows that he is flexible enough to try to see things differently, but strong enough in his convictions to not automatically go with the crowd.

💬 **Action Speak**

Contracted	Installed
Devised	Issued
Drafted	Listened
Employed	Reshaped
Grossed	Restored

Q: Tell me about a time when you had to defend an idea to your boss or someone else in an authoritative position.

How to phrase it: *After working for my current employer for just a few months, I realized that many of our biggest accounts were not happy with the public relations services we were providing. It seemed that our Manhattan-based PR firm was having difficulty satisfying our West Coast clientele. As West Coast companies make up nearly 80 percent of our business, **I approached my boss about** changing PR firms. Because we had been using the same firm for nearly ten years, **he was quite reluctant to change**. When **I showed him** the demographic shift in our customer base **and had him speak with** several of our clients who had voiced concerns to* me in the past, **he agreed that** we might be better off switching agencies.

The most important thing here is to make sure that you describe a time or situation in which—after defending your idea—you were able to see it through successfully. By explaining such a situation, you are telling the interviewer three important things about yourself:

1. You have good ideas;

2. You will fight for what you believe in;

3. Those in higher positions respect your opinion and are willing to take a chance on your ideas.

Q: How did you get along with your last supervisor?

How to phrase it: *We had a great relationship. I really respected him, and I know he respected me, too. **He knew he could trust me with any project, so he always assigned me those that were very challenging.***

This candidate describes his relationship with his boss on a professional level, and while doing that manages to say something very positive about himself.

Q: If you were unhappy with your job, how would you discuss this with your boss?

How to phrase it: ***I've always had good relationships with everyone I've worked for**, so I think **it would be to everyone's benefit** for me to be direct with my boss. First, I would make a list of the things I'm unhappy with, as well as **suggestions for improving each situation**. I would then ask for a meeting with my boss to go over*

the list point by point**, being careful not to place any blame.**

This interviewee smartly points out that she maintains good relationships with her bosses, which can withstand this type of discussion. She explains how she would be proactive in helping to find a solution for the problems she is dealing with at work.

Q: What would your current coworkers say about you?

How to phrase it: ***My coworkers would say I'm very committed to my job.** I work hard to contribute to each project's success, and I always **share credit** with everyone else who contributes to that success.*

This interviewee portrays himself as someone who is a team player. He sticks to talking about work-related matters.

Q: What would you do about a long-term employee whose work has been slipping lately?

How to phrase it: *I would talk to my employee to **find out what was going on**. Obviously if this person always did a good job, something must have happened to change that. As a supervisor, it is my job to find out what that is and **help the employee** fix the problem; it is also preferable to firing someone. It is generally **more cost-effective** to retain a worker who already knows the job than to train someone new. It also is **better for the morale** of that person's coworkers, who don't want to see a coworker lose his job.*

This answer shows that the candidate has good managerial skills. While dismissing an unproductive employee may seem like a quick and easy solution in the short term, it can have a detrimental effect on the company in the end.

Q: What do you do when you have a very unhappy customer?

How to phrase it: *My first step is to let the customer know **I will listen** to what he has to say. If the company has a strict policy regarding customer complaints, I will follow it. However, if I must **use my own judgment**, I will have to **strike a balance** between keeping the customer happy and not costing my employer too much. If I see that the customer's complaint is legitimate, **I will do what it takes to remedy the situation.***

This applicant plays by the rules. He knows a satisfied customer will return, but he also realizes that a company is always concerned about its bottom line.

Q: How are you at delegating?

How to phrase it: *I have such a **high level of trust in my staff members** that delegating to them is easy. **I know each person's strengths and weaknesses**, so I can easily decide who can handle what jobs and duties. I try to give people projects that challenge them but won't defeat them.*

This candidate is obviously a good manager. He puts a lot of thought into how to delegate responsibilities and makes a point of knowing his staff very well.

Creativity and Leadership Skills

Q: What's the most innovative project you've ever worked on?

How phrase it: *When I worked with JLM Company last summer, I noticed that when sales inquiries would come into the office, they would be distributed haphazardly amongst the marketing assistants. **Realizing that there had to be a better, more efficient way of logging these inquiries, I took it upon myself to set up a system**. I organized these inquiries according to region and distributed them to the marketing assistants based on their regions. **This approach enabled** our marketing team to come up with better and more creative solutions to our sales problems, and it also **addressed the specific concerns** of our pre-existing customers.*

Give examples of your initiative and willingness to contribute new ideas. Discuss how your leadership skills have helped you accomplish your goals. Give a specific example that shows a creative, new, or unusual approach you took to reaching your goals.

Q: Describe a time when you've been able to overcome an obstacle in a creative manner.

How to phrase it: *For months, the publishing company I worked for had been trying to get an appointment with a particular Fortune 500 company to talk about a possible advertising campaign. **After several sales representatives tried to no avail, I volunteered to take a crack at the task**. Rather than contact the vice president of advertising himself, I decided to target his assistant. **I was able to** schedule an appointment with the assistant and give her my sales pitch instead. **I must have made*** *quite an impression, because* the assistant immediately scheduled me for a meeting with the VP for that very day. *Two weeks later, we got the order, and* **the deal was made**.

A smart way to answer this question is to focus on how you overcome problems with the help and support of your coworkers. Show that in addition to being a creatively independent thinker, you are concerned about the company and your team as a whole. Also, illustrate your strength as a leader. Think about how you have approached a problem differently from how others might approach it, and how you have achieved success in doing so. Emphasize your creative solution along with its positive results.

Q: How resourceful are you?

How to phrase it: *I consider myself to be extremely resourceful. While product launches at my current company are generally the domain of our chief engineer, the CEO decided to let me conduct one, as I had shown much creativity in other projects. While the chief engineer usually would simply send out a press release describing the new product's virtues, I decided it was time for a change. I contacted three of our largest customers and asked them to try out the new product and let me know what they thought. With an overwhelmingly positive response to the new line, I then asked permission to videotape these real-life testimonials. The customers agreed, and rather than send out just a press release, we were able to create a podcast. The result was a far higher level of credibility for the company and product, and we exceeded our six-month sales quota. Personal endorsements have now become a cornerstone of all of our marketing campaigns.*

This question specifically targets the candidate's level of creativity and initiative. Your best bet is to provide an example of how you've altered the traditional way of doing things at some point and attained the same—if not better—results. Focus on how you obtained crucial information or how you changed your personal style to get someone to cooperate. As always, make sure to sound confident without being cocky, and don't exaggerate the situation just to have a great answer to the question. Employers will find out if you are lying; if you are, you can rest assured you will not be hired.

> **Green Light Phrases**
> Consider myself well versed in
> Made an effort to develop
> Work well on a team
> Have great communication skills
> Prioritize my work.
> Listen to others
> Focus on the positive
> Consult with my team
> Create a positive work atmosphere.
> Find new solutions

Q: Describe an improvement you personally initiated.

How to phrase it: *When I began working for my previous employer, one of my duties was to send out customer satisfaction surveys. This was done as a traditional paper process that seemed cumbersome to me, especially since we had client e-mails in our database.*

I worked with one of the members of the tech team to create an online survey, which was sent directly to the customer's e-mail within ten days of the transaction. This new system saved time, money, and print resources, and it also increased overall customer survey response by 34 percent.

Here's your chance to prove your dedication to your work and your ability to see the entire picture. Show that, given the chance, you can be instrumental in making significant changes to the company or to the way things are done. Highlight your effectiveness in making things happen; express your desire to do the same for this company. Sometimes this same question can be asked in a more specific way. For example, describe a time when you thought an existing process or manner of doing things could have been done better and what you did about it.

Q: How would you describe your own personal management style?

How to phrase it: *Rather than tell someone what to do or answer a question directly, I try to **encourage my employees** to help find the solution. **For example**, if asked a question about how to proceed on a project or task, I will prompt the person to tell me what he thinks we should do. In addition to questions, I want to hear solutions. **I like being able to** lead my team, but I want to know that they are working to help solve problems as well. I like to think that by **involving my staff** in questions and problems that arise in the department, I am **teaching them how to be effective leaders**.*

Talk about your management style and interpersonal skills with your staff. Do you allow them to be creative or are you a take-charge sort of person? Think about how your staff views you. Are you a micromanager? Describe a particular skill you've learned from a leader you admire and discuss how you try to incorporate that into your own management style. Be careful that you portray yourself as a fair leader and not as a tyrant.

Q: Describe a time when you had to alter your leadership style.

How to phrase it: *In my current position, I am **put in charge of** approximately one new project per month. Each month, I am assigned a new group of employees—usually a group of new recruits—to help them learn how to see a project through to completion. **My usual style is** to look the project over beforehand, figure out the best solution, and begin delegating tasks. About a year ago, the assigned group began to question my initial plan to complete the project. They proposed some alternate ideas, and I was quite **impressed by their suggestions.** While it had always been my style to assume that my idea was the right way to approach a project, this team taught me differently. **Since then**, the first step I take when beginning any new project is to **talk with the group and figure out a solution—together**.*

Assure the employer of your willingness and ability to create strong working relationships by making different kinds of people comfortable with your authority. Your answer should indicate a time when you encountered a person or group that questioned your leadership style, and you should illustrate how you worked to change it. Be specific. What initiatives did you take to improve a less-than-ideal situation? What would the other people involved say about you now? Don't make yourself out to be a tyrant, but don't seem like a wimp either. Indicate that the reasons for your change in style were a result of your keen ability to deal with people.

Q: How do you think a past subordinate would describe your leadership style?

How to phrase it: *I think that people who have worked under me have considered it a positive experience. I look at my role as a supervisor as the chance to have a say in something and contribute to the success of the company. I do not believe it is my place to have the final ruling. I am not one of those people who constantly reminds you that I'm in charge. Before making decisions, I consult with my team to see what kinds of ideas they can come up with. This kind of leadership has been key to success in the past, and it's the model I plan to use throughout my career. Colleagues and employees have both commented to me on the positive work atmosphere that I create; I take that as the highest compliment.*

By asking this question, the interviewer is trying to determine what your references would say about you. When describing yourself, be objective and realistic without embellishing—or being overly modest. Describe candidly your leadership style; give specific examples that reflect your personal approach. Even if your style is to retain control, what are its positive aspects? Keep in mind that the employer may very likely call your colleagues to find out the truth from them. Rather than make excuses for your style, explain your leadership approach and why it works. If you can, give examples of how this style has succeeded.

Q: Do you believe that past job appraisals have adequately reflected your abilities as a leader?

How to phrase it: *I think that the many goals I have surpassed and the various projects I have seen through to successful completion are proof of my strong leadership skills. I am sure that any job appraisal would mention how I look to my team for support, as well as how I take the time to clearly define our objectives to all those around me. By creating a certain amount of camaraderie, I have gained the confidence and respect of my coworkers, which, in my opinion, is the real key to success.*

If you've ever had an experience where—under your supervision—a project failed, this is the time to explain that struggle. Even if a project failed, how did you work to affect this project in a positive manner? What were the steps that you took to ensure its success anyway? Just because a project did not turn out as well as you had hoped does not mean that your job appraisal should be negative. Avoid taking offense at this question or blaming someone else. Regardless of your team, you were the leader. Talk about how you would translate your past successes and failures to this job. What lessons have you learned? Which pitfalls do you know to avoid in the future?

Q: Describe the situations in which you feel most comfortable as a leader.

How to phrase it: *I think that one of my talents is the ability to take complex issues and break them down. For this reason, I have always been very good at solving problems that involve facts and figures. As those who work around me are quite aware of this, they usually allow me to emerge as the leader in situations in which there is a complex problem; they look to me to find a solution and instruct them on how to proceed, and I am happy to do so. I am a highly effective leader in these situations. In situations in which there are political or emotional factors to consider, I usually prefer that someone else take the lead. In such situations, I simply resolve to be a good team player. In all other situations, I normally surface as a leader.*

Your answer to this question says an awful lot about you. Do you feel comfortable leading a situation only when it is specifically asked of you, or do you assert yourself in situations in which you think your expertise could help bring a project to a successful conclusion? Talk about the projects you have led and how other people have trusted you. Why do you think people are willing to follow you in situations such as these? The best way to answer this question is to discuss instances when you were recognized as the leader because of your expertise in something, not because you were appointed project leader. If you're asked to describe situations in which you are a better contributor than leader, you can define types of problems that you're less comfortable working on or situations in which you feel you're too opinionated or biased to lead without controlling the group unfairly. Then end by describing instances when you've played the leader well.

Q: Describe how comfortable you are working with people of higher rank versus working with employees of lower rank.

How to phrase it: *I am on a friendly basis with just about everyone I come into contact with throughout the course of my workday. I recently learned that one of the receptionists and I work out at the same gym, so we carpool after work and are becoming friends because of that. On the other hand, the general manager and I also share several common interests. We have golfed together on a few occasions and have spent many a lunch discussing our various common interests. I pride myself on getting to know those around me personally while, at the same time, building strong working relationships.*

Be very specific here in discussing your relationships. Talk about how you have been able to build strong relationships with all those around you. Don't talk as if those who work under you are below you socially, and don't seem too obsequious when talking about your boss. Though those of higher rank should always command respect, you shouldn't let them walk all over you. By discussing all the ways you help out your boss, you may be setting yourself up as the company's next doormat.

Problem-Solving Ability

Q: How do you usually go about solving a problem?

How to phrase it: *The first step I take is to figure out all the possible causes for the problem. I then think about the outcomes that could arise from my* **taking action**; *I consider the best- and worst- case scenarios as well as the things that are likely to occur. I then try to relate this problem—and its possible causes—to a larger problem. When I have everything laid out in front of me, it is much easier to make a logical connection between cause and effect, and I can come up with a practical way of* **resolving the issue**.

The key here is to show the interviewer your initiative and your ability to make logical decisions. Convince the interviewer that you are able to solve a problem successfully and that you already have a set plan for tackling such complex issues. What criteria do you base your decisions on? Do others seem to have faith in your problem-solving abilities? If you can, give specific examples of times when you were able to use these problem-solving abilities to a successful conclusion.

Q: Describe a time when you've used a problem-solving process to obtain successful results.

How to phrase it: *The hotel chain that I work for offers a free night's stay to any customer who has had an unpleasant experience there in the past. As customer service is a top priority of mine,* **I took it upon myself to** *follow up with some of the unsatisfied customers. Upon retrieving the names of all those customers who had complained about our hotels in the past few years, I noticed that several customers were arranging hotel stays around the country through abuse of this policy.* **I suggested that we** *set up a flagging program in our computer that would allow the clerk or person making reservations to recognize this customer as someone who had complained in the past*

Hotel employees were instructed to make mention of this customer's past experience. By stating something as simple as "Mr. Smith, I know that you have had an unpleasant experience with our hotel in the past, and I am happy that you have decided to give us a second chance. If there is anything I can do to make your stay more accommodating, please don't hesitate to contact me." For the customers who have had legitimate complaints in the past, this tactic allows us to be able to **address their concerns** more closely and **make them aware** that we are working to correct any problems they have found. Those customers who chose to abuse our satisfaction guaranteed policy are warned that their name is on record as having complained in the past, making it less likely that they will do so again after this stay. **Because of this new system, our satisfaction rate has improved tremendously,** and fraudulent cases have decreased.

You are trying to establish yourself as a fair employee who uses logic to solve difficult problems. When choosing a situation to describe, make sure it defines a real problem and a good solution that has helped in solving this issue. Describe, step by step, how the process you came up with was able to lead to a successful conclusion. What measures or benchmarks did you use to control or manage the process? What were the results?

Q: Tell me about a time when a problem that you failed to anticipate arose.

How to phrase it: *My boss had asked me to spend a little time trying to find some inventive ways to cut costs in my department. I* ***immediately got to work*** *and found all sorts of ways to cut barely noticeable amounts of money in various areas that would result in an overall 10 percent decrease in costs.* ***What I hadn't realized*** *is that each of the department heads had already been asked to choose one area in which they would be willing to cut costs. The department heads responded that there was no area within their department that they were willing or able to cut any costs. Soon after I submitted my solution to my boss, I noticed the apathetic way in which each of the department heads dealt with me. I failed to realize that my solution had already been attempted and that there were a lot of negative feelings associated with my findings.*

Green Light Allow yourself to stop and think before answering. A little uncomfortable silence while you work out the best answer to an interview question is better than a careless answer that doesn't impress.

Everyone has failed to anticipate a problem at some time, even the interviewer. The question is whether you're secure enough to fess up to it and see it as a learning experience. Discuss an incident in which you failed to see the warning signs that a problem was likely to occur. What did you learn from this experience? How has your judgment changed because of that incident?

Q: Describe a time when a problem wasn't resolved to your satisfaction.

How to phrase it: *During last year's holiday season,* ***we*** *weren't able to complete a customer's order in time.* ***Our*** *production capacity was not sufficient to deliver the entire order on time. As a result, the customer asked for a discount on her order.* ***I was upset by the fact that we did not take initiative*** *and offer the customer a discount at the same time we informed her that her order would not be ready. The sense of goodwill and genuine regret for not having the order ready would have been greater.*

This question focuses on the candidate's standards of quality. Do you let things slide by when there is an easier or better way to solve the problem, or do you work tirelessly to ensure a satisfactory ending? Describe a situation in which you foresaw long-term complications from a problem that was poorly handled. Did you initiate the resolution of this situation? If the solution still wasn't satisfactory, did you do anything else? If there was nothing else you could do, why not?

Q: Describe an opportunity in which you felt the risks far outweighed the rewards.

How to phrase it: *We were given the opportunity to purchase manufacturing equipment at thirty cents on the dollar from a company that had recently dissolved. At the time, we* ***anticipated*** *an overhaul of our manufacturing facility five years down the road.* ***I made the decision that*** *it was too far into the future to spend money* *only to have idle capacity for a five-year period. If market conditions had shown more promise for new sales in the initial two-year period, I would have gone ahead with it.*

The interviewer wants to be assured that the candidate is able to take reasonable risks without being foolish. The best way to answer this question is to offer an example of a time when you were given a decision to make and were able to use good judgment in determining the risks versus the benefits. How was the outcome of your decision preferable to what might have happened? Were you aware of the possible risks? What was the thought process you used to decide against this?

Personal Questions

Q: Tell me about yourself.

How to phrase it: *I attended Ace Business College, where I **earned** my associate's degree in office technology five years ago. I started working as a library clerk right after I graduated, and **after a year I was promoted to** assistant circulation manager. I helped the library switch over to a new circulation system about two years ago. I was **part of the team that** selected the new system, and I helped train our department in its use. In addition to my technical skills, I am **adept at trouble-shooting**. I also **work well with customers**, helping to solve any problems that arise. **I'm now ready to take on a job with more responsibility**, and I know I will make a great circulation manager.*

This candidate tells the interviewer about his skills and experience and shows why he is qualified for the job. He doesn't wander off course, revealing information

that is irrelevant. The answer is relatively short and, more importantly, to the point.

Q: What do you consider to be your biggest weakness?

How to phrase it: *I am very **dedicated to my job**, and I expect the same level of dedication from other people. Not everyone feels the same way about work and **sometimes my expectations are too high**.*

Wouldn't every boss love such a dedicated employee? This interviewee knew she had to find a weakness that her prospective employer would see as a strength. Another option is to pick a weakness that is somewhat innocuous.

Q: How do you handle failure?

How to phrase it: *I give myself a short time to feel sad, **but I don't dwell on it**. Without spending too much energy on it, **I always try to figure out where things went wrong**. If I don't do that, I won't know **what I need to do to succeed next time**.*

This isn't someone who wastes any time feeling sorry for himself. He's also smart enough to learn from his mistakes.

Q: Do you prefer to work alone or as part of a team?

How to phrase it: ***Each situation is different**. Having a team to collaborate with works better for some projects, while it's best for one person to work on other* projects. *I enjoy being part of a team, but I can work independently, too.*

This interviewer shows that she's flexible and can adapt to working in either situation.

Q: What do you consider to be your greatest strength?

How to phrase it: *My greatest strength is my ability to see a project through from its inception to its completion. Each project I am assigned is important to me, and I always make sure it gets the appropriate amount of attention.*

Notice the interviewee said each project gets the "appropriate amount of attention" and not "all my attention." She clearly knows that not all projects need the same amount of attention and indicates that she knows how to prioritize.

Q: Do you like to take risks or are you cautious?

How to phrase it: *I'll take risks, but I always proceed with caution, so I guess I fall somewhere in between. I like to see what my odds are before I take a risk. I also want to know what I stand to gain or lose.*

This candidate is a careful decision-maker who isn't afraid to take risks if there is a high probability of success. He also wants to make sure the risk is worth taking. He's not a gambler, but he's not afraid to take chances when it's appropriate to do so.

Q: We're not one of those companies that do things the same way year after year. How do you react to change?

How to phrase it: *When appropriate, change is important. For example, when I heard about a new payroll system at a conference last year, I did a little investigating, found out it was better than what we were using, and recommended we move over to it.*

This interviewee has shown that she doesn't shy away from change, even providing a good example of how she initiated it at work. She has also shown that she doesn't jump into change just for the sake of doing something different but, rather, does her homework first.

Q: How do you make decisions?

How to phrase it: *I evaluate the situation before I decide what I need to do. If there is someone who has had experience with similar situations, I'm not afraid to ask for advice.*

This interviewee isn't going to make a decision without considering it carefully. She is also very resourceful; seeking advice from people with more experience is always a good idea.

Q: Can you describe your ideal work environment?

How to phrase it: *I want to work in an environment where I can use my presentation skills to help the company increase its client roster. It's important that I work in a fast-paced environment because I like being busy. I want to work somewhere where employees are recognized for their contributions.*

Based on some research, she is able to describe both the job that she's interviewing for and her potential employer. By showing that her ideal fits with what the job requires, she shows that she is the perfect fit for the position.

Q: How do you explain your success in the workplace?

How to phrase it: *In this age of technology, human contact is highly underrated. I know how frustrated I get when I call a company and am met with a barrage of computer voices telling me which number to hit and whom to call. In business, I never assume that a customer is satisfied until she has told me so directly. I take a very **personal approach** to following up with every customer. The feedback that I have received—both positive and negative—has provided valuable insight into the quality and characteristics of our products. **What augments my past successes even more** is how much the customer appreciates these follow-ups, especially when there's been some sort of problem and I still have **the opportunity to correct it** on a timely basis. And the customer feedback doesn't just benefit me; I'm always passing on customer comments to our production and design teams **so that we can ensure we are making the best possible product.***

This question is similar to the question, What sets you apart from the crowd?

Again, the key to answering such personal questions is to be honest but not arrogant. You should not be embarrassed to toot your own horn a little.

Endnote: If you've accomplished something in the workplace (or anywhere else), don't be afraid to talk about it. It's not enough for you to tell the interviewer how great you are. You have to show him specific examples. Discuss the steps you've taken to ensure that you are considered a worthwhile employee, and mention that little bit extra that you do. Talk about observations other people have made about your strengths or talents and you'll continue to make a lasting impression.

Chapter 14

SPEAKING WITH PASSION

. . . About Your Industry Ambition

If there was ever a good time to map out your career plan, the time is now—before your interview. Employers want to be assured that 1) you're the kind of person who is responsible enough to have a career plan and 2) your career plan fits within the parameters of the job they want to fill. Your interviewer will also want to gauge your enthusiasm for the job and your motivation to do it well. Using the phrases bolded in this chapter, you can tailor your answers to prove that you are a goal-oriented worker with a clear interest in the company at hand.

Aside from basic skills, you must show that you are enthusiastic—not just about the prospect of employment but about the industry in general and the company in particular. This is where it's crucial for you to do your research. Find out all you can about a company before you attend the interview. Use your answers to questions about ambition to demonstrate all that you know about the company. It sounds like a cinch, but this chapter will tell you about the potential pitfalls to avoid.

Why You Chose This Industry

Q: What led you to apply for a position in this industry?

How to phrase it: *I've always wanted to work in an industry that makes tools. I enjoy working on home improvement projects, so I've collected a number of saws manufactured by your company. I could be an accountant anywhere, but I'd rather work for a company whose products I trust.*

Talk about how you first became interested in this specific industry. Discuss the similarities between your current job and the job you are applying for. Be sure to emphasize that you are looking for a career, not just a job! Make sure that your enthusiasm for the industry—and work in general—comes through in all of your answers (where appropriate, of course).

Q: Why is it that you have decided to make this industry your career?

How to phrase it: *The technology in the industry is changing so rapidly that I see lots of room for job enhancement regardless of promotions. I'm particularly interested in the many applications for multimedia as a training tool.*

The interviewer wants to make sure that any time and energy spent on training you will be money well spent and that you will remain with the organization for several years to come. Think about why you have chosen this specific industry or job as a career and what it has to offer you in the future. Don't mention money! You want to assure the interviewer that by selecting you for the job, she is selecting a competent and loyal employee who will look forward to many years of continued growth with the company.

Other key factors to keep in mind when answering this question are what expectations you have for the industry as a whole and what aspects of the business excite you. Though it may seem redundant, the key to a successful interview is to drill your "themes" into the interviewer's head. If you need to mention on more than one occasion your deep interest in the industry or your membership in a professional society, so be it. Be sure to offer specific proof of your long-held interest in the industry and not just your very recent decision to make it your life's career. Passion for your work is one thing that should never be taken for granted.

Q: Is there anything you find troubling about this industry?

How to phrase it: Actually, no. **I've been reading a lot about this industry** and everything I've seen so far is positive. **This industry has made a great recovery** after the decline about a decade ago. Since then it has been growing steadily and actually saw record growth last year.

Although this candidate doesn't have anything negative to say, the candidate takes this opportunity to show that she did her homework.

Q: Since all your experience has been in another industry, you must be a little concerned about making this change. What do you think working in this industry will be like?

How to phrase it: *Everything in this industry seems to go at a very fast pace. I think* **the transition will be an easy one for me** *because in the magazine industry, I also worked at a fast pace. There were tight deadlines and sudden changes that needed to be dealt with on a moment's notice.* **From what I have researched, this industry involves the same things**. *I think I will be able to make a seamless transition to this industry.*

This candidate's answer conveys that he feels he can adapt to working in this new industry.

💬 Action Speak

Ascertained	Gained
Began	Informed
Catalogued	Netted
Described	Observed
Diverted	Placed

What You Know about the Company

Q: Tell me what you know about this company.

How to phrase it: *I served as an intern to a restaurant analyst last summer, so I followed all the steak-house chains closely.* **What you've done especially well is** *focus on a limited menu with great consistency among locations; the business traveler trusts* **your product**

everywhere in the United States. **I'm particularly interested in your** *real estate finance group and expansion plans.*

This is one of those open-ended questions that many interviewees hate. It ranks right up there with "Tell me about yourself." Still, if you have done your homework —like you should have—you should have no problem scoring points with this inquiry. Start out by telling the recruiter how you first became aware of the company. Talk about the personal experiences you've had with the company's product or service—whether it be your own experience or someone else's.

Discuss the many reasons why a job with this particular company (and not a competitor) would be ideal. What is this company offering that its competitors are not? While a general knowledge of the company is imperative, avoid reciting the company's mission statement. The recruiter is looking for evidence of a genuine interest in the company (not just a general interest in the industry). Make sure you provide him with the insightful information he is looking for.

Q: What particular aspect of the company interests you most?

How to phrase it: **I'm particularly interested in your** *recent joint ventures with two processing companies in Latin America. When my father was an army officer, we lived in Latin America for three years. I am very interested in what happens with these agreements.* **What are your plans for the next few years?**

This is a great way to showcase your special knowledge of the company. If the company has a website, try to gain access to any recent press releases to learn about the latest happenings. If you've researched the company properly, you should have no problem answering this question quickly and authoritatively.

Q: What do you think it takes to be successful here?

How to phrase it: *I understand that* Q & H Corporation introduced five new products to the market in the last year alone. *To be a successful employee of such an innovative company*, one would have to be very creative. In a competitive industry such as soaps and toiletries, *you need employees who can* keep up with what consumers want.

This person has obviously done her homework. She not only knows about the company, but she seems to know about the industry as well.

Q: How much do you know about our company's recent growth?

How to phrase it: *I know that XYZ Brands is a multinational company. I was particularly* **intrigued by your acquisition of** ABC Corporation last March. It seems like it's going to open up a whole new market for this company.

Not only does the interviewee show that she took the time to learn about the company, she also shows she's kept up with the latest news about it. Notice that the interviewee said "it's going to open up a whole new market for this company" not "your company," so as not to create distance between herself and the employer.

Q: What do you know about some of our major clients?

How to phrase it: *I know your major clients are* all in the canned food industry. BBR represents Heller Foods, Green Products, and Acorn Corp. *I read in* Advertising Digest *just last week that* Heans hired you to run their new broadcast campaign.

This candidate has done his homework, even keeping up with the latest industry news.

Q: What interests you about our products and services?

How to phrase it: *Turning Corporation provides products and services that* help so many people. Just the other day, I was reading about the new motorized scooter Turning developed. Those in health care and advocates for the disabled are very excited about it, *according to everything I've read.*

This candidate has obviously made a point of learning about her prospective employer, including keeping up with news about the latest products.

Q: What is your favorite product made by our company?

How to phrase it: *I have been using your* model X cellular phone for more than two years now. Although friends and colleagues are constantly having problems with cell phones from other manufacturers, I have never experienced any sort of problems. In fact, whenever I head out to buy a new electronic product, *I look for your label*; I know that it is synonymous with "quality."

Whether the company you're applying to is product or service based, describe your related personal experiences. If you are interviewing with a restaurant, talk about your favorite thing on the menu. Think about why you use the company's product/service. If possible, discuss the various other markets that you think the company's product could succeed in. Employers love to hear new ideas from fresh voices.

Q: If you had the opportunity to develop a new product to add to our line, what would it be?

How to phrase it: *Since Perfect Posies currently sells flowers and other gift items, I think a line of chocolate would be a good choice.* **I recently saw a survey that said** *that consumers spend $150 billion on chocolate gifts each year, so this would be a great market to enter. And* **since this company already has a great reputation in** *the mail-order gift industry and the systems in place to handle the addition of this product, this would be a natural expansion of Perfect Posies' product line.*

This is a well-thought-out answer based on this candidate's knowledge of the company and the gift industry in general.

Q: Describe our competitors as you see them.

How to phrase it: **As far as I can tell, your competitors have tried to** *branch out too often and too fast. They have tried to improve upon their main product, and with little success. As a result, they have had a lot of difficulty maintaining a consistent quality. I think that the recent bankruptcy of ABC Company only* **further illustrates** *this point.* **Your company has been smart enough to** *refrain from looking toward this same type of expansion and instead has focused on creating the best possible product.* **It is this kind of dedication that I am looking for in an employer.**

In addition to researching the company extensively, make sure you have a good idea of its competitors and what they do. Know in which areas the competition is beating out this company and in which they are lagging behind. Give evidence that in addition to a vast knowledge of the company, you know a lot about the industry as a whole. Most importantly, discuss how this company's initiatives are better suited to your personal interests.

Q: What do you think our distinct advantage is over our competitors?

How to phrase it: **I think the smartest way to stay ahead of the industry was your choice of** *headquarters location. By operating in a low-cost area and maintaining a low production cost, you are able to spend aggressively on more important aspects, such as research and development and advertising.* **Even when the rest of the industry is showing a dip in sales, your company remains profitable.**

Again, this is the time to highlight your in-depth knowledge of the company, its products, and its operation in general. What things do you think the company does well, particularly when compared to their competitors? Pick one important aspect you see as a real advantage, and discuss it in an informed and intelligent manner.

Green Light Phrases
Always wanted to work in this industry
Look for your label/brand/logo
Strong grasp of the business
Your company's mission
Believe in your products
Ready for the next step
Long-term relationship with my employer
Know this business from the ground up
Know the company and its products

Q: What do you think of our newest advertising campaign?

How to phrase it: *If you are talking about the one with the family at breakfast time, I think it is great.* ***I know that in the past your company has*** *been criticized for offering foods that are high in fat. This comforting campaign—and the new heart-healthy product—was a great way to step away from that issue. It really shows that* ***you care about your customers and take their comments and concerns seriously.***

Make sure to familiarize yourself with the company's latest happenings, including new products, new advertising campaigns, and any recent press (whether bad or good). Know enough about the company's current state to speak in an informed and intelligent manner. Always offer positive comments and make specific suggestions if you think they apply.

Q: Where do you think we're the most vulnerable as a business?

How to phrase it: *The last company I worked for underwent a merger.* ***Based on your cash position and strong product presence, your company*** *would be an attractive target for a takeover. Though we did experience some difficulties in my last company, I also know I* ***can weather the storm*** *of such an occurrence.*

Answering this question requires a relatively strong grasp on the business and a definite knowledge of the firm's competitors. Figure out what the company does not do well in relation to its competitors, and talk a bit about this. Discuss how you would cope if these vulnerabilities were to be fully realized. As an employee with a passion for the business, you should always be thinking of the future of your job.

Q: If you were allowed to run the company, what would you do differently?

How to phrase it: *I might* ***investigate*** *whether to sell off the light-manufacturing businesses and start an* ***aggressive*** *supplier-relations program.*

This is another question in which you must avoid stepping on anyone's toes. For example, if you are being interviewed by the human resources director, you probably wouldn't want to say, "I would change the overall structure of the human resources department. The way you are structured right now I'm surprised anyone gets hired." Rather than concentrate on your own personal experience, look at the company from a business standpoint. To answer this question, it really helps to have some insider information. If you know people who work for the company—or even in the industry—see if they can help you. Make sure you keep the rules of business in mind. Companies don't turn a profit by letting their employees run wild. Keep your changes informed and intelligent; again, this is not the land of make-believe.

Q: Where do you think this company is going to be in five years?

How to phrase it: **Based on what I've been reading**, it seems this company will be fully expanded into the international market by then. Parker Corporation opened offices in Japan and Switzerland last year, and I read that they are looking into opening Canadian offices next year.

This candidate is aware of what his prospective employer has in store for the future because he did his homework.

Q: How well do you understand our mission?

How to phrase it: **From my research, I understand that your mission is to** develop high-quality toys that enhance learning and provide entertainment for children between preschool age and ten years old.

This candidate states the company's mission as she understands it, which is exactly what the interviewer asked her to do.

Q: If you were interviewing potential employees for a job here, how would you describe this organization to them?

How to phrase it: XRT, Inc., manufacturers windows and sells them directly to the consumer. **The company has a sales force of about** twenty people who respond to customer inquiries by visiting their homes or places of business.

This answer shows that this interviewee has a firm grasp of what this business is all about.

Why You Want to Work Here

Q: What makes you think you'd be particularly good at this job?

How to phrase it: **My academic career included** several classes in business and marketing. Additionally, in my current internship, **I have frequently been given the chance to** help promote our products by attending trade shows, helping in the development of flyers and sales catalogs, and **sitting in on meetings with** the company sales department. I have been **commended for my willingness to** voice opinions and offer new ideas on how we could better market our products. **I am forward thinking**, and **I always try to keep up with current trends and tendencies.** I think that my creativity and strong writing skills would **augment the success** I could have as part of your marketing team.

The question is specifically asking about which skills and characteristics you possess that could help you succeed. Think about the kind of person that would be perfectly compatible with the job you are applying for. What skills do you possess that reflect this "perfect candidate"? Discuss how you keep up with the industry. Read the trade magazines and visit various organizational meetings and websites to find out about current trends. Make it part of your job to keep current, and make sure the interviewer knows that you are doing this.

Q: Why do you want to work here?

How to phrase it: *About a year ago, your company beat me out for a bid on a project. To find out why the organization decided in your favor,* **I decided to research your products**. *It was then that I discovered that while many products in the computer industry are becoming increasingly similar,* **your company strives to be** *forward thinking. Since then,* **I have kept a very active interest in your company** *and the steps they have made in the industry as a whole. Your company has maintained a consistently strong service record, and your customer support is unrivaled. I believe that while many bigger companies will come and go, this company will always remain dedicated to the customer. I* **respect** *that kind of personal attention, and it's a characteristic that— unfortunately—is hard to find.*

All aspects of the interviewing company should come into play here. In addition to the actual business, you should talk about the other reasons why you would like to become a part of this particular company. For example, if you are applying to work in an office with just three or four employees, you could mention your preference for small companies. Tell the recruiter about the many reasons that made you apply for this position. If you don't know much about the company culture, look at aspects such as the company's reputation or the job description itself to help you come up with an answer. Customer feedback can also be of value in answering this question.

Q: Why are you leaving your current job?

How to phrase it: *Though, at one point, I made the leap from being a bank lender to working in the human resources department, I am hoping to combine these two experiences. Sure, I can work in human resources anywhere, but* **because of my past experience** *as a lender, I think that* **my skills would be well suited** *to a human resources career within your bank. As I have been on both sides of the traditional job interview, I think I have a* **strong ability** *to find those applicants who are most compatible with the job.*

Give two or three reasons why you are ready to leave your current job. Focus on discussing the lack of growth or responsibility in your current job, and how you think this new job will challenge you. Regardless of your feelings for your current boss or work environment, refrain from making any negative statements about either. Speaking disparagingly of your current job is a red flag to the interviewer that you could have an attitude problem. Your boss isn't there to defend herself, so the interviewer is left to wonder which one of you is the guilty party in all of this.

Q: What are you hoping to get out of your next job?

How to phrase it: *I'd be* **very interested in** *taking control of a segment of the company in which we are really lagging behind. Sure,* **it would be a challenge, but that's exactly what I'm looking for**. *In my current position, I have been able to increase the sales in my territory by more than 30 percent in just a few years.* **If given the opportunity to work with your company**, *I believe I could do that again. I also hope to get a very aggressive* *commission structure if I'm able to turn around a problem territory.*

This question is very similar to the one that asks, "Why are you ready to leave your current job?" Without being negative about your current job or boss, give one or two examples of your current work experience that explain why you are interested in a new position. For this question, it is best to focus on obtaining a greater challenge. For example, telling the interviewer that there is no potential for advancement in your current position conveys that you are a hard worker who wants to advance; it also implies that you have gone as high as you can go in your current position. Make sure you give some reasons why you believe the job at hand will provide the additional responsibilities you are seeking.

Q: What would your dream job be like?

How to phrase it: **My dream job would allow me to be** *creative and artistic on a day-to-day basis. It would be fast paced and deadline driven, as I thrive on pressure. I would like to work for a small start-up company with limitless* **growth potential**. *I would like to be part of a company from the beginning so that* **I could help in the shaping of** *a new business. I know that your company has been around for about a year now, but I think that your potential for growth is endless.* **The reason I am so interested in this position is that it would allow me to do all of these things, and then some**.

This is another question that might tempt you to offer up a bit of your fantasy life to the interviewer. Rather than cite a specific fantasy job title, your best bet is to tell the interviewer the tasks that would be involved in your dream job and how those tasks relate to this job. Tie in the industry, size of the company, or other factors where appropriate.

 RED FLAG!
DON'T TALK ABOUT a job you would like to have that either is close to or involves the same skills as the job you are applying for.

Q: What motivates you to do this kind of work?

How to phrase it: **I have been fortunate enough in my schooling to** *have encountered many wonderful teachers. Each of them has left an indelible mark on me in some way, and I have always longed to do the same for some other child.* **I want to be** *the kind of teacher who not only* **encourages** *kids to learn but also* **sets an example** *that makes others want to teach. The quality of education in this state has been criticized over the past several years, and* **I want to help change** *this negative perception.*

Here is a great opportunity to show your enthusiasm for an industry as well as your belief in the products or services of the company. It is always a wise idea to use personal experiences to underscore your enthusiasm. Talk about your natural interests, as the interviewer is trying to find out if they are compatible with the job.

Q: What interests you most about this job?

How to phrase it: **I would love the opportunity to work under** *Jane Doe, a woman who really helped to build the financial services practice under bank deregulation. I have worked closely with Ms. Doe on projects* before, and *I completely respect her and her opinions*. *I think that in addition to getting along with your boss, it is important to respect that person, and to believe in her. My esteem for Ms. Doe is one of the main reasons I chose to apply for this job.*

Point out the new responsibilities you'll be assuming in this job, as well as the reasons why you are already well suited for it. Mention similarities to some of your past jobs in which you have enjoyed professional success. Do not speak in generalities!

In this case, the interviewee mentioned the name of someone at the company with whom she once enjoyed working.

 RED FLAG!
AVOID USING FIRST NAME ONLY when speaking of a previous colleague or boss. This can be off-putting to some people. Keep it professional by using Mr. or Mrs. or first and last name.

Keep it professional when mentioning a current employee's name at the company where you're interviewing. Give his or her full name first, and then refer to the person as "Ms. Doe" or "Mr. Doe."

Q: What would you like to accomplish in this job that you weren't able to accomplish in your current position?

How to phrase it: *The company that I work for right now is rather small. That said, the budget we had for marketing our products was fairly limited. For the most part, our marketing efforts were limited to print ads and* other traditional resources. *I know that your company dedicates much of its time and energy to* interactive media, targeting the eighteen-to-twenty-five-year-old category. *This is a step that I am looking forward to taking, and it's one that I think I have many good ideas for.*

Answer here in the same way you'd answer the question, Why are you ready to leave your current job? Don't say anything negative, and be sure your answer reflects professional goals! Talk about the goals you have set for yourself and how this job would help you attain them. Discuss the things you enjoy and have an aptitude for, but do not dwell on the limitations imposed by your current or previous job.

What Your Career Plans Are

Q: Where do you see yourself in five years?

How to phrase it: *I would like to think that in five years I could be managing my own department within the company. As I have served directly under department heads in the past, I think that I have learned valuable lessons as to what it takes to be a good leader. I would like to have the chance to use these skills and, I hope, to make a difference within the company.*

Here's one instance in which you don't want your answer to be too specific. If you think you would like to see yourself at a management level, say so, but refrain from giving an exact job title such as senior vice president of financial affairs. Showing that you are achievement motivated is one thing; telling the interviewer that you are out to get others fired is another. Use this question as a way to talk about your greatest skills. Again, be realistic. If you are being hired for the mailroom, it is unlikely that you will be running the show within the next five years. Though confidence and a desire to be promoted are all valuable to an employer, an employee who is living in his or her own fixed reality is another story. One way to surely eliminate yourself from consideration for a job is to state unrelated career goals. If you're applying for a job as an accountant, it is not wise to tell the interviewer that in five years you hope to be the host of your own late-night talk show!

Q: What other firms are you interviewing with, and for what positions?

How to phrase it: *Since **I have definitely decided on a career in** the publishing industry, I am applying strictly for editorial assistant positions. **My most recent interviews have been** with some of the top publishing houses in this market.*

One mistake that interviewees often make is trying to impress the interviewer with the names of big companies. As each of the *Fortune* 500 businesses are unrelated as far as industry is concerned, this would be a mass mailing at its worst. Make sure the companies you mention are all within the same industry as the company you are interviewing with. Don't be afraid to tell the recruiter that you are interviewing with one of the company's biggest competitors. If anything, it will reinforce that this is exactly the kind of business you want to get into and illustrate that you're committed to finding a job in your field of interest, thus showing you to be a low-risk hire.

Q: What would you say if one of our competitors offered you a position?

How to phrase it: *I'd probably say no. **I'm not too interested in working for the other players in this industry.** My desire to work for Nike comes from the many positive experiences I have had with your product. **I truly believe in your products** and would not consider working for a company whose products I didn't believe in. After all, how could I convince someone to buy a product that I myself wouldn't buy?*

It is not always necessary to answer no to this question. Depending on the order of the questions asked, you may have already told an interviewer that you are applying for a position with his competitor. Still, whether you answer this question with a yes or a no, be sure that you let the interviewer know that it is this company you would like to work for. Point out the reasons why you would prefer to work for this company even if a competitor offered you a position. Talk about the advantages this company has to offer you both as an employee and as a consumer. Again, the interviewer is trying to determine whether your interest in the company and industry is genuine. Talk about why you would choose this company over any other, and demonstrate your interest.

Q: How have your career motivations changed over the past few years?

How to phrase it: ***When I first started out**, I worked in sales, which is where I was sure I wanted to be. As I worked very closely with the marketing department, I realized that perhaps that was **where my talents were**.*

*I found out that I could use my creativity and strong writing skills to really help out in the marketing end of things. My boss also quickly realized this and immediately offered me a position within the marketing department. **Since then, my interest in** marketing has only **increased**. I know that your sales and marketing departments rely heavily upon one another to make each other work, as is the case with many companies. Though **I will always love the thrill of** salesmanship, I cannot deny that marketing **is where I need to be**. Working for your company **would allow me to keep a close eye on both of these interests** and, I hope, **help in the productivity of** each of these departments.*

Regardless of whether or not you have changed careers completely, you have probably learned a lot about yourself and your talents since entering the work force. Talk about the things that you have learned from your past work experience, especially where your skills and natural instincts lie. Make sure that your current motivation relates to the job you are interviewing for. Avoid seeming fickle. An employer will not want to take a chance on an employee who can't seem to make up his mind about what he wants to do. Even if you've had various jobs, talking about the goal you have always had in mind will put a positive spin on your varied past.

Q: You seem to be climbing the corporate ladder in your current job. Why leave now?

How to phrase it: ***I'm choosing to leave now because my goals have changed**. I want to use my public relations skills at a nonprofit organization such as this one.*

This applicant is making a change to another industry, but shows how he can still use his skills to meet his new goals.

Q: Your last job was very different than the ones you had before. Why did you take that job?

How to phrase it: *I was thinking of going back to school to be a veterinarian. I mentioned this to my neighbor, a vet, and he offered me a job in his office. I love animals, but **before I made the commitment** to go to veterinary school, I wanted **to make sure I'd be happy working with** them and especially dealing with sick ones. It turned out that wasn't right for me after all.*

This candidate has a good explanation for why she took a job that has nothing at all to do with her current career path. In doing so she also shows off her decision-making skills.

Q: Describe how your career progressed over the past five years. Was it aligned with the goals you set for yourself?

How to phrase it: *When I graduated from the community college**, I knew I wanted to work as a** store manager. I also knew **I would have to work my way up**, so I took a job as a sales associate at Dress Corral. After a lot of hard work, **I was promoted to** assistant department manager after two years. After being in that job for a year, I got a job as manager of the ladies' accessories department at P. J. Coopers, and I've been there for the past two years. **With my experience, I'm ready for the next step**—store manager.*

This job candidate shows exactly how her career has progressed and how she is now ready for a job with this employer.

Q: How does this job fit in with your career goals?

How to phrase it: *As I mentioned earlier, my long-range goal is to be an elementary school principal. Reaching that is several years off, of course. **I have a lot to learn about** school administration. **I've attended several workshops you've run**, and I am always impressed by your knowledge, and **I know I can learn a lot from you**. From what I've heard through the grapevine, you always place a lot of trust in everyone you hire and give employees a chance to grow. **I know I can gain valuable knowledge and experience here** at Oakwood, in addition to **what I can contribute** as an assistant principal.*

This candidate demonstrates her knowledge about her prospective employer. She has personally learned from him in the past. She has also talked to other people who know him and how the school is run.

How You Would Contribute

Q: How do you stay current?

How to phrase it: ***I pore over the** Wall Street Journal, the New York Times, Institutional Investor, and several mutual fund newsletters. **I also have a number of friends who** are financial analysts, and **we often discuss the business** amongst ourselves.*

This question relates to the previous one. Show the employer that your interest in a specific job or field

does not end at 5 P.M. Talk about the many ways that—even outside of work—you keep up with your business. It could be that you spend your lazy Sunday mornings reading trade magazines; there's no shame in sharing this with the interviewer. If you are a member of any professional trade organization, now is the time to talk about it. Do you attend regular meetings or chat frequently with the other members? Show the employer that this position is not just a way to make a living but a way of life for you.

Q: Tell me something about yourself that I wouldn't know from reading your resume.

How to phrase it: *I love snorkeling. **It's my favorite way to relax**. Down there, observing all those strange and wonderful forms of life, it gives a **fresh and upbeat outlook** on my own life.*

Remember that you are being asked to tell the interviewer something about yourself that she wouldn't know from reading your resume. If certain pieces of information were omitted from your resume to keep it all on one page, now is the time to bring them up. For example, if in addition to a part-time job and your full-time studies you were part of an athletic team or organization, talk about it. While the actual organization might be a bit off the topic, you can usually find a way to weave it into the conversation. By participating in a particular event or becoming part of a certain organization, what did you learn? What are some of the skills you acquired that will help you in your professional endeavors? Do not tell the interviewer something that is completely irrelevant (such as, "I have ten cats!"). Above all, remember not to repeat anything that can be found from looking at your resume.

Q: Do you think that you are overqualified for this position?

How to phrase it: *Absolutely not! My relative experience and qualifications will only help me to do this job better.* **Because I have experience in so many different facets of your business**, *I feel that I can help in the overall success of the company, and not just within my department. For example, my business experience can help me to run the art department in a cost-efficient manner, while my creative background will allow me to find the best freelance talent.* **As I have been working in the industry for quite some time, I have many business contacts that I can call upon** *to help me. My qualifications are better for the company, too, since* **you'll be getting a better return on your investment**. *Since I am interested in establishing* **a long-term relationship with my employer**, *I would expect expanded responsibilities that could make use of even other skills when I have proven myself.*

This question intends to catch an interviewee off guard, and it often does. The mistake many people make in answering this question is to automatically take a defensive position. If you do have extensive experience, an interviewer is testing to see whether you would quickly become bored in the position, how much confidence you have in your own skills, and how you plan to let your past experience work for you in this company. When answering this question, be sure to address each of your strongest skills and explain how each could benefit the company. Confidence is the key to answering this question.

Q: What new or unique skills could you bring to the job that other candidates aren't likely to offer?

How to phrase it: *Because the company I currently work for is one of the oldest players in the industry, I think* **I could bring** *the history and experience that goes along with that. I can help this company avoid making some of the same mistakes we have made in our established markets.* **For example, if I were to start work today, I would work at** *retaining your core customer base before trying to secure new accounts.* **It is this kind of experience that you are not likely to find in many other candidates.**

This question addresses your desire to add true value to a job (beyond what is expected of an employee). Imagine that you are being considered for the position alongside one other person with the exact same educational and professional qualifications. What are the things that would make you the better hire?

 RED FLAG!
STEER CLEAR OF VAGUE interview answers such as "I am multitask oriented" and "I wear many hats." These answers tell the recruiter absolutely nothing about your skills and abilities.

Q: Based on what you know about this company, how will you contribute to it?

How to phrase it: *I see that most of your company's clients are in the food industry. Since I spent ten years working for AMJ Bean Company, I am very familiar with that industry. I know my experience in the industry is something your clients will appreciate.*

This candidate has researched her prospective employer and knows that her experience in the food industry will help her should she be hired. She is able to make a point of mentioning that in the job interview.

Q: Do you know what your job duties will be if we hire you?

How to phrase it: *As eligibility clerk, I know I will use my interviewing skills to help determine whether individuals are eligible to receive assistance from various government programs. I will interview people and then write reports that will be sent to the appropriate agencies.*

This candidate knows what the general duties are for the job.

Q: What would you like to accomplish here if we hire you?

How to phrase it: *I read that this company is expanding into the children's clothing market. With my background in that area, I know I can help make that clothing line successful.*

The interviewee bases his answer on what he has learned about this employer. He explains how his experience will help the company reach its goals.

Q: If you were hired here today, what is the first thing you would do?

How to phrase it: *I would help to increase your business within the software market. Though your company is mainly known for its printed products, I believe that your software is one of your greatest assets. I have spent the past four years working as a sales manager for a software developer, so I have a great understanding of how to market these products more effectively.*

In addition to showing your enthusiasm for a job, this question tests your knowledge of a company and its products. Give the interviewer clear, tangible evidence that the company will benefit immediately upon hiring you. Focus your answer on the action you would take, and—above all—make sure your goals are realistic. Is there an area you think could use some improvement? Discuss the steps you would take to achieve maximum results. Do you have a creative way to improve some aspect of the company? Talk about it. If you can, relate what you would like to accomplish in this company to past achievements and experience. A job offer is a cause to celebrate, but the interviewer isn't probing for that kind of response; she wants to know how you can make a difference right from day one.

Q: Our latest venture has been all over the news. What would you do to make the transition go more smoothly for our employees?

How to phrase it: *I would make sure employees know how the merger between this company and Pacific Pencil Company will affect them. I would hold meetings to discuss how procedures will change and schedule workshops to help employees adapt to these changes. When my former employer merged with RQR International, I assisted the vice president who was responsible for handling the transition, so I have experience in this area.*

By referring to the venture by name, this candidate shows he knows what the interviewer is talking about. He has clearly given some thought to how this merger will affect the company and knows how to deal with it, and he can draw upon his experience with a similar situation.

Q: Why should we hire you?

How to phrase it: *My aunt had a company that was a small-scale manufacturer in the industry, and although she later sold the business, I worked there for five summers doing all sorts of odd jobs. For that reason, I believe I know this business from the ground up, and you can be assured that I know what I'd be getting into as a plant manager here.*

Why *should* a company hire you? This question, which is usually the last one asked in a formal interview, is your chance to sum up your skills and value as an employee *without* repeating your resume or employment history. Here's your chance to offer one or two examples that explain why you want to work for this particular company and why they would want you to work for them. What's the most compelling example you can give to prove your interest? Though this question often remains unasked, it's always in the back of a recruiter's mind. If you're lucky enough to get through the interview without hearing it, you should still try to find an opportunity to use your prepared response sometime during the interview, perhaps in your closing remarks.

Endnote: Choose your answer wisely when fielding questions about industry ambitions. Use proper phrasing to expertly showcase how well you know the industry and how passionate you are about working for the company. "Determination" should be the word that comes to mind when they think of you.

Chapter 15

SPEAKING WITH CLARITY

. . . About Your Goals and Interests

During the course of your interview, you want to give the interviewer a clear image of how you would fit into the company. You want them to be able to picture you walking by them in the hallway someday. To do so, you want to present yourself as someone whose values and personality mesh well with the company's and whose career goals coincide with the needs of the company. Do the research required to determine the usual progression of someone in your chosen career path. Consider how your success and this company's success are intertwined and be ready to verbalize it using succinct and powerful phrases.

Be practical and realistic as you practice your own answers to the questions in this chapter. If you are interviewing for the position of mailroom clerk, for example, you should not tell the interviewer that in two years you hope to be CEO. Make sure the goals are attainable and that you can explain the steps that will take you from one goal to the next.

Something you may not be prepared for is the personal questions your interviewer may ask. Finding out what you do in your leisure time is a good and quick way to get to know you as a person, not just a job applicant. Prove to them, in your carefully worded answers, that you have a balanced lifestyle, that your personality is a good match for the job at hand, and that your personal and professional interests are compatible.

Long- and Short-Term Goals

Q: What are your long-term goals?

How to phrase it: *I want to move into a supervisory position eventually. I know that will take time and hard work, but it is something I expect to achieve.*

It's important to emphasize that you have goals—and also that you are willing to do the work to reach them.

Q: What are your short-term goals?

How to phrase it: *I want to work for a company that is growing, in a position that allows me to use my skills to help that growth. I know your company is trying to expand into the teen market. My experience selling to that market will help your company reach its goals.*

This interviewee's goals are aligned with those of the company. By giving an example of how she will help the company meet its goals, she has forced the employer to visualize her as an employee. This answer also shows that the interviewee took the time to research the company before her appointment.

Q: Do you consider yourself a leader?

How to phrase it: *I am willing to take on responsibility, I am persuasive, and I can delegate. All these qualities make me a good leader. If a situation calls for someone to take charge, I will certainly step forward.*

This interviewer states the qualities that make her a good leader but knows to tread lightly here. She wants to show she can evaluate the needs of each situation and

step forward if necessary, while making it clear she's a team player.

Q: Are you a procrastinator or do you like to get things done?

How to phrase it: *Though I've been known to procrastinate on occasion, I don't make a habit of it. When someone hands me a project that needs to be done in a timely fashion, I will get it done.*

Who hasn't procrastinated on occasion? What matters is that this candidate knows the difference between a project that can wait and one that needs to be done right away, and can finish the pressing ones in time to meet deadlines.

> **Green Light Phrases**
> High standards for myself
> Help the company grow
> Find a job suited to my personality
> Know what I want
> Become an industry leader
> Gain experience in many parts of the business
> Move up in the company ranks
> Authoritative position
> Insight into the industry
> Motivated to

Q: I see that you worked full time while attending graduate school. How did you manage to balance everything?

How to phrase it: *It was difficult, but I managed not to fall behind at work or school. I worked five full days a week and took classes two evenings a week. I studied on the other three nights and on the weekends.*

This candidate shows that he was determined to complete his degree but not at the expense of his job.

Q: How do you want your career to progress in the next few years?

How to phrase it: *Over the next few years, I would like to be at the point where I have **bottom-line budget responsibility** and charge of a production unit in which I have labor-relations, quality-control, design, and manufacturing **responsibilities**. I believe **this job will go a long way toward helping me meet my career goals**.*

Avoid the temptation to suggest job titles; this makes you seem unbending and unrealistic since you don't know or control the system of promotion. Likewise, you don't know how long it might have taken your interviewer to reach certain levels, and you wouldn't want to offend her. On the other hand, you don't want to be too general either. The best way to answer this question is to discuss the new experiences you would like to have in the next few years and the responsibilities you would like to acquire.

Q: What new challenges would you enjoy taking on?

How to phrase it: *I've worked in various positions in the hospitality industry **for more than eight years** and have **progressively worked** in larger, more prestigious hotels. I've learned both the food and beverage side of the business as well as the hotel management side. **Armed with that background**, I now believe **I'm ready to** take part in the convention and conference area.*

Based on the skills you have learned and enjoyed using in your current position, describe the new challenges that you would like to take on and that you feel capable of handling. Be as specific as you can, considering what you know about the current or future direction of the position, department, and company as a whole. Think about the duties of the job at hand and which ones might provide you with a bit of a challenge.

Q: What are your long-term career plans?

How to phrase it: *My long-term career goals are to become known as an industry expert and to have earned a respectable **management position** with responsibility for a major piece of the business. I'd like to think I'll have experience in many parts of the business **over time**.*

This question requires you to focus on the experiences you would like to have in your career, and the things you would like to be responsible for. Even though this question does ask about your long-term goals, be sure to stay realistic and keep your goals along the same career path.

 RED FLAG!
DON'T CITE A JOB TITLE as your long-term career goal. You never know what kinds of duties and jobs will be obsolete by the time you reach the end of your career, especially in fields that are always changing (such as computer technology).

Q: Have you ever taken a position that didn't fit into your long-term plan?

How to phrase it: *Though **I had always been drawn to** a high-tech career, I was offered a very lucrative position in real estate several years back. Though I knew that real estate was not my life work, I decided to take the job **for financial security**. Before long, I realized that the work wasn't **fulfilling or challenging enough** to keep me happy. I stayed with the company for two years, but I **remained close with many of my original contacts** in the high-tech industry, and I was **lucky enough** to pick up where I'd left off. I've **since moved up in the ranks**, and my long-term plans include staying in the industry and **assuming greater responsibility** in the area of computer programming and networking.*

Don't be afraid to answer no to this question. Many members of the work force have been lucky enough to develop a strong and compatible career path right off the bat, and stick to it throughout their careers. If this is the case with you, don't be afraid to tell the interviewer so. If you have taken a job that didn't quite fit in with what you hoped to accomplish, talk about the reasons that led to this acceptance. The interviewer is trying to determine how wisely you can pick jobs to match your interests and aspirations. If you've been sidetracked by some job, you'll probably have to convince the recruiter that you are on the right track pursuing this position.

Q: Have you progressed in your career as you expected?

How to phrase it: *My six years with a major gas company have included **solid experience in** price analysis, capital budgets, and financial planning. I now believe **I'm ready to take on** departmental responsibility for the entire finance function within a finance company.*

Think about your past career experiences. Have you accomplished as much as you had hoped to at this point? If not, why do you think that is? Talk about the many learning experiences you've had and what these have taught you about the industry. Be realistic in admitting the areas where you need more experience. Honesty—without demonstrating either pessimism or unrealistic expectations—is important when answering this question.

Interest in Your Chosen Career

Q: Why did you choose this career?

How to phrase it: *When I started college, I wasn't sure what I wanted to do. I visited the career office, and they gave me some self-assessment tests. Based on the results, they gave me a list of **careers that might be suitable** and told me how to **research** them. I did, and this is what I thought I'd like best.*

Great answer. This is someone who knows what steps to take to make an important decision.

Q: Since this will be your first job, how do you know you'll like the career path?

How to phrase it: ***Although it's true that I've never worked in this industry**, I've talked to many friends and alums at my school who've been successful here. I always ask them what the job's greatest challenges* are and what is most rewarding about the job. **From the information I've gained,** I'm confident that I'll be **able to adapt quickly** to your culture and will find the next few years rewarding, **based on my goals and values**.

Unless you've done your research and/or are really familiar with the industry, this can be a difficult question to answer. Before going into an interview, be sure you know what kind of job—or even job title—you would be next in line for. By taking the position you are applying for, what would be the next logical step, according to your industry's general career path? If you have had any experience in the field—an internship, for example—make sure to mention that. You should also feel free to discuss the conversations you had with professionals within the industry and how you gained a better understanding of the job and the career path through those people. Point out why you are interested in this career, how you've learned more about the industry, and how you are able to keep current with the industry trends.

Q: What makes you think that this job is right for you at this point in your career?

How to phrase it: *Though I have never had the title of manager, I think that **my past experiences up until now could have only led me in this direction**. I have spent the past five years working as a corporate trainer for two separate Fortune 500 companies. My job required that I learn the functions and responsibilities of each of the companies' departments well enough that **I could teach others how to do the job**. More than **learning the business basics** of just about every department in a major corporation—from sales and marketing to accounting—I*

have also **learned how to deal with people effectively in an authoritative position**. I still get phone calls from people I have trained in the past asking me questions and telling me about their own promotions. I think that **if you ask any of these people, they would agree that I would make a great manager**.

In addition to addressing your applicable skills, and the logical progression that brought you to apply for this job, address your desire to work for this company in this position. Showcase the knowledge you have of this company and what the specific job entails. Describe the experiences you want to pursue that build on your current skills and interests. Be as specific as you can, based on what you know about the current or future direction of the position and the department. Demonstrate why this position fits with your personal career goals. Talk about how you can create job growth for yourself.

Q: If you could start all over again, which direction would you take?

How to phrase it: *I've always enjoyed consumer sales as I've moved up in my career. Looking back, **I wish I'd gotten a bit more experience in** market research earlier in my career, because **it's important to understand** the types of quantitative models and technical research techniques that a regional sales manager now needs to know.*

The interviewer is trying to figure out if the career path you have chosen to take (including this interview) is ideal for you. Is it this industry alone that you are passionate about, or does your heart lie somewhere else? In answering this question, offer some insight as to why your goals may have changed a bit, given the information you have now. The best way to answer this question is to think of a separate but related task that you enjoy and to talk about how you may have chosen to do something with that. Be honest and insightful, but reassure the interviewer that that only place you want to be is with this company.

Q: How long do you think you'd continue to grow in this job?

How to phrase it: *I define job growth as the process of acquiring new skills, new knowledge, and new insight into the industry. That said, as long as I can manage this type of growth, I consider myself successful. I'm a believer in stretching a job by reaching out to learn more about other areas peripheral to my job.*

This is a variation on the question of where you want to be in five years. Again, when answering, be as specific as you can based on all you know about the position. Make sure that any goals or time frames you state are realistic and well thought out. Don't mention a job title you'd want next, or the interviewer will wonder if you're already preoccupied with moving on.

Q: What career path interests you within the company?

How to phrase it: *I'd like to work toward becoming a senior project manager within your commercial real estate firm. My background includes several areas within commercial real estate, including working in architectural design, with governmental departments and agencies, with banks in the finance area, and,* finally, in sales and leasing. I'd like to pull all this background together **in the next few years** and **eventually have** project management **responsibility**.

In addition to demonstrating your knowledge of the company, or the typical career path within the industry, the interviewer is interested in how realistic you are. Use the knowledge you have of this industry in general and this company in particular to talk about the path you are interested in following. If you're unfamiliar with the typical career path, it's okay to ask a question such as, "What's the typical career path for someone with my skills?" Focus principally on businesses or divisions of the company that interest you, as well as skills and challenges you hope to master in the next few years.

Q: How does this job compare to the other positions you are pursuing?

How to phrase it: *Since I've narrowed my job search to only those large securities firms within the finance industry, this job is very close to the other types of positions I am currently interviewing for. The basic skills necessary with all of these firms are similar: strong quantitative and analytical abilities, the ability to make decisions quickly, and good interpersonal skills to react to customer needs.*

While the interviewer may not want to hear all about your most recent interviews with the company's biggest competitors, he does want to be assured that you are settled on a career path. He wants to make sure that you are not picking job titles and/or companies out of a hat. Some consistency or thread of commonality among your other prospects is important here. Your choices must reflect your career aspirations. Talk about the common skills that are clearly needed in all the jobs you're pursuing.

Q: Have you ever found yourself really burned out from a job, and if so, what did you do about it?

How to phrase it: *Because I know how damaging it can be to begin experiencing those sort of feelings, I don't allow myself to get locked into an unchanging routine. I am the type of person who will continually **ask for new assignments and tasks so that I can keep motivated and challenged**.*

The interviewer is trying to figure out a few different things here. Are you smart and disciplined enough to avoid burnout? When you are not being productive, do you recognize it? What do you do to cope with stress? The interviewer wants to be sure that in a few months you will not be running from this job and company.

Focus principally on businesses or divisions of the company that interest you, as well as skills and challenges you hope to master in the next few years.

Personal Interests, Hobbies, and Activities

Q: Do you have any hobbies?

How to phrase it: *I love woodworking. I've made tables, chairs, and a bookshelf. **I love the satisfaction I get from** taking a few pieces of wood and turning them into something I, or someone else, can use.*

This answer shows that the interviewee can see a project through from beginning to end.

Q: Other than work, tell me about an activity you've remained interested in over several years.

How to phrase it: *I've been **involved in fundraising efforts for** cancer research ever since my grandmother died from breast cancer. I'm hoping that the research can save the lives of others.*

The interviewer is questioning whether you are fickle. Do you take a strong interest in things and stick to them, or do you seem to have a problem with commitment? Prove to the interviewer that you are a solid person who doesn't just jump into something to jump right back out. Talk about your hobbies and favorite activities. Think about the other questions that the interviewer is considering: Are your interests compatible with the job you are applying for? Would they be of value in any way to the company?

💬 Action Speak

Achieve	Judged
Apply	Published
Build	Reached
Displayed	Supervised
Found	Updated

Q: What do you do in your spare time?

How to phrase it: *I am a real sports fan. Whether watching or playing, I enjoy the excitement that sports* such as baseball, basketball, and tennis have to offer. *I especially enjoy team sports. Knowing that a group of people is **working so closely together to achieve a specific goal** is inspiring to me in many ways. **I know that many of your clients are** high-profile sports clubs and companies, and I think that because of my dedication to sports of all kinds, I could definitely bring a unique perspective and insight to the company.*

The interviewer wants evidence that you're well rounded, not one-dimensional. He is looking for shared interests or common ground. Make sure that the personal life you describe is active and fulfilling. Though the interviewer wants to know that you will be dedicated to your job, he does not want to think that this is the only creative outlet you will have. You should always, in some way, relate your answer to the job description.

Q: Tell me about a time when you were in a recreational setting and got an idea that helped in your work.

How to phrase it: *I **was on vacation** in Mexico and saw a woman with a homemade seesaw she was using to lift her laundry basket when she needed something out of it. **It gave me an idea** for a new type of scaffolding that I designed **when I got back to work**. Now our brick masons have a rotating bench that keeps their materials at waist level, which reduces back fatigue.*

The interviewer wants to know that—even when you're not working—you are able to synthesize information and apply what you see to your profession. You want to be sure that you are portraying yourself as an innovative and creative person. While you want to show you can be competitive in business, talking about a great idea that you saw another business doing and chose to copy won't showcase your own creative thinking. Show that your work is something you are naturally inquisitive about rather than something you have to do. Are you able to think outside of the box to come up with fresh ideas? Be sure to give specific examples.

Q: How is your personality reflected in the kinds of activities you enjoy?

How to phrase it: *I love to cook and entertain. That's the salesman coming out in me. **I love sharing experiences with people**, and I'm very **outgoing**.*

Talk about the way your natural skills, values, and ethics are reflected in things you do in your spare time. What do your hobbies and passions outside of work say about your personality? Remember, everything we do says something about us as a person. Think about your words so that the image you portray of yourself is always to your advantage.

Q: What are some of the things you do to relax?

How to phrase it: *The **main thing that helps me to relax is my family**. For me, my weekends are like a vacation. I make the most of all the time I have to spend with my family. **When I'm at work, I focus** on what is going on in my professional life, but when I am at home, it's all about my family. When I began working at my present job, my husband and I decided to buy a home about twenty miles outside of the city. It was really one of the best things we ever did; now, even the drive home is relaxing.*

The interviewer wants to be reassured that you do not spend all of your time—physically or mentally—in the office. Describe at least one part of your life or activity that you engage in that you find to be relaxing. Talking about what you do in your free time is a great way to give the interviewer an insight into who you are as a person.

Q: Our company believes that employees should give time back to the community. How do you feel about that?

How to phrase it: *I completely agree. In my last job* **as a manager, I allowed employees to** *spend one day a month, as long as the entire staff wasn't gone on one day,* **giving back to the community** *as a volunteer. I myself spend one Friday a month working with an adult literacy program.*

If you have spent time giving back to your community in some way, this is a great time to talk about it. Even if you have not, this is a good opportunity for you to discuss the issues, charities, and world problems that concern you. If you were given the time to participate in community outreach, what would you do? Showing a lack of excitement at the prospect of helping others is probably not the type of spirit a company is looking for. Do you use your skills productively? Are you unselfish and a real team player? Demonstrate how your personal interests make you productive even when you aren't being paid. What incentives other than a paycheck inspire you?

Q: Are there any community projects that have benefited from your professional experience?

How to phrase it: *As a marketing professional, I have been able to* **help out at our local high school** *in drumming up publicity and awareness for its fundraisers.*

This question gives the interviewer a sense of your values and lets her know whether you will be a good corporate citizen. Showing that you like to apply your professional expertise to situations in which the only reward is good will impresses an interviewer. Don't get sidetracked describing a cause that doesn't demonstrate job-related skills. Avoid discussing any charity or organization that may be considered controversial; the last thing you want to do is offend the interviewer.

Q: Describe how a sport or hobby taught you a lesson in teamwork or discipline.

How to phrase it: *I used to play football, and* **our coach always taught us that** *the most important part of the game was watching out for the other guy, that if you do that job well, you'll always have someone watching out for you as well.* **It is exactly this strategy that I have tried to apply in my professional life.** *Help out when and where you can, and you'll always have others to rely on as well.*

Remember that the key to this question is teamwork! Rather than focus on how you have applied a certain strategy to work to your advantage, talk about how you have used lessons learned to help your entire department or work group or a time when you had to use teamwork to get a desired result. Tell a specific story, then describe how the same skill or lesson has been used in your work.

Q: Tell me about an interest that you outgrew.

How to phrase it: ***Early on, I wanted to be*** *a research physician. Then I spent time in a chemistry lab and realized that I wasn't looking forward to the next two years of lab work.* ***That's why I've chosen*** *marketing for medical equipment instead. It combines my respect for the medical profession with* ***a job that's more suited to my personality***.

Describe a former interest or hobby that you no longer pursue, making sure that the interest isn't related in some way to the job you're interviewing for. You also don't want to expose a weak skill that the interviewer had never even considered. Talk about why you outgrew that interest and why it's not compatible with your current interests. Be sure to discuss how your current interests are related to your career.

Endnote: The best interviewees are ones that are controlled and articulate in answering questions but can relax just enough to let their unique personality shine through. Nobody wants to hire a robot. Allow yourself to show a more personal side as you answer career goal and interest questions, and you'll come off as a dynamic and appealing candidate.

Chapter 16

SPEAKING WITH SKILL

. . . About Your Education

Recent graduates may not have a lot of work experience to share, but they do have a lot of educational experience to pull from in an interview. Even if your college or graduate school experience seems like old news, it can often provide useful material—especially when your professional experience doesn't provide the material you need to give a satisfactory answer. Dig deep before your interview and begin shaping answers to questions about your coursework, your grades, your teacher's perceptions of you, clubs and organizations you enjoyed, and any internship or volunteer experiences. Your goal is to use carefully chosen words and phrases to illustrate the most important contributions you made to your school's community. After all, a productive and motivated student makes for a productive and motivated worker.

Why You Chose Your Major

Q: I see you majored in English. Are you prepared for a job in marketing and sales?

How to phrase it: *As an English major, I had to do a large amount of reading and needed to retain all of it. Reading and absorbing the literature on the products I'll be selling will be a snap. I believe college also prepared me to manage my time well. I have hands-on experience in this field as well; I worked in various sales positions to put myself through school.*

Notice that the interviewee doesn't make any excuses for working in a field outside his major. Instead, he talks about how his major qualifies him for this job. He also talks about the fact that he has sales experience.

Q: Why did you choose to major in philosophy?

How to phrase it: *From a very early age, I wanted to be a lawyer. When I started to do my research, I found out that undergraduates who want to go to law school should take a lot of liberal arts classes. During my freshman year, I took different courses in the school of liberal arts and sciences, and I liked philosophy the best, so I decided to make it my concentration.*

This applicant shows that she made an informed choice when choosing her major.

Q: What was your favorite subject in high school? What was your favorite subject in college?

How to phrase it: *English was my favorite subject in high school. I did a lot of writing in English. I liked working hard to put together a paper and then getting feedback in the form of a grade. My favorite classes in college were those in my major. I actually took only one marketing class before I declared marketing as my major. I found the subject matter so interesting that I started looking into it as a career choice.*

This candidate explains why English was her favorite subject and in the process demonstrates her skill as a writer, which she knows will be an important part of her job. By stating that her major was her favorite subject in college, she shows that she is dedicated to the field.

Q: What were your least favorite subjects in high school and college?

How to phrase: *My least favorite subject in high school was home economics. I helped with the housekeeping at home; I didn't want to have to deal with it at school, too. I liked most of the classes I took in college. If I had to pick my least favorite, I guess it would have to be biology. We had to dissect a fetal pig, and I had a problem doing that.*

The candidate picked classes unrelated to the job he's applying for. Notice also that he didn't say he disliked the classes because of their difficulty.

Q: Why did you decide to major in elementary education?

How to phrase it: *When I was in high school, I took an assessment test to help me figure out what career I should go into. When I got my results, teaching was one of the occupations on the list, along with several others like psychology, social work, and nursing. When I started researching the occupations in more detail, I discovered that teaching* **was the one that appealed to me most**.

This candidate put a lot of thought into choosing an occupation. This answer not only shows her dedication to teaching but also that she makes decisions carefully.

Q: Are you planning to get your MBA?

How to phrase it: *I would like to do that. I'm trying to find a program with* **a schedule that won't interfere with work**.

This interviewee knows that an MBA is highly valued in her field, but she anticipates that her potential employer might be concerned that her work schedule would be compromised if she pursues one. She heads off those fears.

> **Green Light Phrases**
> Internship taught me
> Extracurricular activities
> Put myself through school
> Studied consistently
> Attentive in class
> Researching my occupation
> Gave as much effort as possible.
> Gained knowledge about this field.
> Manage my own time, budget, and limits
> Grade point average

Why You Chose Your School

Q: Why did you choose Adams University?

How to phrase it: *Adams University has an* **accredited** *business school. It is* **ranked third in the nation**. *The university also has a great cross-country team, and I wanted to try out for it.*

This candidate put a lot of thought into choosing a college, implying that's how she makes all her decisions. She also uses this opportunity to brag about the quality of her education.

Q: I see you transferred to Hamford University from Sannau County Community College. Why did you start at a two-year school?

How to phrase it: **I knew I wanted to earn a bachelor's degree**. *I also wanted to go to Hamford, but the cost of a four-year education there was extremely high. I decided to take my core classes at a community college to* **save money**. *I first checked to make sure Hamford would take my credits. Since Sannau is a very* **well respected community college**, *I knew I would get a decent education there.*

By giving this answer, the interviewee demonstrates that she is a very practical person. She spends money wisely but doesn't compromise her goals. She also doesn't do something without first investigating it.

Q: Why did you choose to go away to college rather than going to one near your home?

How to phrase it: *I wanted to be* **responsible for myself**, *and I knew that wouldn't happen at home. By living in* *the dorms, I had no choice but to **manage my own time, budget my money, and set my own limits**.*

This candidate saw going away to college as a learning experience, both in and out of the classroom.

Courses You Took and Grades

Q: I see you majored in marketing. What courses did you take outside your major?

How to phrase it: *I took a few psych classes because I felt that knowing how people think would be **to my advantage** in marketing. I took some art classes because I really enjoy that. I also **took writing courses because** I thought that was an **important skill to have**.*

Instead of just giving a list of courses, this candidate talks about why she took them. She even explains how two of the subjects will help in her career.

Q: I see it took you four and a half years to graduate. Can you explain that?

How to phrase it: *I had a **difficult time adjusting** during my freshman year. I wasn't quite **ready for** all the demands of college. I had to take a few classes over. During the summer between my freshman and sophomore years, **I went to a few workshops to help me improve my study skills and my time management skills**. By the time I was a sophomore, I was a much more **serious student**.*

This candidate doesn't make excuses for his failings, but rather speaks about how he overcame them and how he succeeded in the end.

Q: What grade did you receive in your favorite class?

How to phrase it: ***My favorite class was** Intro to Journalism. It was actually pretty **tough** at first. Everything I handed in came back marked up in red ink. I must have gotten D's on the first four assignments. There were a few times that I found just the right words to capture an event, though, and **I loved that feeling, so I stuck with it**. Fortunately my professor gave us **the opportunity to redo our work** for a higher grade, and **although it took some extra work**, ultimately **I got an A in the class**.*

💬 Action Speak

Chaired	Joined
Delivered	Mobilized
Eliminated	Prioritized
Enlivened	Outdid
Forecasted	Tested

It's easy to like a class if you don't have to work hard for a good grade. This applicant explains why journalism was her favorite class despite having to work hard.

Never say: "Intro to Journalism. I got an A." Without saying more than that, the interviewer is left to wonder whether the candidate liked that class simply because she got an A in it.

Q: What grade did you receive in your least favorite class?

How to phrase it: *My **least favorite class** was art history. I know other people who took the class with other* *professors, got a C, and loved it. I hated the class and got an A. I didn't learn anything. I just had to show up for every class.*

Clearly this candidate likes to work hard and isn't impressed with getting rewarded for "just showing up."

Q: What courses best prepared you for this job?

How to phrase it: ***I took a course in*** *research and bibliographic methods that* ***provided me with the technical skills to do this job.*** *The most* ***important thing I learned*** *in that class was that there is a resource available to answer almost all questions. I also took several classes in children's and young adult literature. I saw from the job description that the person who takes this position will also have to spend several hours a week in the children's department.*

This candidate not only lists some courses he took but also explains how they will help him do the job should he be hired.

Q. What elective accounting courses did you take?

How to phrase it: *I* ***took three auditing classes*** *because I knew I wanted to work in public accounting. I also took an international accounting class. In this global economy, I knew that* ***would come in handy at some point in my career.***

This candidate explains how she chose courses she would be able to use professionally.

Q. Your GPA wasn't very high. Can you please explain that?

How to phrase it: *During my first two years of college, I was kind of immature and didn't work hard enough. I* ***worked really hard my junior and senior years****, but unfortunately those first two years really brought down my GPA. It was hard to recover from that.*

This candidate acknowledges that he was responsible for his low GPA, but also talks about how he worked hard to raise it.

Q: Why weren't your grades better in school?

How to phrase it: *School was a wonderful experience for me. I really* ***enjoyed learning new ideas****, I* ***studied consistently,*** *and I was* ***attentive in class****. But I never believed in cramming the night before an exam just to get a higher grade or staying up all night to finish a term paper. I really believe I learned just as much as many students who went for the grades.*

If you've made it to the interview stage, it is likely that your qualifications meet what the employer is looking for. In this case, the interviewer is just interested in how you react to her inquiry. The most important thing in responding to this question is not to get defensive or place blame on someone else. Instead, try to put a positive spin on it. For example, you could focus your answer on what you learned and the extra effort you put in to learning, rather than on the actual grades you received. Be aware that your grades could be just fine; don't take this question personally and don't think it is an insult in any way.

Extracurricular Activities and Internships

Q. What extracurricular activities did you participate in?

How to phrase it: *During my junior year of college, I was **president of the psychology club**. Then in my senior year, I was **editor of the yearbook**. I wrote for both my high school and college newspapers, too.*

This candidate highlights his leadership experience. He also calls attention to a very important skill—writing.

Q: Why didn't you participate more in extracurricular activities?

How to phrase it: *I wanted to **give as much effort as possible** to my studies. Though I had done very well in high school, I lived in a very small town, and the school didn't prepare me very well for college. To keep getting **the As I had become accustomed to**, I was forced to study very hard. Luckily, I was able to **grasp material quickly** enough that I found time to explore the city and make new friends. Still, between **studying, working a part-time job**, and socializing with friends, **I never had much time for organized, extracurricular activities**.*

Employers like candidates who are well rounded and have interests outside of work. If you didn't participate in formal extracurricular activities in college, you still may want to talk about some of your interests, such as reading or exercising, that you participated in on a more informal level. For instance, you may have a passion for running, even if you weren't on the college track team.

RED FLAG!

DON'T COME UP EMPTY when an interviewer asks you about extracurricular activities. The interviewer needs to know that you have a balanced life with outside interests and that you won't suffer from burnout.

Q: I see you had an internship in this field. What did you learn from it?

How to phrase it: ***My internship at** Carlson Corporate allowed me to get some **hands-on experience in this field** that I wouldn't have gotten in classes alone. I **learned that jobs in this field are** often stressful, and long hours are often required. On the other hand, I got to find out **how wonderful it is when you're on a team** that helps land a big account as a result of hard work.*

This applicant speaks about what he gained from the internship and what he learned about the positive and negative aspects of working in the field.

Q: Why haven't you done any internships?

How to phrase it: *I **would have loved to have done an internship**, but unfortunately I **had to work my way through college**. Most internships don't pay that well. However, as you can see from my resume, I made a point of finding work within this industry. Even though I was in the mailroom, I was still **exposed to the field**.*

While internships are important, sometimes extenuating circumstances get in the way. This candidate has no choice but to be honest about that. However, she explains how she tried to make up for not being able to do an internship.

Q: How did you spend your summers during college?

How to phrase it: I **worked every summer** to earn money for books and part of my tuition. I had this great job at a day camp. I **started off as a counselor** the summer before my senior year of high school, **moved up to group leader** the summer after I graduated, and then **became assistant director**.

This applicant takes the opportunity to show off a little. He stayed at the same job for several years and was promoted to a supervisory position.

What You Gained from Your College Experience

Q: Did you have any teachers who influenced you?

How to phrase it: Yes, I did. It goes all the way back to junior high school. Mr. Danzer was my earth science teacher. He loved the subject, and he loved teaching. I think both these things came across in his ability to teach. **It showed me that if a person loves what he does, he's more likely to excel at it**. That was good to know when it came time to choose a career.

This candidate tells which teacher influenced him and how.

Q: What did you gain from attending college?

How to phrase it: I **gained knowledge about this field**. I was able to use what I learned in class on the **internship** I did last summer at the Tallahassee Tribune. College is where I **learned to be independent**. There wasn't anyone pushing me to complete assignments on time,

so I had to learn how to **manage my time well** and **stay organized**.

This candidate talks about things he learned both in and out of the classroom. He includes technical skills as well as soft skills—time management and organization.

Q: Aside from coursework, what was the most enriching part of your college education?

How to phrase it: I was **very involved** on the programming committee. As a matter of fact, I was chair during my senior year. We were **responsible for planning on-campus events** for the student body. The **goal** was to hold events that were well attended and safe. That meant hiring entertainment that appealed to the majority of students and making sure campus security was present to enforce the rules.

This applicant talks about her work on this committee as if it were a job. She explains her goals and how she met them.

Q: What would your professors say about you?

How to phrase it: My **professors would say I** always turned in **high-quality work**. They would say I **contributed to classroom discussions** by offering interesting comments and **asking good questions**. They would also say I was **willing to help other students**.

This candidate takes the opportunity to highlight some positive attributes.

Q: Have you ever had a disagreement with a professor? How did you handle it?

How to phrase it: *I **disagreed about a grade** I received once. I spent a lot of time researching and writing a paper for a history class. When I got the paper back with a B, I was very disappointed. After thinking about it for a day, **I decided to talk to the professor**. He asked me what grade I thought I deserved. I said I thought I had earned an A on the paper and explained why. He said he would read the paper over and regrade it if he found my arguments were valid. The next day he told me **he changed my grade to an A**.*

This student knows how to stand up for herself when there is something she feels strongly about. She demonstrates how she persuaded her teacher to change her grade by presenting her arguments in a calm manner after waiting a day to collect her thoughts.

Q: What was the most difficult assignment you had while in school?

How to phrase it: *I took a creative writing class. It was one of several electives I could choose from outside my major. I had to write a poem. I **discovered** I'm not really good at that sort of thing.*

This interviewee chose to discuss an assignment that was entirely unrelated to his major and to anything he would be expected to do at this job.

Q: What did you like most about college?

How to phrase it: *I really enjoyed **playing on the volleyball team**. During my freshman and sophomore years, the team wasn't as strong as it could have been. We **pulled together and worked very hard**, and by my junior year we were ranked number two in our division. By my senior year, we were **ranked first place**.*

This candidate's mention of her participation on an athletic team draws attention to her ability to work on a team. From her research, she knows employees of this company often work on teams.

Q: Why didn't you finish college?

How to phrase it: *I left school because of financial reasons. My parents **couldn't afford my tuition, so I decided to work for a few years**. The experience was actually a great one for me. I learned a lot from it. I'm **planning to take some classes** next semester. I just heard about a great program that offers classes online. I checked the program out with the State Education Department, and it's legitimate.*

Dropping out of school for financial reasons is certainly acceptable. This candidate speaks positively of her work experience, claiming that she gained something from it. Her plan to take some classes won't affect her work schedule.

Endnote: If you're interviewing for jobs straight out of school, you should be prepared to answer a lot of questions about your education. Simply think of your school as a company and structure your answers to sound professional. All of this information lets your interviewer get a better look at who you are and gives you a chance to talk about your skills.

Chapter 17

SPEAKING WITH EASE

. . . About Why You're an Ideal Fit

Before you go on your interview, take some time to think about the personality of the company you're courting. Brainstorm the ways in which you mirror that personality. Be ready to emphasize those parts of yourself in your interview. For example, if you are applying at an internet start-up company, you'll want to emphasize your innovative side and your willingness to work long hours to support your team. What every employer is looking for is someone with good character and ethics. That kind of person is a good fit in any company. If you have the right keywords in mind and you have real-life examples to use as evidence of your professional integrity, then you will ace this part of the interview.

Business Sense and Personal Character

Q: Give an example of how you saw a project through, despite various obstacles.

How to phrase it: **My promotion** *from account representative to account manager required that I pass on many of my oldest accounts to the new account representative. After two years of dealing directly with me, some of these accounts did not take kindly to a new face. Some even threatened to move their accounts if I could not be part of their projects. While I had plenty of work to do adjusting to my new job, I* **assigned myself the role of account advisor** *to all of the accounts who were having problems adjusting.* **I took the time to** *visit each of these accounts personally with the new account rep and* **discuss the changes** *that were taking place within our company. I assured each of the accounts that* **I would be there for them** *if they needed answers, but that they should refer to the new rep with any new business. After a few months of phone calls, they eventually began to stop. The accounts realized that my replacement had a lot of talent, and they began to trust in his abilities. To this day, each of those accounts is still with my company.*

The goal in your answer is to demonstrate your competence and willingness to do well, even when the pressure is on. Don't dwell on the obstacles themselves; the interviewer doesn't care about the problems of your current or former company. Focus your answer on how you approached these obstacles and the results that you got.

Q: Tell me about a time when you showed real determination.

How to phrase it: *A few years back, our work force was predominantly older baby boomers who were not web savvy. When my company went online, nobody seemed to* **appreciate what the technology could do for our business.** *Most of the employees weren't sure what to do. I was convinced that if all staff members took the time to undergo online training, they would all find it* **a much easier way to do business.** *I* **began a promotion** *in which each morning I would send out via e-mail a trivia contest. The first person to get all the answers right and send them back via e-mail would win a prize. As the employees became more comfortable using e-mail to enter the trivia contest, they* **began using the Internet** *to help them conduct business as well.*

Talk about a time when you persevered to accomplish a goal. You can use either a professional or a personal goal here, as long as it reflects an interest in developing new skills. Demonstrate your ability to gather resources, predict obstacles, and manage stress. Talk about the results you obtained.

Q: Tell me about a time when you showed real diligence or perseverance.

How to phrase it: *I was working on an installation project when about halfway through to completion the client decided that he wanted something different.* **While for many this would cause quite an obstacle,** *my partner and I agreed that we could still get the work done by the original completion date. We* **had to put in about seventy hours a week** *for the next few months, but we did it* to **make sure that the client was happy** and the project went **according to plan**.

Talk about your professional character. Describe your focus, diligence, and accountability. Demonstrate how you gather resources, manage your time wisely, or are willing to go the extra mile. Use a specific example from your professional, educational, or personal history. Don't paint a somewhat problematic picture of yourself. There's a big difference between being determined and just plain annoying and tiring.

Q: How many days were you absent from work in the past year, and why?

How to phrase it: *I was absent from work three days last year. I caught the flu early in the year and was forced to miss two days, and I experienced a death in the family just last month and took a day off.*

A history of absenteeism, tardiness, or any indication of a weak work ethic can be detrimental to your candidacy. Answering this question should be an easy way to score points. If you used up all of your sick and/or personal days, tell the interviewer the reason. Be honest; lying will be found out. If you think your poor attendance may be a source of bad references, be prepared to give a detailed and exonerating explanation of why you have missed so much work in the past. Most importantly, convince the interviewer of your dependability and assure her that punctuality and/or absenteeism is not something she should worry about.

> **Green Light Phrases** Adjusting to my new job; Find an easier way to do business; Make sure the client is happy; Act according to plan; Gather resources; Task-oriented; Problem-solving abilities; Mastering new skills; Healthy work-life balance; Natural skills and abilities

Q: Are you punctual?

How to phrase it: *Yes. In the past year, **I have only been late to work on one or two occasions**, and each time I **called my supervisor ahead of time** to let him know. On each occasion, it was a matter of traffic delays.*

This is really just an alternate version of the previous question. The problem here is that whereas there is a definitive answer to the earlier question ("I was out three days."), this question is much more open-ended. Again, to say yes to this question when you know that you are always tardy will certainly come back to haunt you.

Q: We have found that all of our employees fall into one of two categories: concept oriented or task oriented. Which of these categories do you fit into?

How to phrase it: *When given a project, I **like to be involved in every step**. From initial development to final product, I like to be able to **use my creativity and strong problem-solving abilities**. I would definitely consider myself more **concept oriented**.*

Here you have to pick a side and describe some of the personal characteristics that made you choose this orientation. Most importantly, be sure that the answer you choose coincides with the job description. If you are to be engaged in manual labor forty hours a week, it is not likely that your orientation toward concepts will help you in any way. Similarly, if your job entails a lot of creativity, being task oriented is not necessarily the best way to be. Whatever answer you come up with, relate it to the job in some way.

RED FLAG!
DON'T TAKE THE EASY WAY OUT on an either/or interview question by supplying an all-encompassing answer like, "I think it's both!" Choose a side and stay there.

Q: What would your supervisor tell me about your attention to detail?

How to phrase it: *As my supervisor relies heavily on me to think projects through with him, I am confident that **he would praise my attention to detail**. I know how easy it can be for someone to overlook the smallest details of a project, and **I pride myself on** catching any glitches before they find their way into the final results.*

Regardless of the job you hold or the industry you belong to, a strong attention to detail is a great asset. Throughout the day, there are so many small details that often get overlooked that it is comforting for employers to know they have employees they can count on. If your attention to detail track record is not the best, don't try and push off the importance of this trait

by discussing another one of your strengths. Instead, admit that you have let mistakes get past you before, but talk about how you are working to stop this. If you do, in fact, have a strong attention to detail, talk about an experience when this really helped you in some way.

Q: Describe a professional skill you've been able to acquire in your current position or at your current company.

How to phrase it: *While I had **used computers quite extensively** in my previous positions, I had **never been required to use** database technology. As my current company relies heavily upon several different databases to store all of our work, I **have become an expert in programs such as** Access. What used to take me hours of research and data compiling can now be completed with just a few clicks of the mouse.*

The best way to answer this question is to talk about a new skill that you have learned—and worked toward mastering—while at your current job. You want to make sure that the interviewer sees you as a desirable candidate who is able and ready to take on new tasks with enthusiasm.

Q: Why is service such an important issue?

How to phrase it: *Asking why service is important would be the same as asking why customers are important; it is the **heart and soul of any business**. You can't have a business without customers, and you can't maintain customers without a **strong dedication to service**. If a customer isn't receiving a level of service that meets or exceeds his expectations, you can be sure he will take his* business elsewhere. And it's likely that he will relay that information to other would-be customers. On the other hand, if you are **dedicated to providing the best service** you can, customers will keep coming back for more, and they'll still tell others about you. In many instances, service may be the one thing that distinguishes a company from the competition. A bad reputation for service may compromise a company's position in the marketplace.

A question like this gauges your business sense. The interviewer is trying to determine whether you understand the importance of good customer service in establishing a positive image in the marketplace. If possible, talk about how you or your company have taken steps to ensure good customer service and how that has proven beneficial. Show that you understand the impact of repeat business, and convince the interviewer that you will work hard to uphold a standard of good service.

Q: Tell me about a time when you had to deal with an angry customer. How did you handle the situation?

How to phrase it: *As you can imagine, in the retail world, you are* **forced to deal with irate customers** *from time to time, regardless of how strong your product or customer service is.* **I specifically remember one occasion** *in which a customer was angry because the item she had purchased was not working properly once she got it home. The best way to handle these situations, in my opinion, is to remember that* **there is a simple solution***. Products can be fixed, exchanged, or refunded. I try to think of myself in terms of the consumer. When* **discussing the problem** *with the customer, I speak in a*

calm*, even voice, thus prompting the customer to do the same. The main issue to be concerned with is* **solving the problem at hand***, and you need to be professional enough to get that done.*

How you react to an unsatisfied customer is very important in most positions, and it's especially important if you work in a service industry. The interviewer will be looking for evidence of your aptitude for work that involves a great deal of contact with the public, even in situations in which the public isn't being too nice. Give an example of a time when you faced a difficult person and how you handled it. Explain the result of that situation, if in fact something positive came out of it (for example, if the customer reordered a week later). Your answer should illustrate your maturity, diplomacy, and awareness of the needs and feelings of others. Though you shouldn't take such things personally, you should be able to show compassion to the customers who are in need of pacification.

RED FLAG!
KEEP IT TO YOURSELF: Today, most employers respect childcare and eldercare issues, but calling attention to them in the interview is an unnecessary red flag.

Q: Are there any issues in your personal life that might in some way affect your professional career?

How to phrase it: *I really pride myself on* **my keen ability to separate my personal life from my work life***. When I'm in the office, I am an employee of the company. I* *recognize this is not the place for me to deal with or worry about issues in my personal life. I do my best to keep a **strong work-life balance** that keeps both components satisfied.*

The interviewer wants to make sure that you're not going to be bringing your home life to work with you. If you are dealing with stressful personal issues, the company wants to be sure that your time spent at work will be concentrated on work only. Though certain questions about your beliefs or your family are illegal, the interviewer wants to know whether you will be able to perform the duties this job calls for. In the health services industry, for example, personal issues that have not been worked through properly could easily affect your judgment in assessing patients, planning treatments, and making recommendations. Make sure the interviewer knows that you are a fully integrated individual and that your professional life and personal life always remain separate.

Q: Tell me about a time when your diplomacy skills were really put to the test.

How to phrase it: *I **recall one time when** a customer came into the store and demanded his money back on a suit that had apparently been worn. Because this kind of situation happens often—people want a fancy outfit to wear for one night only—we have **a strict policy** that says there are no refunds once the tags have been removed. The man claimed that the suit had become very worn looking after being sent to the dry cleaner and that the cleaner had claimed it was a faulty fabric. **Rather than argue** with the man about the policy and about the fact that the tags had been removed, I refunded his money,*

*though I didn't believe that he was being honest. He was a consistent customer, and **I decided it was more important to maintain his regular business** and to keep the other customers from hearing him complain rather than have them doubt the quality of our merchandise.*

Diplomacy involves using tact, finesse, and good judgment to reach an end that is ultimately beneficial to the entire company. Being diplomatic for selfish reasons is closer to backhandedness. In answering this question, make sure you demonstrate a pragmatic sensibility. Talk about a problem situation with a client or a work associate that you resolved by remaining objective. How did you show empathy and build rapport? What was the end result? How did this help all those involved, including yourself?

Q: What personal skill or work habit have you struggled to improve?

How to phrase it: *I think that **one habit I have worked very hard to overcome is my inability to say no**. I used to be helpful to the point of overextension. It didn't matter that I already had a full plate or whether or not I thought I could do a good job on a project; I would simply always say yes when colleagues asked me for help. Now, when someone asks me to do something for her, I counter with something I'd like help on in return. Since then, **cooperation** in my office has **improved considerably**.*

Here's another one of those questions that forces you to confront a negative aspect of your professional character. The interviewer wants to hear about a particular skill that you have had trouble acquiring, or something about yourself that you have had to change for the betterment of the workplace. The smartest way to answer this question is to find an example from your earliest days in the workplace so that any sort of negative quality can be attributed to your lack of experience. Talking about a problem that you have been trying to overcome in your current job will only show the interviewer that that trait could follow you to your new place of business. In the end, make sure you leave no question in the interviewer's mind as to whether that particular work habit is still an obstacle.

Why You Want the Job

Q: After learning more about this job, which aspect interests you most?

How to phrase it: *I'm **particularly interested in your recent joint ventures with** two processing companies in Latin America. My father was an army officer, so we lived in Latin America for three years. I am **very interested in seeing what happens** with these agreements. **What are your plans for the next few years?***

In the section regarding your motivation, the interviewer asks a very similar question: What particular aspect of the company interests you most? Essentially, there is no real difference between these questions except the way that they are worded. In the question above, you are being asked to talk directly about the company in an effort to prove that you have done your research. In this instance, you should feel free to talk about the company or about the position itself. Describe your qualifications for the job and how well the job fits your natural skills and abilities.

Give evidence that you've performed well in similar work. What proof can you offer that you'll excel in this job? The best answer to this question would address both the company and the position. More specifically, it would focus on what you could do for the company in the position at hand. If you've researched the company properly, you should have no problem answering this question quickly and authoritatively.

Q: After learning more about this job, which aspect interests you least?

How to phrase it: *In my last position, **I was able to find more success by** spending time on my major accounts rather than scheduling one-on-one interviews with smaller accounts. Though every salesperson has her preference, I think that this is really **where my strength lies**. In my time there, I was able to **increase my key account business by 20 percent**. I would like to be able to continue with this personal style within your company **to obtain even better results**.*

This is another one of those questions that job seekers hate to be asked. Forcing you to talk about a potentially negative aspect of the job can be a little intimidating, especially when you're trying to impress this person. One way to skirt the issue is to talk about a situation in your current position that you find to be a negative aspect and find out whether this job would have a similar downside. Another way to counter this question is to ask why the last person left the job. Respond to the interviewer's answer, then go on to discuss what you see as the positive points of this job, even if you've done so before.

Q: What aspects of this job do you feel most confident about?

How to phrase it: *As the companies I have worked with in the past have been engaged in the manufacture of very similar products, I feel that I will be able to **fully integrate myself in no time at all**. With a strong knowledge of your company's products, I think I will be able to **jump right in** with lots of creative and **fresh ideas** and **translate my past success** to your company.*

Make sure that when you answer this question, you sell the skills you have as they relate to this job—and not just sell yourself! The interviewer probably already has a good sense of your personality and you as a person; this is a chance to plug your applicable skills and how they relate to the position at hand. Talk about your skills in relation to the larger scope of things: that is, how they relate to this job, this company, and the industry.

> **Green Light** When answering a complicated interview question, try to respond with a step-by-step answer. It will keep your thoughts organized and show the interviewer that you are practical and methodical.

Q: What concerns you most about performing this job?

How to phrase it: *As my past experiences relate directly to this position, I am **confident** that I could perform the job well. Other than that, I have never been the key manager of a department, and I am **a little concerned** as to whether or not there will be a large enough customer service network. As **one of the key points of this company** is a twenty-four-hour service line, I just want to be sure that there are always enough people here to answer the phones.*

Even if the job you are interviewing for will bring about many brand-new responsibilities and is not something you have much experience with, you should never say the word "failure." Always project an air of confidence. One way you can answer this question is to turn it around and say, "Nothing that you have mentioned so far concerns me. I am fairly confident that I could perform the job really well. Are there any aspects of this job that you are concerned with me performing?" If the interviewer comes back with a few questions, respond with the same confidence in your abilities. Address each one of the interviewer's concerns and make her sure that your interests are compatible with the position. Offer proof that will dispel any doubts she may have.

Q: Why is this a particularly good job for someone with your qualifications?

How to phrase it: ***Based on what you've told me about the last person who held—and excelled in—this job**, I believe we share many similarities and, therefore, am confident that I would do a great job. We seem to have the same educational qualifications and similar work experience. I also think that I would **work well with** your audit **team**. I come from a similar kind of environment and know exactly what a client can do to make the consulting relationship more **productive**.*

The key to answering this question is to draw upon experiences from your current or former job and talk about the positive experiences you have had. If you know anything about the success and background of the person who formerly held this position, that's also a great way to prove that you are a great match for the job. Being too specific can be detrimental to this question, as it indicates that you may not quite understand what this position is all about.

What You'd Bring to the Company

Q: The department you would be in charge of hasn't had a supervisor in months. This is going to be a big transition for the staff. How will you handle it?

How to phrase it: *I wouldn't want to make any big changes for at least the first two weeks. I find it's **better to just observe how** things are done before trying to make any improvements. I want to **gain the staff's trust** first and **listen to their concerns**.*

This candidate has a plan in place, and she lays it out step by step. She knows that employees who have been unsupervised for a long time need to get used to having someone overseeing their work.

Q: Senior citizens represent a huge market now, and we want to convince them to buy our product. If we hired you, how would you help with that?

How to phrase it: *In addition to being a very big market, the senior market also continues to grow. They are a group with a very active lifestyle. Many have expendable income, and they choose to use their savings on travel,*

so it's clear **we have a product they will want**. We have to determine how to **reach them**. I would first want to do **research** to find out what publications seniors read and what television shows they watch. Only then can we **embark on** an advertising campaign.*

This candidate demonstrates that he would take a methodical approach to this project. He also shows that he understands the market very well.

💬 Action Speak

Amplified	Executed
Briefed	Harmonized
Conferred	Instituted
Edited	Promulgated

Q: We're about to change over to a new software program for our shipping and receiving department. We'd like the person we hire for this position to do the training. Are you the right person for that job?

How to phrase it: *I am definitely **the right person** for this job. **As you can see on my resume**, my last job was with a software distributor. One of my responsibilities was to travel to our clients' offices to provide software training.*

This is one confident candidate.

Q: The person who last held this position took ill and has only been able to work off and on for the last three months and has finally resigned. Things are a huge mess, which the person we hire will need to sort out. Are you up for the challenge?

How to phrase it: *I love a good challenge. First I'll sort through the mess to* **organize** *it. Then* **I'll see which things require immediate attention** *and which things I can work on later.*

The interviewee, by giving this answer, shows that she knows how to both organize and prioritize. These are two skills that are extremely important for someone taking over a job that has been neglected.

Q: The person we hire will have to respond to customer complaints occasionally. Will you be able to do that?

How to phrase it: *Years ago I worked in customer service. I'll be able to* **put that experience to good use.**

The interviewee finds some past experience that will help her with this aspect of the job.

Q: In about a year, we want to open a new branch on the other side of town. We plan to train the person who takes this position to run that office. Is that something you'd be interested in?

How to phrase it: *I would welcome that opportunity* **if it arises.**

Notice the applicant says "if it arises." She wants to express her eagerness to take on more responsibility with this employer without sounding like she'd leave if that opportunity didn't come up, or if such an opportunity came up sooner with another company.

Q: If we hire you, will you be willing to get your certification? You have all the skills we're looking for, but we really need someone who is certified.

How to phrase it: *I was* **planning to take my certification exam** *in June. That's the next time it's being given.*

While it would have been okay for this candidate to say he would get his certification because the client has asked him to, it's even better that he said he was planning to do it anyway.

Q: We have several clients with outstanding bills. If we hire you, how will you handle this situation?

How to phrase it: *First, I would* **want to go through the paperwork** *to make sure these clients were properly notified their accounts are delinquent. If I find out they were notified, I'll* **call each one personally** *to discuss this. There might be extenuating circumstances. It's* **important not to be too heavy-handed** *in dealing with* **these types of situations**. *After all, these are our clients. We don't want to lose them entirely.*

This candidate gives a clearly thought-out answer. She knows how important it is to be diplomatic when dealing with clients.

Q: Our clients expect a very quick turnaround on the projects we do for them. Can you handle that?

How to phrase it: *Yes, I can.* ***While I was in graduate school****, I had several professors who assigned projects that were due only a few days later. I became an* ***expert at scheduling*** *my time around completing these assignments.*

Since this interviewee doesn't have work experience to draw upon, she talks about her experience as a student. In the process she highlights a valuable skill—time management.

Q: If you are hired for this position, you will go from managing your current staff of ten to managing fifty people. Will you be able to oversee a substantially larger staff?

How to phrase it: *Yes, I will.* ***Although I've never managed a staff of that size before****, I know I have the* ***skills necessary*** *to do it. I am a* ***strong leader****. I am good at* ***communicating*** *what each member of my staff needs to accomplish. I am good at* ***delegating*** *responsibilities, which will be even more important with such a large staff.*

This candidate lets the interviewer know that he has all the skills that a good manager should have, even though he doesn't have experience with the exact situation he will face.

Q: When we are in the process of developing a new product, it's essential that information about it doesn't leak out. How are you at keeping secrets?

How to phrase it: *After working in the technology field for the past three years,* ***I know how important it is to keep information confidential*** *until a product is released.*

This candidate knows from experience that keeping secrets is important.

Q: We currently have several employees who have problems with things like tardiness and excessive personal phone calls. How would you deal with this if we hired you as supervisor?

How to phrase it: *First, I would need* ***to find out exactly what is occurring****. Then, prior to singling out any one employee, I would* ***circulate a memo*** *to the entire department that reiterated the rules. If the behavior continued, I would have a* ***private meeting*** *with each employee who isn't following the rules. I would stress* ***the importance of following the rule*** *they are breaking, and I would try to find out if there are extenuating* ***circumstances that could be remedied****. If the employee continues to break the rules, there would be repercussions.*

This interviewee is clearly not one to "leap without looking." She knows how important it is to evaluate a situation before taking action. However, she will take action in an expedient manner.

Q: Four times a year we work around the clock for about a week. Will that be a problem?

How to phrase it: *That's fine with me. **I understand** that the beginning of each season is a very busy time.*

Not only is this job candidate willing to work late, he knows enough about the industry to know what times of year this would be expected of him.

Q: As my assistant, would I be able to trust you to take over for me whenever I'm out of the office?

How to phrase it: *Absolutely. **I would follow whatever rules you set forth**. I also have **excellent judgment**, so I can handle whatever comes up.*

The applicant uses this opportunity to highlight her skills.

Q: Whoever fills this position will need to write next year's budget, which needs to be 10 percent lower than the current one. Could you do this?

How to phrase it: ***I had to do something similar when** my department went through funding cuts last year and I was **in charge of** writing the new budget. First I reviewed the current year's budget and removed amounts that had been budgeted for one-time events. Then I found a few areas where our actual expenditures were lower than we had **budgeted** for, and I was able to bring the amount down to more **realistic levels**, of course accounting for possible price increases. Finally, I went through it to see what cuts would have a minimal effect on services. I cut a program that traditionally had very low attendance. This eliminated the need to hire a part-time instructor. I was **able to submit a budget that was 12 percent lower** than the one for the previous year.*

This candidate demonstrates how he takes a practical approach to trimming a budget. He shows how he is able to get the job done with a minimal effect on service.

Q: As a contact person for our clients, you might have to tell them little white lies to keep them happy. For example, we never would want a client to know about a mishap that occurred with a project we were working on for them. Would you be comfortable with that?

How to phrase it: *I'm always **inclined to be honest**. However, I know that little white lies **come with the territory** in this field. If not telling a client the whole truth keeps them calm and happy, then **I can do that**. No need to worry anyone unnecessarily. Of course, I will work to **make sure the problem is resolved** as quickly as possible.*

Knowing what common practice is in her field helps this candidate answer this question. By telling the interviewer that she always tries to be honest but is willing to tell a client a white lie to keep him happy, she essentially says to the interviewer, "I'll always be honest with you, but I'll also help protect your relationship with clients even if it means telling the occasional half-truth."

Q: The students in this school can be very challenging to manage. As a teacher here, will you be able to handle them?

How to phrase it: *I worked with special-needs children when I was an assistant teacher at Ardsley School. I* **learned that it is important to** *look at each child as an individual. Each one has different strengths and weaknesses. If you look at it that way, you can* **figure out what strategy you need** *to use to work with each child. Children will* **trust** *you when they know you see them as individuals and will usually respond by doing what you need them to do.*

Although this candidate is applying for his first professional job, he is able to draw on his past experience. He explains what he learned from his previous experience as an assistant teacher.

RED FLAG!
DON'T GET STUCK talking at length about obstacles you dealt with at your past company. Keep the conversation focused on how you overcame them, not how annoying they were.

Q: In this fast-paced environment, we need someone who can think on her feet. Are you that person?

How to phrase it: *Yes, I am. I have* **experience making thoughtful decisions under pressure**. *I worked at a daily newspaper for five years. Every day we had to make last-minute decisions about what to include in the* next day's edition. There was no time to waste when the paper had to go to press within the next half-hour.

This candidate shows how her experience has enabled her to be decisive.

Your Past Work Experiences

Q: What was your first job?

How to phrase it: *My very first job was in a deli. I worked there every summer from ninth grade until I graduated from college. At first I was hired to do odd jobs, but once I was old enough, I worked behind the counter, serving customers. I was the youngest employee there, but* **my boss always said I was the hardest-working one**.

Although this job was unrelated to his career, his longevity there, as well as his former boss's opinion of him, lets the interviewer know that he was a valuable employee.

Q: Out of the jobs you've had, which was your favorite?

How to phrase it: *My favorite job was teaching at the Wee Ones Preschool.* **I like my current job** *at Parkside Elementary, but* **I realize now that I prefer to** *work with preschoolers.* **That's why I want to work here.**

This candidate has chosen a job that is related to the one that she is being interviewed for.

Q: What kinds of jobs did you have during college?

How to phrase it: *I had a variety of jobs while I was going to college, and since I was **paying my own way**, I sometimes had more than one job. I worked as a waiter, a door-to-door salesman, and a data entry clerk. I learned a lot about **interacting tactfully with different people**, and I also **developed my office and computer skills**.*

In addition to demonstrating how industrious he is (working his way through school), this candidate shows how he developed skills in different areas through his experience.

Q: I see three jobs listed on your resume. Can you tell me what you learned from each of them?

How to phrase it: ***I learned a lot on each of my jobs**, so it's hard to pick one thing from each, but I'll try. When I worked in customer support at CSV, I learned how to help our software users **troubleshoot problems**. When I worked as a software trainer at Circle Tech, I learned that I needed to **find a common ground** when teaching a large group of people, because not everyone has the same level of skills. I **learned to manage** employees at my job as assistant to the head of training at APCO.*

Knowing about the job that he's applying for helped the applicant answer this question. He has picked one skill from each job that will be required for the job with this employer.

Q: Do you find your job rewarding?

How to phrase it: ***I found my job very rewarding** for a long time. It hasn't been as rewarding lately. While **I love**

*my new responsibilities**, I miss working with clients. That is what **attracted me to this position**—the combination of supervisory responsibilities and client contact.*

It's okay for the interviewee to say she doesn't find her current job rewarding. She explains why she feels this way without placing blame anywhere. With this answer, she also shows that she knows about the position she's interviewing for and explains why she is better suited for it.

Q: What about your current job isn't very rewarding?

How to phrase it: *I think every job has something about it that isn't rewarding. There is a lot of paperwork, and I don't find that particularly rewarding, but I know it **needs to be done**.*

This candidate understands the reality of work. Some job duties are rewarding, while others are not. She chose something that many people don't find particularly rewarding—paperwork.

Q: How have your other jobs prepared you for the one at this company?

How to phrase it: *I've worked on the retail end of the office supplies industry **for the past ten years**. I know what customers want and in turn what the retail outlets want. **I know the industry, and I know the products.** That is what qualifies me to be a sales rep for Roxy Staple Company.*

This candidate is confident of his abilities and that comes across in his response.

Q: Have you had to do any traveling for work?

How to phrase it: *I've had to do some traveling for my job. I went to Asia several times. I **enjoy traveling** and hope to do more of it on this job. I find it helpful to have **face-to-face meetings with clients** periodically rather than doing everything through conference calls.*

This applicant knows that his potential employer requires extensive traveling, and although he hasn't done a lot of it, he makes sure to point out that it's something he wants to do more of.

Q: You've never worked in widget manufacturing before. How have your jobs in the publishing industry prepared you for this?

How to phrase it: *Taking a product, whether it's a widget or a book, from its inception to the hands of the consumer takes a lot of **planning**. You have to put together a budget and **set deadlines**. You need to make sure your current staff can handle the work and hire consultants if necessary. You may even have to **handle crises** along the way, should problems arise. I dealt with such things on a daily basis while working in publishing, and I would be able to use the same **planning and management skills** to help your company.*

By focusing on his job responsibilities and talking about them in general terms, this candidate is able to show how he can transfer his skills from one industry to another.

Q: What decisions have you had to make in your current job?

How to phrase it: *When I **planned** career workshops for students, I had to **decide** what topics to feature, when to hold the workshops, and who would speak at them. I had to decide what software to purchase for our public computers, **within the constraints of our budget**. I also **made decisions about hiring and firing** student aides.*

By giving specific examples, this candidate highlights her skills in planning events, making purchasing decisions, working within a budget, and making personnel decisions.

Q: How is your present job different from the ones you had before it?

How to phrase it: *As a senior accounting clerk, I **supervise** three payroll clerks and a bookkeeper. This is the first time I've had to supervise other people.*

This applicant talks about how she has increased responsibilities at her job.

Q: What duties of your last job did you find difficult?

How to phrase it: *I found it difficult to fire people. Even though I always **put a lot of thought into** deciding whether or not to terminate someone, I knew I was affecting someone's livelihood.*

No one could fault someone for disliking this unpleasant duty.

Q: What do you think this job offers that your last job did not?

How to phrase it: *This job **offers me the opportunity to** use my **research skills**. I have mostly administrative duties on my current job, with some research duties. I **look forward to** a job that is primarily research oriented with some administrative duties.*

This applicant has both administrative and research skills, as she points out to the interviewer. She wants to use them in a different way than she does on her current job.

Endnote: You'll be asked a variety of questions about your past work experience and professional decision-making in your job interview. Frame your answers in a way that convinces them of your integrity and, ultimately, your compatibility with the company.

Chapter 18

SPEAKING WITH GRACE

. . . When It Comes to Hard Questions

There is always a chance that you'll be sideswiped by a particularly difficult question when you're interviewing. This is what makes interviews so scary for some people. If you've adequately prepared yourself, there is no reason to feel anything but confident walking into an interview. The key to rising above difficult questions is to take the time you need to formulate your answer and be diplomatic and positive in your response.

You can't prepare for every challenging question out there, but you can prepare for the most common ones. This chapter gives examples of some frequently asked zingers. All of them require careful consideration and a calm and collected interview persona. Reading them ahead of time puts you one step ahead of the competition in terms of preparation. Jotting down key phrases and practicing the best answers to them puts you miles ahead.

Discussing Frustrations and Failures

Q: Tell me about a project in which you were a bit disappointed in your own performance.

How to phrase it: *In my last job with a manufacturing company, I had to analyze all the supplier bids and present recommendations to the vice president of logistics. **Because the supplier bids weren't in a consistent format**, my analysis often consisted of comparing dissimilar items. **This caused some confusion in my final report**, and by the time I'd reworked it and presented it to the vice president, we'd lost the critical time we'd needed to improve our approval process for these bids. **In hindsight, I should have** set the bid format so that we could assess similar items. **Ever since, I've used a request for proposal process** consistent with the results we are looking to **achieve**.*

Describe the barriers you've come across in past experiences and how you've worked around them. How have your skills come into play? In hindsight, what could you have done differently? Most importantly, turn this roadblock into a lesson and tell the interviewer what you learned from having gone through the experience.

Q: Which aspects of your work are most often criticized?

How to phrase it: *In my first job as marketing assistant, I spent endless hours analyzing a particular problem for which I knew there was a better solution. I **came up with a revised marketing plan** that was extremely **well received** by my coworkers. Unfortunately, when it came time to present the plan to the top-level management, I **wasn't well versed in** PowerPoint. My presentation was*

*dull, and the proposal was turned down. **I'd failed to effectively** market and showcase the real benefits of my plan, such as the savings that would result from implementing it. I spent the next two weeks working on a presentation with a bit more sizzle, and **on my second try,** management approved it; **my recommendations were carried out to everyone's satisfaction**. I was very grateful to have been given that second chance. **Since then, I certainly make sure that** all the details have been taken care of when I am proposing something new to a group so that there are **no questions left unanswered**.*

Though the answer given here seems to skirt the issue a bit, that's okay. The best way to answer this question is to give an example of something you overlooked—or a mistake that you made—earlier in your career. Discuss the ways in which you worked to overcome the situation and to improve your work. Talk about how the failure has changed the way you work now, or how it has caused you to pay more careful attention to detail in all your work.

Q: Tell me about a situation that frustrated you at work.

How to phrase it: *I was frustrated once when a client who had insisted on purchasing a high-growth stock called in a panic because the stock had dropped more than twenty points in one day. I had a **hard time convincing her** to ride it out rather than cut her losses. I think what frustrated me most was that this happened **despite my attempts** from the beginning to explain the short-term volatility of that stock.*

This is another question designed to probe the candidate's professional personality. The interviewer will want reassurance that you are able to withstand pressure on the job. Describe how you've remained diplomatic, objective, or professional in a difficult situation. Pick a situation in which, again, you will not raise any major doubts or concerns in the mind of the interviewer. Depict yourself as able to work through the problems that arise in any job with tact and no hard feelings.

Q: Tell me about a time when your employer wasn't happy with your work performance.

How to phrase it: *When I first began working* as a paralegal, I handed in two letters with typos in them during my first week on the job. Perhaps my nervousness at beginning a new career contributed to my carelessness, *but I soon learned to be an excellent* proofreader. After that first week, *my boss told me regularly how happy he was with my work.*

Talking about your role in causing a company to go bankrupt certainly will not win you any points here. Instead, try to think of a relatively minor incident in which you made a mistake but were able to learn from it. Simply describe what happened and what you did to successfully resolve the situation. In the time since that incident, how have you redeemed yourself or improved upon your past mistakes?

Q: Give me an example of a time when you were asked to complete a task but weren't given enough information to get it done.

How to phrase it: At *my first job as* a publicity assistant, I was given the task of assembling 500 press kits for immediate mailing. The work had already been done, but I was *unsure of* whether or not there was a specific order in which each of the pages needed to be arranged. My supervisor had already left for a meeting, but I was *able to track her down* in her car. She explained to me the order in which the kits needed to be assembled, and the work was completed fairly quickly. In the end, I *managed to prevent a problem* that would have cost several hours of time to rectify, not to mention a bunch of headaches.

In answering this question, you want to reassure the interviewer that you are mature and responsible enough to handle problems that are likely to occur. Think of a situation in which you were able to think quickly enough to prevent a problem. Talk about your own resourcefulness and initiative in getting the job done in a timely and professional manner.

Q: Tell me about a time when you failed to resolve a conflict that had arisen.

How to phrase it: I *wasn't able to* keep a good employee who had been working in one of my company's manufacturing facilities for more than twenty years. As part of the company's modernization policy, all job descriptions were rewritten to require some sort of computer skills. *Though I offered to* pay the cost of classes so that he could gain these skills, he refused. Unfortunately, I *had*

no other option than to replace him, as the new technology we were using required these skills. **When I look back** on the experience, I really **wish I had been more vocal** to him and the other employees about acquiring new training periodically. That way, when new techniques were introduced, he may not have been so overwhelmed. Now I am **vigilant about** encouraging those in my work group to attend seminars and training classes to enhance their job skills. I have even had various professionals come into the office and teach some classes on-site.

The best way to answer this question is to discuss a difficult situation but one that was not really yours to solve in the first place. Briefly introduce the problem, but focus more on the steps you took to solve the problem. What was the result of your work? What did you learn from the experience? How has that experience changed your professional behavior today?

Q: How do you feel when things go wrong on a project? How do you handle it?

How to phrase it: *Though I would obviously prefer that all of the projects I work on run smoothly, I am **realistic enough to know** that this cannot happen. This is especially true in the case of the biotechnology industry, in which changes can and will happen to any plan at any time. I **try to realize from the outset of any project** that the plan we come up with is only the best-case scenario plan and that it **may need to be changed** at any given moment. When plans begin to unravel, my approach is just **to cross each bridge when I come to it** and not obsess about it beforehand. One of the ways in which I **try to prepare for complications** is to **come up with**

some alternative plans. Though this does work in some cases, it doesn't help in all; sometimes you can't prepare for a problem until it's right there in front of you. My basic attitude is to **take it all in stride**.*

This is a very tricky question. As the interviewee, you should understand that from the outset. What the interviewer is really trying to get at here is whether you have the ability to work under pressure. Without going into too much detail about all the projects that have somehow gone wrong in your professional history, reassure the interviewer that you can and do handle pressure with ease and professionalism.

 RED FLAG!
WHEN TALKING ABOUT problems you faced in past jobs, avoid blaming others or making excuses for the problems. Take responsibility and focus on the lesson you learned.

Q: Have you ever been passed up for a promotion you thought you deserved?

How to phrase it: ***A couple times** in my early career, I thought I was unfairly passed up for a promotion. However, **in retrospect**, I now **realize that I probably wasn't ready** to perform those jobs. In fact, the **additional training I received** remaining where I was proved invaluable in the last few years, as I've made **significant progress moving up the corporate ladder**. I've also learned to **appreciate** that being ready for a promotion doesn't necessarily mean it will happen. There are many external factors aside from a person's performance and capabilities that need to be taken into consideration.*

The interviewer wants to gauge the candidate's self-confidence and objectivity about personal or professional limitations. Be sure to give evidence here that you have enough patience to learn what is important before you get bored in one position or frustrated because you have not been promoted. After you've mastered your own job, would you stay motivated long enough to be productive? If you've never been passed up for a promotion—or if you've never been up for a promotion at all—it's okay to say so. Perhaps you've only been in the work force for a short period of time and don't think you've acquired strong enough skills to be promoted. Whatever the case, be honest.

Q: Tell me about your least favorite manager or professor.

How to phrase it: *Well, I've been* **pretty fortunate as far as managers go**, *and I didn't have any problems with my professors. In my first job out of college, I worked with a manager who was pretty inaccessible. If you walked into her office to ask a question, you got the sense that you were bothering her, so* **my coworkers and I just learned to get help from each other** *instead. She was good in a lot of ways, but I would have* **preferred** *that she'd been* **more available to us** *and given us more direction.*

Answering this question will be a little bit like walking across a minefield, so be careful! Keep in mind that the interviewer doesn't really want to learn about your former supervisors but about the way you speak of them. Though the interviewer may bait you to make a negative statement about your former employer, doing so can create a host of problems. Even if your claim is completely true and entirely justified, the recruiter may conclude either that you don't get along well with people in general (or specifically with those in authority positions) or that you often shift blame to others. The best way around this dilemma is to choose an example that's not too negative, touch upon it briefly, then focus the rest of your answer on what you learned from the experience.

Q: Who's the toughest employer you've ever had to work for and why?

How to phrase it: *The most difficult employer I've ever had would* **definitely** *have to be Mr. Rogers at the Brady Project. He would push people to their limits when things got busy, and he was a stickler for detail. But he was always* **fair**, *and he always rewarded people when they* **worked hard** *and did a good job.* **I'd** *definitely call him a tough boss,* **but I'd also call him a good boss**.

This question is another in which the interviewer is sort of daring you to make negative statements about a previous employer. Just remember that even the most difficult of bosses has taught you something new, so focus on that part of the experience.

Q: Have you ever had to work with a manager who you thought was unfair to you or who was just plain difficult to get along with?

How to phrase it: *Fortunately, I've* **never really run into that problem**. *Of course, my current boss has to work under time constraints—just like everyone else—and she sometimes has a* **tendency to phrase things rather bluntly** *to push our department to meet its goals. But I've never considered that unfair or hard to handle; it's* just **part of the job**. My supervisors and I have always **gotten along quite well**.

Again, no matter how many times an interviewer gives you the opportunity to do so, never criticize a current or former employer! The interviewer is not really interested in finding out whether or not you have worked for difficult people in the past; we all have. What he is trying to discover is whether or not (and how easily) you are willing to badmouth these people.

Q: What are some of the things your supervisor has done that you disliked?

How to phrase it: *The only thing I really don't like is to get feedback in front of others. I want to hear good or bad feedback in private so that I have time to think and react to the issue without other distractions. I believe that's the **fair** way to **improve learning** or to change future behavior.*

Again, avoid being overly negative about your ex-boss or manager. Discuss a relatively minor example of one with which the interviewer is likely to empathize. Put a positive spin on your answer by describing what you learned from this difficult situation.

Q: Tell me about two or three aspects of your last job that you never want to repeat.

How to phrase it: *One of the skills that I am most proud of is **my fairly extensive background in** credit collections; it has **enabled** me to make better risk assessments in my everyday job. **Though I really enjoyed the experience** I received from having worked in collec-*

tions, it was **not a job that I particularly enjoyed**, and it isn't something that I would want to do again.

In a completely constructive way, describe one or two things you've done that you didn't especially enjoy or that didn't play upon your greatest strengths. Though this question specifically targets a negative topic, it's easy to turn this around: After talking about why you didn't like a particular job or task, describe your strengths and their relevance to the job you're applying for.

Special Situations

Q: You were at your last job for only six months. Why so short a time?

How to phrase it: *Unfortunately, the job turned out to be much different than what I thought it would be. Fortunately though, I found this out early on—before the employer invested more time in me and I invested more time in the company. I know I **could put my editing skills to much better use in this position**.*

Notice the interviewer places no blame on either herself or the employer. She doesn't say that the employer didn't tell her the truth about the job or that she misunderstood what she'd be doing. She also shows how she looked out for both her employer and herself by leaving before more time was invested.

Q: I see from your resume that you've had five jobs in five years. Why have you moved around so much?

How to phrase it: *When I first graduated from college, I wasn't sure what I wanted to do. Five years later **I'm committed to working in this field**. I even took some courses to **enhance my skills**. I know I can do a good job here.*

This is an honest answer. The candidate states that she is now committed to the field and proves it by talking about classes she has taken.

Q: Why did you stay in your last job for such a long time?

How to phrase it: *I was in my last job for more than seven years. During that time, I **completed an advanced technical degree** at an evening university and also had two six-month assignments in which I was loaned out to different departments. As a result, I **acquired some additional skills** that normally aren't associated with that job. Therefore, I think I've **made good progress** and am **ready to accept the next challenge**.*

An interviewer may also be curious as to why you would stay in one particular position for too long. If you've been with the same company for an extended time, the interviewer may be curious about your interest in personal improvement, tackling new assignments, and so on. He may also be concerned about whether you have a tendency to get too comfortable with the status quo. Demonstrate how you've developed job responsibilities in meaningful new ways in your many years on the job

and that you are expecting to do the same with this company.

Q: Why do you want to leave your current position?

How to phrase it: *My current position **has allowed me to learn a great deal** about the plastics industry, and I am very **glad to have had that opportunity**. However, I've also found that my interests really lie in research and development, which my company has recently decided to phase out over the next two years. That is why I am **so interested in your organization**. As I understand, your company places a great deal of importance on research and development and is also a highly respected leader in the industry.*

The interviewer's foremost concern with career changers will always be why they want to switch careers. But people do it every day, so don't think you will not get the job just because you don't have any hands-on experience in the field. Show the interviewer that your decision to switch careers has been based on careful consideration. Explain why you decided on this particular position and how the position will allow you to further your skills and interests.

Q: Why would you want to leave an established career at an employment agency for what is essentially an entry-level marketing job?

How to phrase it: *During my many years at the agency, I have **acquired many valuable skills**. At the same time, **I feel as if I've stopped growing**. There's only so far you can go in such a career, and I am nearing the end of the career path. I am no longer challenged by my work,* and *being challenged is what keeps me motivated*. *I've thought about this for a long time, as switching careers is not an easy decision to make. Still, I am confident that I am doing the right thing by looking for a job within another industry, even if it means starting over.*

My interest in marketing arose last year when a local family lost their home to a fire. A group of people from my community decided to pitch in and help this family raise enough money to rebuild their home. I helped by designing and distributing posters, placing advertisements in local newspapers, and selling T-shirts outside grocery stores and shopping malls. When I began to see the result of what my work was doing, I became very excited about this task. I learned that you can have a great product and a great cause but that if nobody knows about it, you are dead in the water. I felt as if the work I was doing was making a difference, and I was good at it, too.

Since then, I have taken two introductory marketing courses and am planning to enroll in a part-time degree program this fall. Also, I'll be able to use many of the skills I've acquired working at an employment agency to benefit me in a marketing career as well. After all, working in an employment agency is marketing—that is, marketing the agency to corporate clients and job seekers, and marketing the job seekers to corporate clients.

The interviewer wants to determine two things: the candidate's motivation for choosing a new career and the likelihood that the candidate will be comfortable in a position in which she will probably have less power and responsibility than in previous jobs. To dispel the interviewer's fears, discuss your reasons for switching careers and be sure to show that you have a solid understanding of the position and the industry in general. Many candidates expect to start their new careers in jobs comparable to the one they held previously. The truth is that most career changers must start in a lower, if not entry-level, position in their new companies to gain basic experience and knowledge in the field.

> **Green Light** When you're asked a question with a negative spin, try to turn it around with a positive, upbeat response.

Q: According to your resume, you were a manager at Crane Computer Store from 1990 through 1995 and then assistant manager at a different branch of the store starting in 1995. Were you demoted?

How to phrase it: *This **wasn't a demotion**. I was originally manager of the Paper Products Department. It was a very small section. When an opening came up for an assistant manager in the Home PC Department at another store, I **jumped at the chance**. It was a **much better opportunity** because it was a much larger department, and I knew I would have **greater responsibilities**.*

Although the candidate's job title would indicate that she had been demoted, she explains why this wasn't actually the case. She was willing to trade the "manager" title for a job with more responsibility. If she had been demoted, however, she would need to explain why.

Q: Your resume says that you are an administrative assistant, yet you're applying for a job that has much more responsibility. What makes you think you can handle it?

How to phrase it: *Even though my job title is administrative assistant, I have many* **more responsibilities than that title usually implies***. I train all new support staff and supervise junior clerks.*

This answer explains how this candidate's responsibilities differed from what one might assume from her job title. She chooses to discuss the aspects of her current job that are related to the job she is interviewing for.

Q: Have you ever been fired?

How to phrase it: *When I was in college, I was fired from a summer internship. I was working for a software consulting company, and midway through the summer a new president was appointed because of some financial difficulties. As one of his first orders of business, he requested the resignation of my entire work group. I was unexpectedly swept out* **with everyone else***, though* **my work performance had never been criticized***.*

If you've never been fired, this should be an easy question to answer. If you have been fired, you'll need to be prepared to discuss the situation in detail and possibly answer a series of specific follow-up questions. If the termination was the result of a situation beyond your control, such as corporate downsizing, most interviewers will be understanding. If you were fired due to poor performance or some other personal problem, you'll need to admit your fault and convince the interviewer that you've corrected the problem. Although this may

be a difficult question to answer (and one that makes you—ultimately—nervous about the overall impression you will leave behind), you should be completely honest. If you aren't honest and the recruiter finds out as much from your references, you will definitely not be offered the job; if you have been made an offer or have already accepted one, it may be revoked or you may be subject to an immediate dismissal.

Q: Your resume states that you were fired from your last job. I admire your honesty, but can you explain why this happened?

How to phrase it: *A* **new manager** *came in.* **I liked him***, and I thought we worked well together. But a month after he arrived, he fired me. I heard afterward that* **many of the people I'd worked with were fired also***, and he'd filled the empty slots with people from his previous job.*

Understanding why you were fired is the first important step to take if you want an employer to hire you. Any employer would be nervous and, in fact, foolish to hire someone who doesn't have a clue as to why she was fired. Own up to your mistakes; you'll stand a better chance of being hired.

Q: In checking your resume we found that you were fired—and for a serious offense. Can you explain what happened?

How to phrase it: *It happened about five years ago. I got in with the wrong crowd; they would go out for drinks every night, and I wound up joining them. They were a rowdy bunch, not the kind of friends I would have picked if I could, but they were my colleagues, and I didn't have* *the courage to refuse them. But one night we stayed too late at a club and drank too much, and a fight started. One woman got hurt, and they had to rush her to the hospital. I didn't have anything to do with it, but the cops took us all in. I spent the night in jail, got bailed out in the morning, and when I went into work later that day, I got a pink slip. It was a **hard lesson** for me, but it **changed my life**. Since then, I've had two jobs, and though I'm always friendly with all my colleagues, when I walk out the door at night I don't socialize with them. I head home.*

Both situations are difficult for a prospective employer to accept. However, when a job hunter admits her mistake and has changed her ways, she stands a much better chance than someone who refuses to admit she might have been responsible for a serious offense.

Q: Would you be able to work extended hours if the job needed you to?

How to phrase it: *I'm **accustomed to working long hours** during the week. I usually work until at least 6:30 because I get a lot done after the office closes at five. I can make arrangements to be available on weekends **if necessary**, though I do **prefer to have at least twenty-four hours' notice**.*

Your response should match closely the position you are applying for and should reflect a realistic understanding of the work and time required. Ask about seasonality of your work if you're unsure, and show a willingness to work occasional extended hours. If you are completely unwilling to work any overtime, it's not likely that many companies will consider you a very valuable asset. Recent studies have shown that a large majority of Americans are working, on average, closer to fifty hours per week than to forty.

Q: What are your salary requirements?

How to phrase it: *If hired, I would **expect to earn** a salary that is **comparable to the going rate** for someone in my field, with my same skills, amount of experience, and expertise. However, the salary of the job is **not my only consideration**. The opportunity, as you have presented it, is much more important to me. I really believe that this job is exactly **in line with what I hope to accomplish**, and that is the most important thing to me. **What kind of range do you have in mind?***

Recruiters weed out people whose financial goals are unrealistic or not in line with what the position at hand is offering. This question is a direct hit, and both the interviewer and the candidate know that. It forces you to respond—directly—to a question relating to a very touchy subject. On the one hand, you may cite a salary that is too low. As a result, you will seem uninformed or (even worse) desperate. On the other hand, if you throw out a salary amount that is too high, you may immediately eliminate yourself from any further consideration. The best way to handle the salary question is to turn the question back on the recruiter. Mention that the salary isn't your primary consideration, and ask what the salary range for the position is. Next, ask the recruiter to consider how your qualifications compare to the average requirements for the position and go from there.

Q: What is your current salary?

How to phrase it: *I currently earn an annual salary of $45,000 per year with comprehensive company paid benefits.*

If you're asked a question this direct, consider yourself lucky. Telling the recruiter how much money you make now is a heck of a lot easier than trying to negotiate a salary with absolutely no information to go on (as in the previous question).

 RED FLAG!

DON'T EMBELLISH when asked about your most recent salary. More and more companies are starting to verify applicants' pay history, some even demanding to see W-2 forms from job seekers.

Q: Would you be willing to relocate to another city?

How to phrase it: *Though I would **prefer to remain here**, it's certainly a possibility I'd be willing to consider **based on the scope of the opportunity**.*

Just because you're asked this question does not mean that the interviewer wants to fly you off to the other side of the country for a job. You may, even in some first interviews, be asked questions that seem to elicit a tremendous commitment on your behalf, such as this one. Although such questions may be unfair during an initial job interview, you may well conclude that you have nothing to gain and everything to lose with a negative response. If you are asked such a question unexpectedly during an initial job interview, simply say something like "That's certainly a possibility" or "I'm willing to consider that." If and when the interviewer says something along the lines of "Well, we have nothing for you in our Anchorage office, but our outfit in Mobile would certainly benefit from someone with your experience!" then you can begin to panic.

If you do receive an offer, you can find out the specific work conditions as far as relocation goes and then decide whether you wish to accept the position. Remember, at the job-offer stage, you have the most negotiating power, and the employer may be willing to accommodate your needs. If that isn't the case, you explain that upon reflection, you've decided you can't relocate but you'd like to be considered for other positions that might open up in the future.

Q: Does the frequent travel that is required for this job fit in with your lifestyle?

How to phrase it: *The frequent travel in this consulting position is **no problem** for either me or my family. I was recently married, but my wife is an airline flight attendant, so neither of us follows the typical routine.*

If you feel comfortable enough to divulge information about your family situation, now is the time to do so. The interviewer's main concern here is that the candidate may not be able to travel as much as the job requires. To alleviate this concern, emphasize your flexibility or explain why travel wouldn't be a problem. Remember to be honest. If you were unaware that the job required any sort of travel—and if it would most likely be a problem—say so.

Q: Sell me this stapler.

How to phrase it: *This professional quality stapler is both functional and attractive. It will help you reduce clutter on your desk by enabling you to fasten pages together. Since papers relating to the same subject will now be attached, you'll be **more efficient**, and you will **spend less time** searching for papers. Finally, its sleek shape and black color are coordinated to match the rest of your office furniture.*

The interviewer is curious as to how quickly you can react to a situation. Do you have the ability to think on your feet? Do you know how to communicate effectively and succinctly? This is one question that you're likely to be asked if you're applying for a sales or marketing position in particular. If you want to get into either of those industries, be prepared to give a thirty-second sales pitch on the benefits and advantages of any common office staple, from a paper clip to a BlackBerry.

Q: Prove to me that your interest in this job and company is sincere.

How to phrase it: *I know that many people would like to work in television because of large income potential or the opportunity to be on camera, but **my reasons go far beyond that**. To me, communication is an art form, and the television industry is the ultimate test of how well one communicates. Working in television isn't like working for a newspaper, where, if a reader misses a fact, he can just go back and reread it. A television news story can go by in a flash, and the **challenge** is to make sure the audience understands it, learns from it, and, in a broader sense, can use the information **to better**
their lives or their situations. It's the way television can evoke action **that's always made me want to be a part of the industry**. I'm particularly interested in this station because **I like your focus on** the community. Though the on-air products have a great look, the station seems to remain focused on the tradition of local news and what matters to its audience. The special reports that emphasize town politics and explain the big issues facing a community make the viewer feel that the station is a part of the community. **In my opinion**, this is a great way to maintain a loyal audience.*

Being unprepared to answer this question can eliminate you from further consideration. On the other hand, if you are able to demonstrate a strong interest in the company and the position, you'll have an advantage over the competition. Be sure to talk about the specific position and give the details of the company that make you want to become an employee.

Let's say you are faced with this statement: "You have seven minutes to convince me you're the best candidate for the job. Go." How would you react? The question is essentially the question that can determine whether you're paying attention to the material in this book. This is the question that only the most prepared of all job interviewees will survive, and that's exactly what the recruiter is looking for. In answering this question, you should refer back to everything this book has taught you. Review your personal themes and touch upon each and every one of them. Assure the interviewer that you know all there is to know about the job, the company, and the industry. Essentially, you are trying to be every recruiter's dream candidate. It's not an easy thing to pull off, but have faith; you can do it. You can win that job!

Q: You've been working outside the banking industry for the past year. Can you explain why you want to return now?

How to phrase it: *Yes, I can. The **job market**, as you know, has been bad for the past year and a half. It's been **impossible for someone with my qualifications to find a job** in the banking industry. **To support my family**, I had to take jobs in retail sales. I was **happy to see your ad** for a banking job that **needs someone with my skills** in branch management.*

This candidate's only choice is to be honest. He is not to blame for the bad job market, so he makes no excuses for working outside his field for a year.

Q: Your resume states that when you got caught up in the burst of the tech bubble you decided not to look for a job but to freelance as a consultant. How did that work out for you, and why are you back in the job market?

How to phrase it: *I **enjoyed** consulting. It worked out well for almost two years. But I found it hard to do everything— to keep looking for clients and at the same time service the ones I had. I also **missed the collegial atmosphere of working with a team**. I'm **eager** to return to that atmosphere. I **don't regret** the two years I spent consulting, however. I think I learned a lot during those years, and I'm bringing with me the **valuable lessons I learned**.*

No one likes to feel second best. Why should an employer hire anyone who isn't fully committed to the company and his job? Most employers, however, would be intrigued by a prospective employee who is bringing new skills and ideas to the job.

Q: I see from your resume you were laid off from your job six months ago. Why haven't you taken another job?

How to phrase it: *I decided I needed to **brush up on some skills** that might have prevented my being laid off. Also, I thought these skills would help me in my job search and, ultimately, **prove an asset in my career.***

Six months is a long hiatus between jobs. Your prospective employer is right to be curious about what you were doing during that time. He's not interested in the time you spent on the beach. He wants to know what skills you learned that might help him in his business. Also, he might see behind that Mexican trip and decide that you're having trouble finding a new job. If so, this makes one more reason you won't be hired.

Q: Your resume indicates that you have not worked for several years. Would you mind explaining this absence?

How to phrase it: *I have spent the past five years raising my son, Liam, who's now in kindergarten. **Leaving the workplace was a very difficult decision** for me, but as this was our first child, I didn't think I would be able to commit to my career 100 percent, knowing the **responsibilities I had at home**. Since I didn't think it would be fair to my employer to give any less than 100 percent,*

*I believe it was **the right decision for me at the time**. Now that my son is old enough to be in school, I feel refreshed and am completely **ready to devote myself** to a full-time career.*

Whatever the reason for your hiatus, be honest. The interviewer has the right to know why you have not worked in so long, as it could relate to the job you are being considered for. Discuss the decisions behind your absence, whether they were to stay at home and raise a family or recuperate from a debilitating injury. Be sure to emphasize the reasons why you want to return to work and why you think you are ready. Most importantly, stress your eagerness to resume your career.

Q: What made you decide that you were now ready to pursue full-time employment again?

*How to phrase it: I took a leave of absence to care for my elderly father. This was prior to our family making arrangements for his transfer to an adult home. It took some time to find the appropriate residence and get him settled in comfortably, **but now I am confident** he is getting good care and that I **can focus on work** and **not be distracted** by personal issues.*

While you don't have to defend your absence, your response should make good sense to the interviewer so that you can dispel any fear of an inability to commit to the job at hand. Sometimes candidates are uncomfortable giving up too much information about their personal lives, but providing a few sentences on this absence justifies the time frame and offers a "that was then, this is now" validation.

Q: Have you kept current with what is going on in the field?

*How to phrase it: Absolutely. Even though I have been out of the industry for several years, I continue to read all the **trade journals** and subscribe to current Internet newsletters on **emerging trends** and new case studies. I'm very eager **to put some of these ideas into practice** now and can see how they would be very applicable to **your company's growth mission**. I've also maintained my membership status in the **professional association** for my skill area, so I still have **networking access** as well.*

Employers want to know you have something to contribute from day one. A returnee who needs time to get up to speed will not appear as desirable as one who has done her homework. Additionally, if your time off has been of a significant length, you need to project flexibility. Nothing scares an employer more than thinking you might be stuck in old ways of doing things or have difficulty adapting to new processes.

Q: I see you were manager at Wanda's Whispers. What type of business is that and what did you do there?

*How to phrase it: Wanda's Whispers is a retail store that sells women's lingerie. I was the store manager. I **interviewed, hired, and trained** the store's sales team.*

Although the candidate may be embarrassed to discuss the nature of the business, she proudly discusses her responsibilities there.

Q: I see you have a GED. Why did you drop out of high school?

How to phrase it: *I guess I was young and foolish then. It was a long time ago. I thought I didn't need school anymore, but I was **sadly mistaken**. I got my GED three years later and then **went on to college**. I'm looking forward to **applying my training** as a registered nurse to this position.*

Youthful indiscretions can be forgiven. Although this candidate dropped out of high school, he did continue his education and is planning to move forward with his career.

Q: Why are you applying for a job outside your major?

How to phrase it: *I know I can use the **skills I developed** as a psychology major **to succeed** in marketing research. I have taken courses in consumer behavior, statistics, and research design, which I know will be **useful** in this field.*

This candidate shows how her skills are transferable to this field. She makes no mention of what her future plans are for staying in this field or going back to psychology.

Q: You didn't start working until two years after you got your degree. What were you doing?

How to phrase it: *I **traveled extensively** the year after I graduated from college. I backpacked across Europe for three months, and then I spent four months in Australia. After that, I traveled throughout the United States.*

Had this candidate said that she sat at home watching television for a year after graduating, the interviewer would have assumed she was a little low on motivation. However, she explored the world, which was an admirable use of her time.

🗨 **Action Speak**

Aided	Detected
Cooperated	Explained
Completed	Orchestrated
Checked	Prescribed

Q: Your resume doesn't show any formal training in this field. What do you think qualifies you for this job?

How to phrase it: *While I don't have formal training in this field, I do have a lot of **practical experience**. As you can see from my resume, on my last job I spent a tremendous amount of time doing research. I plan **to begin taking some courses** so I can **get my degree** in this field.*

This interviewee explains how her experience has given her the skills she needs to do this job. She also talks about her intention to get some formal training.

Q: You're so young. What makes you think you can do a good job?

How to phrase it: *I have **a lot of experience** in retail. I started working as a retail clerk straight out of high school, and over the past three years I **worked my way up** to assistant manager.*

Rather than letting the interviewer lead her into a discussion about her age, this candidate leads him into a discussion about her experience.

Illegal Questions

Q: How old are you?

How to phrase it: *I prefer to* **think of myself in terms of experience** *and not age. I have worked in this industry for quite some time. I have seen it go from a small playing field to what it is today. Fortunately I have* **kept up with all the changes** *by taking classes and constantly* **updating my skills***.*

Rather than address the issue of age, or the inappropriateness of this question, this candidate has instead decided to address some positive things about himself. He has a lot of experience, and he strives to keep himself abreast of changes in the industry by taking classes.

Q: How much do you weigh?

How to phrase it: *My weight isn't an issue. I have* **never had a problem performing my job duties***.*

This question is not only rude, it may be illegal as well. This candidate explains how her weight doesn't affect her ability to do her job.

Q: What is your race?

How to phrase it: *I'm African-American and Asian.*

If an employer asks a question about race, his intentions are usually not good, so make a mental note that you were asked. If the employer discriminates against you based on your race, the information you provided in this answer can be used as evidence against him if you file a complaint with the Equal Employment Opportunity Commission.

Q: Were you born in the United States?

How to phrase it: *I'm not sure why you're asking me that.* **Can you explain?**

This question is inappropriate, and the employer probably knows that. The candidate gives him a chance to correct himself. Perhaps all the employer needs to know is that the candidate is eligible to work in the United States.

Q: Where were your parents born?

How to phrase it: *My parents came to this country thirty years ago. They worked very hard to put me through school and are very* **proud of my successful career***. They passed their* **work ethic** *down to me.*

This candidate chooses not to reveal his national origin and instead manages to talk about his own qualities. There is nothing that says a candidate shouldn't reveal his national origin, just that he doesn't have to.

Q: Your last name sounds Spanish. Is it?

How to phrase it: *Yes, it is.*

The applicant has a choice to make. She can refuse to answer, or she can just give a simple answer, as she did. If this was the only question of this type, the interviewer may have just been trying to make conversation.

Q: What is your sexual orientation?

How to phrase it: *I don't think that has anything to do with this job.*

Sexual orientation isn't something that should be discussed on a job interview.

Q: What is your religious background?

How to phrase it: *I consider religion a very personal thing, so I would **rather not discuss** it.*

The applicant can always choose to politely refuse to answer a question she considers improper. That is what she decides to do.

Q: Do you have any children?

How to phrase it: *I understand that you may be concerned that having a family might get in the way of someone's career. However, that has never been the case with me. I'm very **dedicated to my career**.*

Without giving a direct answer to this question, the candidate has chosen to reassure the employer that having a family, or not having one, will not influence her career.

Q: Are you planning to have children?

How to phrase it: *I am very **committed** to my career. Whether or not I have children will not affect that.*

This interviewee tells the employer the only thing he has the right to know—that she is dedicated to her career.

Green Light Phrases

In hindsight
Don't make excuses
Improve on my past mistakes
Accept responsibility
Brush up on my skills
Take it all in stride
Alternate plans
Committed to working in this field.
Make a difference
Greater responsibilities
Better opportunity
I'm accustomed to working long hours
Salary is not my only consideration

Q: Are you married?

How to phrase it: *No, I'm not.*

Although this question is inappropriate and may be illegal, depending on where you live, the candidate sees no harm in answering it.

Q: Do you belong to a union?

How to phrase it: *Will I be required to join a union?*

The National Labor Relations Act prohibits employers from questioning applicants about their union sympathies. This candidate chooses to avoid the question by asking her own.

Q: Are you a Democrat or Republican?

How to phrase it: *I've always felt that it's a bad idea to discuss religion or politics with anyone. Therefore, **I'm going to refrain from answering that question**.*

The candidate has given a polite answer but has refused to provide the information the interviewer improperly requested.

Q: Will your religion keep you from working on Saturday or Sunday?

How to phrase it: *Perhaps we can **discuss the details of my schedule** after we both confirm that I'm **the right candidate** for this position.*

This candidate knows Title VII of the Civil Rights Act requires that an employer reasonably accommodate the religious practices of an employee or applicant as long as doing so doesn't pose a hardship. He also knows that an employer cannot decide to reject a candidate based on the knowledge that this accommodation will be necessary. However, he chooses to wait until he receives an offer before discussing this.

Q: Have you ever been arrested or convicted of a crime?

How to phrase it: *No. I have never been convicted of a crime.*

An employer may not ask you if you have ever been arrested, but you can be legally asked if you've been convicted of a crime. Notice how this candidate avoids the arrest question. She doesn't want to lie or discuss an arrest that she was not convicted for.

Q: Have you ever committed a crime?

How to phrase it: ***If you're asking if** I've ever been convicted of a crime, no I haven't.*

An employer may ask if an applicant has been convicted of a crime, but he may not ask if he has committed one or if he has been arrested.

Q: I see you're limping. Did you hurt yourself?

How to phrase it: *I'm fine, thank you.*

The employer, according to the Americans with Disabilities Act, cannot inquire about an applicant's injury, and the candidate is under no obligation to reveal it.

Q: Do you have a heart condition?

How to phrase it: ***With all due respect**, I don't have to answer that question.*

The applicant has a right to refuse to answer this question. The ADA makes questions about one's health illegal.

Q: Will you need us to make any accommodations for you to do your job?

How to phrase it: *I am **able to perform all functions of the job** as you described it.*

ADA prohibits the employer from asking this question, even if she asks it of all applicants. The only reason an employer may ask this question is if the applicant's disability is obvious and the employer has good reason to believe she will need accommodation.

Q: Have you ever been treated for mental health problems?

How to phrase it: *I have, but everything is **under control** now. I have always performed well at work, and I know I will continue to.*

Although the candidate is under no obligation to reveal this information at any time, he knows he may need reasonable accommodation in the future.

Q: Have you ever been treated for drug addiction?

How to phrase it: *That was some time ago, and **I prefer not to discuss it**.*

This candidate is within her rights not to discuss this. People who have been treated for drug addiction are covered by the ADA, and a hiring decision cannot be based upon this.

Q: Travel is a big part of this job. Will your family be okay with that?

How to phrase it: ***I can assure you that** traveling will not be a problem. I traveled extensively on my previous job.*

This candidate has chosen to let the employer know that her family status will not affect her job. She mentions the fact that her previous job had similar requirements, and it wasn't a problem.

Q: You're a young single guy living in the city. How do you handle having women chase after you?

How to phrase it: ***Work has always been my priority**.*

It is inappropriate for the employer to ask a question regarding the applicant's sex life. The candidate chooses to evade the question by talking about work.

Endnote: Stay calm and collect your thoughts when your interviewer throws tough questions your way. If you can answer the sample questions in this chapter using some of the savvy wording in bold, then you are more prepared then the average candidate. If a questions is asked that seems too personal, it may be illegal for him/her to require a response. A simple "I'd rather not answer that" is sometimes the most appropriate response.

ASKING YOUR OWN QUESTIONS

Chapter 19

Smart Queries

Most of the words and phrases provided in this book are chosen because they help to define you as a proactive person. What better way to show this side of yourself than to turn the tables and start asking the interviewer some tough questions! You may find that asking questions in an interview can boost your sense of confidence. It's a subtle reminder that they're not the only ones making a big decision. You are determining whether this company is a good fit for you. When you ask questions in an interview, you show that you are paying close attention and that you're a careful decision-maker who gathers information before making a decision.

Prepare four or five questions before the job interview. Pinpoint the kind of information that will help you decide whether you want to work for this employer. Some things to consider: the company's future plans for growth, its current financial health, rates of employee turnover, levels of job satisfaction among employees, and what your chances for advancement are.

Why the Job Is Open

Q: Why is this job open?

This information will help you understand how you will be received should a job offer be made to you and should you accept it. If the person you will be replacing has left under difficult circumstances, that is, if he was fired or was otherwise forced to leave, his former coworkers may be resentful of anyone who fills his place. If the previous employee was promoted within the company, you taking the job may give you a chance for similar advancement down the line.

💬 Action Speak

Improvised	Revamped
Prepared	Sustained
Questioned	Worked
Regulated	Yielded

Q: How many people have held this position in the past three years? Why did they leave?

If there is a high rate of turnover in the position you are interviewing for, you should be suspicious. You should try to find out why this is the case. Is this a difficult employer to work for? Or perhaps the company has expectations that are impossible for employees to meet, and they are fired for not meeting them. If you haven't already, access your network to find out if anyone has had any experience with this employer.

Q: How will you decide who to hire?

The answer to this question will let you find out if you missed something during the interview. Was there another skill or qualification the employer is seeking that you didn't get to talk about? By the time you get to ask this question, the interview will be drawing to a close. However, you can still follow up by sending a thank-you letter that will highlight the particular qualifications that you have and the employer is seeking.

Q: When will you make a decision?

If you know when the employer will make a hiring decision, you won't be left in a state of limbo waiting for the phone to ring. You can call the employer yourself, but it's best to wait one day after the employer says the decision is going to be made. If you are continuing to interview for other jobs, which you should do until you receive and accept a job offer, you might decide to schedule future interviews after that date, if it is close.

Job Responsibilities

Q: Is there a written job description? May I see it?

You will ask this question simply because you need this information to make an informed decision about whether or not to accept the job.

Q: You mentioned something about a training period. How long is it?

This question indicates your interest in the job and shows that you were listening during the interview. It allows you to get clarification.

Q: Are there any other opportunities for training?

An employee who inquires about training opportunities is willing to learn as much as possible to do a good job.

Q: What types of assignments will I have?

This question indicates that you are interested in the job. It also allows you to learn what you will be doing if you are hired.

 RED FLAG!

HOLD OFF ON ASKING any questions about salary, benefits, and vacation time until an official job offer has been made.

Q: What improvements do you want to make here and how can I help you make them?

You will phrase this question the same way you phrased the previous one, allowing the employer to envision you as the person he will hire. It will give you a glimpse into the job and the company's plans for the future.

Opportunities for Advancement

Q: What does one need to do to advance?

Asking this question shows that you will be a productive employee who is interested in doing the best job possible. You will do what you need to do to move up.

Q: What are the chances for advancement?

Similar in nature to the previous question, this question shows the employer that you are motivated. It also allows you to find out if you will have the opportunity to advance should you work for that employer. That information will help you decide whether to accept a job offer, since you don't want to languish in the same position for a long time.

Q: How often are performance evaluations conducted and how are the evaluations made?

You will ask this question to learn what working for this company will be like. You may get a sense of how strict the managers are or how closely the staff is monitored. If you are interviewing for a management position, you will get a sense of how much of your time you will spend on evaluation paperwork.

Who Your Supervisor Is

Q: What is the chain of command?

Whenever you ask questions about the inner workings of the company, it indicates to the employer that you are interested in the job.

Q: Who will I be reporting to?

If you find out who your immediate supervisor is, you can try to learn about that person. Don't forget that you should be gathering information that will help you decide whether to accept an offer if one is made.

Company History and Growth

Q: How long have you worked here?

The person interviewing you is in a job that is probably several steps above the one that you are interviewing for. Given that fact, the answer to this question will indicate how employees typically advance within the company. If the owner of the company is interviewing you, there is no reason to ask this question.

Q: What do you like most about your job with this company?

The interviewer is likely one of the few employees of the company with whom you will have contact before making your decision. See what she has to say about working there. The answer to this question, if the interviewer is honest, will weigh in to your decision about accepting a job offer. As with the previous question, ask this only of employees and not of the owner of the company.

Q: How long do most employees stay?

Learning about turnover is a good way to gauge whether employees enjoy working for the employer. A high rate of turnover indicates that most employees aren't satisfied with their jobs, while a low rate of turnover demonstrates a high level of job satisfaction.

Q: What reason do most employees give for leaving?

The answer to this question expands on the answer to the prior question. Knowing why employees leave the company helps you find out what you may or may not like about working there. Of course, the interviewer may not know the answer to this question or may not be willing to share it.

> **Green Light** It's likely that you'll generate more questions during the course of the interview. Don't be afraid to ask for clarification of anything you didn't understand.

Q: How has the company grown over the past five years? Is it profitable?

A company's financial health will help you decide whether to accept a job offer. If the company hasn't grown over the past five years or if it isn't profitable, this should signal that it might not be in the best financial health. Should you accept a job offer, you may be looking for work again soon.

Q: What does the company plan to do to keep growing and what role would I play?

The answer to this question will give you information about your prospective employer and the job. You will learn what expectations the employer has for you. By phrasing the question like this, you give the interviewer the chance to picture you in the job he is interviewing you for.

Q: In your opinion, how does this company compare to its major competitors, like Activate, Pump, and Dragon Works?

In preparing for the interview, you should have researched the prospective employer. When you ask this question, you are saying to the interviewer, "Look at the research I've done. I know who your competitors are." The answer to this question will also help you learn more about the company.

Q: From my research, I learned you sell your products both in the United States and Canada. Do you plan to expand into any other markets?

Again you are stating something you uncovered in your research. You are also trying to learn something further about the company.

Q: I know you sell hair-care products. What are the demographics of your customers?

Your reason for asking this question is similar to your reason for asking the prior one. If you have experience with the demographic this company targets, that is something you can talk about in your thank-you letter or in any follow-up interviews.

Q: You mentioned that several of your clients are in the apparel business. What industries are your other clients in?

This question shows you were paying attention during the interview. You also want to learn more about the company's other clients, which demonstrates your interest in the company.

Endnote: There are a lot of important questions to ask your interviewer before you shake hands and part ways. It is imperative that you are ready for that opportunity when it comes. The quality of your questions will reflect how much you know about the job, the company, and the industry.

Chapter 20

DESCRIBING YOUR SKILLS

Industry-Specific Wording

Buzzwords are key at every stage of your job search. You put them in your cover letter and your resume. Don't forget to utilize them during your interview. Using the industry's own unique language to talk about your experience and interest in a job can help you solidify a connection with your interviewer who is (most likely) very familiar with this language. This chapter contains a list of fifteen common industries and some well-known buzzwords associated with their professions. Each section also lists examples of phrases you can use when answering questions about your work experience. Practice using them before the interview so that the words and phrases sound natural as you speak them.

Accounting and Finance

Accounting and finance buzzwords highlight experience with accounting, budgeting, treasury, auditing, and information systems activities. This includes collection, documentation, and analysis of financial data and the use of this data to make strategic decisions and share pertinent information with investors, regulators, and government entities. It also includes allocation of capital required for annual operations as well as growth.

Buzzwords

Accounting

Analytical services

Asset management

Audits

Bonds

Brokerage services

Budgeting

Capital

Client relations

Commodities

Consumer Confidence
  Index (CCI)

Corporate and municipal
  securities

Credit analysis

Derivatives

Financial analysis

Foreign markets

Global markets

Home loans

Insurance products

IRS filing

Lending

Management services

Managerial accounting

Mergers and acquisitions

Online investments

Payroll

Private client services

Real estate and mortgage
  loans

Retail banking

SEC reporting

Securities services

Tax filings

Transaction management

Trust and banking markets

Underwriting

Real Phrases to Use When Describing Your Skills and Experience

- **Managed all aspects of** finance, accounting, foreign exchange dealings, marketing, and data processing of company and its overseas offices.

- **Reviewed finances and securities** pertaining to advances and shipping for client.

- **Audited** private companies; listed companies, partnerships, and individual business.

- Prepared financial statements and schedules.

- **Settled bond and equity transactions** in the United States markets.

- Generated income statements, balance sheets, general ledger, checks, and reports.

- Entered payable vouchers.

- **Performed all accounting functions** to include journal entries, accounts payable and receivable, petty cash, deposits, bank reconciliations, and trial balance.

- Controlled budget, cash flow, and capital expenditures.

- Developed corporate and **project-oriented financial strategies**.

Administrative

These buzzwords are for applicants looking for general management and office positions. They reflect an involvement and familiarity with general office management as well as oversight of facilities and systems associated with the day-to-day organizational activities. Important skills include administrative, project management, customer service, and light labor.

Buzzwords

Administrative support services	Office management and operations
Association membership	Organization policies and procedures
Business administration	Procedural enhancement
Client relations	
Customer service	Public relations
Data entry	Reconciliation
Database management	Report generation
Event planning	Sales support
File maintenance	Supervisory skills
Information trafficking	Travel arrangements
Invoicing	Troubleshooting
Mass mailings	Vendor relations
Meeting planning	Word processing
Meetings	

Real Phrases to Use When Describing Your Skills and Experience

- **Translated** survey data into numerical code for data entry.

- Designed forms for archive.

- Assisted in **revising** physical inventory procedures.

- Served as principal consultant on plant inventory systems.

- Developed **nationwide** relocation policy and procedures for new employees.

- Provided word processing, customer relations, and some accounts payable processing.

- **Handled incoming calls**; scheduled appointments.

- Supervised employees to ensure observation of rules/regulations.

- Provided customer service; **resolved complaints**.

- **Coordinated** catering for special events.

- Budgeted and facilitated four-day professional seminar.

- **Secured new business** using customer inquiries and mass mailing responses.

- Scheduled site visits and installations.

- Collected, sorted, and **distributed** incoming mail.

- Created effective product displays.

- Monitored equipment and supply inventories.

- **Performed analysis of** client files.

Biotechnological and Pharmaceuticals

The buzzwords in these industries are often highly technical, and they exhibit a science background with in-depth familiarity of biology and chemistry. Resumes may demonstrate experience with cell biology, vaccine research, prescription drugs, over-the-counter medicines, chemical compounds used in pharmaceuticals, and tools used to diagnose diseases. Relevant experience includes synthesizing new drugs, testing of drugs, determination of dosages and delivery forms (such as liquid or tablets), calculating cost-effectiveness of a proposed drug, and selling/marketing of pharmaceuticals.

Buzzwords

Advanced cellular and molecular biology	FDA compliance strategies
Agricultural biotechnology	Genetics
Biomedical research	Health care policy
Biostatistics	Immunology
Chemical manufacturing	Infectious diseases
Clinical trials	Metabolic diseases
Critical care products	Patient care
Development and consulting	Pharmaceuticals
	Public health research
Diagnostic tests	Reproductive disorders
Drug optimization programs	Tissue and organ replacement
	Urology/gynecology studies
Epidemiological research	Veterinary applications

💬 Action Speak

Implemented	Ran
Marketed	Related
Operated	Simulated
Proofread	Totaled

Real Phrases to Use When Describing Your Skills and Experience

- Contributed to the discovery and **preclinical development of** antiviral compounds.

- Designed and implemented in vitro and in vivo drug metabolism and pharmacokinetic experiments to facilitate the selection and **optimization** of drug candidates.

- Identified potential metabolites by using state-of-the-art technologies from in vitro and in vivo studies.

- Performed tasks that support study conduct, **according to all applicable regulations** and operations procedures.

- Used and maintained standard Medical Affairs tracking tools.

- **Performed initial review of** regulatory and required study documents.

- Responsible for inventory management of nonclinical supply materials.

- Applied knowledge of therapeutic area and drug development (**investigational**, **observational**, **surveillance**).

- Trained others on job-related functions.

Communications

Industry buzzwords in the area of communications highlight writing, graphics, public relations, publicity, and promotions skills and experience. This includes activities associated with creating, distributing, and transmitting text and graphic information via varied print, video, audio, computer, and web-based media.

Buzzwords

Acquisition of titles	Layout
Book production	Marketing proposals
Casting contracts	Media relations
Communications management	Periodical publishing
Content development	Publishing process
Data management	Standards and procedures
Desktop publishing	Story development
Editorial direction	Trade magazines
Fact checking	Trade newspaper
Health care communications systems	Workflow systems
	Writing

Real Phrases to Use When Describing Your Skills and Experience

- **Proofread** archaeological monographs and museum catalogues.

- **Edited and typed** grant proposals, research papers, and reports.

- Researched and wrote items for annual fact books and their weekly supplemental updates covering the communications industry.

- Reported and **wrote articles and columns** for twice-monthly newspaper for the arts and entertainment industry.

- **Supervised the design and production of** titles for two continuity programs.

- Acted as **liaison** for Marketing Director, Editor, and advertisers.

- Edited three medical textbooks.

- Wrote campaign letters; ordered all campaign materials; staffed Campaign Advisory Committee; coordinated and directed chapter-wide meetings; **conducted** staff meetings.

- **Drafted** press releases and speeches.

- Researched and **generated story ideas**.

- Assisted in the production of industrial films, business presentations, videotaping of plays, fashion shows, and more.

Computers and Mathematics

For positions in the computer industry, buzzwords are highly technical and change fairly rapidly. Effective buzzwords highlight experience with defining, analyzing, and resolving business problems and using knowledge of computer systems to examine problems and design solutions. Important skills and experience include planning new computer systems or devising ways to apply existing systems to operations that are still done manually.

Resumes for positions in mathematics should spotlight activities ranging from the creation of new theories and techniques to the translation of economic, scientific, engineering, and managerial problems into mathematical terms.

Buzzwords

Algorithms	IT planning
Backup and multiplatform connectivity systems	LAN management
	MIS
C++	Network configuration
CMS-2	Networking solutions
COBOL programming	Operating efficiencies
Computer systems	Preproduction testing
Data acquisition	Real-time computer programs
Database management	
Database repair/ troubleshooting	Software development
	Software testing
Developmental math	System design engineering
DOD telecommunications technology, architecture, policy, and standards	Systems test and integration
	Technology integration
Drivers	Video communications
Information architecture	Workstation maintenance

Real Phrases to Use When Describing Your Skills and Experience

- **Designed network-based applications for** manufacturing process control and test data collection, improving product quality and manufacturing efficiency.

- Designed and maintained computer-based electronic test hardware.

- Developed online message system for members of the programming group.

- Supported existing clients and **resolved critical issues**/problems in a timely fashion.

- **Maintained and supported** the existing COBOL mainframe online and batch systems.

- Researched and identified modern replacement hardware architecture for existing real-time simulation.

- **Researched**, **identified**, **and developed** a high-speed data communication system connecting an Intel Hypercube and Sun Sparc Workstation.

- **Managed** large data migration effort.

- Assisted sales force in technical presentations for prospective clients.

- **Reduced process time** and purchasing errors by developing an online program, allowing the purchasing department to track the status of all invoices.

Engineering

Buzzwords from the various fields of engineering demonstrate experience with the theories and principles of science and mathematics and with designing machinery, products, systems, and processes for efficient and economical performance. This includes designing industrial machinery and equipment for manufacturing goods, defense systems, and weapons for the armed forces. Other important skills and experience include planning and supervising the construction of buildings, highways, and rapid transit systems and also designing and developing consumer products and systems for control and automation of manufacturing, business, and management processes.

Buzzwords

3D modeling	Manufacturing
Assembly design	Mechanical and control
C programming	systems
C4 navigation and	Performance
intelligence	characteristics
Complex electromechani-	Process and procedure
cal systems	development
Conceptualization	Professional consulting
Data collection and	Research and development
analysis	(R&D)
Design methodologies	Structural design
Electrical design	Test planning and field
Engineering management	operations
Facilities engineering	Top-level system
Geological formations	architecture
High-temperature	Vendor and partner tech-
environments	nology relationships
Injection molding design	

> **RED FLAG!**
> DON'T DRAW ATTENTION to negative aspects of your professional abilities like skills you lack or even those you lacked in the past. Talk instead about a skill you already have that you've improved upon.

Real Phrases to Use When Describing Your Skills and Experience

- **Applied knowledge of** thermodynamics, reactor design, phase separation, fluid compression and expansion, and process control to complete simulation from preliminary coding.

- **Provided structural design** and engineering estimates, and specifications for industrial, laboratory, commercial, and power facilities.

- Evaluated new computer product designs, solving environmental problems on prototype computers.

- Assisted engineers working on load monitors, which gauge weight and distribution properties on heavy machine presses.

- **Conducted a variety of tests including** Tensile, Compression, and Creep tests on modeled parts.

- **Assembled** machines from drawing specifications, wire electrical boards, test and trace defects.

- Observed and participated in exploration of mines surrounding Great Salt Lake.

- **Repaired** generators, electrical motors, and mechanical systems in shop, yard, and aboard rail units for public transport.

Executive and Managerial

Executive and managerial positions exist in all types of businesses. The "Administrative" section earlier in this chapter contains a number of words that are also relevant to applicants seeking to be managers in an office setting. Executive buzzwords should highlight experience ranging from general supervisory duties to running an entire company. Relevant skills include management of individual departments within a larger corporate structure, motivating workers to achieve their goals as rapidly and economically as possibly, budgeting and directing projects, and evaluating company processes and methods to determine cost-effective plans.

Buzzwords

Account management	Major accounts
Asset management	New business development
Benefits coordination	Product awareness
Branch management	Provider/client
Budget development	communication
Business development	Relationship management
Client relations	Revenue development
Contract management	Sales objectives
Customer service	Team management
Franchise management	Troubleshooting
Lead development	Yearly transactions

Real Phrases to Use When Describing Your Skills and Experience

- **Obtained new accounts** to replace lost business and maintain profitability.

- Used sales expertise and account management to develop 80-percent-new client base and **maintain profit margins**.

- **Administered and directed** marketing activities of banking operations.

- Organized and planned actions impacting on various sectors of bank's markets.

- Worked with other internal divisions and outside agencies to **develop plans** that supported division's activities.

- Planned and **supervised** training activities.

- Organized a smoothly functioning administration and operational division.

- **Maintained detailed knowledge of** all aspects to include maintenance, logistics, and communications.

- **Trained and supervised** three claims adjusters.

Government

For people interested in positions in politics and government, buzzwords highlight experience in executive, legislative, judicial, or general government agencies as well as with public agencies, such as firefighting, military, police work, or the United States Postal Service. This includes researching and evaluating military materials; cleaning, maintenance, and general service for public works; participating in political campaigns by networking, fundraising, or organizing; and working to control narcotic and dangerous drug use through prevention and law enforcement. It also includes mail pickup and delivery experience, public relations and press work, and public outreach activities.

Buzzwords

Administrative services	Maintenance and
Agency management	improvement
Briefing reports	Medicaid services
Central management	Metropolitan development
agencies	National health programs
Consumer rights	Nonprofit
Defense contract	Organization analysis
management	Political and legislative
Department of Labor and	support functions
Workforce Development	Productivity of natural
Economic and educational	resources
support	Public works
Environmental studies	Recycling services
Field offices	Regulatory commission
Foreign intelligence	Security products
Governmental organization	State government
Human health protection	Transportation planning
Information services	U.S. policy
Issuance of licenses	Urban development
Local government agency	Work force conditions

Real Phrases to Use When Describing Your Skills and Experience

- **Demonstrated problem-solving skills** and **diplomatic capabilities** in dealing with federal labor-management relations.

- **Campaigned for** the Democratic Party, focusing on significant economic changes, recycling services, regulation of companies, and safe living conditions.

- **Processed** incoming and outgoing mail for sorting and distribution; updated postal rates and sold stamps.

- Managed fire prevention activities and the protection of citizens in fire or medical emergencies.

- **Dispatched** law enforcement officers and rescue personnel in emergency situations.

- Supervised daily functions at national park, including trash pickup, water supply, and repair services; managed park headquarters.

- **Volunteered** at center for senior services and welfare. Responsibilities included helping to ensure safe living conditions, tracking Medicaid services, and being on call for emergency situations.

- **Investigated** cases of worker's compensation claims for public defender and **compiled** statistical material into spreadsheets.

- Raised drug prevention awareness by organizing support functions and seminars.

- Practiced law as a public defender in district court for ten years, primarily handling cases concerning domestic disputes and custody battles.

Health and Medical

Buzzwords from the vital health and medical fields demonstrate experience with illness, working toward achieving and maintaining healthy lifestyles, and helping to address and resolve related issues, such as insurance and medical claim forms. This includes working directly with patients and their families in dealing with health problems; assisting patients by providing medical advice regarding prescriptions, insurance claim forms, and related issues; and researching medical treatments and techniques.

Buzzwords

Ambulatory services

Appointments

Behavioral programs

Budget responsibilities

Business management
  activities

Case management

Clerical support

Clinical instruction

Comprehensive care

Crisis intervention

DEA regulations

Discharge planning

Disease research

Educational counseling

Emergency care

Formal education
  programs

Hematology and serology
  testing

Human services

In-patient and outpatient
  care

Laboratory operations

Medical management

Multidisciplined practice

Nursing services

Patient services

Pediatric/emergency
  medicine

Pharmacology and
  behavioral modification
  methods

Policy and procedures
  development

Private practice

Psychiatric care

Referring physicians

Respiratory therapy

Social services

Surgical procedures

Therapy

Ultrasound

X-ray department

Real Phrases to Use When Describing Your Skills and Experience

- **Provided** spinal manipulation and handled necessary muscular-skeletal needs of sports-injured patients.

- **Provided information for** insurance companies, workman's compensation, and third-party billing procedures.

- Supervised seventy-five clinical, administrative, and staff employees.

- Coordinated treatment and discharge planning.

- **Prepared patients for** surgical procedures, recorded temperature and blood pressure, inserted intravenous units, and administered sedatives.

- Scheduled patients for appointments.

- **Monitored** radiographs and administered Novocain prior to procedures.

- Assisted dentist in prophylactic procedures: **provided necessary tools**, sterilized equipment, and comforted patients.

- Taught intensive aerobics, calisthenics, and stretching to co-educational classes of up to twenty-five adults in all physical conditions.

- **Organized labs for** veterinary students and for clinical instruction.

- Directed hygienic procedures on 300 animals, including surgical and necropsies.

- **Instructed and supervised** home health aides.

- Served as clinical instructor for physical therapy students and pulmonary clinic.

- Drafted physical therapy **standards of care** for selected surgical procedures.

- Requisitioned all laboratory supplies; participated in conferences with medical staff on patients with special laboratory needs.

- Conducted hematology and serology **testing**, as well as test sample photography.

- **Operated** hematology laboratory, using haemacount machine, leitz photometer, and EKF machine.

Insurance

For the insurance industry, appropriate buzzwords highlight experience with contracts, claims, personal injury, workman's compensation, and assets. This includes knowledge of different areas of insurance, such as fire, theft, automotive, property, business, health, and disability. Familiarity with premiums, appraisals, policies, financial planning services, and insurance sales should also be noted.

Buzzwords

Accounts receivable

Auto insurance claims

Broad-based customer group

Caseload

Claims management services

Commercial and individual financial services

Credit associations

Credit insurance

Credit life insurance

Dental care services

Dental insurance firm

Buzzwords *continued*

Disability income insurance

Emergency coverage

Estate planning

Financial and insurance operations

Health care delivery

Health plan coverage

High exposure claims

Investment planning

Lending organizations

Loss prevention

Malpractice insurance

Permanent insurance

Personal insurance

Product portfolio

Professional liability insurance

Professional medical services

Property and casualty reinsurance

Regional and specialty property and casualty insurers

Risk management programs

Search and examination services

Title insurance

RED FLAG!

IF YOU ARE BEING interviewed by the only supervisor in your department, avoid saying that you want to move into a supervisor position someday. It may sound like you're after the interviewer's job.

Real Phrases to Use When Describing Your Skills and Experience

- Evaluated client portfolios for claims; **filed** regarding personal injury and negligence.

- Worked as an actuary; computed premiums and insurance risks **in conjunction with supporting team**.

- Interacted with customers daily to explain annuity plans, real estate transactions, and claims.

- Adjusted premium rates for commercial and individual financial services; **notified clients of** renewal periods.

- Updated records regarding policies and procedures to be ready for use by real estate brokers.

- **Recorded** proof of loss and delivered reimbursement checks.

- Assisted individuals in selection of insurance policies. **Worked to ensure** lowest rates and highest coverage possible to fit individual needs.

- **Computed settlements** for homeowners after major disasters.

- **Implemented** employee wellness programs for special accounts during renewal periods.

- Conducted automotive claims investigations to determine net loss.

- Worked in professional liability insurance, **advocating the rights of** policyholders.

Legal and Protective Services

In these fields, buzzwords highlight experience with interpreting and enforcing the laws. This includes supporting the legal system; patrolling and inspecting property to protect against theft, vandalism, and illegal entry; and ensuring the safety and security of persons who have been arrested, are awaiting trial, or who have been convicted of crimes and sentenced to serve time in correctional institutions. It also includes maintaining order, enforcing rules and regulations, and supplementing counseling.

Buzzwords

Administrative support services
Attorney-client conferences
Clerical support
Community outreach
Copyright registration and licensing
Courtroom activity
Criminal investigations
Crisis intervention
Custody/traffic direction processes
Drafting wills
Extensive corporate dealings
Fire fighting
Fire prevention
Human services
Interviewing of witnesses
Legal research
Licensing
Medical documentation
Modernization of office procedures
Notarizing legal documents
Paralegal services
Permitting processes
Polygraph techniques
Preparation of cases
Prisoner visitation
Public utility litigation
Record filing
Resident and building security
Safety and crime prevention
Security programs
Training workshops
Trial preparation
Vandalism and theft deterrence
Weaponry training

Real Phrases to Use When Describing Your Skills and Experience

- **Prosecuted** criminal cases at district court in conjunction with Urban Violence Strike Force.

- **Prepared and presented** civil and criminal motions before district and superior courts.

- Presented public-safety workshops and lectures.

- Supervised criminal investigations and trained assistant district attorneys.

Retail

Retail industry buzzwords demonstrate experience in the sale of clothing, goods, or appliances, either directly to consumers or to the retail stores, or the buying of such products for sale in stores. They also demonstrate knowledge of customer service, handling transactions, complaints, and returns, and the management of a retail environment.

Buzzwords

Accessories	Factory-direct
Apparel	Fashion
Appliances	Food services
Beauty care products	General merchandise
Brand names	Gross margin
Catalog retailer	Independently owned
Children's products	Leading retailer
Consumer advocate	Marketing research
Design professionals	Mass merchandisers
Direct marketing	

Buzzwords *continued*

National direct sales company	Soft-goods products
Price marketing	Specialty retailer
Promotional advertising	Trade
Retailer	Value-priced
	Wholesale

Real Phrases to Use When Describing Your Skills and Experience

- Explained brands of televisions, videos, cellular phones, computers, and other electronics to customers.

- **Filled orders**, shipped products, and answered calls for women's intimate apparel catalog retailer.

- **Operated cash register**, ringing both cash and credit card transactions, with responsibility for knowledge of discounted prices, clearance items, ad items, and changes in universal product codes (UPCs).

- Managed specialty fashion store carrying private label product lines of **nationally recognized brands**.

- Sold wide assortment of primary apparel in mall-based retail outlet at value prices.

- Bought women's, men's, and children's apparel for independently owned retail store.

- **Excelled in suggestive selling of** sales promotions, as well as customer service duties, such as layaways, returns, and exchanges.

- Organized shipments of accessories, stocked shelves by categories in different departments, and **took inventory of** all items annually.

- Oversaw all aspects of managing one location in major bookstore chain, including verifying barcodes, organizing category sections by book title, scheduling employees, and handling all accounting.

Science

For scientific positions, each particular field will have many specialized technical terms aside from those listed here. Science industry buzzwords, in general, display experience with research and development. This includes research to develop new medicines; increase crop yield; improve the environment; study farm crops, animals, and living organisms; and explore practical use and knowledge of chemicals, as well as the atmosphere's physical characteristics, motions, and processes.

Buzzwords

Agriculture	Geological aspects
Air pollution	Horticulture
Animals	Instrumentation
Bacteria	Materials research
Biological research	Microprocessors
Cleanup procedures	Mineral content
Drainage	Natural disasters
Ecosystem	Oceanic research
Firefighting techniques	Pest control
Fisheries	Plant acquisition
Forecasting weather	
Forestry	

Buzzwords *continued*

Quality control systems	Veterinary medicine
Raw material	Waste disposal
Satellites	Weather conditions
Soil testing	Wildlife activities
USDA regulations	

Real Phrases to Use When Describing Your Skills and Experience

- **Ensured smooth running of** the lab and orderly maintenance of telescopes; ordered equipment and supplies.

- **Conducted more than** 500 manual and computerized assays of steroids, carcinogenic analysis, vitamins, fibrinogens, and other chemicals in hospital laboratory.

- **Developed laboratory microcomputer systems** for instrument automation and custom and specialized instrumentation/test equipment.

- Designed and **built** a continuous viscometer detector for gel permeation chromatography to provide absolute molecular weight and branching data.

- Performed set funnel extractions, **creating** surrogate solutions and maintaining laboratory inventory of glassware and chemicals, waste disposal, and cleanup.

- **Managed the operation of** a livestock and production farm, its marketing and accounting tasks, selling beef, lamb, and produce to supermarkets, restaurants, and roadside vegetable stands.

- Researched sources for tree and plant acquisition.

- **Made written**, **editorial**, **and research contributions** to ten briefing papers and a **comprehensive management plan** for Puget Sound.

- Worked directly with doctors of veterinary medicine and racehorse trainers in the breeding and grooming of **top-quality** thoroughbreds.

Technical

Technical industry buzzwords highlight experience with applying specialized knowledge of technology, systems, engineering, and science. Potential applications for technical skills and experience exist in virtually all industries, including transportation, building design and inspection, engine repair and maintenance, electrical systems design, and communications.

Buzzwords

Aircraft maintenance	Equipment application
Analytical attributes	Final product design
Architecture	General construction
Artistic illustration	Hand tools
Blueprints	Hardware
Building codes	Hybrid microcircuit design
Codes and standards	and drawing
Compliance procedures	Illustration
Data testing standards	Inspection
Design development	Inventory
Drafting	Lock repair
Drafting technology	Maintenance
Electrical regulations	Mechanical aptitude

Buzzwords *continued*

Multimedia product	State rules and regulations
Operations	System design
Plumbing regulations	Technical drawing
Product development	Technical illustration
Quality assurance	Technical writing
Real estate development	Troubleshooting
layout	Zoning laws

Real Phrases to Use When Describing Your Skills and Experience

- **Trained in maintenance**, **servicing**, **and troubleshooting** on all areas of aircraft from wing tips to landing gear, nose to tail, interior and exterior, including removals and replacements of component parts, repairs, lubrications, refueling, and flight-line launching and recoveries.

- Worked within **both the public and private sectors**. Required knowledge of local government agency procedures (e.g., obtaining permits and variances and interfacing with the building, planning, and engineering departments).

- Created and interpreted testing programs to **evaluate and modify product performance and reliability** for manufacturer of commercial kitchen equipment.

- Developed standard designs for retaining walls and reinforced-concrete bridge abutments, the design of which are still currently being used.

- **Used verbal specifications to develop** electronic illustrations for new and changed products.

- Researched the effect of worldwide television deregulation on broadcast, cable, and satellite television, as well as international broadcasting and advertising.

Transportation and Travel

In the transportation and travel industries, buzzwords highlight experience with conveying passengers or goods, providing or controlling means for transportation, and coordinating or advancing the travel of others. They also include knowledge of various transportation methods, either from the customer service side or the transporting side.

Buzzwords

Airports
Bus service
Cargo services
Charter services
Communities
Commuter train lines
Construction services
Cruise line
Dinner/theater events
Domestic travel
Emergency road services
Executive travel
Express services
Flat rate
Freight service railroad operations
Global transportation
High-speed rail
Highways
International travel
Light rail transit
Limousine transportation services
Mass transportation
Moving
Off-road divisions
Passenger service
Public transportation firm
Railroad industry
Safety policies and procedures
Sightseeing activities

Buzzwords *continued*

Specialized transportation services
Subways
Tow services
Transportation services
Travel
Vacations
Vehicles
Warehousing
Weddings
Worldwide supply chain solutions

Real Phrases to Use When Describing Your Skills and Experience

- **Planned** vacations and business trips, both foreign and domestic, for discount service travel agency.

- **Confirmed** ticket purchases, **scheduled** connecting flights, and **contacted** transportation services for passengers.

- Mapped out route systems for buses in coordination with peak periods.

- Operated commuter rail, **adhering to all** mass transit regulations.

- **Enforced safety policies and procedures** for specialized vehicles.

- Sold passes for incoming and outgoing trains, handled switching track operations, and was responsible for general managing of station.

- Programmed self-propelled vehicles and self-unloading bulk carriers; **performed maintenance when necessary**.

- Coordinated sightseeing activities, made restaurant reservations, and **arranged** other local services for tourists.

- Drove public shuttle bus on express service route with designated drop-off locations.

- **Filed reports** on average weekly traffic and planned traffic routes with fluctuating rush hour schedules.

Endnote: Make your mark on the interviewer by showing him or her that you know the language of your industry. The right words and phrases signify the breadth of your knowledge. They can open all the right doors for you.

Chapter 21

WRITING THE THANK YOU

Thoughtfully Crafted Letters

Some job seekers are under the false impression that thank-you letters and cards are too old fashioned for today's workplace. Those who know the truth can bump those other applicants right out of the competition. You should always take advantage of this simple but powerful gesture to set you apart from the rest. The key to thank-you letter writing is to keep it short and professional. Don't write to the interviewer as if you are writing to your best friend. Maintain a polite distance and simply state your appreciation for her time. Injecting a specific detail from the interview using phrasing like "as you explained in our meeting" or "as I mentioned during the interview" shows that you were paying close attention and that you truly care about the job.

Here are four sample thank-you letters. The first three are written to the actual interviewer, and the final one is written to an administrative assistant who showed the candidate around the office. This letter is significantly shorter than the others, and it does not make a point of reiterating any of the writer's skills, since its recipient will not be making the hiring decision and never discussed those skills with the candidate.

SAMPLE THANK-YOU LETTER #1

Joseph R. Green
14 Willow Street
Hoboken, NJ 07030

June 5, 2012

Ms. Maria Sanchez
Production Manager
Artistic Media
515 Madison Avenue
New York, NY 10022

Dear Ms. Sanchez:

Thank you for meeting with me this afternoon **regarding** the assistant production manager position at Artistic Media. I **appreciate the time** you spent getting to know me and explaining the specifics of the job.

I feel strongly that my experience and skills will allow me to make significant contributions to the production team. Artistic Media **seems to be a company that** values creativity, which is definitely one of my strengths.

I am **looking forward to hearing from you** within the week, as we discussed. Thank you again for your time and for considering me for this position. You can **reach me by phone** at (212) 555-4444 **or by e-mail at** *jgreene@rcat.net.*

Yours truly,

Joe Green

SAMPLE THANK-YOU LETTER #2

Beverly Smith
1524 South Jefferson Street
Williams, AZ 86046

September 21, 2012

Mr. Connor Shmedley
Customer Service Manager
Smart Mart Stores, Inc.
250 Adams Avenue
Flagstaff, AZ 86001

Dear Mr. Shmedley:

I appreciate your meeting with me this morning regarding the assistant customer service manager job at Smart Mart Stores. I **enjoyed having the opportunity to talk to you** about the improvements you have planned for the customer service department.

As I mentioned to you during the interview, before I moved to Williams, I worked at Bullseye Stores, which, as you know, has a great reputation for providing customer service. I worked closely with the department manager in implementing many of the procedures that earned Bullseye that reputation. I **hope to have the opportunity to work with you** to implement such procedures at Smart Mart.

Once again, **thank you for taking time out of your busy schedule** today. If you have any further questions, you can reach me by phone at (520) 555-5151 or by e-mail at *bevsmith@netco.com.* I **look forward to hearing your decision soon**.

Sincerely,

Beverly Smith

SAMPLE THANK-YOU LETTER #3

Sandy Beane
37 Oak Drive
Portland, OR 97205

June 24, 2012

Dr. Pat Lee
26 Tulip Street
Portland, OR 97201

Dear Dr. Lee:

Thank you for taking time out of your busy schedule this afternoon to interview me for the office manager position. I would **welcome the opportunity to work with you** and the members of your staff.

As you expressed in your interview, you are looking for someone who can manage a very busy office while showing compassion for your patients. **As we discussed** during the interview, though I did not work in a medical office, my experience managing a law office has **provided me with the skills necessary** to do this job well.

Again, thank you for meeting with me. **If you have additional questions**, you can reach me by phone at (503) 555-1234 or by e-mail at *sbeane@horizon.net*. I look forward to hearing from you **regarding your decision**.

Yours truly,

Sandy Beane

SAMPLE THANK-YOU LETTER #4

Rose Thornton

105 Peyton Place
Chicago, IL 60637

April 19, 2012

Mr. Richard Rheinhardt
Executive Assistant
Turning Corporation
1543 48th Street
Chicago, IL 60637

Dear Mr. Rheinhardt:

I just wanted to send **a quick note to thank you** for showing me around your offices on Tuesday **after my interview with** Janet Parker.

As Ms. Parker mentioned to you, I am interviewing for the bookkeeper position. **Perhaps we will get to work together**.

Yours truly,

Rose Thornton

Green Light Phrases
Regarding the position
Hope to hear from you
Thanks for your time
Look forward to hearing from you
Appreciate the time
As we discussed
Welcome the opportunity
Enjoyed speaking with you

Endnote: Graciousness goes a long way when you're looking for a job. The best way to make a lasting positive impression on an interviewer is to show your appreciation with a thank-you letter. If properly executed with the right wording, a good thank-you letter can actually seal the deal and get you hired.

Appendix

JOB SEARCH RESOURCES

Career-Related Websites

6FigureJobs
www.6figurejobs.com
Executives can post their resumes and search for jobs for free on this website.

About Career Planning
http://careerplanning.about.com
The Everything® Practice Interview Book author Dawn Rosenberg McKay's site covers all aspects of career planning including career choice, job hunting, job training, legal issues, and the workplace.

About Job Searching
http://jobsearch.about.com
Alison Doyle, the guide to this excellent site, helps you with all aspects of online job searching, writing resumes and cover letters, references, interviewing skills, and unemployment.

About Job Searching: Technical
http://jobsearchtech.about.com
Guide J. Steven Niznik keeps you updated on the technical job market. Get the latest information on health care, engineering, semiconducter, science, Internet, and telecom jobs.

CareerMag.com
www.careermag.com
At this site, you can search for jobs by career, industry, keyword, or location.

CareerBuilder.com
www.careerbuilder.com
Through its partnerships with newspaper publishers Tribune, Gannett, and Knight Ridder, CareerBuilder. com lists local jobs from newspaper help wanted sections from around the country. Search this huge jobs database by location, company, job type, and industry. You can even search in Spanish.

Career Journal

www.careerjournal.com

Career Journal is the *Wall Street Journal*'s executive career site and is geared toward executives, managers, and professionals. It includes salary and hiring information, job search advice, and career management help. There is also a searchable database of jobs in select fields.

CollegeGrad.com

www.collegegrad.com

This job board targets college graduates and recent graduates. In addition to job listings, you'll find information on career choice, job search advice, and salary information.

Company Research from About Career Planning

http://careerplanning.about.com/cs/companyresearch
Find out what resources you can use to do company research. Learn how to access business directories and news sources.

The Equal Employment Opportunity Commission

www.eeoc.gov
Use this website to learn more about the laws that protect workers from discrimination at work.

ExecutivePlanet.com

www.executiveplanet.com
This website includes business culture guides for international businesspeople.

FlipDog.com

www.flipdog.com
FlipDog.com collects job announcements from company websites. Search for jobs by employer, keyword, and category. Post your resume.

JobStar Profession-Specific Salary Surveys

www.jobstar.org/tools/salary/sal-prof.cfm
Get salary information for dozens of professions.

Knock 'em Dead

www.knockemdead.com
Author Martin Yate's website includes information on constructing resumes and cover letters as well as webinars on all aspects of job searches.

Monster

www.monster.com
Search for jobs by location or job category. You can also enter keywords to search by job titles, company names, and requirements. Post your resume online so employers can find you.

Monster Career Advice

http://content.monster.com
Resume and job interviewing tips, salary information, relocating advice, and diversity advice from Monster.com.

NewsLink

http://newslink.org
This site provides links to business journals around the country.

Occupational Outlook Handbook

www.bls.gov/oco/home.htm

Use this resource, published by the U.S. Bureau of Labor Statistics, to find out what workers do on the job. Learn about working conditions, training and education needed, employment outlook, salary, and expected job prospects for a wide number of occupations.

Public Service Employees Network

www.pse-net.com

You'll find links to local government job listings on this site.

Quintessential Careers

www.quintcareers.com

Get job search and career advice. You'll find links to job banks, career advice for teens and college grads, and tutorials to help you with job interviews and writing a resume and cover letter.

Riley Guide

www.rileyguide.com

Librarian Margaret F. Dikel has organized myriad sites that can help you with your job search.

Salary.com

www.salary.com

Get salary information for a variety of occupations.

SEC Filings and Forms (EDGAR)

www.sec.gov/edgar.shtml

The Securities and Exchange Commission requires publicly held companies to file information about finances quarterly and information about material events or corporate changes as they occur. You can retrieve this information from the EDGAR database.

USAJOBS

www.usajobs.opm.gov

This is the official website of the U.S. federal government. Job listings for all federal jobs are posted here. Post and store a resume that you can use to apply for jobs on this site.

Vault

www.vault.com

When you're preparing for a job interview, Vault.com is the place to go. You'll find company and industry profiles. There are message boards where employees share information about their employers. There's also a free job board that lists thousands of openings.

Yahoo! HotJobs

www.hotjobs.com

Search for a job by keyword, job category, or location. Post your resume and let employers find you. You can cut and paste your current resume or use Resume Builder to get help creating a new one.

Books

Job Search

The Back Door Guide to Short-Term Job Adventures, by Michael Landes. CA: Ten Speed Press, 2002.

Cyberspace Job Search Kit: The Complete Guide to Online Job Seeking and Career Information, by Mary B. Nemnich and Fred E. Jandt. IN: JIST Works, 2001.

Federal Civil Service Jobs, by Dawn Rosenberg McKay and Michele Lipson. NJ: Peterson's, 2002.

JobBank Series, Adams Media, Annual.

Job-Hunting for the So-Called Handicapped or People Who Have Disabilities, by Richard Nelson Bolles and Dale S. Brown. IN: JIST Works, 2001.

Knock 'em Dead 2010: The Ultimate Job Search Guide, by Martin Yate. MA: Adams Media, 2009.

Cover Letters and Resumes

101 Best Cover Letters, by Jay A. Block and Michael Betrus. NY: McGraw-Hill, 1999.

101 Grade A Resumes for Teachers, by Rebecca Anthony and Gerald Roe. NY: Barron's Educational Series, 2003.

201 Killer Cover Letters, by Sandra Podesta and Andrea Paxton. NY: McGraw-Hill, 2003.

Ace the IT Resume!, by Paula Moreira and Robyn Thorpe. CA: Osborne/McGraw-Hill, 2002.

Adams Cover Letter Almanac, Second Edition, MA: Adams Media, 2006.

Adams Resume Almanac, Second Edition, MA: Adams Media, 2005.

America's Top Resumes for America's Top Jobs, by Michael Farr. IN: JIST Works, 2002.

Best Resumes for $100,000+ Jobs, by Wendy S. Enelow. VA: Impact Publications, 1997.

Best Resumes for College Students and New Grads, by Louise M. Kursmark. IN: JIST Works, 2003.

Blue Collar Resumes, by Steven Provenzano. NJ: Career Press, 1999.

The Damn Good Resume Guide: A Crash Course in Resume Writing, by Yana Parker. CA: Ten Speed Press, 2002.

Designing the Perfect Resume, by Pat Criscito. NY: Barron's Educational Series, 2000.

The Edge Resume and Job Search Strategy, by Bill Corbin and Shelbi Wright. IN: JIST Works, 2000.

The Everything® Cover Letter Book, Second Edition by Burton Jay Nadler. MA: Adams Media, 2005.

The Everything® Resume Book, Third Edition, by Nancy Schuman. MA: Adams Media, 2008.

Expert Resumes for Computer and Web Jobs, by Wendy S. Enelow and Louise M. Kursmark. IN: JIST Works, 2002.

Expert Resumes for Health Care Careers, by Wendy S. Enelow and Louise M Kursmark. IN: JIST Works, 2004.

Expert Resumes for People Returning to Work, by Wendy S. Enclow and Louise M. Kursmark. IN: JIST Works, 2003.

Gallery of Best Resumes, by David F. Noble. IN: JIST Works, 2001.

Gallery of Best Resumes for People Without a Four-Year Degree, by David F. Noble. IN: JIST Works, 2000.

The Insider's Guide to Writing the Perfect Resume by Karl Weber and Rob Kaplan. NJ: Peterson's, 2001.

Knock 'em Dead Cover Letters, 8th ed. by Martin Yate. MA: Adams Media, 2008.

Knock 'em Dead Resumes, 8th ed. by Martin Yate. MA: Adams Media, 2008.

Real Resumes for Financial Jobs, edited by Anne McKinney. NC: Prep Publishing, 2001.

The Resume Catalog: 200 Damn Good Examples, by Yana Parker. CA: Ten Speed Press, 1996.

Resume Magic, by Susan Britton Whitcomb. IN: JIST Works, 2003.

Resumes That Get Jobs, 10th ed., edited by Ray Potter. NJ: Arco, 2002.

Sales and Marketing Resumes for $100,000 Careers, by Louise Kursmark. IN: JIST Works, 2000.

Top Secret Executive Resumes: What It Takes to Create the Perfect Resume for the Best Top-Level Positions, by Steven Provenzano. NJ: Career Press, 2000.

Vault Guide to Resumes, Cover Letters and Interviewing 2002 Edition, by the editors of Vault. NY: Vault, 2001.

Interview Etiquette and Style

Adams Job Interview Almanac, 2nd Ed, MA: Adams Media, 2005.

Business Etiquette: 101 Ways to Conduct Business with Charm and Savvy, by Ann Marie Sabath. NJ: Career Press, 2002.

Chic Simple Dress Smart for Men: Wardrobes That Win in the Workplace, by Kim Johnson Gross and Jeff Stone. NY: Warner Books, 2002.

Chic Simple Dress Smart for Women: Wardrobes That Win in the Workplace, by Kim Johnson Gross and Jeff Stone. NY: Warner Books, 2002.

Emily Post's the Etiquette Advantage in Business, by Emily Post and Peter Post. NY: HarperCollins, 1999.

Esquire's Things a Man Should Know About Handshakes, White Lies, and Which Fork Goes Where, by Ted Allen and Scott Omelianuk. NY: Hearst Communications, 2001.

Gestures: The Do's and Taboos of Body Language Around the World, by Roger E. Axtell and Mike Fornwald. NY: John Wiley & Sons, 1997.

Your Executive Image: How to Look Your Best and Project Success for Men and Women, by Victoria A. Seitz. MA: Adams Media Corporation, 2000.

International Job Searching

Best Resumes and CVs for International Jobs: Your Passport to the Global Job Market, by Ronald L. Krannich and Wendy S. Enelow. VA: Impact Publications, 2002.

Dun and Bradstreet's Guide to Doing Business Around the World, by Terri Morrison, Wayne A. Conaway, and Joseph J. Douress. NJ: Prentice Hall Press, 2000.

Global Etiquette Guide to Europe: Everything You Need to Know for Business and Travel Success, by Dean Allen Foster. NY: John Wiley & Sons, 2000.

International Jobs: Where They Are and How to Get Them, by Nina Segal and Eric Kocher. NY: Perseus Publishing, 2003.

General

The 7 Habits of Highly Effective People, by Stephen R. Covey. NY: Free Press, 1989.

Building Your Career Portfolio, by Carol A. Poore. NJ: Career Press, 2001.

Communicate with Confidence, by Dianna Booher. NY: McGraw-Hill, 1994.

The Everything® Get-a-Job Book, 2nd Ed by Dawn Rosenberg McKay. MA: Adams Media, 2007.

Get Paid What You're Worth: The Expert Negotiators' Guide to Salary and Compensation, by Robin L. Pinkley and Gregory B. Northcraft. NY: St. Martin's Press, 2003.

How to Say It at Work: Putting Yourself across with Power Words, Phrases, Body Language, and Communication Secrets, by Jack Griffin. NJ: Prentice Hall Press, 1998.

Kick off Your Career: Write a Winning Resume, Ace Your Interview, Negotiate a Great Salary, by Kate Wendleton. NJ: Career Press, 2002.

Make a Name for Yourself: 8 Steps Every Woman Needs to Create a Personal Brand Strategy for Success, by Robin Fisher Roffer. NY: Broadway Books, 2000.

Negotiating Your Salary: How to Make $1000 a Minute, by Jack Chapman. CA: Ten Speed Press, 2000.

The Networking Survival Guide: Get the Success You Want by Tapping into the People You Know, by Diane Darling. NY: McGraw-Hill, 2003.

Power Interviews: Job-Winning Tactics from Fortune 500 Recruiters, by Neil Yeager and Lee Hough. NY: John Wiley & Sons, 1998.

The Smart Woman's Guide to Resumes and Job Hunting, by Julie Adair King and Betsy Sheldon. NJ: Career Press, 1995.

SuperNetworking, by Michael Salmon. NJ: Career Press, 2003.

Targeting the Job You Want, by Kate Wendleton. NJ: Career Press, 2000.

Women for Hire: The Ultimate Guide to Getting a Job, by Tory Johnson, Robyn Freedman Spizman, and Lindsey Pollak. NY: Berkley Publishing Group, 2002.

INDEX